always up to date

The law changes, but Nolo is on top of it! We offer several
ways to make sure you and your Nolo products are up to date:

1 **Nolo's Legal Updater**
We'll send you an email whenever a new edition of this book is
published! Sign up at **www.nolo.com/legalupdater**.

2 **Updates @ Nolo.com**
Check **www.nolo.com/update** to find recent changes
in the law that affect the current edition of your book.

3 **Nolo Customer Service**
To make sure that this edition of the book is the most
recent one, call us at **800-728-3555** and ask one of
our friendly customer service representatives.
Or find out at **www.nolo.com**.

please note

We believe accurate, plain-English legal information should help
you solve many of your own legal problems. But this text is not a
substitute for personalized advice from a knowledgeable lawyer.
If you want the help of a trained professional—and we'll always
point out situations in which we think that's a good idea—consult
an attorney licensed to practice in your state.

5th edition

Music Law
How to Run Your Band's Business

By Attorney Richard Stim

Fifth Edition	SEPTEMBER 2006
Book Design	SUSAN PUTNEY
Production	MARGARET LIVINGSTON
Proofreader	EMILY K. WOLMAN
CD-ROM Preparation	ANDRÉ ZIVKOVICH
Indexer	MEDEA MINNICH
Cover Photography	TONYA PERME (www.tonyaperme.com)
Printing	CONSOLIDATED PRINTERS, INC.

Stim, Richard.
  Music law : how to run your band's business / by Richard Stim.-- 5th ed.
    p. cm.
  Includes index.
  ISBN 1-4133-0517-2 (alk. paper)
    1. Band musicians--Legal status, laws, etc.--United States--Popular works. 2.
  Performing arts--Law and legislation--United States--Popular works. I. Title.

  KF390.E57S87 2006
  344.73'097—dc22

                                                                    2006046425

For information on bulk purchases or corporate premium sales, please contact the Special Sales department. For academic sales or textbook adoptions, ask for Academic Sales. Call 800-955-4775 or write to Nolo at 950 Parker St., Berkeley, CA 94710.

Acknowledgments

Thanks to those who provided me with helpful information in various chapters: Craig Leon, Kathryn Roessel, George (area 51) Earth, Frank Gallagher, Andrea Ross, Andy Olyphant, Lindsay Hutton, Howard Thompson, Don Ciccone, and Marc Weinstein.

This book is dedicated to Joseph D. Stim and Roberta Stim.

About the Author

Richard Stim is a lawyer and musician who, for the past 25 years, has written and performed with two bands, angel corpus christi (www.angelcorpuschristi.com) and MX-80 (www.MX-80.com). He is also the author of eight other books including *License Your Invention* (Nolo), *Getting Permission* (Nolo), *Your Crafts Business: A Legal Guide* (Nolo), *Whoops! I'm in Business* (Nolo), and *Patent, Copyright & Trademark* (Nolo).

Foreword

"The conventional wisdom in the music industry is to 'get a good lawyer.' My advice to the contrary would be to have no truck with lawyers at all."

—Steve Albini

Steve Albini is a successful musician and producer. He has produced or engineered over a thousand records—many on his own record label—with international sales in the millions. As musicians, he and his bandmates in Big Black and Shellac have toured the world and sold hundreds of thousands of records of their own. What sets Albini apart from lots of other musicians today is that he's reached success on his own terms—which, in most of his business dealings, involves no lawyers or written contracts. Rather than relying on legal protection against the sharks in the music industry, Albini's strategy is to be careful to work only with trustworthy people.

Although we take a fundamentally different approach in this book and recommend easy-to-understand written contracts for your business agreements, we agree with his advice that the trustworthiness of the parties is the most important aspect of any agreement. A contract, no matter how carefully drafted, cannot completely insulate you from the dishonest acts of an individual or company. As you proceed through this book, keep in mind that the key to a satisfying and successful music career is not on the dotted line, but in the company you keep.

Richard Stim, August 2006

Table of Contents

1 Yes, Your Band Is a Business!

2 Band Partnerships and Beyond

8 Publishing Your Band's Music

9 Band Names

10 Album Artwork

11 Recording

Index

 # Forms Included on CD-ROM

Artwork Agreement

[Abbreviated] Artwork Agreement

Band Partnership Agreement

[Abbreviated] Band Partnership Agreement

Notice of Intention to Obtain Compulsory License for Making and Distributing Sound Recordings

Consignment Form

Independent Distribution Agreement

Mechanical License and Authorization for First-Time Recording of Song

Independent Label Recording Agreement

Independent Label License Agreement

Invoice

Label-Shopping Agreement

Management Agreement

[Abbreviated] Management Agreement

Model Release Agreement

Musician Release Agreement

Performance Agreement

Blank Recording Budget

Agreement With Music Publisher for Use of Song Sample

Agreement With Record Company for Use of Master Recording Sample

Tour Budget

Application for Employer Identification Number

Form PA

Form CA

Chapter 1

Yes, Your Band Is a Business!

> *"It's very easy in this business to find people who are willing to put their arm around you and tell you how great you are. Unfortunately, their other hand is in your pocket."*
> **—Paul Stanley of KISS**

Lou Reed once told an audience, "Give me an issue and I'll give you a tissue." Many music business executives have a similar attitude—they have little sympathy for the moral, business, or ethical issues faced by a band competing in the music business. The sole concern for most music industry companies is whether or not the band will make a lot of money. Therefore, bands should not expect much help (or sympathy) from their label, distributor, or booking agent when dealing with common problems. Even if your band can afford accountants, business managers, and lawyers to help you with problems, you'll save considerable time and money by making your band as self-sufficient as possible.

Taking On the Music Industry

Some people perceive the music industry as a bunch of cigar-smoking sleazy guys who steal artists' songs and recordings. Popular films and books reinforce these stereotypes. Why? Is the music business more unethical than other industries?

No, the music industry is probably not that much different from others. All businesses are opportunistic. If there is an opportunity to get ahead, then you can bet someone will take advantage of it. The problem in the music industry is that getting ahead often means taking advantage of musicians who aren't experienced in the business side of music. But if a musician learns the basics about business and law, there is less of an opportunity for a sleazy guy with a cigar to screw him over. That's what this book is about: protecting yourself and minimizing your damages.

This isn't to say that you can always avoid getting screwed. Be prepared for some setbacks. In this chapter we'll ease you into the different aspects of your band's business, and we'll try to help you decide on the business form that is best for your band.

Your Band Is a Business

The first and most important step in running your band's business is to accept the fact that it *is* a business. Producing music is your band's creative work, and selling that music is a business venture. As long as your band is interested in selling its music, business knowledge is as essential to your success as musical creativity!

You may be surprised to learn that taking care of business actually involves creativity and is not quite as boring as you may believe (ask Mick Jagger—a business school graduate). In fact, your band may well enjoy the power that comes with understanding how to run a business—and to do it successfully. This doesn't mean your band must micro-manage every detail of its business. As your band develops, you will delegate power and responsibilities. But, especially at the beginning, it's important for you to understand basic contract and accounting principles in order to make smart decisions and avoid the many pitfalls that often trap bands and their members.

Apathy Is Not the Answer

There is a joke that asks for the definition of "apathy." The answer: "I don't know and I don't care." Unfortunately, many musicians take this attitude toward the business dealings of their band. Don't be one of them.

The "I Don't Know" Excuse

Some musicians believe that they are unable to understand business principles.

This is *not* a valid excuse. Scientific studies have shown that many of the same cognitive skills that are used in music are used in mathematics and business. That is, if you can mix eighth and sixteenth notes and still land on the downbeat, then you probably possess the skills necessary to understand a spreadsheet.

Cutting Through the Legal Jargon

Sometimes, failing to understand business principles is really nothing more than not knowing the language. As in many other industries, the music industry often uses a smokescreen of strange terms (such as "compulsory license," "mechanical royalties," and so on) and legalese (such as "the band hereby indemnifies" and so on) that can make otherwise simple concepts incomprehensible. In this book, we'll discuss business and legal issues without relying on jargon, plus we'll introduce you to the terms you need to know.

The "I Don't Care" Excuse

It only takes getting burned once before a musician realizes, "I *do* care about business." Most musical careers are relatively short, and the only way to make a career last longer is to devote equal time to music and business. Without business knowledge, you may soon find that the glory days have ended and you're broke.

Do the Old Rules Still Apply?

When the first edition of this book debuted in 1998, few bands had websites, and it took hours to download a song (assuming you could find a song to download). Two years later, thanks to the Internet, many people proclaimed that the 20th century music business—as personified by the major labels—was officially dead. The new mission for bands was to bypass the middleman and sell direct or through downloads. We wondered whether the old rules about touring, promotion, and releasing recordings were still valid.

In 2004, we informally surveyed musicians and music industry honchos to find out what they thought. The results indicated that little had changed for working bands, other than the emergence of band websites as a vehicle for marketing and distribution. We asked people to list in descending order the factors that would help a band succeed in the 21st century. All but one identified songwriting as the most important factor for a band's success. Strong musical skills and a compelling live performance were near the top on everyone's list; "physical appearance" and "luck" were near the bottom. In other words, the old-fashioned

approach to success still pays off: write great songs, play well, and give the fans a great show.

Everyone also agreed that getting a contract with a major label was more of a stumbling block than a goal for success. Thirty-year music business veteran Christopher Knab, whose website, FourFront Media & Music (www.4frontmusic.com), is one of the top music resources for indie musicians, wrote that for most bands today, major labels are "worthless, and in so much trouble they have no time to properly develop you."

His advice for new bands remains timeless: "Build from a local, break-out geographical area near a large city where you can plug into a local scene, and slowly over years develop a loyal following. Keep in contact with your fan base, all the while being very well funded to properly promote your indie releases."

Industry veteran Howard Thompson agreed that for most bands, major labels are "irrelevant." As for the current state of the music business, Thompson added, "The saddest thing about the music business right now is that the stories aren't as good [as they used to be], and books like this exist." Ouch!

Nancy Kravitz, aka Mr. Nancy, the self-described "poppy-punk" bass player for numerous San Francisco bands, has been gigging around the country for over a decade. She's been signed to major and indie label bands and still believes in the traditional approach, including "a lot of radio and video exposure, a great live show, and touring to support a well-recorded record, all with lots of promo." Mr. Nancy, like other musicians surveyed, believes in the power of the Internet. "It provides widespread attention," she says, "which lets you do your own thing more easily."

We concluded in 2004 that although the Internet is helpful to a band's promotional arsenal, it hasn't dramatically altered the essential elements for a band's success.

In 2006, as we complete the fifth edition of this book, we are seeing (finally) true self-sufficiency in terms of music production and promotion. It is now possible to compose, record, mix, master, duplicate, promote, and distribute an excellent recording without leaving your garage. And the same is true for the creation of music videos and merchandise. With the proliferation of web services such as iTunes, MySpace, YouTube, and Blogger, a band can build a following in their hometown or around the world. And even more unbelievable: some bands can even make a living solely from digital downloads.

Making the music industry more accessible has also made it more competitive. There are thousands of bands competing for the attention of music fans. And in the end, success in the music business depends on the same crucial elements: good tunes, great performances, and smart business sense.

How This Book Can Help

This book can help steer you through some of the common problems and crises experienced by most bands. These include:

- **Disputes between band members.** Few bands get along harmoniously all the time. Sometimes confrontations are good, because they may spark the band creatively. Most of the time, however, confrontations are bad for band business because they distract the group from its major purpose—making music. Chapter 2 offers a simple band agreement that can help prevent disputes over money, ownership of the band name, and ownership of band equipment. Chapter 11 provides suggestions for avoiding disputes in the recording studio. Chapters 7 and 8 have tips on avoiding fights over song ownership and division of song income.

- **Management issues.** A manager can be an excellent buffer between your band and the business. A bad manager, however, can be a major disaster. Chapter 3 provides background on the common ways that managers screw bands and how to avoid them.

- **Lawyers.** Depressing as it may seem, lawyers run a large portion of the music business. There are occasions when your band must hire an attorney—for example, to negotiate a major contract, or to sue or to defend your band in a lawsuit. In Chapter 4 we discuss when a lawyer might be necessary, suggest ways to choose the right one, and provide tips on how to avoid being overbilled.

- **Song ownership and music publishing.** Ownership and publishing of songs results in the largest revenue in the music business. For that reason, it is potentially explosive territory for bands. Everybody wants a piece of the band's songs. And often band members can't seem to agree on who wrote a song or how to split the revenue. Chapters 7 and 8 deal with these issues and offer some practical alternatives on how bands can divide songwriting income.

- **The making and selling of your band's recordings.** Some bands make a comfortable living without ever signing with a major label. They perform for years, surviving on the sale of their own recordings. It's not that hard to master the business of making and selling your band recordings. In Chapters 11, 12, and 13 we offer recording tips, suggestions for duplication, and methods of distributing and selling your music online and off.

- **Record companies and distribution.** Many bands are surprised to find that their troubles really begin

once they get signed to a record company. As Kurt Neuman of the BoDeans put it, "We had it made and then we got a record deal." In Chapter 14 we address most of the important issues for an independent record deal, and in Chapter 13 we explain the principles of independent distribution.

⚠️ **Major record deals should be handled with an attorney.** Major label agreements are outside the scope of this book. If your band has been offered a recording contract with a major label, you'll need an attorney or an experienced manager to help you negotiate the deal. These agreements often run as long as 100 pages and contain hundreds of provisions that could have seriously negative consequences for your band.

- **Taking your band online.** The Internet has made it possible for you to bring your band to a global audience without leaving home. Regardless of whether you're tech savvy or a technophobe, you'll need to follow some basic rules for staying out of trouble with website developers, hosts, and domain name users. In Chapter 15 we talk about issues involved when taking your band online, and in Chapter 13 we explain how to sell CDs and downloads online.

- **Band names.** The right to use a band name has caused problems for many bands. The country band Shenandoah paid over $500,000 to settle three lawsuits over its name. The lawsuits were so burdensome that the band ultimately filed for bankruptcy. In Chapter 9 we'll explain trademark and other basic band name issues and provide you with a method of researching and registering your band's name.

Have a Hit! Go Broke

Many musicians believe that having a hit record is financial salvation. Consider these sobering facts:

- Meat Loaf, whose albums sold over 20 million copies, filed for bankruptcy in 1983.
- Jerry Lee Lewis didn't receive royalty payments for over a decade because the IRS had a lien on his income.
- Singer Toni Braxton lost millions in bad business deals and filed for bankruptcy in 1998.
- Rap star Luther Campbell gave up his 36-hole golf course and other assets when he filed for bankruptcy in the 1990s.
- As a result of legal hassles with MCA Records, Tom Petty filed for bankruptcy in the 1970s, a half million dollars in debt.
- The IRS challenged Willie Nelson's tax reports and demanded $9 million in back taxes.
- Faced with a breach of contract lawsuit, funk music superstar George Clinton was prohibited from recording and forced into bankruptcy in 1985.
- Mick Fleetwood of Fleetwood Mac fame ran into financial problems when his real estate and oil investments bottomed out. He filed for bankruptcy in 1984.
- Bankruptcy and tax debts forced Marvin Gaye to leave the U.S. in 1982.
- Ray Sawyer, aka Dr. Hook, had a monster hit with "The Cover of the Rolling Stone," but the band went broke due to financial mismanagement. The band's first album after emerging from bankruptcy court was titled "Bankrupt."

Written Agreements: Your First Line of Defense

Putting agreements in writing will go a long way to avoid misunderstandings and nasty contract disputes. A contract sets up rules for doing business and makes it easier for your band to go after people who have ripped you off. This book provides samples of several common agreements that bands enter into, such as partnership deals, compulsory licenses, and independent record deals. Most of the chapters in this book include a sample agreement that deals with the issues covered in that chapter. Whenever a sample agreement is provided, we explain how to fill it out and modify it to fit your needs.

An ounce of prevention is worth the strongest contract. You should always remember that a contract is not a bulletproof method of protecting yourself. While the contracts in this book will help you protect your band's interests if a dispute arises, the costs of filing or defending a lawsuit in court will often dwarf the benefits even if you win. We urge you to try to prevent problems in the first place by developing "business radar" to help you determine which people and companies are more trustworthy than others. In each chapter, we offer suggestions on researching individuals and companies so that you can make educated guesses as to who is the best match for your band.

Below are some of the agreements you'll find in this book:

- **Partnership agreement:** for all band members, covering how to divide expenses and profits, rights to songs, rights to the band name, and related issues.
- **Management agreement:** for your band and your manager, covering commissions, length of representation, and post-termination issues.
- **Label-shopping agreement:** for your band and your attorney (or whoever is shopping your band to record companies), covering issues such as the extent and length of payment for the representation.
- **Performance agreement:** for your band and the venue that is booking your band, covering the payment and other performance details.
- **Model release agreement:** for your band and any person whose image is used on band artwork or merchandise, covering the extent of the use and the payment.
- **Artwork agreement:** for your band and those providing artwork for recordings or merchandise, covering the extent of the artwork use and payment.
- **Musician clearance agreement:** for your band and any nonband musician providing a performance for recordings, covering the extent of the musical use and payment.

- **Compulsory license agreement:** for your band and any nonband songwriter or copyright holder, dealing with the right to "cover" their song on your band's recording.
- **Distribution agreement:** for your band and distributors of your band's recordings to stores, covering the length, payment, and territory where your record will be sold.
- **Independent label record agreement:** for your band and an independent record label, covering the details of ownership and making of recordings. ∎

Chapter 2

Band Partnerships and Beyond

Okay, you've accepted the fact that your band is a business. But what kind of business is it? Every business has a legal structure, which we refer to as a business form. You've probably heard of most of the common ones:

- **Sole proprietorship.** In a sole proprietorship, you own and operate the band by yourself and are personally liable for business debts. You pay the other band members, either as employees or as independent contractors. You don't file a separate business tax return. You report business income on your individual tax return. (This type of arrangement is referred to as a "pass-through" entity because the income passes through the business to the owners before it is taxed.)
- **Partnership.** If you form a partnership, your band splits the profits and losses among the band members, and each member is personally liable for all partnership debts. The partnership is also a pass-through tax entity (see above).
- **Limited liability company (LLC).** To form an LLC, your band must file papers with the state government. The LLC operates like a partnership—profits and losses are shared, and income is reported on each partner's individual tax return. But, unlike a partnership, each band member is shielded from personal

liability for many business debts—a legal theory known as "limited liability."

- **Corporation.** To create a corporation, the band must file papers with the state government. Your band will have to file a corporate tax return (and pay taxes at corporate tax rates). (A corporation is not a pass-through entity.) The band members (who are shareholders in the corporation) have limited liability for band-related debts.

That's a snapshot of the various business entities. Later in this chapter, more information is provided on each entity's advantages and disadvantages. By default, most bands qualify as partnerships—an informal business entity that's easy to form and manage.

Since your band is likely to be a partnership, most of this chapter is geared towards creating a band partnership agreement (a BPA). A BPA defines the rights and obligations of the band members. Think of it as the band's business rule book. While there's no requirement that your band must have a written BPA, it's recommended. As with any type of venture, it's always best to make sure everyone is clear on the arrangement and that everyone knows their rights and responsibilities, which reduces the chances of a dispute later. And if a dispute does erupt, it will be easier to solve if you have a written agreement as a guide.

In this chapter, you'll find two types of band partnership agreements: a short-form agreement that establishes some basic rules, and a long-form partnership agreement that is more comprehensive and deals with more contingencies. A bare-bones agreement might be fine in the beginning, but as the stakes grow, so should your BPA.

It's also possible that your band business has progressed beyond the partnership stage. Perhaps you are touring regularly or have experienced a serious jump in band income. As a result, band members may be concerned about personal liability. We will help you analyze which business form is best for your band. In the event your band wants to limit personal liability, the most common approach is to convert the band partnership to a band limited liability company (LLC). The conversion process is discussed at the end of this chapter.

Who Needs a Band Partnership Agreement?

Any business that operates as a partnership is advised to execute an agreement among all the partners to make sure that everyone understands and agrees to certain terms, such as shares of ownership, shares of profit distribution, and rules for joining or leaving the partnership. A band partnership agreement (BPA) is simply a partnership

agreement that is tailored to the needs of a band. Typically, a BPA:

- provides a method for resolving disputes
- sets standards for firing and hiring band members
- creates a system for dividing band income and expenses, including future royalties
- establishes guidelines for when members depart or the band breaks up, and
- defines who may use the band name and songs.

 BPAs are used only for bands that operate as partnerships. If your band is operating as a sole proprietorship, corporation, or limited liability company (LLC), you should not use a BPA.

Many bands get along fine without a written BPA, especially small bands that play just as much for fun as for business. They have adopted commonsense principles and work out business deals as they go along. Some bands wait until they have a record deal before formalizing their arrangements with a written BPA.

But, while winging it might work for a while, forging ahead without an agreement can be risky. Countless bands have been unpleasantly surprised at how an unforeseen conflict can suddenly swoop in and cause chaos, or even destroy a band. Putting your agreement in writing sooner rather than later helps to avoid such disputes, because it forces you to deal with issues before they become threatening problems.

Besides the common wisdom that a written agreement is always a good idea among business partners, another reason to enter into a BPA with your bandmates is that if you don't, the laws of your state will have the final word on how your partnership is run. All states except Louisiana have adopted the Uniform Partnership Act (UPA) in some form, which provides standard, default rules for partnerships that haven't executed their own agreements. In the absence of your own agreement, for example, the UPA says that profits must be shared equally and that each member has an equal voice in running the business. If that's not the arrangement you and your bandmates want, you won't want to be caught without a written agreement.

Aren't Oral Agreements Valid?

Oral contracts and agreements—including oral BPAs—are legally binding. But without a written document, band members may have different recollections of the terms of the oral agreement. Especially in the heat of a dispute, different memories and misunderstandings among band members will leave an oral agreement meaningless and unenforceable. Keep in mind the old saying that an oral agreement isn't worth the paper it's written on.

The abbreviated short-form agreement is quite simple and easy to complete. If your band is just starting out, or is undecided on whether to use a BPA, take a look at the short-form agreement. It's not very complex and will provide a minimal, but significant, level of protection for band members. Even if you decide not use it, your band should at least discuss some of the issues raised in it, such as who owns the band name or what type of vote is necessary to kick out a band member.

The second (or full-length) agreement is more complex and covers a wider range of potential problems. If your band is growing as a business—such as earning regular income of more than $2,000 a month—you should consider adopting the long BPA. As your revenues increase, the long BPA is designed to preserve each band member's rights. You should also use the long BPA if your band is preparing to sign a record deal, because the agreement will safeguard each member's right to royalties, even after a member leaves the group. (See Chapter 14 on independent record deals.)

⚠️ **Get professional help with major label record deals.** Signing a record deal with a major label is beyond the scope of this book. If you're being offered a deal with a major label, you'll need a lawyer or sophisticated manager to negotiate the contract. See Chapter 4 for information on hiring and working with lawyers, Chapter 14 on independent record deals versus major label deals, and Chapter 17 for other resources beyond this book.

Using a BPA to Avoid Getting Screwed

Most of the chapters in this book describe how a band gets screwed by forces outside the band such as a record company, manager, retail store, or music publisher. In this chapter, however, we deal with situations in which the band can be harmed by internal forces—that is, by a band member or ex-member. The following situations are unfortunately all too common:

- An ex-band member claims a right to use the band name or band logo.
- The band breaks up and there is a dispute about dividing the assets.
- A dispute between the band and an ex-member results in a costly lawsuit.

Thankfully, you can help avoid these and most other ugly situations by covering them in your BPA.

Situation #1: *An ex-band member claims a right to use the band name or logo.*

A band can get screwed when ex-members begin using the band's name or a substantially similar name. The similarly named band confuses fans, dilutes the strength of the original band's drawing power, and may generate merchandise sales that are not shared with other members of the original band. For example, ex-members of Creedence Clearwater Revival used the name Creedence Clearwater Revisited—without the consent or participation of founder John Fogerty. He sued to prevent the band's use of the name but lost the case on appeal. In 2005, Dave Mustaine, lead singer of Megadeth, sued David Ellefson, the band's former bass player, for allegedly using the name of the group without permission in an ad for musical equipment. Tina Weymouth and Chris Frantz were sued by ex-bandmate David Byrne when they used the name Heads as a truncated version of their former band name, the Talking Heads. The lawsuit settled and Weymouth and Frantz were permitted to use the name. In 2003, John Densmore, former drummer and co-founder of the Doors, sued to prevent keyboardist Ray Manzarek and guitarist Robby Krieger from playing shows as the Doors (with singer Ian Astbury and drummer Stewart Copeland). If bands such as Creedence Clearwater Revival, the

Talking Heads, and the Doors had agreed upon ownership of the name, a great deal of litigation (and aggravation) could have been avoided.

How to avoid getting screwed:

In your BPA, be sure to cover two things: 1) whether the band as a whole owns the name, or whether specific individuals in the band own it; and 2) which band members (if any) can continue to use the name of the band in the event that the band splits up or members leave the band. Dealing with this issue in your BPA will help to avoid disputes over who owns the name and will help prevent unauthorized—and potentially damaging—use of the name by former band members.

Situation #2:
The band breaks up and there is a dispute about dividing the assets or debts.

Bands have a notoriously difficult time staying together. But common as they are, band break-ups can be complex. The band may be earning record royalties or have outstanding debts. When there is no BPA and the band members cannot agree how to divide the assets and debts, an ugly break-up can quickly go from bad to worse. If there are assets, they may be held by the courts until the matter is resolved—which sometimes can take months or years.

How to avoid getting screwed:

Establish a system in your BPA for dividing assets and debts. The most common arrangement is for a band to split the band's assets (usually equipment) after paying off people to whom the band owes money (referred to as creditors). The sample long BPA at the end of this chapter provides a common asset and debt division system for your band to adopt.

Situation #3:
An ex-band member sues the band.

There are a variety of reasons why an ex-band member might sue the band. Take the case of Guns 'N' Roses drummer Steve Adler. In 1990, the band asked Adler to sign an agreement terminating his partnership interest in the band and agreeing to a lump sum as settlement for leaving. Slash, the guitarist for Guns 'N' Roses, later testified that Adler was strung out on heroin when Adler signed the termination agreement. Adler sued, claiming that the termination agreement was invalid because he was not mentally capable at the time he signed it. He claimed that the band owed him money and drum equipment. To avoid a court judgment, the band settled with Adler in 1993, agreeing to pay him $2.5 million. The band also had to pay its own legal costs.

Whatever the dispute, fighting it out in court is the most expensive and time-consuming way to resolve disputes. Paying legal fees, even for a relatively short case, can quickly put a band into bankruptcy. The Guns 'N' Roses dispute might have been avoided, for example, if the band had established a system for distributing income to terminated members in their BPA.

How to avoid getting screwed:

A BPA can avoid disputes in the first place by establishing the rules of the band at the outset. A thorough, written agreement is often enough to resolve a conflict before it gets ugly and ends up in court. Even if a dispute does arise, a BPA can help the band avoid a lawsuit by establishing a method for resolving disputes such as arbitration or mediation.

What About Songwriting?

Under our model BPA, each songwriter owns their own songs. However, many bands decide to share songwriting income in some way. The long-form BPA below includes two optional provisions that can be inserted if your band wants to share songwriting income. We provide more information about dividing songwriting income in Chapter 7.

Abbreviated Band Partnership Agreement

If your band is just starting out or not earning much income (say, under $2,000 a month), or if you're just not ready to deal with a long agreement, we recommend you execute at least a basic BPA covering the essentials. In this section, we'll walk you through the simple task of putting together a short BPA. A sample form appears below. You can modify the form to fit your needs, though if many modifications are necessary you may want to use the long form that is covered in the next section.

 This agreement is included on the forms CD in the back of this book.

Names of Partners

Enter the names of the band members who will be included in your partnership. You should include the names of only those members who will actually be full partners who will share band profits and debts. Other musicians who may sometimes play with your band, but to whom you don't intend to give an ownership interest in your band, should not be included.

Partnership Name

You will need to create a name for your band partnership. Most bands usually use the band name and add the word "partnership" at the end (for example, "The Smashing Pumpkins Partnership").

Band Name and Ownership

Enter the name of your band as you will use it in public. If you haven't already discussed ownership of the band name, now is the time. See instructions for the long BPA later in this chapter, or refer to Chapter 9 on protecting your band name. Depending on how your band wants to deal with name ownership, choose one or more of the alternative provisions, or create your own. If one person owns the name, enter that person's name.

Profits and Losses

This clause establishes that band members will share all profits equally. If you want a different arrangement, you should use the long BPA, below.

Partnership Voting

Indicate whether a unanimous vote or just a majority vote is required to expel a band partner, to add a new band partner, and to enter the band into an agreement that will last longer than one year.

Tie-Breaker

This is an optional provision in which you can name one band member whose vote will have the power to break a tie. (In essence, that member's vote would count twice.) If you do not want to name a tie-breaker, enter "none."

Addition of Band Partner

This clause simply states that any new band members will be bound by the terms of this agreement.

Leaving Members

This clause establishes that the partnership will stay in effect when a member leaves. It also says that a band member may voluntarily quit the band, and that a leaving member is entitled to her share of the net worth of the partnership as well as her share of royalties. Any payments will be made only after the band has actually received the income and deducted expenses.

Mediation; Arbitration

Under this clause, if a dispute arises, the band members agree to try to resolve it through mediation or, if that fails, binding arbitration, rather than immediately going to court. Mediation can save thousands of dollars in legal fees and often produces better results than court verdicts. Enter the location where you agree to mediate, most likely the city where you all live.

Signatures

Have all band members sign and date the agreement, and enter their personal addresses and social security numbers.

[Abbreviated] Band Partnership Agreement

Band Partners

Names of band members ("Band Partners"):

_____

_____

Partnership Name

The Band Partners establish themselves as a general partnership (the "Band Partnership") known as the _____

Band Name

The Band Partnership will do business under the name _____ (the "Band Name"). Each Band Partner acknowledges that (check appropriate box):

○ Band Partners who leave the band will have no interest in the Band Name.

○ No individual member will have a right to use the Band Name in the event the band breaks up.

○ The Band Name is the exclusive property of _____.

Profits and Losses

The Band Partners will share equally in all payments that are paid to the Band Partnership or to any Band Partner as a result of Band Partnership activities. After deducting Band Partnership expenses (for example, reasonable salaries, rent, promotional costs, travel costs, office expenditures, telephone costs, and accounting and legal fees), these payments will be distributed in cash to the Band Partners.

Partnership Voting

Check either "unanimous vote" or "majority vote" for each issue.

	Unanimous Vote	Majority Vote
• Expelling a Band Partner (unanimous except for party to be expelled)	○	○
• Admission of a new Band Partner	○	○
• Entering into any agreement that binds the Band Partnership for more than one year	○	○
• Dissolving the Band Partnership	○	○

Tie-Breaker (optional)

In the event that a majority cannot be achieved, the decision of _____ will prevail.

Addition of a Band Partner

Each new Band Partner must agree to be bound by all of the provisions in this Agreement. The addition of a new Band Partner will not end the Partnership, which will remain in full force.

Leaving Members

A Band Partner may leave the Band Partnership (a "Leaving Member") voluntarily (by resignation) or involuntarily (by reason of death, disability, or being expelled). A Leaving Member is entitled to a proportionate share of the net worth of the Band Partnership as of the date of leaving, and to the Leaving Member's share of any future royalties or fees earned from sound recordings that include the Leaving Member's performance. These payments will be made when actually received by the Band Partnership and after subtracting a proportionate deduction of expenses. If a member leaves, the Band Partnership will remain in full force among the remaining members.

Mediation; Arbitration

If a dispute arises under this Agreement, the parties agree to first try to resolve the dispute with the help of a mutually agreed-on mediator in _____ . Any costs and fees other than attorney fees will be shared equally by the parties. If it proves impossible to arrive at a mutually satisfactory solution, the parties agree to submit the dispute to binding arbitration in the same city or region, conducted on a confidential basis under the Commercial Arbitration Rules of the American Arbitration Association.

Amendments

This agreement may not be amended except in writing signed by all Band Partners.

Band Member Signature _____

Address _____

_____

Date _____ Soc. Sec. # _____

Band Member Signature _____

Address _____

_____

Date _____ Soc. Sec. # _____

Band Member Signature _____

Address _____

_____

Date _____ Soc. Sec. # _____

Band Member Signature _____

Address _____

_____

Date _____ Soc. Sec. # _____

Band Member Signature _____

Address _____

_____

Date _____ Soc. Sec. # _____

Full-Length Band Partnership Agreement

Use the long-form BPA if your band income is growing or if your band has signed a publishing or record company deal and the members are comfortable discussing and negotiating the details. The following instructions explain how to fill out the BPA and what the various clauses mean. Many clauses have alternative provisions for you to choose from, which are explained in the instructions. Some clauses, as noted in the instructions, are optional altogether. A sample appears below. You can modify the form agreement to fit your needs.

 This agreement is included on the forms CD in the back of this book.

In the Introduction clause, fill in the names of the band members who will be included in the partnership. Don't include any musicians to whom you don't want to give an ownership interest in the band.

The Band Partnership

You will need to create a name for your band partnership. Most bands usually use the band name and add the word "partnership" (for example, "The Smashing Pumpkins Partnership"). You also need to insert the state or province in which the band resides. If different members live in different areas, choose the state or province in which the band meets to practice. Finally, insert the location for the band's headquarters (usually an address where the band gets its mail).

Band Partner Services

This provision explains what types of services are expected from the band members. The "merchandising rights" section refers to the band partnership's right to use the band member's name and picture on products such as T-shirts.

Nonband Partnership Activities

Under this provision, band members can participate in side projects such as solo recordings or playing in other bands, provided that these activities don't interfere with the band. The obligations of being in this band must take priority over all other activities. Without this essential commitment, it will be difficult to coordinate touring and recording.

Band Name, Domain Name, and Logo

This provision deals with ownership of the band's name and, if you have them, your band's domain name and logo. Enter the band's name. If you don't have a domain name or logo, don't check those sections— leave them blank. If you do have a domain name for your band, enter it. If you have a logo, enter "see attached." Then be sure to attach a copy of the logo to the completed agreement. Staple a clean, final version of the logo to the agreement.

If you haven't already discussed ownership of the band name (see Chapter 9), now is the time. Any logo and domain name should also be considered when determining ownership rights. The person in the band who thought up the name does not automatically get any special ownership rights. As we explain in Chapter 9, the primary issues are whether the band, or specific individuals in the band, own the name; and which band members (if any) can continue to use the name of the band in the event that the band splits up or if members leave the band. Sometimes (particularly in the event of band names that feature one performer, such as the Jimi Hendrix Experience or Jon Spencer Blues Explosion), the name of the band may be owned and controlled by one member.

 If one person owns the domain name, have that person listed as owner and contact person with the domain name registry. As we explain in Chapter 15, domain name registries issue domain names and manage domain name renewals. Therefore, if your band agrees that one person is the owner, that person should be listed with the registry. Otherwise, the owner may have difficulty transferring and renewing the domain name.

Depending on your band's determination, choose one of the alternative provisions or create your own. The three alternatives given are:

1) The band owns the name even if members leave; if the band breaks up, no member may use the band name.
2) The band owns the name but only if certain members remain in the band. If the band breaks up, no member may use the band name.
3) One person in the band owns the name and controls its use.

Warranties

Warranties are contractual promises. If a band member breaks one of these promises (for example, by driving drunk to a gig), that can be the basis for expulsion. You can add other promises if you want. For example, "... will appear punctually for all performances, recording sessions, and rehearsals."

The last sentence of this provision ("Each Band Partner indemnifies each other Band Partner from all claims ...") refers to a legal principle known as indemnification. If a band partner breaks one of the promises—for example, gets in a fist fight with a club manager—and the band partnership is sued, partnership law says that every partner of the band is liable for any damages awarded. If each band partner indemnifies the other partners, however, then ultimately only the band partner who caused the problem will pay the damages and legal fees by paying back the others. Of course, this clause must be considered in a real-world perspective. A partner may be "judgment proof"—that is, the band member may not have the ability to pay. In that case, the indemnity clause will fail to shield innocent band members.

Profits and Losses

This provision includes a standard definition of net profits. It provides that before the band members are paid, the band's debts and other reasonable expenses must be deducted.

Practically, the issue of profits and losses is a matter of maintaining a bank account and making regular accountings of expenses and income. Bands that can afford it hire an accountant to handle these details and to make the payments to the band partners. If you cannot afford an accountant, there are many popular off-the-shelf accounting software programs (such as *Quicken, QuickBooks,* and *M.Y.O.B.*) that make managing your band's money quite easy.

Ownership of Recorded Compositions

If your band wants to create its own publishing company and share songwriting income, check "will" in this clause to create a band partnership publishing company. If you don't want to share songwriting income or create a publishing company, check "will not" or delete the language. This clause and the next two ("Division of Publishing Revenue" and "Publishing Administration") only affect songs written by band members that are recorded and released under the band name.

The issue of whether to share songwriting income is sometimes controversial for band members, and we have devoted Chapter 8 to this issue. You should review that chapter prior to making a decision. If an agreement on songwriting cannot be reached right now, leave this and the next two provisions blank or remove them from your BPA.

Division of Publishing Revenue

If you did not create a publishing company with the previous clause, this provision will not apply to you. You can delete the language altogether if you use the form on the disk in the back of the book.

When your band shares song income through a publishing company, there are many ways to divide the money. You can choose from three alternatives, or create your own. Your three alternatives in the agreement are:

- all money divided equally
- writers split writer share, and band splits publisher share, or
- a compromise system in which band members receive one credit for performing a song, and two credits for both writing and performing a song. We have provided a detailed explanation of dividing song income in Chapter 8.

Publishing Administration

If you did not create a publishing company, this provision will not apply to you. You can delete the language altogether if you use the form on the disk in the back of the book.

This provision permits the band's publishing company to "administer" the songs. Administration is explained in Chapter 8, but generally it means the band has the right to enter into contracts regarding the songs, make decisions about the use of the songs, collect royalties for the songs, and sue infringers of the songs. This provision also guarantees that the band can continue to administer the songs even after a member departs, and establishes the publishing rights for the departing member.

Meetings and Voting

This provision establishes the type of vote—majority or unanimous—that is required for different band actions. You are free to decide which issues require a majority or unanimous vote. However, we recommend that the first one (expelling a band partner) be done by unanimous vote. A unanimous vote should also be required to dissolve the band partnership. It's also wise to require at least a majority vote for purchases above a certain amount. Purchases between $200 and $500—depending on your band's financial situation, of course—typically warrant a majority vote.

Your band is also free to "skew" the voting. That is, one member may be granted two or three votes for every other member's one vote. This may be the case, for example, in a band that is centered around one founding individual. This can be accomplished with the optional statement, by filling in the name(s) of who gets extra voting power and how many votes they get. If you don't want to skew the voting, leave the clause blank or delete the clause.

In addition, in the event that the band partners cannot reach a majority agreement on a band partnership issue, you may choose an individual who acts as the tie-breaker. Often this is a founding member, but it can be any band partner—or it can be a nonpartner such as a manager or advisor. Enter the name of the tie-breaker in the blank, or if you don't want to designate one, either leave it blank or delete the clause.

Books of Account and Records

This accounting provision sets out some rules for band bookkeeping. The fiscal year is based on a calendar year. However, you may want to consult with your tax preparer or accountant in case there is an advantage for having a fiscal year that ends on another date (for example, April 15). The accounting statement that must be furnished to band members is just a spreadsheet that details the band's income minus the band's expenses during the preceding period.

Ending the Partnership

Without a written BPA, a partnership would end if one of the members quit or died. This clause establishes that your partnership will not terminate simply because a member leaves (or when a new member joins). The language referring to "operation of law" simply reaffirms the power of any other partnership laws to terminate your partnership in certain situations (such as a lawsuit being filed), depending on the laws of your state.

If your band is built around a key performer, the partnership can also provide for termination if that member departs. If you wish to use such a provision, fill in this section. Otherwise, leave it blank or delete the language.

Distribution of Band Assets After Termination

This provision explains how the band's money is used to pay off debts and obligations before repaying band partners. It is divided into three sections, which deal with current assets and debts, band equipment, and future income and royalties. This pay-off system is based on partnership laws that require that creditors get paid before partners. It is standard for all forms of partnerships and should not be changed. The term "capital contributions" refers to the contributions that band partners make, usually when they join the band partnership. For example, members may contribute money or equipment.

Addition of a Band Partner

This establishes the obligations of a new band partner. Generally, the new band partner cannot share in previously acquired assets or property and has no share in any recordings (or their royalties) created prior to joining the band.

Leaving Members

This provision helps to head off problems by providing a system to deal with band members who leave. It provides for a 30-day notice period for leaving members (whether expelled or quitting) and gives the band the option to exclude the leaving member from performances during the notice period.

A leaving member, whether expelled or quitting, is entitled to a payment. If the leaving partner has an interest in song ownership, then you will have to pay the share of the income earned from those songs. The amount you pay depends on the partner's proportionate share.

If you want to list reasons that justify expelling a member from the band, note them in this optional section. If you don't want to specify reasons for firing a member, either leave the section blank or remove the language altogether. You can choose one or both of the reasons supplied in the agreement, or you can write in your own. The ones we've supplied are all financial. Under many state partnership laws, a partner's personal bankruptcy causes the partnership to dissolve. Therefore, some partnerships like to include a provision that provides for immediate expulsion in the event of financial problems such as bankruptcy or insolvency. If you add your own specific criteria, be careful not to be too specific, as this may limit your ability to fire someone. We suggest you include general language such as: "or for any reason that appears sufficient to the remaining Band Partners."

Determination of Net Worth

This provision provides a method of paying off the ex-band partner. Usually the band partnership cannot afford to pay off large sums at one time, so payments above $10,000 are staggered over several years.

Band Partnership Bank Account

Your band will need to decide who has "signing power." This is who has the authority to sign checks to buy things, to endorse checks for deposit, and to sign for withdrawals from the partnership account. Insert the name or names of the band partners who will be allowed to sign band partnership checks. Sometimes two signatures are required, or required on checks over an amount like $500.

Mediation; Arbitration

This provision gives alternatives to resolving your dispute in court that may be significantly less expensive. (See the sidebar "What Are Mediation and Arbitration," below.) We highly recommend you include this provision in most, if not all, of your contracts.

We recommend that you choose the county, province, or city in which the band resides for arbitration. If all the members do not reside within one area, choose a place that is convenient. Enter your location of choice in the first blank.

In some states there are organizations that specialize in arbitration for people in the arts, such as California Lawyers for the Arts (CLA) (www.calawyersforthearts.org) and, in New York, Volunteer Lawyers for the Arts (VLA) (www.vlany.org). You can substitute the rules of such an organization for those of the American Arbitration Association in your agreement. If your band is based in Canada, you can still use the AAA's rules, as they perform arbitration in all major Canadian cities. (For more information on the AAA, see Chapter 17.) Check one of the choices or delete the unwanted alternative.

What Are Mediation and Arbitration?

In mediation, a neutral third party, called a mediator (usually an attorney or expert in the music business), helps the parties reach a solution. The mediator is trained in getting parties to discuss issues that are in dispute and to reach mutually satisfactory agreements. Arbitration is a similar process, except that while a mediator is only a facilitator for the parties who ultimately reach their own agreement, an arbitrator actually decides how the case should be resolved. The decision of the arbitrator is "binding" and is as enforceable as a court judgment. Unlike a court judgment, an arbitrator's decision normally cannot be appealed by the loser.

General

This section contains standard contractual provisions (called "boilerplate") that appear in most contracts, regardless of the subject matter. Boilerplate provisions are explained in the sidebar "What Do These Boilerplate Provisions Mean?," below.

In the blank space, insert the state of residence for the band partners (Canadian bands should enter their province). In the event of a dispute, this determines which law will govern the arbitration or lawsuit.

We have included language advising each band partner to hire an attorney.

It's unlikely that each band partner will do this, but the language reminds the partners they have a right to have the agreement independently evaluated.

Signatures

Have all band members sign and date the agreement, and enter their personal addresses. The birthdates of band members are optional. A person under the age of majority is considered a minor and lacks the ability to enter into a binding contract. The age of majority varies from state to state, but is usually 18 or 21 years old. If a minor signs an agreement and later wants to get out of it (referred to as "disaffirming the agreement"), a court will usually permit the minor to do that. Therefore, if one of the band partners is under 18, it is wise to have both parents or a guardian sign on behalf of the minor. In some states—California, New York, Tennessee, and Massachusetts, for example—if the parents sign the agreement, the minor is prohibited by law from disaffirming it.

What Do These Boilerplate Provisions Mean?

Standard, or "boilerplate," provisions in contracts establish important rules and can affect how disputes are resolved and how the contract is enforced by a court. Here's an explanation of some of the most common boilerplate provisions you'll find in contracts:

- The sentence that begins "The Agreement may not be amended ..." establishes that the agreement is the final version and that any further change must be in writing.
- The sentence dealing with "waiver of any right" allows a band partner to permit something that is otherwise prohibited by the agreement without permanently giving up that right. For example, say your BPA establishes that each band member has an equal vote in all important matters. Under the waiver provision, if a member misses a vote, that doesn't mean that she has lost her voting power under the agreement.
- The sentence that starts "If a court finds any provision of this Agreement invalid ..." permits a court to delete an invalid provision and still keep the rest of the agreement legal and intact.
- The sentence dealing with "successors and assigns" provides that if a band member's interest is transferred to someone else (for example, a band member dies and his interest goes into an estate), then whoever acquires that interest must abide by the terms of this agreement.

Band Partnership Agreement

Introduction

This Band Partnership Agreement (the "Agreement") is made by and between _____,
(collectively referred to as "Band," individually referred to as "Band Partners"). This agreement will be effective as of the date of the last signature below (the "Effective Date"). The Band Partners agree as follows:

The Band Partnership

The Band Partners establish themselves as a general partnership (the "Band Partnership") to be known as _____ under the laws of _____ for the purposes of musical and related entertainment activities. The Band Partnership will commence on the Effective Date and will continue until it is ended according to this Agreement. The principal place of business of the Band Partnership will be at _____ or at any other place the Band Partners determine.

Band Partner Services

In order to fulfill the Band Partnership purposes, each Band Partner will contribute musical entertainment services to the Band Partnership. Such contributions will include, but not be limited to, services:

- as a recording artist with respect to sound recordings
- as a musical performer in all media and on the live stage, and
- related to merchandising rights solely with respect to activities as a member of the Band.

Nonband Partnership Activities

Each Band Partner is permitted to engage in one or more businesses, including other musical entertainment efforts, but only to the extent that such activities do not directly interfere with the business and obligations of the Band Partnership. Neither the Band Partnership nor any other Band Partner will have any right to any income or profit derived by a Band Partner from any nonband Partnership business activity permitted under this paragraph.

Name and Logo

The Band Partnership will do business under the name _____ (the "Band Name") as an assumed name and as its trademark and service mark.

(Check if applicable and fill in.)

❍ The Band also uses the following logo (the "Band Logo") as a trademark and service mark:

_____

❍ The Band also owns and uses the following domain name:

_____

Each Band Partner acknowledges that the Band Name as well as any Domain Name and Logo the Band may have are (select one):

❍ the exclusive property of the Partnership and not owned by any individual member, and, unless otherwise authorized in writing, departing Band Partners will have no interest whatsoever in the Band Name, Domain Name, and Logo, apart from the limited right to be known as an ex-member of the Band. If the Partnership dissolves, no individual member will have a right to use the Band Name, Domain Name, and Logo, apart from the limited right to be known as an ex-member of the Band.

❍ the exclusive property of the Partnership and not owned by any individual member, except that if _____ and _____ cease to be members of the Partnership, the Partnership will cease use of the Band Name, Domain Name, and Logo (including "formerly [Band Name]" or similar references) in connection with any offering of entertainment services. Departing Band Partners will have no interest whatsoever in the Band Name, Domain Name, and Logo, apart from the limited right to be known as a former member of the Band. In the event that the Partnership dissolves, no individual member will have a right to use the Band Name, Domain Name, and Logo, apart from the limited right to be known as an ex-member of the Band.

❍ not assets of the Band Partnership, but rather are the sole and exclusive property of _____ (name of person who owns Band Name, Domain Name, and Logo) and, unless otherwise authorized in writing, will remain that person's sole and exclusive property during and after the term of this Agreement. The other Band Partners will have no interest whatsoever in the Band Name, Domain Name, and Logo, apart from the limited right to be known as former members of the Band.

Warranties

Each Band Partner warrants that the Band Partner:

• is free to enter into this Agreement

• is under no restriction that will interfere with this Agreement

• has not done nor will do any act or thing that might hurt the Band Partnership

- will not sell or transfer any interest in the Band Partnership without the prior written consent of the other Band Partners, and
- will refrain from activities that could prohibit the Band Partner from performing.

Each Band Partner indemnifies each other Band Partner from all claims that may arise from any breach of these warranties.

Profits and Losses

Unless agreed otherwise in writing by the Band Partners, the Band Partners will share equally in all of the Net Profits, losses, rights, and obligations of the Band Partnership. "Net Profits" will mean all payments that are paid to the Band Partnership or to any Band Partner as a result of Band Partnership activities, after deducting Band Partnership expenses (that is, reasonable salaries, rent, promotional costs, travel costs, office expenditures, telephone costs, and accounting and legal fees). The Net Profits will be distributed in cash to the Band Partners.

Ownership of Recorded Compositions

The Band Partners ○ **will** ○ **will not** create a publishing entity (the "Band Partnership Publishing Company") that will own all rights to "Recorded Compositions." Recorded Compositions are songs:

- recorded by the Band
- released for sale on sound recordings under the Band Name, and
- that were written or cowritten in whole or in part by one or more Band Partners.

Each Band Partner agrees to assign any ownership interest in each Recorded Composition to the Band Partnership Publishing Company and to sign any documents necessary to show the transfer of ownership to the Band Partnership Publishing Company.

Division of Publishing Revenue

Revenue from the Band Partnership Publishing Company, if such publishing company has been created, will be distributed as follows:

○ All music publishing income derived from Recorded Compositions, including both writer's and publisher's shares, will be divided equally among the band members.

○ The Band Partners will share equally in the publishing income from all Recorded Compositions. The writers of each Recorded Composition will receive an equal prorata share of the songwriters' income with respect to each Recorded Composition. By way of example, if two Band Partners write a Recorded Composition, each will share equally in the songwriters' income from that song. The publishing income from that song will be distributed equally to all Band Partners.

○ All revenue derived from Recorded Compositions will be pooled (whether it is characterized as publishing or songwriter revenue). Each Band Partner will receive one credit for performing on each Recorded Composition. The writers of each Recorded Composition will receive one credit for writing each Recorded Composition. Each Band Partner's total number of credits equals the numerator (top number of a fraction). The total number of credits equals the denominator, or bottom number of a fraction. Each Band Partner then receives this fraction of the song income. By way of example, if all four Band Partners perform on a song and one Band Partner has written that song, the songwriter Band Partner would receive 2/5 of the revenue, and the other three band members would each receive 1/5 of the revenue.

Publishing Administration

The Band Partnership Publishing Company, if such company has been created, will have the worldwide, exclusive right to:

• administer and control the copyright ownership to the Recorded Compositions

• designate all persons to administer the copyrights to the Recorded Compositions, and

• enter into agreements to copublish, subpublish, or otherwise deal with the copyrights in the Recorded Compositions.

In the event that one of the Band Partners leaves the Band Partnership (a "Leaving Member"), the control of the jointly owned copyrights will vest exclusively in the remaining Band Partners for the term of this Band Partnership.

The Leaving Member's interest in the Band Partnership Publishing Company will extend only to those Recorded Compositions that were commercially released for sale during the Leaving Member's period as a Band Partner ("Leaving Member Recorded Compositions"). The Leaving Member will receive semi-annual accountings and payments with respect to any income due on Leaving Member Recorded Compositions.

Meetings and Voting

Each Band Partner has the right to participate in the business of the Band Partnership. Meetings of the Band Partners can be called by any member of the Band Partnership on reasonable notice.

(Check "unanimous vote" or "majority vote" for each issue.)	Unanimous Vote	Majority Vote
Expelling a Band Partner (unanimous except for party to be expelled)	○	○
Admission of a new Band Partner	○	○
Entering into any agreement that binds the Band Partnership for more than one year	○	○
Additional capital contributions by any Band Partner	○	○
Receipt of any bonus or goods or other assets of the Band Partnership in excess of that received by any other Band Partner	○	○
Any expenditure in excess of $ _____	○	○
Incurring any major obligation such as borrowing or lending money	○	○
Selling, leasing, or transferring any Band Partnership property	○	○
Entering into any contract that takes more than a year to complete	○	○
Check-signing rights	○	○
Amendment of this Agreement	○	○
Dissolving the Band Partnership	○	○

(Check and fill in blanks if applicable.)

○ In matters that require a majority vote, _____ shall be entitled to extra voting power, in the amount of _____ votes for every other Band Partner's single vote.

○ In the event that a majority cannot be achieved, the decision of _____ shall prevail.

Books of Account and Records

The books of the Band Partnership and all other documents relating to the business of the Band Partnership will be maintained at its principal place of business and be available for inspection at reasonable times by any Band Partner (or any designated representative of any Band Partner). The fiscal year of the Band Partnership ends on December 31. The Band Partnership will provide an accounting statement to each Band Partner twice a year, at the end of June and December.

Ending the Partnership

This Agreement and the Band Partnership will not terminate if a Band Partner leaves the Partnership. If a member leaves, the Band Partnership will remain in full force among the remaining members.

This Agreement will terminate, and the Band Partnership will end, on the first to occur of the following events:

- the written agreement of the Band Partners to end the Band Partnership, or
- by operation of law, except as otherwise provided in this Agreement.

(Check and fill in blank if applicable.)

○ If _____ leaves the Band Partnership, the Band Partnership shall end. The addition of a new Band Partner shall not end the Partnership, and it shall remain in full force among the remaining Band Partners.

Distribution of Band Assets After Termination

Income and Debts. After termination of the Band Partnership, any income that is owed to the Band Partnership will be collected and used first to pay off debts to people outside the Band (creditors), and any remaining money will be used to pay debts (loans in excess of capital contributions) to Band Partners. If money remains after paying off these debts to Band Partners, it will be distributed equally to the Band Partners.

Band Property. Any property owned or controlled by the Band Partnership (for example, musical equipment) will not be sold but will be evaluated, by an accountant if necessary. The property will then be distributed, as nearly as possible, in equal shares among the Band Partners.

Royalties and Future Income. If, at the time of termination, the Band is entitled to royalties or owns property that is generating income or royalties, the Band Partnership will vote to either establish an administrative trust or designate an individual (for example, an accountant) to collect and distribute the royalties on an ongoing basis to the Band Partners according to their respective interests.

Addition of a Band Partner

Each new Band Partner must agree to be bound by all of the provisions in this Agreement. A new Band Partner has no rights to the Band Partnership property or assets existing at the time of admission to the Band Partnership ("Existing Property") or in any of the proceeds derived from the Existing Property (for example, revenue or royalties generated by recorded compositions, sound recordings, or other materials created prior to the new Band Partner's admission).

Leaving Members

A Band Partner may leave the Band Partnership (a "Leaving Member") voluntarily (by resignation) or involuntarily (by reason of death, disability, or being expelled). A Band Partner who resigns must give thirty (30) days' prior written notice. The Band Partnership will provide thirty (30) days' written notice if it expels a Partner. The Band has, at its option, the right to immediately exclude any expelled partners from live or recorded performances during this 30-day notice period. A Leaving Member is entitled to:

- the Leaving Member's proportionate share of the net worth of the Band Partnership as of the date of disassociation
- the Leaving Member's share of any royalties, commissions, or licensing fees earned from sound recordings that include the Leaving Member's performance. These payments will be made when actually received by the Band Partnership and after subtracting a proportionate deduction of expenses. The Leaving Member's record royalties will be paid only after the record company has recouped the band's recording costs for the respective recording.

An expelled Partner will be entitled to receive the value of his or her interest in the partnership according to the provisions of this Agreement.

(Check and fill in blank if applicable.)

A Band Partner may be expelled from the Partnership if:

○ the Band Partner seeks protection under the federal bankruptcy code

○ the Band Partner makes an assignment for the benefit of creditors, or

○ _____

_____

Determination of Net Worth

If the Leaving Member and the Band Partnership cannot agree on the net worth of the Band Partnership, then it will be determined by a mutually agreed-on accountant. The net worth will be determined as of the date thirty (30) days after receipt of the written notice of leaving, whether voluntary or involuntary. The Leaving Member's share will be paid in installments starting one month after determining the net worth and be payable as follows:

- If the share is less than $10,000, it will be paid in 12 monthly installments.
- If the share is more than $10,000 but less than $25,000, it will be paid in 24 monthly installments, or

- If the share is more than $25,000, it will be paid in 36 monthly installments.

The share payments will include interest at the prime interest rate.

Notices

All accountings and notices required under this Agreement will be given in writing by personal delivery, mail, or fax at the addresses of the Band Partners set forth below (or at any other addresses designated by a Band Partner).

Band Partnership Bank Account

A Band Partnership bank account may be opened by the Band Partners. _____ has the right to sign any checks drawn on the Band Partnership bank account, endorse checks for deposit, or make any withdrawals from the Band Partnership bank account.

Mediation; Arbitration

If a dispute arises under this Agreement, the parties agree to first try to resolve the dispute with the help of a mutually agreed-on mediator in _____ . Any costs and fees other than attorney fees will be shared equally by the parties. If it is impossible to arrive at a mutually satisfactory solution within a reasonable time, the parties agree to submit the dispute to binding arbitration in the same city or region, conducted on a confidential basis pursuant to:

◯ the Commercial Arbitration Rules of the American Arbitration Association, or

◯ the rules of _____ .

Any decision or award as a result of any arbitration proceeding will include the assessment of costs, expenses, and reasonable attorney's fees and a written determination by the arbitrators. Absent an agreement to the contrary, any such arbitration will be conducted by an arbitrator experienced in music industry law. An award of arbitration will be final and binding on the Band Partners and may be confirmed in a court of competent jurisdiction. The prevailing party has the right to collect from the other party its reasonable costs and attorney fees incurred in enforcing this Agreement.

General

This Agreement may not be amended except in a writing signed by all Band Partners. No waiver by any Band Partner of any right under this Agreement will be construed as a waiver of any other right. If a court finds any provision of this Agreement invalid or unenforceable as applied to any circumstance, the remainder of this Agreement will be interpreted to best carry out the intent of the parties. This Agreement is governed by and interpreted in accordance with the laws of _____. The provisions of this Agreement are binding on the successors and assigns of the Band Partners. In the event of any dispute arising from or related to this Agreement, the prevailing party is entitled to attorney fees.

Signatures

MY SIGNATURE BELOW INDICATES THAT I HAVE READ AND UNDERSTOOD THIS AGREEMENT AND HAVE BEEN ADVISED OF MY RIGHT TO SEEK INDEPENDENT LEGAL REPRESENTATION REGARDING THIS AGREEMENT.

Band Member Signature _____

Address _____

_____

Date _____ Soc. Sec. # _____

Band Member Signature _____

Address _____

_____

Date _____ Soc. Sec. # _____

Band Member Signature _____

Address _____

_____

Date _____ Soc. Sec. # _____

Band Member Signature _____

Address _____

_____

Date _____ Soc. Sec. # _____

What's the Right Business Entity for Your Band?

Most of this chapter focuses on the band partnership—the most common type of business entity for musical groups. But there is a world beyond partnerships and your band may want to explore some of the alternatives.

There are three important factors in choosing a business form: personal liability, taxes, and the relative difficulty and expense of formation. Below, we discuss personal liability and difficulty of formation. The tax issues regarding business forms are discussed in Chapter 16. If your band doesn't choose a business form, it's probably a partnership by default.

Talk with an expert. An accountant or tax preparation expert can best advise you on the tax pros and cons of sole proprietorships, corporations, partnerships, and LLCs.

Personal Liability: Can They Take My Amplifier?

Liabilities are debts, or money, that you owe. Most band businesses carry some liabilities—for example, monthly rent for rehearsal space, installments due on a band van, or payments due to a recording studio. Additional liabilities may arise if your band is devastated by theft, if a fire or flood ruins your band equipment, or

if you are the victim of a lawsuit—for instance, because someone is injured in your rehearsal studio and sues you (as well as the building owner) for damages.

If you operate your band business as a partnership—the most common business form for bands—then each partner will be personally liable for all band business debts. In other words, a creditor can collect a partnership debt against any band partner, regardless of which partner incurred the debt. That means that if your guitarist orders $50,000 worth of sound equipment for the band without telling you and then moves to Venezuela, you could be on the hook. You can create a partnership agreement in which the partners apportion or share their potential liability—for example, the agreement may state that each partner is liable only for certain debts. But this agreement is enforceable only among the partners; it won't eliminate your personal liability to people outside the band who are owed money.

Limited liability companies (LLCs) and corporations are created to shield band members from personal liability. In theory, forming an LLC gives its owners "limited liability." This means that the band members/owners are not personally liable for business debts or lawsuits. The main reason most bands go to the trouble of forming LLCs and corporations is to get this limited liability. But that's not to say you should rush out tomorrow and turn your band partnership into one of these entities. As explained below, limited liability can sometimes be more of a myth than a reality for most bands. For practical reasons, you may not get the benefits you want from the LLC or corporate form of business, so it's often not worth the time, trouble, and expense of converting to an LLC or incorporating.

 Many major label bands create subsidiary companies that deal with specific business issues. For example, to limit its liability, a band may create an LLC solely for touring or selling merchandise. Consult an attorney and tax expert if you want to form an LLC or corporation for these specific purposes.

Business Debts

LLCs and corporations were created to help people invest in a business without risking all their personal assets if the business failed or was unable to pay its debts. In an LLC or corporation, musicians may lose what they invested in the band, but band creditors can't go after personal assets such as band members' bank accounts or homes.

This theory may not work for your band, especially if you're just starting out. Major creditors such as banks don't want to be left holding the bag if your band business goes under. To help ensure payment, they will want to be able to go after your personal assets as well as your business assets. If your band forms an LLC

or corporation, creditors may demand that one of you *personally guarantee* business loans, credit cards, or other extensions of credit by signing a legally enforceable document pledging your personal assets to pay the debt if your business assets fall short. This means that the band member who gives the personal guarantee will be personally liable for the debt, just as if he or she were a sole proprietor or partner. In that case, the so-called protections of limited liability are irrelevant.

EXAMPLE: The members of the band Faith & Sadie form an LLC to run their band business. When the band applies for a business credit card from the bank, they learn that the application contains a clause providing that the signatories—the people who sign the application—will be personally liable for the credit card balance, even though the credit card will be in the LLC's name. When the band asks the bank to remove the clause, the bank refuses, stating that its policy is to require personal guarantees from all small businesses. Two band members sign the application. Now, if the band LLC fails to pay off the credit card, the bank can go after the signatories personally and collect against their personal assets, such as personal bank accounts.

Lawsuits

Forming an LLC or corporation can shield you from personal liability from many business-related lawsuits. That's one of the main reasons for choosing these types of entities. As explained below, however, the members of a band LLC or corporation won't be shielded from some suits.

Corporation and LLC Owners are Personally Liable for Their Own Negligence: Band members who have an ownership interest in a band corporation or LLC are personally liable for any damages caused by their own personal negligence or intentional wrongdoing in carrying out band business. If your band forms a corporation or an LLC, and it doesn't have the money or insurance to pay a claim, the lawyer suing the band will seek a way to collect against your personal assets. Here are some ways that may happen:

- A visitor slips and falls at your rehearsal space and breaks his hip. His lawyer sues the band LLC and the members personally for negligence claiming the band members failed to keep the premises safe.
- Your band LLC hires a driver to take you on a tour. The driver accidentally injures someone while running an errand for you. The injured person sues the band LLC and you personally for damages claiming you negligently hired, trained, and/or supervised the driver.

- Your band creates an album and licenses it to a record label. Another musician claims that a song on the album infringes on her copyright. Even if you've formed a corporation or an LLC, the copyright holder can sue you personally for causing copyright infringement. This is so even though your corporation or LLC owns the copyright, not you personally.

Piercing the Corporate Veil: Another way that the band members can be personally liable even though you've formed an LLC or a corporation is through a legal doctrine called "piercing the corporate veil." Under this legal rule, courts disregard the corporate entity and hold its owners personally liable for any harm done by the corporation *and* for corporate debts.

Generally, the courts say that corporate limited liability protection will be disregarded—that is, the owners will be held personally liable for business debts and claims—only in extreme cases. Most typically this occurs when owners fail to respect the separate legal existence of their LLC or corporation, but instead treat it as an extension of their personal affairs, for example, if band members fail to follow routine corporate formalities, such as adequately investing in or capitalizing (putting money in) the business. You can avoid this result by taking the following actions:

- **Act fairly and legally.** Do not conceal or misrepresent material facts or the state of your finances about your band to other businesses, creditors, or outsiders. Or put more bluntly, don't engage in fraud.

- **Fund your LLC or corporation adequately.** You don't have to invest a lot of money in your band business, but do try to put enough cash or other liquid assets in at the beginning so your band will be able to meet foreseeable expenses and liabilities. If you fail to do this, it is possible that a court faced with a balance sheet that shows a very minimal investment may disregard your limited liability protection. This is particularly likely if you engage in a risky venture that everyone knows needs a large investment.

- **Keep band business and personal business separate.** Get a federal Employer Identification Number for your LLC or corporation and open up a separate band checking account. (For an explanation of EINs and how to get one, see below.) As a routine business practice, write all checks for business expenses or payouts of profits out of this account, and deposit all revenue into it. Keep separate accounting books for your band—these can consist of a simple single-entry system, such as your check register and deposit slips, but a double-entry system will serve you better when it comes time to prepare your end-of-year income tax returns. Lastly, you should keep written records of all major LLC and corporate decisions.

Liability and Bankruptcy

In olden days (the 19th century and earlier), a musician who owed large sums of money could lose everything he owned and even be thrown in debtor's prison by creditors. In our modern society, however, there is no such thing as unlimited liability. First of all, some of your personal property is always safe from creditors' reach. How much depends on the state in which you live. For example, creditors may not be allowed to take your car, your business tools (musical equipment), or your home and furnishings depending on how much each is worth.

Moreover, bankruptcy is always an option if your debts get out of control. By filing for bankruptcy, you can partly or wholly wipe out your debts and get a fresh financial start. Since a partnership is a separate entity for bankruptcy purposes, a partner's personal bankruptcy doesn't bankrupt the partnership, and vice versa.

For a complete discussion of bankruptcy and the types and amounts of property that your creditors can't reach, see:

- *How to File for Chapter 7 Bankruptcy,* by Stephen Elias, Albin Renauer and Robin Leonard,
- *The New Bankruptcy: Will It Work for You?,* by Stephen Elias, and
- *Chapter 13 Bankruptcy: Repay Your Debts,* by Robin Leonard. (All published by Nolo.)

The Role of Insurance

If incorporating or forming an LLC won't always relieve the band members of personal liability—except perhaps in the event of bankruptcy—what else can you do to protect your band and yourself from business-related lawsuits?

First, consider the likelihood of a lawsuit. Most bands rarely get sued unless a particularly awful event has occurred, for example, an accident on the way to a gig. One solution is to maintain insurance for certain types of liabilities.

 If you're looking for insurance for musicians, review the information at MusicPro Insurance (www .musicproinsurance.com) or Clarion Associates, Inc. (www.clarionins.com), where your band may be able to obtain insurance for instrument and equipment loss, tour liability, composer's liability, and travel and accident insurance, health insurance, or term life insurance.

You can also maintain separate auto or business liability for other potential mishaps. Even if auto insurance is mandatory in your state, you may want to check with your insurance agent to be sure that your policy covers your vehicle for band business use. If the vehicle is owned by the band, make sure that you have discussed the possible contingencies—uses of the vehicle, passengers, and traveling out of state—with your insurance agent.

Similarly, if band members are concerned about accidents in the rehearsal space, consult an insurance agent about getting a business policy. Bands rarely get sued for copyright or trademark infringement, but if, for some reason, you're concerned about these types of disputes, you may want to consider carrying a policy that covers your band in the event of these disasters. As for loss of equipment, in Chapter 5 we discuss methods of insuring against that loss.

Insurance has its drawbacks: periodic payments, annoying deductibles, and hard-to-read policies. But insurance is a tried and true way to protect against business disasters such as fire, theft, injury to visitors, and even claims that you stole someone else's music.

Keep in mind that sometimes your band *must* get insurance—for example, if you have employees, state laws may require that you obtain worker's compensation coverage. Your band may have to sign a practice studio lease requiring you to have business and personal property coverage. In other cases, insurance may prove too expensive and you'll have to forgo it. A good insurance agent can help you make the right decisions. If you do acquire insurance, here are some additional tips:

- Maintain enough property and liability coverage to protect your band from common claims—for example, fire, theft, or accidental injury.

- When possible, keep insurance costs down by selecting high deductibles.
- Do your best to reduce hazards or conditions that can lead to insurance claims.

If you are concerned about being sued over band debts—for example, you fail to pay back a credit card or a loan, or you default on a lease—note that insurance won't protect you from liability for these business debts. This is where bankruptcy comes in (see the sidebar, "Liability and Bankruptcy," above).

Expense and Difficulty of Forming Your Band Business

Another factor that may affect your choice of business structure is how hard it is to form that type of business. For example, creating and maintaining a corporation requires some diligence and paperwork. Creating and maintaining an LLC is quite a bit easier. Creating a sole proprietorship or partnership is the easiest; just start performing or selling your CDs and you've done it.

You can create each type of business without the help of an attorney. Nolo (www.nolo.com), the publisher of this book, offers books on forming partnerships, corporations, nonprofits, and LLCs. Generally, if you're confused, too busy, or unsure of how to form a business entity, see an attorney and a tax consultant. Even if you decide to use an attorney's services, continue reading this section to inform yourself on what you're getting into.

Required Paperwork for All New Businesses

If you're starting a new business from scratch, you'll have to take care of some paperwork no matter what business form you choose. Many businesses will need to obtain one or more of the following:

- **EIN.** An Employer Identification Number (EIN) is required for partnerships, LLCs, and corporations. (If you're a sole proprietor without employees, you can use your social security number.) To obtain an EIN, complete IRS Form SS-4. A copy is included on the disk at the back of this book or can be downloaded from the IRS website (www.irs.gov). Additional information is provided in Chapter 16.
- **DBA.** If you're doing business under an assumed name (and—with the exception of Crosby, Stills & Nash— most bands are), local governments require that you file a DBA ("doing business as") statement. You can find out the details from the county clerk at your local courthouse. If you're doing band business as a sole proprietorship under your own name (that is, your last name—for example, The Mark Mellosohn Band), you won't need to file. (For more information on band names, read Chapter 9.)

- **Local Permits.** In addition to filing a DBA, your local or state government may have other permit or licensing requirements. You can usually find out those details at your county clerk's office.

! **Business names versus trademarks.** Registering your business name as a DBA with your county clerk or filing incorporation papers does not guarantee your right to use your name in business or to use that name to identify your products. Before choosing a name for your band business, review the rules regarding trade names and trademarks in Chapter 9.

How to Create a Sole Proprietorship

Forming a sole proprietorship is effortless. If you're running your band business by yourself—that is, without anyone sharing the expenses and profits—you've already created a sole proprietorship.

How to Create a Partnership

Like a sole proprietorship, you don't have to do anything (other than sell your band's music) to create a partnership. No written agreement is required among the partners—although a written agreement is strongly recommended. One reason for using a band partnership agreement (BPA) is to establish each partner's share of the income; another is to guarantee the continued existence of the partnership in the event one partner leaves or dies.

Without a BPA, the departure of a partner ends the band partnership.

How to Create a Limited Liability Company

You can form an LLC in every state. Creating an LLC requires formal filing procedures, and the rules differ from state to state.

Creating an LLC requires filing a document—called Articles or Certificate of Organization—with the state's corporate filing office, usually the Secretary of State. The owners (known as members) can manage the business or designate others to do so. In general, there is far less formality to maintaining an LLC than a corporation.

How to Create a Corporation

Each state's incorporation laws may differ. Therefore, providing detailed instructions for incorporating in your state is beyond the scope of this book. However, here are the basic rules followed in most or all states.

One person, or many, can incorporate a band business. The process starts when an incorporator—any of the owners—prepares and files Articles of Incorporation with the state's corporate filing office, usually the Secretary of State. Bylaws—rules that establish the voting, directors, equity, and other rules—must be prepared (but not filed).

Once the state certifies the Articles of Incorporation, the corporation's board of directors is chosen, the bylaws are adopted, and stock is issued to the owners (one person can own 100% of the stock). The directors manage the business and choose officers who manage the day-to-day operations.

What's Right for Your Band?

In general, we recommend the following approach to choosing a business form:

- **Single owner—keep it simple.** If liability is not a major concern and one person runs the band, keeps all the money, and pays salaries, then maintain the arrangement as a sole proprietorship. Each salaried band member is either an employee or an independent contractor. Salaried musicians who are paid to practice and perform are probably classified as employees. Musicians who are added just to play an occasional gig are probably classified as independent contractors. This classification can make a big difference when it comes time to pay taxes.
- **Band members share expenses and profits—keep it simple.** If liability is not a major concern and the members share in expenses and profits, keep things simple as a partnership. For most bands, a partnership arrangement works fine, because you don't have to do anything to exist as a partnership

(although we recommend creating a band partnership agreement). Some bands are partnerships that employ side musicians. For example, the three core members of a band may be a partnership, and the hired drummer and bass player may be employees of the partnership.

- **Getting bigger or incurring liability is a concern—consider an LLC or a corporation.** If your band is signing a major label agreement or touring regularly and has serious concerns about taxes and liability, you should look into insurance and/or forming an LLC or a corporation.

Honey, I Incorporated the Kids: Family-Owned Bands

If you're one of the many family-owned band businesses, you may wonder how your family fits into the world of business forms. Here are some things to consider.

If a band is comprised solely of a husband and wife and they operate their band business in a community property state (Arizona, California, Idaho, Louisiana, Nevada, New Mexico, Texas, Washington, and Wisconsin), they can operate as a sole proprietorship for federal-tax-filing purposes. They can report all band income and expenses on Schedule C (Profit or Loss From Business), which is then attached to their Form 1040. If a band is comprised of a husband and wife and they operate their band business in a noncommunity property

state, or if a husband and wife have a band with others in any state, then theses bands should form a partnership and file a partnership return (IRS Form 1065) that lists the partnership's income and deductions and each partner's share of partnership profits or losses. (This form is more commonly known as Schedule K1.) The partners use this information to report partnership income or losses on their personal tax return (IRS Form 1040). The same rule holds true if other relatives join in the musical effort: They should also be made partners and given Schedule K1s.

Family members can also operate as an LLC or corporation. One of the advantages of the corporate business form is that the family can provide and fully deduct employee health benefits.

Converting From a Partnership to an LLC

During the years that this book has been available, one business form—the LLC—has grown in popularity. The popularity of the LLC is due to the fact that it allows all owners of the business to quickly and easily achieve the dual goals of "pass-through" tax treatment (the same tax treatment sole proprietors and partnerships receive) and limited personal liability protection (which means owners aren't personally liable for business debts and claims).

As a result of its ease of formation and liability shield, many bands have converted from partnership status to an LLC. If you want to convert your band partnership to an LLC, you'll need to transfer the assets of the band partnership to the LLC, and you should consult with a tax advisor as to state tax rules.

It's possible to accomplish the conversion on your own. But if you prefer making music to filling out legal and tax forms, then leave these tasks to a professional.

Factors to Consider Before Converting

Below is a checklist, borrowed from Anthony Mancuso's *Form Your Own Limited Liability Company* (Nolo), that can help you decide whether your band should make the conversion to an LLC.

- **Is your band involved in extensive touring or is it incurring business debts and claims that could threaten personal assets?** If your band is at a higher risk for lawsuits and claims, consider limiting personal liability by forming an LLC.
- **Do you own sufficient personal assets that would be at risk (such as equity in a house) if a band lawsuit resulted in a judgment that could be collected from your personal assets?** If the answer is yes, an LLC may be the proper route for your band.
- **How much does your state charge for creating an LLC?** Does your state also charge an annual fee? This information can be located at your state government website. High fees may dissuade you from forming an LLC.
- **How are LLCs taxed in your state?** Again, the information is located at your state government website. A tax advisor may help you determine if the conversion is worthwhile.
- **(Optional) Have you consulted with an accountant or lawyer on any complex tax and legal issues surrounding your band's business formation?** If you haven't, you may want to seek some consultation before proceeding. For help in dealing with attorneys, see Chapter 4.

What's involved in converting from a partnership to an LLC?

A band partnership can convert to an LLC in most states with a modest amount of paperwork and fees, and with no change to income tax treatment and filing requirements. That said, as with all legal and tax rules, there are numerous exceptions and strategies that affect a partnership's conversion to an LLC.

Legal Considerations

In order to change a general partnership to an LLC, the partners must take the following action:

- **Terminate the partnership and convert to an LLC.** Your BPA probably requires the unanimous consent of all partners to dissolve or change the form of the business. Even if your BPA states a lesser vote requirement, it's probably best to get everyone onboard by obtaining unanimous approval. (You don't want to drag a reluctant band member into your new LLC.) Additional paperwork may be required to legally terminate a partnership when it is converted to an LLC. For example, your state may require a notice of dissolution of partnership to be published in a newspaper of general circulation in the county where the principal office of the band partnership was located—a routine filing that most newspapers are set up to handle for

a modest fee. A phone call to the legal notice department of your local newspapers should tell you whether this procedure is required in your state and, if so, how much you have to pay to publish this notice.

- **File Articles of Organization.** Your band must file LLC Articles of Organization with the state filing office (typically, the Corporations Division of the Secretary of State's office handles LLC filings). Many states provide an online LLC Articles form specifically designed to handle the conversion of a partnership to an LLC.

- **Prepare Operating Agreement.** The band members should create an LLC Operating Agreement similar to a band partnership agreement. This documents ownership interests, profits, losses, voting and liquidation rights, and other rights and responsibilities of the members. Most bands, when converting to an LLC, set up an LLC that will be managed by all band members (owners), in a system known as member-management (versus management by a select LLC management team, which is called manager-management). Although the LLC Operating Agreement usually contains many of the same provisions found in the BPA, some fine-tuning of the LLC operating agreement may be appropriate to reflect the nuances of LLC tax treatment. This is true even though co-owned LLCs generally are treated the same as partnerships under federal and state law. For that reason, it's best to check with a tax advisor when making the conversion.

- **Revise licenses, permits, and registrations.** Your band LLC should obtain new permits, licenses, and registrations in the name of the band LLC and should cancel old licenses and permits taken out in the name of the now defunct band partnership. If the LLC will do business under a name different from the name of the LLC specified in its Articles of Organization, it should file a fictitious business name statement with the county clerk.

- **Get an EIN.** If the band partnership had an EIN, the band LLC can continue to use it. Otherwise, the band must obtain an EIN to prepare its annual IRS and state information returns.

States May Impose Special LLC Tax Return Filing Requirements and Fees

Most states treat LLCs the same as the IRS—that is, they treat them either as a sole proprietorship (if an LLC has one owner) or a partnership (if it has more than one owner). However, some states may impose special LLC tax return and LLC annual tax and/or fee annual requirements. In other words, if you convert a partnership to an LLC in some states, your annual state tax or fee payments can change. For example, the California Franchise Tax Board requires LLCs that are formed or earn income in California to file Form 568, Limited Liability Company Return of Income, and pay an $800 minimum tax each year, plus an additional annual fee if gross receipts exceed certain thresholds. Check with your tax advisor to find out whether special LLC fees and tax information apply in your state and whether your state imposes a separate entity-level tax or fee on LLCs.

Income Tax Consequences of Conversion

Generally, there are no income tax consequences when a band partnership is changed into a band LLC, provided that the band members keep the same capital, profits, loss, and liability sharing ratios in the band LLC that they had in the band partnership. There may be variations in some state laws regarding the tax consequences of forming an LLC, and your band should speak with a tax professional before making the conversion.

Tax Filing Procedures

After your band partnership is converted to a band LLC, you continue to file a partnership tax return, IRS Form 1065, U.S. Return of Partnership Income at the end of each tax year. (There are no special LLC federal tax forms—LLCs use federal partnership tax forms. An explanation for tax-filing requirements is provided in Chapter 16.) The LLC also continues to prepare a 1065 Schedule K-1, Partner's Share of Income, Credits, Deductions, etc., for each LLC member. The K-1 shows the amount of band LLC income or loss, deductions, and credits each band member must report on their individual 1040 tax returns. The basic income tax treatment of profits earned in the business remains the same after the conversion to an LLC. Band members continue to report and pay income tax on all profits earned each year in the business, whether or not profits are actually paid out in cash by the business to the members.

Band members who receive a share of the LLC profits are not considered employees for payroll tax purposes. However, payroll taxes must be withheld and paid for anyone who receives a salary or other type of guaranteed payment from the band LLC. In other words, if you not only pay out profits to a member, but also employ a member and pay for actual services performed for the LLC, payroll taxes must be withheld from (and paid) on the salary amount.

Beware of Securities Laws

Normally, a member-managed band LLC does not have to be concerned with federal and state securities laws. (A "security" is defined as a sale of an interest with the expectation of earning profits from the efforts of others.) However, if the band creates a manager-managed LLC, the sale of LLC interests probably will be considered a sale of securities under the federal and state rules. That's because the nonmanaging members are investing with the expectation of earning profits from the efforts of others—the classic definition of a "security." In that case, you will need the assistance and advice of an attorney.

Resources for Forming an LLC

The prospect of forming an LLC can be a challenging experience; many people find the legal paperwork less than thrilling. Fortunately, there are plenty of resources available to you to help you handle some, most, or all of the legal paperwork necessary to form your own LLC. In this section, we will list several of the most helpful of these resources.

State Websites

Each state office that accepts LLC filings maintains a website. One way to locate the state filing office is to go to the website for the National Association of Secretaries of State (NASS) (www.nass.org), select the "Business Registration and Filing Services" tab at the top of the page, then select "Corporate Registrations." This will take you to the page for the section or division that handles LLC and corporate filings in the state, where you can look for a downloadable forms link to obtain the official state LLC or corporation Articles form.

Most states provide fill-in downloadable standard Articles to form LLCs. Download the form, fill it in on your computer according to the instructions provided with the form, then print and mail the form together with the required filing fee to the office for filing. The turnaround time in most states to process and file Articles is one to two weeks.

States also are starting to provide online Articles filing services. If your state provides this service, just fill in the Articles form within your browser, then submit the form for filing (you don't have to print and mail the form to the office). The filing fee is charged to your credit card. Typically, online filing is accomplished on the same day or within a few days, and you'll receive a filing receipt from the office either by email or by snail mail within a week of the submission date.

Legal and Business Self-Help Books and Software

There are several publishers of books and software that give you background information on LLCs, plus the forms necessary to organize your own business entity. Nolo (www.nolo.com), the publisher of this book, is a leading source of self-help business formation and operation books and software. Below is a partial list from their catalog of business entity formation and operation resources (see additional Nolo catalog and ordering information at the back of this book).

- *Form Your Own Limited Liability Company*, by Anthony Mancuso. This national title shows you how to form this newest type of business entity under each state's LLC law and the latest federal rules. If you don't need the formality of the corporate form, but would like to have limited personal liability for business debts, this book is for you. Includes instructions for preparing Articles of Organization plus CD-ROM Operating Agreements for member-managed and manager-managed LLCs.

- *LLC Maker*, by Anthony Mancuso. A 50-state Windows software program that leads you through LLC formation process and automatically assembles the state-specific Articles plus an LLC member-managed or manager-managed Operating Agreement to form an LLC in each state.

- *Your Limited Liability Company: An Operating Manual*, by Anthony Mancuso. This book with CD-ROM provides ready-to-use minutes forms for holding formal LLC meetings; it also contains resolutions to insert in your minutes to formally approve standard legal, tax, and other important business decisions that arise in the course of operating an LLC.

Business Entity Formation and Compliance Services

If you're one of the many entrepreneurs who prefer to handle the big decisions and delegate the routine paperwork to others, you may prefer to pay a business formation service to form your LLC or corporation. A leading business entity service provider is The Company Corporation (800-209-0128; www .incorporate.com or www.llc.com), which can handle the formation of an LLC or corporation. ■

Management

I n the motion picture *Stardust*, a British band hires an American manager who tells them they need never worry about business again. It's a jungle out there, explains the new manager, "and I'm the biggest ape in the jungle." For many bands, this is the ideal image of a manager: an assertive, aggressive "ape" who intimidates everyone around him. We will see, however, that managers come in various forms, and a manager's effectiveness is not always related to shouting power.

In this chapter, we offer information about hiring (and firing) a manager. We'll provide an explanation of what a manager does and how to avoid the problems created by handshake deals or management agreements that last too long. We will examine the manager's commission payments and advise how to avoid getting screwed by deductions or commission payments that continue after the management agreement is over. In addition, we provide two sample management agreements: a short-form agreement and a long agreement with more options.

What Is a Manager?

A manager (often referred to as a "personal manager") secures opportunities for earning money, develops a career plan for the band, acts as a liaison between record companies and the band, and shields the band from business pressures. When a manager is doing everything right, it's like cruising on the *Love Boat*. But when a manager is bad, it's like being trapped on the *Titanic*.

The arrangement between the manager and the band is known as the management agreement (or management deal). The management agreement is usually a written document, but it can be oral. As with other agreements, we recommend that you put your agreement in writing. We'll go through the provisions of a sample agreement in this chapter.

A band's arrangement with the manager is almost always exclusive. That is, you can sign with only one manager at a time. Managers, on the other hand, can—and often do—represent more than one band. If you're concerned that a manager might not be loyal to your band or might have a conflict of interest, you'll need to use your best judgment as to whether to hire that manager. (Conflicts of interest are also discussed in Chapter 4.)

The manager's compensation (known as a commission) is negotiated at the beginning of the relationship between the band and the manager. Most managers earn a commission of between 15% and 25% (15% to 20% is most common) of the band's income after certain deductions have been subtracted. Many management agreements state that the commission is a percentage of "gross revenues," which is slightly misleading. The term "gross revenues" usually refers to total income with no deductions taken out. However, in management agreements with bands, the term "gross revenues" often refers to band income *after* deductions. We'll discuss the intricacies of gross revenues later in this chapter.

A personal manager is generally one person. However, sometimes a manager works for a management company that consists of many personal managers. If a band signs with a management company, it can preserve its relationship with an individual manager through a contract provision known as a "key person" provision. We'll discuss key person provisions when we go through the long form sample agreement.

Personal Managers, Road Managers, and Business Managers

Personal managers should be distinguished from business managers and road managers. A personal manager is the mastermind behind the band's business, developing a career plan for the band and acting as a liaison between record companies and the band. The business manager (usually an accountant or tax attorney) handles only finances and investments. For example, the business manager does the band's tax returns and distributes income to the band members and the personal manager. The road manager travels with the band and supervises the day-to-day activities of touring. In the early stages of a band's development, when there is not much income and the band has not signed a record deal, the personal manager may perform all three jobs. We discuss road managers in Chapter 6, and we discuss business managers throughout this chapter.

Avoiding Common Management Problems

There are innumerable ways that managers have screwed bands; we highlight some of the most common examples below.

Situation #1:
There's no written agreement.

A handshake deal is an oral agreement with no written contract. Although at one time handshake deals were standard, that's no longer the case. As we've said before, oral agreements are an invitation to trouble, particularly with important deals like your management agreement. Written management contracts are now the standard in the music business, and we highly recommend that you use one.

If you have a dispute with your manager, the details of a handshake deal may be difficult and time-consuming to prove in court. If you need convincing, ask Bruce Springsteen. In 1976, he planned to record his fourth album but ran into a problem after a falling-out with his manager, Mike Appel. It took lawyers over a year to disentangle the artist and the manager. At one point in the legal mess, Springsteen was so frustrated he jumped on a table in a law office and began screaming at the lawyers. Finally, after his record company stepped in to help negotiate, a settlement was reached with the ex-manager.

How to avoid getting screwed:
If you are dealing with an inexperienced manager, you will have more bargaining power and should insist on a written agreement.

Unfortunately, you may find yourselves dealing with an experienced manager who may insist on a handshake deal. If your band can't persuade the manager to sign a written agreement, you should write down the key terms of the deal on a piece of paper and keep that paper as a record of the agreement. You should also confirm the details of the arrangement in a letter to the manager (for example, "Dear Tom: Our band wanted to summarize the terms of our oral agreement with you. We agreed that … and so on"). Keep a copy of this letter. In addition, you should make an effort ahead of time to understand basic management principles such as gross revenues and the length of the agreement. Be sure to read the sample agreements (below) and review the commentary, which explains the most common provisions of a management deal.

Situation #2:
The management agreement lasts too long.

The length of the management deal—how long the manager will manage the band—is referred to as the term of the agreement. The band and manager can always extend the term if they mutually agree to do so. But the term can be shortened only if there is a method provided in the agreement for early termination. Agreements usually run from one to three years, and often there is an option for the agreement to be extended for an additional two-year period.

Often, a band finds itself unhappy with its manager well before the term of management is over. If, for instance, a manager with a three-year term does a lousy job for a year and fails to bring the band any opportunities, the band might want to find a different manager. However, if the band fires the manager after only one year, the manager can sue the band for damages for the band's breach of the three-year contract.

How to avoid getting screwed:

If possible, try to limit the length of the term to one or two years. You can always renew it if everybody's happy with the arrangement. If your manager insists on three years (or longer), try to establish money standards—also known as earning plateaus—for each year. If the manager doesn't generate a certain amount of money for the band during a specific year, then the band can terminate the arrangement. For example, you can include in your agreement that if the band earns less than $50,000 during the second year, the manager can be fired.

Another solution is to require the band to obtain a record deal by a certain date. If the goal is not reached, the band can fire the manager. Keep in mind, though, that a manager might take *any* record deal in order to meet this requirement. However, this isn't terribly likely because a manager is interested in making money, and if the record deal is bad, the manager won't earn much. In addition, if the band is unable to attract a deal, the manager will probably want to extricate himself or herself from the arrangement as well.

Situation #3:
The manager's commission is calculated from too much income.

A manager is paid by commission, which is a percentage of the band's income. For example, if a band earns $100,000 in one year and the manager earns a 20% commission, the manager would receive $20,000. Often the commission is calculated after certain deductions have been subtracted from the band's income, such as tour expenses or promotion costs. The deductions that are taken from the band's income before the commission is calculated will depend on your agreement with the manager. The more deductions that are taken, the less money gets paid to the manager and the more money your band gets to keep.

An Unusual Definition of "Gross Income"

The terms "gross income" and "gross revenue" usually mean income before any deductions have been taken. However, in music management deals, these terms are typically used even though they often refer to band income after deductions have been made. Since you can't rely on these terms having their usual meaning, it's doubly important that everyone understands what they mean before you enter into a management deal.

A manager should not take a commission on money that is used to pay for crucial band services, such as recording expenses. A band can be screwed when its manager takes a commission "off the top" without permitting the band to first deduct or exclude certain payments or expenses. These amounts, sometimes referred to as "pass-through" income, should be deducted before the manager takes a commission. Including or excluding certain money when calculating a manager's commission can make a big difference in the band's income.

EXAMPLE 1: *Manager Takes It Off the Top*

The band earns $100,000 and has to spend $50,000 on recording expenses.

Manager's commission = $20,000 (20% of *off the top* $100,000)

Band's income = $30,000 (after deducting manager's commission ($20,000) and recording expenses ($50,000))

EXAMPLE 2: *Manager Takes Commission After Deductions and Expenses*

The band earns $100,000, deducts $50,000 for recording expenses, and then pays the manager's commission.

Manager's commission = $10,000 (20% of $100,000– $50,000)

Band's income = $40,000 (after deducting recording expenses ($50,000) and manager's commission ($10,000))

As you can see, the band takes home a lot more money if it pays its bills before the manager takes a commission. By taking the money off the top, the manager is unjustly enriched, because the manager is in effect getting a cut of the recording budget. This leaves the band with less money to pay its operating expenses.

How to avoid getting screwed:

In your management agreement, don't let the manager take a commission on income off the top. Instead, try to have some (or all) of the following sums deducted before the manager takes a commission:

- recording funds advanced by a record company to pay for making recordings (for more information on these payments, see Chapter 14)
- money paid by the record company to make videos (for more information on these payments, see Chapter 14)
- payments for roadies, sound, and light services (for more information on these payments, see Chapter 6)
- payments to record producers, mixers, remixers, engineers, or others who are employed in the production of the band's records (for more information on these payments, see Chapter 11)
- payments to cowriters or co-publishers who are not members of the band (for more information on these payments, see Chapters 7 and 8)
- tour support (for more information on these payments, see Chapter 6)
- booking agent fees (for more information on these payments, see Chapter 6)
- payments to musicians who are not members of the band (for more information on these payments, see Chapter 11)
- payments to acts that open for your band (for more information on these payments, see Chapter 6)
- expenses in connection with promotional and marketing activities (for more information on these payments, see Chapter 14)
- any reimbursements received by your band for expenses paid out of gross income. These occur when you are paid back for something you didn't have to pay in the first place. For example, if your band paid for the shipping of master tapes, which was supposed to be paid by your record company, you may receive reimbursement later. The manager should not receive a commission on this payback.
- income from recording studios, acting, or other entertainment or music sources. The manager should not receive a payment when band members earn money from nonband sources of income.
- packaging income. The manager receives income directly from the ticket sales for a show that the manager is presenting. And
- songwriting income (music publishing) (for more information on these payments, see Chapter 8).

If you have an oral agreement, make sure that the band and manager have agreed on what can or cannot be included in the band's commissionable income, and keep a record of this list.

When Does the Manager Get Paid?

As a practical matter, the calculation of the manager's commission is usually done by the band's accountant or business manager on a monthly basis. In other words, the manager does not simply deduct a percentage from any check that arrives for the band. Instead, all checks for the month are deposited in an account, and the band's business manager or accountant then subtracts those amounts that the manager cannot commission. The manager receives a percentage of the remaining money, and the band receives the rest.

Situation #4:
Commission payments continue too long after the management term ends.

A manager will often get continued commission payments *after* the management deal has ended. These payments are referred to as "post-term commissions." Most managers believe that post-term commissions are fair compensation because they negotiated the original deals that earned—and continue to earn—the income. Sometimes these post-term commissions continue *forever* (in legal lingo, "in perpetuity"). For example, Pink Floyd's ex-manager still receives a commission from some of Pink Floyd's income (income from deals he negotiated) for records made over 25 years ago.

There are two common ways that post-term commissions are calculated. In one, the manager gets a post-term commission from all albums created during the time when he or she was manager. In the other scenario, the manager gets a commission on all albums recorded under a record deal negotiated by the manager—no matter when the albums are created. In other words, if the manager negotiates a three-record deal, the manager would get a cut of the income from all three record deals, even if the management agreement ended after only one album was recorded and the other two were recorded a year or more after the manager left.

As you can see, these types of deals can be quite expensive for a band. If a band is paying a 20% post-term commission to an ex-manager and a 20% commission to a new manager, then 40% of the band's income is being paid out before the band gets its cut.

How to avoid getting screwed:
If possible, limit post-term commissions to *only* albums created during the term. That way, the manager gets paid only for records that are created while the manager is actually performing services. Second, try to negotiate a decreasing percentage after termination. For example, if the manager's commission was 20%, it could decrease in 5% increments over a two-year period as

follows: 20% for the first six months after the termination, 15% for the next six months, 10% for the next six months, and 5% for the last six months. After that, the manager receives no more income. How many managers will accept this? Many bands have been happily surprised to learn that it is often not too difficult to obtain this concession, particularly if the manager does not have a major label track record (that is, the manager does not represent any major label artists).

Situation #5:
The band pays too many of the manager's expenses.

A personal manager will require that the band reimburse the manager for certain management expenses, such as traveling on behalf of your band to meet with record company executives. It is standard to reimburse the manager for all reasonable expenses. It is also standard that the manager must obtain the band's consent before incurring any single expense above a certain amount (say, $200).

Bands can easily get screwed when their manager's expenses get out of control. Sometimes a manager runs up a tab for many smaller expenses that don't each require band approval. Many bands have been shocked to learn how quickly small expenses can add up to several thousand dollars. A manager may travel to a music convention on behalf of two bands he represents and bill one band for the entire trip (or worse, bill both bands for the entire trip). The manager may bill the band for expenses even when the band has no income, creating a personal debt.

How to avoid getting screwed:
Establish rules in your management agreement for which expenses the band will cover. The manager should obtain the band's written approval of either any expense over $200 *or* any total expenses over $1,000 in any month. If the manager has expenses involving two bands or more, those expenses should be prorated. That is, if 30% of the manager's time on a trip to Los Angeles was for your band and 70% was for another band, then the expenses should be split 30-70 between the two bands. Expenses should be paid only when the band earns money and actually receives payment, and band members should never have to dig in their own pockets to pay management expenses. Much of this is monitored by the business manager, who reviews expenses and income and pays the band and manager accordingly.

Situation #6:
The band wants to fire the manager.

If your manager isn't working hard enough for your band (for example, the manager is devoting more time to another band), or your manager has made offensive career choices (for example, booking your band on a one-year tour of Alaska opening for Vanilla Ice), then you need to consider your options. Firing a manager is a last resort and should be considered only after you have exhausted every other option, such as discussing the problem with the manager, amending the agreement, attending mediation, and so on. Consider your decision carefully, because firing a manager is usually a messy and contentious procedure that can disrupt band activities for several months or even much longer. The Jefferson Airplane's management dispute was a particularly nasty one—it lasted 21 years, during which time they received no record royalties.

How to avoid getting screwed:

Review your management agreement and consult with a music business attorney to determine if there is a legitimate basis for termination (Chapter 4 provides information on finding an attorney). For example, your band may have the right to fire the manager because the manager failed to achieve a certain earnings plateau. Before making a final decision to fire the manager, your band should also consider the following:

- **Dispute resolution procedures.** Your agreement may provide for a method of resolving disputes, such as mediation or arbitration. You will have to pursue those dispute resolution methods before terminating the manager. We discuss dispute resolution in the sample management agreement.

- **Post-term commissions.** Even if your band has the legal right to terminate the manager, your band will still be on the hook for post-term commissions. If you hire a new manager, you will have to pay both the old and new manager.

- **The term.** If several years are left on the term, then the fired manager may claim more than post-term commissions. The manager may claim that there are two or three additional years of future records, concerts, and other possible band income that have been denied to the manager. In other words, the more time that is left on the agreement, the more damages that the fired manager may claim.

These contract provisions will affect your decision to fire the manager and your bargaining power if you want to negotiate a termination. Consider that most managers don't go willingly and that it is likely your manager will seek additional compensation. Even so, it's possible to work out a termination without resorting to litigation. In order to do this, you will have to negotiate with the manager and reach a settlement of your differences. Usually this means some form of payment or promise of payment in the future. You should document this termination in some way, possibly by a letter in which you list the terms of the settlement. If you are having trouble reaching a decision, consult a music business attorney. It may be expensive, but it will guarantee that your arrangement is terminated properly.

Abbreviated Management Agreement

This section walks you through the simple task of putting together an abbreviated (or short-form) management agreement. The short-form agreement has mostly fixed terms without much choice. It is suitable if you want to work with a new or inexperienced manager, if you want to have a one-year trial arrangement with a manager, or if you're just not ready to use the long agreement. Keep in mind, though, that the more detailed and customized your agreement, the more protection your band will have. (The long agreement is covered in the next section.) A sample appears below.

 This agreement is included on the forms CD in the back of this book.

Canadian Readers

If you are a Canadian resident, any reference to "state" or "county" in the model agreement should be changed to "province." Occasionally, Canadian contract and partnership laws differ from American law, and when that occurs, we provide an explanation for the difference.

Introduction

Insert the name of the manager and, if applicable, the management company. You should also insert the type of business form and address of the manager or management company (for example, "Mary Smith and Mental Midget Management, a New York corporation, with its address at 47 Prospect Street, Huntington, NY 11743"). If you are signing *only* with a management company and not a specific manager, insert only the name of the company.

Insert your band's name, business form, and address (for example, "Petty Larceny, a general partnership, with its address at 5678 Hempstead Turnpike, Wantagh, NY 11793"). If you are unsure of your business form, review Chapter 2. After that, insert the names of the band members.

Obligations of Manager

This section lists the manager's obligations. The obligations listed in this short agreement are standard for managers. Your band may not like the idea of someone providing "guidance and advice" as to the proper method of presenting the band's music, but this is exactly what a manager is supposed to be doing: studying your band's performance and the audience's reaction to determine how to make your band more successful. A band's arrangement with the manager is almost always exclusive. That is, you can sign with only one manager at a time, and the band cannot make music business deals without the manager.

The Term

This provision (the "term") establishes how long the manager has the job with your band, which in this case is one year. If your band and the manager want to renew at the end of the year, you can do so on the same terms for additional one-year periods. If you want to change the terms, you should execute a new agreement—most likely a longer, more customized one, such as the long-form agreement discussed below.

Commission During the Term

In the blank, enter the commission percentage your manager will receive. The standard commission percentage is between 15% and 25%. A manager who demands 25% should have a successful track record—otherwise your band is paying too much. This provision establishes a number of deductions that must be made before a manager can calculate his or her cut. If the manager will not agree to one or more of these, you may cross them out and have each person who signs the agreement initial each cross-out.

Note that, in this provision, songwriting income is not deducted from the manager's commission. If you do not want your manager to be able to commission songwriting income, or if you want different deductions to be taken from the band's income before the manager's commission is calculated, you should use the long agreement, which is covered in the next section.

Commission After the Term

Managers typically earn post-term commissions—income from the band *after* their job as manager has ended. This provision allows the manager to receive post-term commissions on income from only those records created during the management term. The manager may not receive any commissions on income from records created before or after the term.

Earlier in this chapter, we suggested a descending system for post-term commissions. This provision allows you to choose the descending rate (such as 20%, 15%, 10%, 5%) and the periods that each rate will be paid (usually three- or six-month terms). You can negotiate the numbers according to your bargaining power. We have given space for up to four periods over which to lower your commission rate. If you do not use all four, just cross out the remaining language, enter "N/A," or remove the language altogether. After the last period is over, no more payments are due to the manager.

EXAMPLE:

"These post-term commission payments will be at the following rates during the specified periods:

20% of the Gross Revenues from the first six-month period after termination

10% of the Gross Revenues from the second six-month period after termination

~~____% of the Gross Revenues from the third _____ period after termination~~

~~____% of the Gross Revenues from the fourth _____ period after termination.~~

Thereafter, manager will receive no further post-term commissions. "

Manager's Expenses

Bands are usually obligated to pay their manager's reasonable expenses in promoting the group. This provision sets limits on how much the manager can spend before getting the band's permission. This provision also prevents the band members from becoming personally obligated for management expenses.

Mediation; Arbitration

This provision gives a less-expensive method of resolving disputes than filing a lawsuit. (See the sidebar in Chapter 2 for an explanation of mediation.) We recommend that you use this provision in order to help avoid an expensive lawsuit.

We suggest that you choose the county, province, or city in which the band resides for arbitration. If all the members do not reside within one area, choose a place that is convenient. Enter your location of choice in the blank.

General

The following provisions are standard contractual provisions referred to as boilerplate. Boilerplate provisions are explained in Chapter 2.

Insert the state (or province, in the case of Canadian bands) of residence for the Band Partners. In the event of a dispute, this determines which state law will govern the arbitration or lawsuit.

Signatures

Have all band members and the manager fill in the signature section with signatures, addresses, and dates. Enter the same address for all the band members: the mailing address for the band. Be sure to use an address that will be able to receive mail for two to three years. If there is no such address, use a post office box or an address for the parents of one of the members.

[Abbreviated] Management Agreement

Introduction

This Management Agreement is between _____

_____

("Manager") and _____

_____ ("Band"), comprising the following

members: _____ ("Band Members").

Band agrees to have Manager serve as its exclusive personal manager.

Obligations of Manager

Manager will guide and advise Band in the music business. Manager will serve as Band's exclusive agent for the exploitation and promotion of Band's music services and products throughout the world. Manager will work in association with Band in the negotiation of recording, merchandising, or other agreements affecting Band.

The Term

The term of this agreement will continue for one year after the date of execution of this agreement and may be renewed by mutual consent of the parties on the same terms for subsequent one-year terms.

Commission During the Term

Manager is entitled to _____ percent of Gross Revenues received by Band during the term. "Gross Revenues" are all moneys, including advances and fees, received by Band in connection with Band's entertainment-related activities, but excluding recording funds advanced by a record company, money paid to make videos, payments to record producers, musicians, mixers, remixers, directors, engineers, or any other individuals involved in the creation of audio or audio-visual recordings, payments to nonband member cowriters or copublishers, tour support, and any reimbursements received by Band for expenses paid out of Gross Revenues.

Commission After the Term

Unless Manager has been terminated for a material breach of this Agreement, Manager is entitled to post-term commission payments derived from master recordings created during the Term. Under no circumstances will Manager be entitled to income from albums created before or after the Term. These post-term commission payments will be at the following rates during the specified periods:

_____% of the Gross Revenues from the first _____ period after termination

_____% of the Gross Revenues from the second _____ period after termination

_____% of the Gross Revenues from the third _____ period after termination

_____% of the Gross Revenues from the fourth _____ period after termination

Thereafter, Manager will receive no further post-term commissions.

Manager's Expenses

Band will pay documented reasonable and necessary costs incurred by Manager in connection with Manager's duties on behalf of Band. Band will pay such expenses only out of Gross Revenues commissionable under this Agreement, and no members of Band will be personally liable for any such expenses. Manager will not incur expenses in excess of $200 in any single transaction, or $1,000 during any calendar month, without Band's prior written consent.

Mediation; Arbitration

If a dispute arises under this Agreement, the parties agree to first try to resolve the dispute with the help of a mutually agreed-on mediator in _____ .
Any costs and fees other than attorney fees will be shared equally by the parties. If it is impossible to arrive at a mutually satisfactory solution within a reasonable time, the parties agree to submit the dispute to binding arbitration in the same city or region, conducted on a confidential basis under:

○ the Commercial Arbitration Rules of the American Arbitration Association, or

○ the rules of _____ .

General

This Agreement may not be amended except in a writing signed by all parties. If a court finds any provision of this Agreement invalid or unenforceable as applied to any circumstance, the remainder of this Agreement will be interpreted so as best to effect the intent of the parties. This Agreement will be governed by and interpreted in accordance with the laws of the State of _____. This Agreement expresses the complete understanding of the parties with respect to the subject matter and supersedes all prior proposals, agreements, representations, and understandings.

Signatures

Band Members

Band Member Signature _____

Address _____

_____

Date _____ Soc. Sec. # _____

Band Member Signature _____

Address _____

_____

Date _____ Soc. Sec. # _____

Band Member Signature _____

Address _____

_____

Date _____ Soc. Sec. # _____

Manager

Band Manager Signature _____

Address _____

_____

Date _____ Soc. Sec. # _____

Full-Length Management Agreement

The long-form agreement below covers many more details than the abbreviated form. It includes options and alternatives to deal with most of the situations that may arise between a band and manager. A sample appears below. The following instructions explain how to fill out the form and what the various clauses mean. Many clauses have alternative provisions for you to choose from, which are explained in the instructions. Some clauses, as noted in the instructions, are optional altogether.

 This agreement is included on the forms CD in the back of this book.

Introduction

Insert the name of the manager and, if applicable, the management company. You should also insert the type of business form and address (for example, "Mary Smith and Mental Midget Management, a New York corporation, with its address at 47 Prospect Street, Huntington, NY 11743"). If you are signing only with a management company and not a specific manager, insert only the name of the company. You will not need the optional "Key Person Provision."

Insert your band's name, business form, and address (for example, "Petty Larceny, a general partnership, with its address at 5678 Hempstead Turnpike, Wantagh, NY 11793"). If you are unsure of your business form, review Chapter 2. After that, insert the names of the band members.

Obligations of Manager

This section lists the manager's obligations. These include:

- **Guidance and advice.** Your band may bristle at the idea of someone providing "guidance and advice" as to the proper method of presenting the band's music, but this is exactly what a manager is supposed to be doing— studying your band's performance and the audience's reaction to determine how to make your band more successful.

- **Engagement of services.** A band's arrangement with the manager is almost always exclusive. That is, you can sign with only one manager at a time, and the band cannot make music business deals without the manager. Your band cannot hire another manager until you terminate this relationship. Many managers handle more than one band, and this provision guarantees the manager's right to represent a "stable" of artists.

- **Negotiation and execution of agreements.** This provision provides that the manager oversees every band contract. It does not mean that the manager can sign agreements without your consent. That depends on the "power of attorney" provision, which appears later in the sample agreement.
- **Other obligations.** If your band wants specific tasks to be listed, you can add them here (for example, "Manager will perform regular radio promotion at regional college radio stations for all band recordings").

Key Person Provision

This is an optional provision. If a band prefers to work with only one manager at a management company, that arrangement is sometimes known as a "key man" or "key person" relationship. This provision allows your band to terminate the relationship with the management company (including post-term commissions) if your personal manager is no longer associated with the management company. If you want to name a key person, check the box and fill in that person's name. Otherwise don't check the box and leave the clause blank, or delete the clause altogether.

The Term

This provision (the "term") establishes how long the manager has a job. We recommend that you keep it as short as possible—perhaps one or two years. You can always renew it if the manager is performing successfully. Most managers want a minimum of three years.

As mentioned earlier in this chapter, your band can establish some criteria for keeping the manager. Choose one of the options for the term of the management agreement. Either check the option you want and fill in the blanks or delete the other, unwanted options and fill in the blanks of your choice.

- **Option 1** simply establishes a fixed term for the agreement. Enter the number of years it will last if you choose this option.
- **Option 2** gives the parties a one-year period to determine if the relationship is working before continuing for the full term, which is presumably longer than one year (most likely three years). Enter the full term in the blank if you choose this option.
- **Option 3** establishes one earning goal that must be reached before renewal. Enter the earning goal if you choose this option.
- **Option 4** sets two yearly earning goals in order for the manager to continue. If you choose this option, enter the earning goals.

- **Option 5** sets a "signing" goal. The manager must obtain a recording contract in order for the manager to continue. Enter the time limit for the manager to secure a record deal if you choose this option.
- **Option 6** is similar to Options 4 and 5. In Options 4 and 5, if the goal is not reached, the agreement is terminated. Option 6 is a "flip" version, using a record deal as a goal. If the goal is reached, then the management agreement is renewed. That is, instead of using the goal as a basis for termination, it's used as a basis for renewal.

Commission During the Term

The standard commission percentage is between 15% and 25%. A manager who demands 25% should have a successful track record—otherwise, your band is paying too much. In this agreement, the manager cannot commission the band's income "off the top." Certain payments—generally income that "passes through" the band and is used to pay for crucial band services such as recording expenses—are excluded before the manager gets a cut. Check the exclusions that your band has negotiated.

- **Recording funds advanced by a record company.** A manager should never commission the money received to pay for making recordings (the "recording fund" or "recording advance"). Sometimes the band does not use all of the recording fund to make the recording and the manager may try to commission the surplus. If you decide to allow the manager to commission the surplus, change the language to read as follows: "recording funds advanced by a record company and actually used to create master recordings."
- **Money paid to make videos.** This is "pass-through" income, and it would be unfair for the manager to obtain a commission on it. This should not be commissioned, since the band cannot keep this money.
- **Payments to record producers, website developers, musicians, and so on.** Same as above.
- **Payments to nonband member cowriters or copublishers.** A manager should not commission payments to nonband members who collaborate on songs (see Chapter 7).
- **Tour support.** These payments, made by a record company, are to assist the band in meeting cash shortages while touring. A manager should not commission these payments.
- **Booking agent fees.** Many managers will not agree to this, as they prefer to commission gross revenue before booking agent fees are paid.
- **Payments to opening acts.** Your band, as the headlining act, usually pays the opening band when touring. A manager should not commission these payments.

- **Expenses in connection with promotional and marketing activities and so on.** We recommend that the manager should not commission these independent promotion payments, because promotion is for the benefit of both the band and manager.
- **Income from music publishing and songwriting.** If you have the power to exclude this income from a manager's commission, check this exclusion. If a manager insists on receiving some income from music publishing and songwriting, look at the optional compromise provision below ("Commission on Publishing Income"). Note: If you fill in the optional provision below, you should *not* check this exclusion.
- **Income from any entertainment presentations which manager packages and so on.** We recommend that a manager should not commission income from a manager-owned or controlled production (for example, a packaged tour) as the manager would be paid twice (referred to as "double-dipping"): once from ticket revenues, and once from your band's show income.
- **Payments to nonband member musicians.** This is "pass-through" income, and it would be unfair for the manager to obtain a commission on it.
- **Reimbursements received by band for expenses paid out of gross revenues.**

Sometimes, a band must pay for expenses out of its own pocket (such as artwork for an album) and is later reimbursed by the record company. We recommend that the manager not commission these reimbursements.
- **Expenses in connection with establishing a band website.** The band website has become de rigueur as a promotional and communication tool. As such, it benefits both band and manager, and, if possible, expenses for creating and maintaining the site should not be commissioned.
- **Income from recording studios, acting, and so on.** Band members who earn income from another entertainment source should not allow the manager to commission this income. For example, if a member works as an actor or author, owns a recording studio or a music label, or performs in a side project or produces other artists, that income should not be commissioned.

Commission on Publishing Income

Band members often believe that the success of songwriting has nothing to do with the manager's work. Many managers, on the other hand, believe that songs become popular partly through their work. One possible compromise is to set a management goal. If the manager achieves that goal, then the band will permit the manager to take a commission on the music publishing income. If the manager does not achieve the goal, the band retains all of the publishing income. This way, the manager must prove himself before getting publishing income. If you want to do this, check this provision and fill in the goals and commission rate you and your manager agree to. Note: If you use this provision, you should *not* check the exclusion "income from music publishing and songwriting" in the Commission During the Term section above. If you do not use this clause, either leave it blank or delete the clause. For more on music publishing, see Chapter 8.

Commission After the Term

Managers typically earn income from the band *after* their job as manager has ended (sometimes referred to as post-term commissions).

Earlier in this chapter, we suggested a descending system for post-term commissions. This provision allows you to choose the descending rate (such as 20%, 15%, 10%, and 5%) and the periods that each rate will be paid (usually three- or six-month terms). You can negotiate the numbers according to your bargaining power. We have given space for up to four periods over which to descend your commission rate. If you do not use all four, just cross out the remaining language, enter "N/A," or remove the language altogether. After the last period is over, no more payments are due to the manager.

EXAMPLE:

"These post-term commission payments shall be at the following rates during the specified periods:

 20% of the Gross Revenues from the first six-month period after termination

10% of the Gross Revenues from the second six-month period after termination

____% of the Gross Revenues from the third _____ period after termination;

____% of the Gross Revenues from the fourth _____ period after termination.

Thereafter, manager shall receive no further post-term commissions."

or

"These post-term commission payments shall be at the following rates during the specified periods:

 20% of the Gross Revenues from the first three-month period after termination

 15% of the Gross Revenues from the second three-month period after termination

 10% of the Gross Revenues from the third three-month period after termination

 5% of the Gross Revenues from the fourth three-month period after termination

Thereafter, manager shall receive no further post-term commissions."

Leaving Member

In Chapter 14, we discuss the "leaving member" provision. If the band breaks up or a member leaves, this provision gives the manager the right to manage the leaving members under the same terms and conditions.

> **EXAMPLE:** Dawn and Joanna leave the group The Bird Feeders. The "leaving member" provision allows their manager to continue managing either of them in their solo career or new musical ventures. In other words, the manager can still earn a percentage of Dawn and Joanna's income.

In order to put some restrictions on the manager's leaving member rights, this member provision is "tied" to the band's recording agreement, if any. That is, if you don't have a record deal or if the record deal doesn't include a leaving member provision, your band would have no obligations.

If any band members are uncomfortable with this provision, they should attempt to strike it completely or have themselves excluded from this provision. Generally the manager seeks to latch on to the songwriter and vocalists in the group, as they tend to be the ones with the most earning potential.

Manager's Expenses

The band is usually obligated to pay the manager's reasonable expenses in promoting the group. This provision sets limits on how much the manager can spend before getting the band's permission. This provision also prevents the band members from becoming personally obligated for management expenses.

Business Manager

The business manager is usually an accountant who acts as a neutral party, dividing up band income and paying band members and the manager.

Power of Attorney

When your band grants a "power of attorney" to the manager, the manager has legal authority to act on your behalf. A "special power of attorney" (also known as a "limited power of attorney") allows the manager to handle specific tasks incurred in the daily business, such as signing booking contracts and endorsing checks. A "general power of attorney" is much broader and allows the manager to sue people on your behalf or bind the band to long-term contracts.

We recommend that you grant the manager only a special power of attorney and list the activities that are permitted.

This provision allows the manager to sign touring contracts and requires that the manager make a good faith effort to show the contract to the band for its signature first. In addition, the manager cannot book the band until the band has designated the periods when it will tour.

Not Theatrical or Talent Agency

This provision is primarily for the benefit of the manager. Three states—California, New York, and Massachusetts—have laws known as "talent agent laws" that require a license for anyone who obtains employment for an entertainer. For example, a booking agent who obtains a series of concerts for a band or a talent agent who obtains a movie part for a band would have to be licensed under these laws.

There are some exceptions. For example, in California, a person does not need a license to obtain a record deal on behalf of a musician. In New York, a person does not need to be licensed to perform incidental booking (for example, a special record company showcase). Because these laws vary and the exceptions are not always interpreted in the same manner, most managers want to make it clear that they are not acting as talent agents. That's why this provision is inserted. Regardless of the contract provision, if a manager violates the law and engages in the booking business, the manager would be subject to the talent agency laws.

Mediation; Arbitration

This provision provides a less-expensive method of resolving disputes than filing a lawsuit. (See the sidebar in Chapter 2 for an explanation of mediation.) We recommend that you use this provision in order to help avoid expensive lawsuits.

We suggest that you choose the county, province, or city in which the band resides for arbitration. If all the members do not reside within one area, choose a place that is convenient. Enter your location of choice in the blank.

In some states there are organizations that specialize in arbitration for people in the arts, such as California Lawyers for the Arts (CLA) and, in New York, Volunteer Lawyers for the Arts (VLA). You can substitute the rules of such an organization for those of the American Arbitration Association in your agreement. If your band is based in Canada, you can still use the AAA's rules, as they perform arbitration in all major Canadian cities. (For more information on the AAA, see Chapter 17.) Check one of the choices, or delete the unwanted alternative.

General

The following provisions are standard contractual provisions referred to as boilerplate. Boilerplate provisions are explained in Chapter 2.

In the blank space, insert the state (or province, in the case of Canadian bands) of residence for the band partners. In the event of a dispute, this determines which state law will govern the arbitration or lawsuit.

Signatures

Have all band members and the manager sign and date the agreement. Enter the same address for all the band members: the mailing address for the band. Be sure to use an address that will be able to receive mail for two to three years. If there is no such address, use a post office box or an address for the parents of one of the members.

Management Agreement

Introduction

This Management Agreement is between _____

_____

("Manager") and _____ ("Band"),

comprising the following members: _____

_____

_____ ("Band Members").

Band agrees to have Manager serve as its exclusive personal manager.

Obligations of Manager

Manager will use its best efforts to perform the following services:

- **Guidance and Advice.** Manager will give guidance and advice in order to enhance Band's career in the entertainment, music, and related industries. This guidance and advice includes methods of presenting Band's music and talents and the selection and coordination of business managers, accountants, and booking agents who may obtain employment for Band.

- **Engagement of Services.** Manager will serve as Band's exclusive agent for the exploitation and promotion of Band's music services and products throughout the world. Nothing contained in this Agreement limits Manager's right to represent other musicians, bands, or entertainers.

- **Negotiation and Execution of Agreements.** Manager will work in association with Band in the negotiation of recording, merchandising, or other agreements affecting Band.

- **Other Obligations (optional).** _____

Key Person Provision *(Check if applicable and fill in blank.)*

○ _____ ("Key Person") of Manager's company will directly oversee the day-to-day performance of its services under this Agreement. In the event that Key Person is not directly involved in the day-to-day activities, Band is entitled to terminate the management relationship.

The Term

The term of this Agreement will continue for (select one):

○ _____ years after the date of execution of this Agreement.

○ _____ years after the date of execution of this Agreement, except that either party may terminate the Agreement within one year of the date of execution by sending written notice to the other party.

○ _____ years after the date of execution of this Agreement, except that Band may terminate this Agreement at the end of any year if the band fails to earn gross income (as defined in this Agreement) of at least $_____ during that year.

○ _____ years after the date of execution of this Agreement, except that Band may terminate this Agreement at the end of any year if the band fails to earn gross income (as defined in this Agreement), according to the following schedule: (a) at least $ _____ during the first year of the Management Agreement; or (b) at least $_____ during the second year of the Management Agreement.

○ _____ years after the date of execution of this Agreement, except that Band may terminate this Agreement if the band has failed to sign a record agreement with a major label within _____ years of signing this Agreement.

○ _____ years after the date of execution of this Agreement, and Band agrees to renew the Agreement under the same terms and conditions for an additional two years if the band has signed a recording agreement with a major label within _____ years of the execution of this Agreement.

Commission During the Term

Manager is entitled to _____ percent of Gross Revenues received by Band during the term. "Gross Revenues" is all money including advances and fees received by Band in connection with Band's entertainment-related activities, but excluding:

Check if excluded

○ recording funds advanced by a record company

○ money paid to make videos

○ payments to record producers, musicians, mixers, remixers, directors, website developers, engineers, or any other individuals involved in the creation of audio or audio-visual recordings

○ payments to nonband-member cowriters or copublishers

○ tour support

○ booking agent fees

○ payments to opening acts

○ expenses in connection with promotional and marketing activities and independent promotion, marketing, or publicity

○ income from music publishing and songwriting

○ income from any entertainment presentations that Manager packages or presents and for which Manager receives a portion of the ticket revenues for packaging or presenting the event

○ payments to nonband-member musicians

○ any reimbursements received by Band for expenses paid out of Gross Revenues

○ payments for Band website creation and maintenance

○ income from recording studios, acting, or other entertainment or other nonband sources of revenue

Commission on Publishing Income *(Check if applicable and fill in blanks.)*

○ Manager is not entitled to commission on revenue from music publishing in any year of the Term unless Band has received Gross Revenues in that year in excess of _____ (the "Publishing Cap"). In the event the Publishing Cap is reached, Manager is due _____ % of the Band's publishing income paid that year. In no event shall Manager take a commission on: (a) what is commonly known as the "writer's share" of the song-writing; (b) performance royalties from BMI or ASCAP; (c) any royalties from synchronization rights other than for Band videos; or (d) cover recordings by other artists.

Commission After the Term

Unless Manager has been terminated for a material breach of this Agreement, Manager is entitled to post-term commission payments on any type of income that was subject to commission during the term. Under no circumstances is Manager entitled to income from albums or videos created before or after the Term.

These post-term commission payments will be at the following rates during the specified periods:

_____% of the Gross Revenues from the first _____ period after termination

_____% of the Gross Revenues from the second _____ period after termination

_____% of the Gross Revenues from the third _____ period after termination

_____% of the Gross Revenues from the fourth _____ period after termination

Thereafter, Manager will receive no further post-term commissions.

Leaving Member

The terms and conditions of this Agreement will continue to apply only for the remainder of the Term and only with respect to the services of any member of Band whose recording services are retained by a record company under the "leaving member" provisions of any recording contract entered into by Band during the Term.

Manager's Expenses

Band will pay documented reasonable and necessary costs incurred by Manager in connection with Manager's duties on behalf of Band. Band will only pay such expenses out of Gross Revenues subject to commission under this Agreement, and no member of Band is personally liable for any such expenses. Manager must not incur expenses in excess of $200 in any single transaction, or $1,000 during any calendar month without Band's prior written consent. If Manager's expenses are incurred in connection with its services to other clients of Manager, the expenses must be prorated between Band and Manager's other clients based on the amount of time Manager rendered its services on behalf of Band and other clients. Under no circumstances will Manager's overhead be characterized as expenses reimbursable by Band.

Business Manager

All Gross Revenues subject to commission under this Agreement will be collected by an accountant or business manager experienced in the music business and designated by Band after consultation with Manager.

Power of Attorney

During the Term, Manager will have a special power of attorney to execute standard performance contracts relating to any live performance agreement during any touring period approved in writing by Band, provided that Manager uses reasonable good faith efforts to submit these contracts to Band for execution.

Not Theatrical or Talent Agency

It is understood and agreed that Manager is not licensed as a theatrical artist agency or talent agency and will not perform services that require a professional license.

Mediation; Arbitration

If a dispute arises under this Agreement, the parties agree to first try to resolve the dispute with the help of a mutually agreed-on mediator in _____. Any costs and fees other than attorney fees will be shared equally by the parties. If it is impossible to arrive at a mutually satisfactory solution within a reasonable time, the parties agree to submit the dispute to binding arbitration in the same city or region, conducted on a confidential basis under:

○ the Commercial Arbitration Rules of the American Arbitration Association, or

○ the rules of _____.

Any decision or award as a result of any such arbitration proceeding will include the assessment of costs, expenses, and reasonable attorney's fees and a written determination of the arbitrators. Absent an agreement to the contrary, any arbitration must be conducted by an arbitrator experienced in music industry law. An award of arbitration is final and binding on the Band Partners and may be confirmed in a court of competent jurisdiction. The prevailing party has the right to collect from the other party its reasonable costs and attorney fees incurred in enforcing this agreement.

General

Nothing contained in this Agreement is meant to establish either Manager or Band a partner, joint venturer, or employee of the other party for any purpose. This Agreement may not be amended except in a writing signed by both parties. No waiver by either party of any right will be construed as a waiver of any other right. If a court finds any provision of this Agreement invalid or unenforceable as applied to any circumstance, the remainder of this Agreement will be interpreted to best carry out the intent of the parties. This Agreement is governed by and interpreted in accordance with the laws of the State of _____. This Agreement expresses the complete understanding of the parties with respect to the subject matter and supersedes all prior proposals, agreements, representations, and understandings. Notices required under this Agreement can be sent to the parties at the addresses provided below. In the event of any dispute arising from or related to this Agreement, the prevailing party is entitled to attorney's fees.

If these terms and conditions are agreeable, please sign and execute both copies of this Agreement and return one copy to Manager.

Band Members

Band Member Signature _____

Address _____

_____

Date _____ Soc. Sec. # _____

Band Member Signature _____

Address _____

_____

Date _____ Soc. Sec. # _____

Band Member Signature _____

Address _____

_____

Date _____ Soc. Sec. # _____

Manager

Band Manager Signature _____

Address _____

_____

Date _____ Soc. Sec. # _____

Variations on Management Arrangements

There are many variations on management agreements. For example, Jon Landau, who manages Bruce Springsteen, is also Springsteen's record producer and is personally involved in what ends up on his albums. Sometimes a band member manages the band. For example, Elvis's first manager was a member of his backup band. Below, we discuss some of the variations on management agreements.

Member-Managed Bands

Except for a major label signing, a band does not have to hire a manager and can probably manage itself (we will refer to this situation as a "member-managed" band). The difficulty with member-management is usually finding someone in the band who is willing to handle the business side of things (it's probably the person who is reading this book!). The member-manager carries a double load—performing and managing—and is usually not compensated for management duties.

Here are some suggestions for a member-managed band:

- Have only one member-manager, because, as a general rule, having several persons in the band handling business doesn't work.
- Provide incentives for member-management, such as offering 5%

or 10% of show income for booking gigs.

- Have regular meetings to discuss current band business; otherwise, band members may feel out of the loop.
- Hire a manager if member-management is not working out. It's better to pay someone 20% than have your band break up over member-management problems.

Producer/Manager Deals

Some bands sign production company/management agreements or production company/management/music publishing arrangements. Under these arrangements, the band signs with a company that manages the band, produces recordings, and also owns a piece of the band's music publishing. This "Swiss Army knife" approach, in which your band puts three different functions in the hands of one company, is especially common in country music. It is also used by successful record producers who have a knack for producing popular recordings and want a piece of the resulting publishing income.

These agreements require an enormous amount of trust, because the band is picking a manager, a producer, and a music publisher all in one shot. As a rule of thumb, you should disregard the deal completely if the production/management company has not had any previous success (for example, has never placed a record on the Billboard charts). You should also attempt to speak with any other artists handled by the same production/management company to find out what it's like working with the company.

Attorney/Management Deals

If your manager is an attorney, there is a potential problem if the manager is giving you legal advice such as reviewing your band's recording agreement. The attorney/manager's advice may be influenced by the potential commission, not by a desire to protect the band. For example, an attorney/manager may agree to less favorable terms and conditions in order to get the deal done quickly—that is, to receive the management commission. It is always better to have an attorney who is not your manager (or your manager's attorney) look over your band's recording agreement. ∎

Chapter 4

Attorneys

At some point in your band's career, you may find yourself sitting in an attorney's waiting room preparing to hire someone who charges more per hour than your band earns in one night. Perhaps your band has been threatened with a lawsuit, or perhaps you need help negotiating a big contract.

How do you choose an attorney? And if things don't work out, how do you fire one? In this chapter we will prepare you for dealing with attorneys. We will help you find, evaluate, and fire an attorney, and we will also discuss what to do about issues such as large legal bills, unending lawsuits, and terminal contract negotiations.

Entertainment Attorneys

When it comes to music attorneys, one size does *not* fit all. Your band's choice of an attorney usually depends on the situation. The most common reason that a band hires a lawyer is to review, draft, or negotiate a contract. To some extent, we have made that task easier by providing you with background contract information in this book. However, there may be situations where your band needs more legal help—and in that case you would seek an attorney knowledgeable in negotiating entertainment contracts. This type of attorney is often referred to as an entertainment attorney or a music attorney.

However, there are different types of entertainment lawyers. Some of them only negotiate contracts; some only handle lawsuits between entertainers and companies; and some are in the business of shopping music. (Shopping is the process of soliciting labels on behalf of a band.) Some attorneys perform all of these functions and more. We will walk you through the procedure of finding the entertainment attorney that is right for your band.

Often a band maintains an ongoing relationship with an entertainment lawyer (much like a patient with a family doctor), and if special problems arise, such as tax problems, criminal charges, or bankruptcy, the entertainment attorney will help the band find a specialist. For example, if a band faces a lawsuit, the entertainment attorney can help the band find a lawyer who specializes in litigation (a litigator).

Locating, Hiring, and Firing an Attorney

The first step in finding an entertainment attorney is to be sure you know what you want to accomplish. "This sounds obvious," said one music business attorney, "but every lawyer has had the experience of being interviewed by a band that has heard that they need an entertainment lawyer, but have no idea what they want that lawyer to accomplish." Therefore, before you begin your search, have a discussion with your band members as to exactly why you need an attorney.

Locating an Attorney

The best way to locate an attorney is through referrals from other bands. It is also possible to locate, interview, and hire a music attorney through a state bar association or through a local county or city bar association. Since you are seeking an attorney for a specific reason, you should express that reason to the referral service. For example, explain that you need an attorney to review a music publishing contract or to assist in a tax audit. These bar association referrals can be helpful, because many referral systems permit you to interview two or three attorneys at a reduced hourly rate.

Check your local Yellow Pages and ask the bar association if they have a lawyer referral service. The Volunteer Lawyers for the Arts (VLA) in New York City (www.vlany.org) maintains a national directory of various organizations offering legal assistance for musicians. You should always be aware that bar associations cannot guarantee the quality of the attorney's services.

How to Interview an Attorney

"Once you know what you need," a music business attorney told us, "then, the first questions you will ask prospective lawyers will have to do with the specific job at hand." For example, do you need

advice reviewing and negotiating a contract, protecting the band name or song copyrights, or shopping a tape to managers or to record companies? "Unless the attorney has a solid reputation in the music community as an entertainment lawyer," the attorney told us, "ask whether he is experienced in that specific type of work. Get a feeling for his experience level by asking what other bands in your genre he represents, and what he has done for them. If you are determined to achieve a specific result (for example, changing the seven-record deal you've been offered into a two-record deal), discuss whether he believes your expectations are realistic. If you are looking for someone to shop your tape, ask which bands he has succeeded in placing. Also ask questions such as 'Will you return all of our phone calls personally?' 'What record executives or record labels do you represent?' 'Do you represent other bands on the label that wants to sign us?' 'How long will it take you to get us a first draft of a contract?' 'Have you listened to the tape we sent you?'"

Talking About Money

After you have discussed the legal tasks required, it's time to start talking about money. You should understand up front that most attorneys bill an hourly fee of $200 to $300 an hour and send a bill at the end of each month. Some attorneys bill on a fixed-fee basis in which your band pays a set fee for services (expect to pay $5,000 to $25,000 to negotiate a major label deal). Most attorneys ask for a retainer, which is an advance payment for legal work (see the sidebar "What is a Retainer?," below). The amount of the retainer is included in the attorney-client fee agreement.

The fee agreement is negotiated between you and your lawyer and establishes the payments and the lawyer's responsibilities. Read it and understand your rights as a client. If you sign a fee agreement, be sure to include a provision stating you have the right to drop your attorney at any time. (In many states, such as California, a client always has the right to terminate the attorney for any reason or no reason.)

Don't be embarrassed to get specific about billing. It's important for all concerned to know whether you can afford the services. Ask how charges are calculated, and what the estimated cost for the job at hand will be. Is a retainer required? If the lawyer bills by the hour, ask if you can get a cap on the price in case negotiations are unusually protracted. Find out if you can use a credit card, or pay over several months, and whether interest will be charged if your payments are late. Be sure you will be provided with a written retainer letter outlining payment terms.

Beware, however: Some attorneys in the music business use unique billing systems. An attorney may, for example,

charge the band a percentage of the "value" of a deal. This "value billing" system is an unpredictable combination of hocus-pocus and greed. Only the powerhouse firms engage in value billing. Beware of attorneys who may attempt to switch to value billing during the period of legal representation. Every lawyer should provide a retainer letter up front saying how charges will be calculated.

Below are some billing tips that will help protect your band:

- **Understand exactly how you're being billed.** In your initial meeting with the attorney, ask how you are being billed. If you are billed on an hourly system, find out the increments. For example, some attorneys charge a minimum of one-quarter of an hour (15 minutes) for a phone call, no matter how short the conversation.

- **Watch out for hidden expenses.** Find out what costs and expenses you must pay other than the fees for the lawyer's work, such as costs for copies or faxes, travel expenses, or court costs. Watch out if your attorney wants to bill for services such as "word processing" or "administrative services." This often means you will be paying the secretary's salary.

- **See if you can avoid hourly rates.** If you can, get your attorney to agree to fixed fees for certain work rather than hourly billings. For example, if your attorney is negotiating a merchandising deal, get a flat rate for the whole job. That way you'll know exactly what to expect. If you can't get fixed billings, ask your attorney to estimate fees for work and ask for an explanation if the bill exceeds the estimate.

- **Review billings carefully.** Billings should be prompt and clear. Do not accept summary billings (for instance, one sentence such as "litigation work"). Every item should be explained with rate and hours worked, including fractions. Late billings are not acceptable, especially in litigation. When you get bills you don't understand, ask the attorney for an explanation—and request that the attorney not bill you for the explanation.

What Is a Retainer?

A retainer is an advance payment to an attorney. The attorney places the retainer in a bank account (in some states, this must be an interest-bearing account) and deducts money from the account at the end of each month to pay your bill. When the money is depleted, the attorney may ask for a new retainer. If the retainer is not used up at the end of the services, the attorney must return what's left. The amount of the retainer usually depends on the project.

For example, retainers for litigation are typically between $2,000 and $5,000. Some attorneys use the term "retainer" to refer to a monthly fee that the attorney gets regardless whether any legal services are performed. In other words, you are paying a monthly fee just to keep the attorney available to you. We recommend against this type of arrangement.

Attorney Style

Choosing an attorney is also a matter of style. Your band may prefer to be represented by an attorney whose style and demeanor correspond with the band's approach. Among those factors that a band may consider when determining style are whether the attorney has clout in the industry; whether the attorney understands the band's music; whether the attorney is aggressive, ethical, knowledgeable, affordable, and impresses friends or terrifies adversaries. After you talk to a number of different lawyers, you can take a band vote on which feels the most right for you. You'll probably wind up hiring the guy with whom you obviously click.

Three Tips for Saving Money With Your Attorney

It's common for a band to feel overwhelmed by a lawyer's bill. Often, that's because the band is not using the attorney's services efficiently. To get the most bang for your legal buck, you need to be organized. Disorganization is unprofessional and can kill careers. Several years ago we spoke with Kathryn (Cassie) Roessel, a New York–based music business attorney who represented Barry Manilow, Diamanda Galas, "and a lot of people who fall between these extremes." Here are some tips Cassie provided for saving money with an attorney:

- **Elect a contact person.** Elect one member to be the "contact person" with the attorney, to ask questions and relay information to the rest of the band. Lawyers charge for telephone time, so don't duplicate your effort. The contact person should keep a written list of "questions for the lawyer," ask them all in one telephone call, and take notes on the answers. Because many lawyers charge in 15-minute increments, five three-minute questions will cost the same as one five-minute question.

- **Keep track of documents.** Documentation is the heart of legal work, and your band needs to have a system to keep track of the papers. Buy a filing cabinet or accordion folder just for band business. Put that folder in the hands of the person in the band who has the neatest bedroom. Place all important papers in this file and nowhere else. Put a copy of all lawyer correspondence, copyright registration papers, and contracts in the file in a well-organized manner, where you can refer to them or produce them if a new lawyer ever needs them. Duplicating records costs money.

- **Prepare for attorney meetings.** Have a band meeting an hour before a meeting at the lawyer's office. Make a written list of any questions or problems you need to cover during the meeting. Travel to the meeting together, so that you aren't billed for time spent reexplaining things to the guy who arrives a half-hour late.

Evaluating Your Attorney's Services

How do you know if your lawyer is doing a good job? Generally the measurement of a professional's performance (whether it is a doctor, lawyer, or dentist) is that he or she:

- provides you with accurate and understandable advice
- permits you to make informed decisions as to how to proceed, and
- works with you to efficiently resolve conflicts and solve problems.

If your attorney is not fulfilling all three of these requirements, then there is a problem in the attorney-client relationship. For example, there is generally a problem if:

- your attorney is not returning phone calls within 48 hours
- your bills are disproportionate to what the attorney predicted and there is no plausible explanation, or
- you are unable to understand why your attorney is doing things or your attorney speaks down to you.

As a general rule, if you leave the lawyer's office confused or unclear of your course of action, then there is a problem. After all, the primary purpose of an attorney is to counsel you as to your legal options. If you don't understand these options, then the attorney has failed. This doesn't mean that the lawyer will always present a black-and-white explanation. There are many gray areas in the law. For example, the law regarding band names is often murky. However, a good attorney will explain this murkiness and evaluate your chances if there is a dispute over the use of a name.

It's sometimes hard to judge the quality of the work an attorney is doing. However, at a minimum, your lawyer should return your phone calls (or have an associate or an assistant deal with them) within one business day ... two at the most. If the lawyer doesn't, you should get a new lawyer. Your attorney should be taking the time to carefully explain the deals you are signing in language that you can understand. You should also receive regular progress reports on your band matters, if you ask for them. If weeks are passing without any apparent progress, there should be a legitimate explanation for the delay. "I've been too busy to get to it" is not a legitimate explanation.

Firing Your Attorney

A band doesn't have to love its attorney, but the members should respect and trust the attorney's abilities as a hired professional. As a general rule, you should switch attorneys if you are unhappy with your lawyer's services. Switching attorneys means that you fire one attorney and hire another. However, since switching attorneys is a nuisance and your band may lose time and money, you should carefully discuss the situation with your band.

How do you fire an attorney? You should notify the attorney by letter that you are terminating services and that you want your files returned. The attorney will probably retain a copy of your files and return the originals to you. You may be asked to pay any outstanding bills. However, an attorney cannot withhold your files because you have failed to pay your bills.

If your attorney is representing you to a third party (for example, to a record company), you should notify the third party that you are no longer working with the attorney and that future correspondence should be sent to you (at least until you retain a new attorney).

The easiest way to switch attorneys is to find a new attorney and ask the old attorney to send the file to the new attorney. In that case, before terminating your current attorney you would have another attorney prepared to take over any outstanding legal work.

How to Avoid Getting Screwed by Your Attorney

Sadly, there are a number of common situations that result in disputes between bands and their lawyers. The best way to protect yourself from an ugly dispute with an attorney is to approach all relationships with lawyers carefully and anticipate problems before they catch you.

Situation #1:
A contract negotiation goes on forever.

Lawyers' fees can quickly get out of control if negotiations for recording or other contracts drag on too long. During this time a band may be missing other, better opportunities or simply paying too much for legal fees.

How to avoid getting screwed:
It's normal for recording contracts to go through many drafts to correct errors and ensure the language is exactly how everyone wants it. While it would be foolish to rush into signing a contract without examining it carefully and making appropriate changes, you also don't want the revision process to go on forever. As long as you and your attorney are conscientious, the fewer drafts, the better. It is common for major label record deals to take four to six months to negotiate. Indie deals should take less— usually under three months.

Make sure your band and the attorney are in agreement as to the goals of the contract negotiation. For example, if getting a guaranteed two-record deal is most important, tell your lawyer that is your number one priority. Once you have achieved most or all of your goals, then be flexible on remaining issues so that you can save time.

Situation #2:
A lawsuit goes on forever.

If you are involved in a dispute that's made it to litigation, it may take months or years to resolve. Some lawsuits, such as the Jefferson Airplane's dispute with its former manager, can go on for decades. During the dispute, the Airplane's record company, RCA, refused to pay over $1.3 million in royalties and $700,000 in interest to the band, claiming it could not make the payment unless the management problems were resolved. After 20 years, a San Francisco judge finally ended the lawsuits, and the record company was required to make the payment. As you can imagine, bands can easily get buried in legal fees during even a medium-length lawsuit. Plus, during the period of the dispute the band may be under legal restrictions that cut into its profit-making ability—such as a ban on using a name or releasing a new recording.

How to avoid getting screwed:
Beware of litigation! One lawsuit can easily cost $10,000 to $50,000, and often the only ones who profit are the lawyers. If you're in a dispute, before screaming "I'll see you in court!" ask your attorney for a realistic assessment of your odds and the potential costs. The assessment and underlying reasoning should be in plain English. If a lawyer can't explain your situation clearly to you, he or she won't be able to explain it clearly to a judge or jury.

Also ask your attorney about alternative dispute resolution methods such as arbitration and mediation. Often these procedures can save money and are generally much faster than litigation. Mediation is a procedure in which a neutral person, experienced in resolving disputes, helps the parties find a solution. The mediator doesn't make a decision or ruling; the mediator only helps the parties settle their controversy. Arbitration is similar to mediation except that the arbitrator makes a decision that is binding on the parties. In some states there are organizations that specialize in these alternative dispute resolution procedures, such as California Lawyers for the Arts and the Volunteer Lawyers for the Arts in New York. (Contact information for these and other resources is found in Chapter 17.)

Situation #3:
Your lawyer represents both sides in a negotiation and you feel like you got screwed.

Lawyers are bound by ethical rules to disclose if there is a potential conflict of interest. A conflict of interest occurs whenever the lawyer represents adverse interests; for example, if your attorney also represents your record company or manager. When there is a conflict of interest, there is the potential that your attorney may not battle as forcefully for your position. For example, if the attorney represents you and a record label, it is possible that the attorney will be apprehensive of endangering a lucrative relationship with the record label for the sake of your band. Another danger is that the attorney you use may enter into an unethical relationship with a band's manager or record company. For example, in 1992 Billy Joel sued his former attorneys, alleging that the attorneys gave his manager payoffs and kickbacks. Evidence surfaced that the attorneys had loaned money to Joel's manager to buy a racehorse (which allegedly was killed to recover insurance money). The attorneys denied all of Joel's allegations, and the case was eventually settled in 1993.

How to avoid getting screwed:

Attorneys should disclose a conflict without being asked, but they don't always do so. Always ask your attorney if there is a potential conflict. Always investigate possible conflicts. If there is a conflict, discuss the matter with bandmates. It's possible that an attorney can vigorously represent both your interests despite a potential conflict of interest. This is a judgment call that should be made based on your feeling for the attorney and any other information you have obtained, such as references from other clients.

Many bands proceed in the face of a potential conflict because they have faith in their attorney's ability to protect the band's interests and perhaps because

they believe that such so-called conflicts can be helpful. Keep in mind that many people shop for a lawyer because he or she has conflicts (also known in our business as "relationships"). These relationships can be great and provide otherwise unavailable access, until it becomes a double-edged sword.

If your band wants to proceed, your attorney may furnish you with a waiver in which the band gives up any right to complain about the situation later. The waiver is used to protect the attorney from a malpractice claim. You don't have to sign the waiver, but the attorney will probably not go ahead if you don't sign it. If your band does not want to sign, find a different attorney.

Having an Attorney Shop Your Music

Some entertainment attorneys shop the band's music to record labels and music publishers. (Nonattorneys also shop music; see the sidebar "Label-Shopping Agreements and Lawyers," below.) These "shoppers" use their industry connections to obtain deals for the band and are paid with a percentage of the band's income from the deal (typically 5% to 10%). This is referred to as a label-shopping deal, and the income may continue for the life of the deal, or for a limited period of time, depending on the arrangement with the attorney.

Label-Shopping Agreements and Lawyers

You might wonder why we discuss "label-shopping agreements" only with reference to lawyers, when in fact nonlawyers can—and often do—perform the task of shopping your band's music for you. The answer is really just a matter of terminology. When a nonattorney manager shops your tapes, that's just part of his job, so the band doesn't execute a specific label-shopping agreement for that job. A separate agreement isn't usually necessary, because shopping music is most likely part of the management agreement, and is probably one of the main reasons the band hired the manager in the first place. But while it's at the heart of a manager's job to try to secure record deals for your band, attorneys usually have a different role with a band. Shopping music isn't generally part of an attorney's job description, so separate shopping agreements are necessary.

For example, an attorney may shop your band's music around and draft your contract in return for a percentage of the band's income from that deal. The attorney may charge $5,000 plus 5% of your record deal. Every time your band receives a payment from the record deal, the attorney would receive 5%. Your band may have to continue paying this percentage even after you switch attorneys.

You may wonder why attorneys shop music. After all, this is not a task that requires a legal education—managers and bands themselves often perform the same function. The reason is that attorneys have assumed a unique position of power in the music business: They're well-connected and have knowledge about contracts. Since many labels are run by attorneys, this creates a situation that many musicians find very depressing—attorneys shopping music to other attorneys. After all, where are the people who are passionate about music? Unfortunately, you will have to put aside such concerns and accept music shopping by attorneys as a business reality.

On the other hand, some attorneys report that less importance is now placed on music-shopping arrangements. That's because, as one lawyer told us, "[Labels] have discovered what pathetic taste most lawyers have. Therefore, they don't pay much attention to the tapes that lawyers send in unless there's some other evidence that the band has something going for it."

What Should You Pay for Label Shopping?

There are several important variables when determining how much to pay a label shopper:

- the size of the percentage
- what deductions are made before the percentage is calculated, and

- whether there is a limit as to how much the shopper receives.

Shoppers traditionally receive 5% to 10% of the record deal, with most deals closer to 5%. Sometimes (but usually not often) a band can make certain deductions before the percentage is calculated. For example, if the label is advancing $50,000 to the band to make a video, the band should try to exclude such payments from the shopper's income. As you can see, the issue of deductions and commissions affects label-shopping agreements in the same way that it affects management agreements (see Chapter 3).

The total amount to be paid to the shopper is also an important factor. Many shopping arrangements are for the length of the record deal. Therefore, if you sign a six-record contract, each time your band receives an advance, the person who shopped the music would get a cut. For that reason, some bands attempt to limit the total payments by placing a limit or "cap" on the money paid to the shopper. For example, your agreement could give the attorney 5% of the income from the record deal up to $20,000. After that, the attorney would receive no more of the payments.

Sometimes the decision of how much is fair is based on the band's circumstances. As one attorney explained, "If a band has never played anywhere besides the drummer's garage and they find a lawyer who procures a major label deal based on a demo tape, I would say that 5% over the life of the deal would be a bargain. On the other hand, if they've already sold 5,000 units of their [do-it-yourself] record in their hometown, it's a complete rip-off."

Potential Pitfalls of Label-Shopping Arrangements

Label shopping used to be a function of the band's manager, but the lines between managers and attorneys have blurred in the past two decades. There is often a large gray area between managers and attorneys—some managers are lawyers, and some lawyers perform management functions. In the past, when the functions were always separate, a band could use the attorney and the manager as a system of checks and balances. That is, the attorney could review the management agreement on behalf of the band, or the manager could advise the band when to switch attorneys.

Whether the same person should perform both functions is a matter that your band must decide based on your knowledge of—and trust in—the attorney. It can be a boon for musicians who can save money on legal bills, but it can also be a risky proposition, particularly when the manager/attorney is getting a percentage of a record deal. Why? Because whenever the manager/attorney is getting a percentage of the deal, there is always the possibility that the band won't get the same impartial legal advice as they would if they retained a separate attorney who was paid on an hourly basis. As is often the case in the music industry, it comes down to greed. An attorney who is getting a percentage of a record deal may forgo other contract considerations (such as length of the contract or song ownership) in order to get the highest possible payments.

As you can see, potentially sticky issues may arise when an attorney shops a demo. Consider the following potential situations:

- **The attorney does not take a personal interest in your band's career.** Sometimes, an attorney who shops music does not use discretion. The attorney simply dumps demos with many record companies in the hopes that one of them connects.

- **The attorney has a conflicting interest.** Since the attorney is earning a percentage from the deal, it is possible that the attorney's major concern is the size of the advance. Your band may have other priorities, such as obtaining a higher royalty rate, getting a guaranteed second record, or getting a good royalty rate for songs written by the band (referred to as "controlled compositions" and discussed in Chapters 8 and 14).

- **The attorney mixes business and legal services.** When an attorney performs nonattorney services, such as shopping music, the attorney is mixing legal and nonlegal services. In some states, such as California, the law requires that before an attorney enters into such a relationship, the client must be advised in writing to seek the advice of another (independent) attorney and that the terms of the business arrangement must be in writing and should be in a manner which "should reasonably have been understood" by the client. In other words, you should understand everything you sign and, if necessary, seek independent advice.

- **The band overpays for the shopping services.** The attorney may continue to earn a percentage of the band's income for years—even after the band breaks up. This sum may be unfair in proportion to the services performed by the attorney.

Musicians should also be aware that most states have rules that prohibit attorneys from "soliciting" business. "So if a lawyer calls you, or comes charging into the dressing room after a gig with a fist full of business cards, check him out carefully," warns attorney Roessel. "Interview a few other attorneys before you make up your mind. By the time that happens, you will have come too far to risk trusting your progress to someone unsavory."

Despite these potential problems, attorney-shopping agreements are still common in the record business. It is difficult for bands to obtain access to record companies, and an attorney may be the only available gatekeeper.

Label-Shopping Agreement

We have drafted a model label-shopping agreement that includes some provisions that will protect your band. The agreement we have provided can also be used if someone besides an attorney is shopping your music. For that reason we have chosen to use the term "representative" rather than attorney.

The following instructions explain how to fill out the label-shopping agreement and what the various clauses mean. Many clauses have alternative provisions for you to choose from, which are explained in the instructions. Some clauses, as noted in the instructions, are optional altogether. A sample appears below. You can modify the form agreement to fit your needs.

 This agreement is included on the forms CD in the back of this book.

Introduction

Insert the name and address of the representative. If the representative is an attorney, you can also indicate where the attorney is licensed to practice (for example, "Gilbert Grand, an attorney licensed to practice in the State of California, whose address is 34 West Pier #103, Sausalito, California").

Insert your band's name, its business form and mailing address, and the names of all the members.

Obligations of Representative

This section establishes some basic responsibilities of the representative.

- **Representation.** Most representatives will want the exclusive right to solicit on behalf of your band. This is reasonable so the representative doesn't have to worry about being undermined by another representative.

- **Solicitations and Reports.** This clause establishes that the representative must give you written reports on whom he or she has solicited. *It is crucial that the representative furnishes your band with proof of each solicitation.* As you will see later in this agreement, the proof of solicitation may make a difference as to whether your band has to pay the representative. For example, say this label-shopping agreement ends and, on your own, your band solicits and obtains a deal with a record company. If your former representative suddenly appears and claims a piece of the deal, you could quickly find yourselves in an ugly dispute. Under a later provision in our label-shopping agreement, the representative would be entitled to a cut only if he or she could prove a direct solicitation with the record company *and* that your new deal occurred within a specific number of months after the end of the agreement. *Watch out for language that allows the representative to get a cut of any deal regardless of whether the representative solicited the company.*

Percentage Payments and Cap

This section establishes the payment structure between the band and the representative. We strongly recommend using Alternative A, which caps the payment at a specified amount. Many representatives, however, will not accept that provision and will insist instead that the representative should be entitled to income from any deal that is made during the six-month term of the label-shopping agreement. If the representative refuses to agree to a payment cap, use Alternative B, with a lower percentage commission. Check and fill in the alternative you want to use, or delete the unwanted alternative altogether.

- **Alternative A—Payment Cap.**
  Under this payment system, the representative's payment is capped. A payment cap prevents the rep from earning an unfair amount, because after a certain amount

(the "Representative Band Income Cap"), the payments will stop. We recommend a commission percentage of 10% to 20%, and a cap somewhere between $10,000 to $20,000. The exact numbers you're able to negotiate will depend on the bargaining power of your band and the representative.

- **Alternative B—Continuing Payments.**
  If the representative is unwilling to agree to the payment cap, you may agree to pay the representative a continuing payment, in which case you should use Alternative B. In the case of continuing payments with no cap, 5% is a typical and fair amount.

Exclusions From Representative Band Income

The representative should not get a percentage of certain band income that is categorized as "pass-through income." Generally speaking, pass-through income is money that the band uses for crucial expenses such as recording costs or payments to nonband musicians. These costs should be subtracted from the band's income before the representative takes his or her commission. (For more information on deductions and commissions, see Chapter 3.) Check the costs that will be deducted from the band's income before the representative calculates a commission. The number of exclusions you're able to get the representative to agree to will depend on your bargaining power.

Payments to Business Manager

If your band has a business manager, that person will be in charge of receiving money on behalf of the band and distributing it to the appropriate people. This clause simply notes that a business manager may be in charge of collecting income from record labels and making payments to the representative. Check this clause if you have a business manager; otherwise leave it blank or delete it altogether.

Costs and Expenses

The band is usually required to pay the representative's reasonable expenses. This provision sets limits on how much the representative can spend before getting the band's permission.

Disclaimer

This is a standard disclaimer telling the band that the representative can't guarantee a deal.

Term

We recommend a six-month term, as that should provide sufficient time for a representative to contact music companies. You may, however, enter a different term length.

Termination

Either party can terminate the agreement, but there are financial consequences for the band if it terminates prior to the end of the term—specifically, that the band will have to pay the value of the representative's services.

- **Termination by Representative.** If the representative terminates, your band has no obligation to pay for his or her services.
- **Termination by the Band.** If your band terminates the agreement early, you'll have to pay the "value of his or her services." If a representative is an attorney, that person may wish to set the value of those services at his or her usual hourly billing rate—which for attorneys is often between $150 and $500. We recommend establishing a lower rate in the agreement if possible, since an attorney is not providing legal services when sending music to A&R representatives.

Agreements Not Resulting From Representative Solicitation

This clause establishes that your representative will not receive any income from a deal in which a record company contacts your band independently, without having been solicited by the representative.

Agreements Occurring After Termination

Under this provision, if you enter into an agreement within a certain number of months (we recommend six months) of termination, you will have to pay the representative a fee if the representative had solicited the company during the term of the label-shopping agreement and reported the solicitation in a monthly report.

Dissolution of the Band

This provision protects band members by preventing the representative from getting rights over members after the band dissolves.

Mediation; Arbitration

This provision provides a less-expensive method of resolving disputes than filing a lawsuit. (See the sidebar in Chapter 2 for an explanation of mediation.) We recommend that you use this provision in order to help avoid an expensive lawsuit.

We suggest that you choose the county, province, or city in which the band resides for arbitration. If all the members do not reside within one area, choose a place that is convenient. Enter your location of choice in the blank.

In some states there are organizations that specialize in arbitration for people in the arts, such as California Lawyers for the Arts (CLA) and, in New York, Volunteer Lawyers for the Arts (VLA). You can substitute the rules of such an organization for those of the American Arbitration Association in your agreement. If your band is based in Canada, you can still use the AAA's rules, as they perform arbitration in all major Canadian cities. (For more information on the AAA, see Chapter 17.) Check one of the choices or delete the unwanted alternative.

General

The following provisions are standard contractual provisions referred to as boilerplate. Boilerplate provisions are explained in Chapter 2.

In the blank space, insert the state (or province, in the case of Canadian bands) of residence for the band partners. In the event of a dispute, this determines which state law will govern the arbitration or lawsuit.

Signatures

You may wish to have an attorney review this agreement before you and your band signs it. That may seem odd, since the other party is an attorney/representative. However, as we mentioned earlier, an attorney who is shopping your music may have interests adverse to your band.

Once you're satisfied that you want to proceed, have all band members and the representative sign and date the agreement. Enter the same address for all the band members: the mailing address for the band. Be sure to use an address that will be able to receive mail for two to three years.

Label-Shopping Agreement

Introduction

This agreement (the "Agreement") is between _____

("Representative") and _____ ("Band").

The Band consists of _____

_____ ("Band Members").

The Band owns certain musical recording, songwriting, and related rights referred to in this Agreement as "Band Rights." The Band desires to have Representative "shop" the Band to companies in the music business.

Obligations of Representative

Representative shall perform the following services:

- **Representation.** Representative will contact and solicit potential licensees or music industry companies on behalf of the Band. This representation is solely for the purpose of soliciting agreements for the Band in the music business (referred to in this Agreement as "Band Agreements"). During the term of this Agreement, Representative will have the exclusive right to solicit on behalf of the Band.

- **Solicitations and Reports.** Representative will, on a monthly basis, provide to Band a list of companies solicited by Representative, the name of the person to whom the solicitation was made, the manner of solicitation, and follow-up ("Monthly Reports"). Monthly Reports will also provide an estimate of time spent and expenses.

Percentage Payments and Cap

As compensation for the services provided above, Representative will receive (select one and fill in blanks):

- ○ **Alternative A.** _____ percentage of income from each Band Agreement (the "Representative Band Income") up to a total of $_____ (the "Representative Band Income Cap"). Once the Representative has received total payments equaling the Representative Band Income Cap, the Band will have no further payment obligations to Representative from that Band Agreement.

- ○ **Alternative B.** _____ percent of income from Band Agreements (the "Representative Band Income").

Exclusions From Representative Band Income

Representative Band Income shall not include the following payments made under a Band Agreement:

Check if excluded:

❍ video production costs

❍ tour shortfall advances

❍ union or guild payments

❍ nonband songwriter or cowriter payments

❍ payments to other musicians performing with Band

❍ pension or health contributions

❍ other: _____

Payments to Business Manager *(Check if applicable.)*

❍ All advances must be paid directly to a mutually agreed-on business manager or accountant, who will issue payments to Representative within thirty (30) days of receipt of Representative Band Income along with any accountings as provided by the licensee, music publisher, or record company.

Costs and Expenses

Regardless of whether a Band Agreement is secured, the Band will pay all reasonable costs incurred by Representative in pursuit of Band Agreements. Such expenses do not include travel and living expenses unless they were incurred at the Band request or approved by Band. Representative will not incur any individual expense in excess of $50 without prior approval of the Band. The Band will promptly pay Representative costs and expenses on receipt of Representative invoice and itemized statement reflecting such costs and expenses.

Disclaimer

Representative makes no guarantee as to the likelihood of success regarding exploitation of the Band Rights. Representative is free to conduct business other than on the Band's behalf including relationships with third parties in the same field as the Band.

Term

The term of this Agreement shall be for _____ months unless terminated earlier, as provided below.

Termination

This Agreement may be terminated at any time at the discretion of either the Band or Representative, provided that written notice of such termination is furnished to the other party thirty (30) days prior to termination.

- **Termination by Representative.** If this Agreement is terminated by the Representative, the parties will have no further obligation to each other, and the Band is free to contract with any third party without any obligation of payment of any fees to Representative.

- **Termination by the Band.** If this Agreement is terminated by the Band, the Band agrees to pay to Representative the reasonable value of any services rendered by Representative. The parties agree that Representative's hourly rate for rendering services shall be _____.

Agreements Not Resulting From Representative Solicitation

If a potential licensee or music company contacts the Band without any direct or indirect solicitation by the Band or Representative, then Representative shall have no rights to any income resulting from any agreements resulting from that unsolicited contact.

Agreements Occurring After Termination

If within _____ months of termination of this Agreement, the Band enters into an agreement to exploit any Band Rights with any company directly contacted by Representative and included in a Monthly Report, the Band agrees to pay the fees established in the "Percentage Payments and Cap section," above.

Dissolution of the Band

If, during the term of this Agreement, the Band dissolves and determines not to continue as a performing or recording entity, this Agreement shall terminate, and no Band Member shall be personally bound or personally liable to Representative for work performed.

Mediation; Arbitration

If a dispute arises under this Agreement, the parties agree to first try to resolve the dispute with the help of a mutually agreed-on mediator in _____. Any costs and fees other than attorney fees will be shared equally by the parties. If it proves impossible to arrive at a mutually satisfactory solution within a reasonable time, the parties agree to submit the dispute to binding arbitration in the same city or region, conducted on a confidential basis pursuant to:

○ the Commercial Arbitration Rules of the American Arbitration Association, or

○ the rules of _____.

Any decision or award as a result of any such arbitration proceeding will include the assessment of costs, expenses, and reasonable attorney's fees and a written determination of the arbitrators. Absent an agreement to the contrary, any arbitration shall be conducted by an arbitrator experienced in music industry law. An award of arbitration is final and binding on the Band Partners and may be confirmed in a court of competent jurisdiction. The prevailing party has the right to collect from the other party its reasonable costs and attorney fees incurred in enforcing this Agreement.

General

Nothing contained in this Agreement is meant to establish either Representative or Band a partner, joint venturer, or employee of the other party for any purpose. This Agreement may not be amended except in a writing signed by both parties. No waiver by either party of any right shall be construed as a waiver of any other right. If a court finds any provision of this Agreement invalid or unenforceable as applied to any circumstance, the remainder of this Agreement shall be interpreted to best carry out the intent of the parties. This Agreement is governed by and interpreted in accordance with the laws of the State of _____. This Agreement expresses the complete understanding of the parties with respect to the subject matter and supersedes all prior proposals, agreements, representations, and understandings. Notices required under this agreement can be sent to the parties at the addresses provided below. In the event of any dispute arising from or related to this Agreement, the prevailing party is entitled to attorney's fees.

If these terms and conditions are agreeable, please sign and execute both copies of this Agreement and return one copy to Representative.

Band Members

Band Member Signature _____

Address _____

_____

Date _____ Soc. Sec. # _____

Band Member Signature _____

Address _____

_____

Date _____ Soc. Sec. # _____

Band Member Signature _____

Address _____

_____

Date _____ Soc. Sec. # _____

Representative

Representative Signature _____

Address _____

_____

Date _____ Soc. Sec. # _____

Band Equipment

I f you're in a band, then you know that it's musical equipment—not sex—that's usually the number one topic backstage. Musicians love to swap details about the virtues of their guitars, amps, and effects pedals. When they have a day off, many musicians spend their free time at local music shops hunting for a great deal. This chapter provides information about your legal rights when buying new or used equipment. We will also discuss how to insure band equipment against theft and explain how to keep an inventory of band equipment.

Equipment Ownership

When drummer Steve Adler sued his former bandmates in Guns 'N' Roses, one of the things he asked for was the return of drum equipment. That is, part of the dispute was whether Adler or the band owned the drums. Ownership of musical equipment can be confusing in a band, particularly if the group has failed to establish ownership principles in a partnership agreement. Below we will discuss how to determine ownership and some of the differences between group and individual ownership.

Band Ownership of Equipment

Band equipment is owned either by the band or by an individual member. If equipment is owned by the band, then:

- The equipment stays with the band even if an individual member leaves. (However, the band agreement may provide for a method of reimbursing leaving members for a percentage of the value of the equipment.)
- The cost (or a portion of the cost) of the equipment is deducted from the group's partnership income tax form, and all of the band partners can claim the deduction on their individual returns.
- If the band breaks up, the equipment is divided among band members according to the partnership agreement.

Equipment Contributed by a Member

There are two ways a band acquires equipment: The band purchases it with band money (for example, with income from a show), or an individual member gives equipment to the band. Often when a band uses a member's equipment, it's not clear whether the equipment has actually been "donated" or whether it still belongs to the band member. When using equipment purchased individually by a band member, you should try to establish who officially owns the equipment.

If the band member is okay with the band keeping it, then that member has contributed something of value to the band, which may affect his or her rights if the member leaves or if the group breaks up. That's why it's important to keep track of band equipment with a band inventory form (a sample is provided below).

EXAMPLE: All of the band members have contributed equally to the group, except that the bass player also contributes a P.A., valued at $5,000, to the band. Therefore, the bass player has given $5,000 more to the band than the other band members and (depending on the partnership agreement) would be entitled to be repaid the value of the P.A. equipment at the time the bass player left or the band broke up. **Note:** The P.A. system's value decreases or depreciates over time.

When Should Bands Own Equipment?

We recommend band ownership of equipment if the equipment will be used by all members (for example, a P.A., van, or recording equipment) *or* if the band is filing a partnership tax return. Group ownership of P.A.s and vans is a good idea, because this equipment stays with the band even though individual band members come and go. However, a departing member may claim a right to be repaid for any ownership interest in band property.

EXAMPLE: Four band members are equal partners in a band, which means they share equally in the band's income and expenses. The band pays $5,000 for a P.A., and the bass player is fired a week later. Under the band partnership agreement, the bass player is owed $1,250 (a payment equal to one-quarter of the value of the P.A.).

Buying Band Equipment

Buying band equipment can be tricky. Many musicians, particularly guitarists, favor vintage equipment rather than a newly made instrument. They may appreciate the sound of the guitar or may buy it as an investment (rare guitars increase dramatically in value). When buying equipment, whether new or used, your band should consider some of the legal issues related to equipment purchases. For example, some purchases come with warranties; some do not. And you may run into legal problems if the equipment you are purchasing is stolen.

Legal Protection When Buying Equipment

There are various laws protecting your band when it purchases equipment.

- **New Products.** As a general rule, almost all new musical equipment comes with a full or limited warranty from the manufacturer that covers the property for a specified time period (the "warranty period"). Under most state laws, you are entitled to see the warranty before purchasing the equipment. A **full warranty** provides that the product will be repaired or replaced for free during the warranty period. A **limited warranty** places restrictions on repair and replacement (for example, you may have to pay for labor costs). *You do not have to return a warranty card to assert your rights (no matter what the warranty card may say).* In addition to the manufacturer's warranty, in most states new merchandise is covered by an **implied warranty**. This means that regardless of the manufacturer's warranty, the store or manufacturer must repair or replace the equipment if it is defective. The implied warranty lasts as long as the manufacturer's warranty period. If the manufacturer has not provided a warranty period, the implied warranty is for one year. Some stores offer—for a price—extended warranties, which increase the time period for protection. Unless a product has a likelihood of malfunction or a very short warranty period (for example, 30 days), we do not recommend paying extra for extended warranties.

- **Used Equipment.** Generally there are no warranties for used or second hand equipment sold "as is." For example, if you buy a second hand amplifier, you won't have a legal right to return it unless the seller gave you a warranty in writing or as a matter of store policy. Even if the seller didn't guarantee the equipment, you would have a legal right to return it if the seller deliberately deceived you—for example, by switching the amplifier you purchased with a different one before delivering it to your practice space.

- **Credit Card Purchases.** We recommend using a credit card to make purchases and to pay for repairs. If you use a bank credit card such as Visa, MasterCard, American Express, or Discover to purchase equipment within your home state or within 100 miles of your residence, and the purchase is for more than $50, you can refuse to pay for it if the company won't repair or replace defective merchandise. In other words, the charge will be reversed until the dispute is resolved. However, in order to use this system, you should notify your credit card company promptly when the charge first appears on your bill. Usually, the credit card company prints a telephone number for reporting such problems on the back of the bill.

Some credit card companies also insure new purchases made using the card (see below).

- **Mail Order and Online Purchases.** If you purchase equipment by mail order or online, the equipment must be shipped within the time promised at the time of ordering. If no time was promised, the company must ship the item within 30 days. If the item can't be shipped to you within the promised time or 30 days, then you have the right to cancel the order and get a refund or agree to a new delivery date. If the item is not in stock, find out if your credit card will be charged *before* the item is shipped. If you have the option, we recommend that you not be charged until the item is shipped. The company's return policy is usually printed in the company's catalog or is posted on their website.

- **Retail Store Purchases.** What if you purchase some musical equipment that works fine, but you're just not happy with it and you want to return it? A store does not *have* to give you a refund or a credit for an item (although most stores do). In some states, the store can simply refer you to the manufacturer for repair or replacement. Rules on refunds vary from store to store and state to state. In many states, such as California, a store can maintain a "no-refund" policy only if that policy is posted at

the sales counter or on order forms. In those states, if the policy isn't posted, you have the right to return merchandise within 30 days.

Stolen Equipment

If you buy, trade, or receive property that you suspect is stolen, you could be liable for a crime known as "receiving stolen merchandise." In some states, for example, if you acquire stolen merchandise worth more than $500, you could be sentenced to more than a year in prison. In order to be convicted of the crime of receiving stolen property, you must know (or have a good reason to believe) that the equipment you are acquiring is stolen. If you have a suspicion it's stolen but you're not sure, then you have an obligation to investigate.

One common indicator that equipment is stolen is when it is offered at a ridiculously low price. If suspicious, ask the seller to furnish you with valid photo identification such as a driver's license. A dealer in stolen merchandise will generally not be willing to do so. In many states, dealers in used merchandise have the same obligation to investigate ownership. That's why pawn shop owners routinely require valid identification before taking items.

Buying Used

If you're buying vintage equipment, you can check market prices by reviewing print and online publications such as *Vintage Guitar* magazine. Similar publications exist for drums and amplifiers. You can also check out Daddy's Junky Music (www.daddys.com) and eBay (www.ebay.com) to compare prices for used gear.

Insurance, Maintenance, and Inventory of Your Equipment

A few years ago, the only musicians who had instrument insurance were classical players seeking to protect their 100-year-old cellos and violins. Nowadays, with the proliferation of musical equipment theft (see below), insurance is common among all types of musicians. Below we provide some background on insuring your equipment and protecting it while under repair. We also provide a method of keeping track of your equipment inventory.

Equipment Insurance

Most insurance companies offer insurance, known as business insurance, that covers your band property. Talk to an insurance broker and find out what type of protection is available. Make sure

that the coverage includes protection of your property wherever you perform, including out-of-state locations. Online, consider Music Pro Insurance (www.musicproinsurance.com). The rates are reasonable—for example, expect to pay approximately $300-$400 a year to insure $20,000 worth of equipment. (Another source of insurance against musical equipment loss is Music Agency, Inc. (www.musicagencyinc.com).)

There are other insurance possibilities. Some credit card companies offer theft insurance for equipment that was purchased using the card. Check your credit card agreement to see if this type of coverage is available to you. It's also possible that individual band members' homeowner insurance or rental insurance will cover the theft of equipment. For example, a homeowner's policy may cover equipment stolen from a band member's home or vehicle. Check your homeowner's or renter's policy to determine if it extends to stolen equipment used for a business.

Valuing Music Equipment

The U.S. Internal Revenue Service usually discounts one-seventh of the purchase price each year over a seven-year period. (Note that in many cases, you can deduct the whole price of some equipment from your income tax in one year. See Chapter 16 for more information.) Many insurance companies use the same system. For example, if a band bought a $700 amplifier, then each year it would lose one-seventh of its value, $100. If the band kept it for two years, then it would be valued at $500. To determine the value of your equipment for inventory purposes, you can either apply the depreciation value (deduct one-seventh of the price for each year of use) or have the band reach an agreement as to the equipment's value.

Repair Shops

Here are three basic rules for repair shops:

- *Always* obtain a claim check or repair invoice with the repair shop's name and address when dropping off equipment for repair.
- *Always* obtain a repair estimate.
- *Always* request that if the work exceeds the estimate by a certain amount (for example, more than $50 over the estimate, or more than 10% over the estimate), your approval must be obtained before proceeding.

Have the repair shop write the estimate and approval information on your check or invoice.

Sample Band Inventory

As part of your equipment maintenance and protection program, your band should create an equipment inventory. If all that your band owns is a P.A. system, then your task is fairly simple: Keep

track of the receipt for the purchase of the P.A. However, if your band owns more equipment or has invested in a vehicle such as a van, you should keep an inventory of all equipment and keep the inventory updated and filed in the band business folder. The following sample band inventory contains all the important information about band equipment.

In the Equipment/ID column, give a brief but clear description of the equipment. In the Value column, insert the value of the equipment as of the date that the band acquired it. This will be either the price paid by the band for the equipment (whether new or used), or the value of the equipment as of the date that it was contributed by a band member. Also indicate whether it was bought new or used. In the How & When Band Acquired column, be sure to enter the date that the band acquired the equipment. You need a date to correspond with the value in order to keep track of the equipment's depreciation. Finally, enter the serial number for each piece of equipment.

Preventing and Dealing With Theft

In one year, London Suede had its equipment stolen from a van in Boston; the Fureys had their musical instruments stolen in London; They Might Be Giants' band equipment was stolen in

Massachusetts; and Radiohead's van filled with equipment was stolen in Denver. These thefts forced some tour dates to be canceled and, in some cases, the whole tour. Theft of band equipment can be traumatic financially and otherwise, and has even caused the breakup of a band.

Generally, there isn't much to do *after* your equipment is stolen. Stolen equipment is difficult to recover, and the only thing that will assist in recovery is equipment serial numbers and proof of ownership. For that reason, it helps to inventory your equipment and to keep track of sales receipts. Also, it's wise to label your equipment. This may not prevent a theft from your van, but it can deter "stage thefts" when a member of another band attempts to walk off with your equipment.

Some bands maintain insurance for their musical instruments. While insurance compensation can certainly help your band get back on its feet, the insurance payout may not reflect the full value of the stolen instruments—especially in the case of vintage equipment—and it may take several months to get the payout.

Frank Gallagher is a tour manager and sound engineer who has worked with a wide range of bands including the Talking Heads and Buddy Guy. According to Gallagher, most equipment theft is not planned, but done by opportunists— unscrupulous people who simply take advantage of a situation. He offers the following tips to prevent losses from theft:

Sample Band Inventory			
Equipment/ID	**Value**	**How & When Band Acquired**	**Serial Number**
Alessis RA-100 power amp	$410 new	Band purchased 12/15/05 at Lucky Music	AL22-789
Hartke bass cabinet	$450 used	Contributed by John on 4/1/06	HB25436
2 Fender Sunn 1212 speaker cabinets (woofers replaced with Case custom subwoofers)	$800 used	Band purchased 1/22/06 at used equip. sale at Rocket Studios	LO91084 LO61743
2 Shure 58 microphones	$210 new	Band purchased 5/1/06 from The Musician's Friend (mail order)	SH4567 & SH4536

- **Avoid thefts from vans.** Since most musical equipment is stolen from vans, you can take some common-sense precautions. Gallagher's number one rule is *never* leave your van unattended while loading in or out. If possible, use a van that allows you to load only out the back, and, if you must store equipment overnight, back the van against a building or wall so that the rear doors are inaccessible.

- **Hang on to the small stuff.** According to Gallagher, many thieves won't steal anything big because they can't carry it. "Cymbals and microphones are stealable and expendable. Write your name on [the bottom of] your cymbals with a magic marker. Keep an inventory of all equipment. Stencil and identify every case." Gallagher also advises parking outside the city you are playing. "Don't stay downtown. *Never!* After your gig, get on the highway in the direction you're headed for the next day and find a motel out of town. Get a room on street level and back your van up to the door. Stay on the highway. It's cheaper than downtown, too."

- **After the theft.** After equipment is stolen, you should contact the local police and file a police report. If you have insurance, a police report is usually a requirement for you to recover. Gallagher advises calling the local radio stations. In addition, you should contact local pawn shops and used music equipment stores to determine if any of your equipment has been offered for sale. Many music magazines also have a section listing stolen equipment. For example, *Bass Player* magazine has a feature called "Police Blotter." Some websites also list stolen merchandise. And of course, check eBay (www.ebay.com) and other auction sites in case the thief is attempting to unload the purloined instruments on the Web.

Be Careful in Church

Gospel bands should take note: More musical equipment is stolen from churches than from clubs or concert halls. For example, in less than one year, musical equipment thieves broke into 30 North Carolina churches and 21 Arkansas churches. Although it is a sad commentary on the times, musicians should be careful leaving instruments unattended in houses of worship.

Chapter 6

Performance and Touring

Every band loves the thrill of performing. Unfortunately, the business of performing is not as exciting. For every hour a band spends on stage, it probably spends at least five to ten hours getting the gig, promoting the show, loading and moving equipment, doing sound checks, and waiting to get paid and load out. On top of this, club owners may not pay your band, and sound and light people may make your band sound and look terrible. If you're on tour, the daily grind can break your band's spirit and bankbook.

The information in this chapter will help make your live performances and tours both profitable and enjoyable for your band. We will review the procedure of getting gigs and getting paid, and provide you with information regarding some of the business issues that may arise at shows. We will also provide a sample performance agreement and offer advice on preparing a tour budget.

Getting Gigs and Getting Paid

It's getting harder and harder for a band to land a gig. The number of live music venues is steadily decreasing, and competition for bookings among bands is fierce. Since it's a buyer's market, many club owners pay tiny amounts ($50 to $100) for a band's performance. Some clubs have even instituted a demeaning "pay to play" system in which the band must buy a block of tickets and attempt to sell them themselves. Under these circumstances, it is easy to understand why bands feel that live performing is a rip-off. Below, we provide some background information on getting gigs and protecting your band's interests.

Getting Gigs

As in dating, there is no surefire way to get a gig. It's a matter of luck, timing, and making the right impression. If you're used to booking your band, you're probably aware that you need patience, persistence, and a good demo tape.

Never booked a show before? First, you must identify the person who makes the booking decisions at the venue. Then, learn the procedure for dealing with the booker. Every experienced booker has some system for submitting demo tapes (for example, "Do not mail more than two songs." "We do all listening on Wednesdays."). You should submit a professional quality demo, and your band's style of music should match the genre or types of bands that are commonly booked at the club. Beware: Sometimes a band's demo remains unheard for weeks or months. A manager with connections may help to open the door for you, or, if you have friends in another band, they may be able to help get the booker's attention.

If a national touring band is headlining in your town, the booker at the club usually doesn't have the freedom to choose an opening act. The touring band either brings the opening act or chooses the opener. If the booker does have the freedom to choose the opener, then you need to somehow demonstrate that your band's music complements the music of the headliner without getting in the way. In addition, the simpler the setup and breakdown for an opening act, the easier it is to get the gig.

If you're trying to get a headlining gig at a local club, then your task is simple, though not necessarily easy: You have to demonstrate that your band is a money-maker.

How Bands Get Paid

Bands are commonly paid in four ways: 1) a percentage of the gate; 2) a flat fee with no percentage; 3) a guaranteed fee or a percentage of the gate, whichever is higher; or 4) a guaranteed fee plus a percentage of revenues above the guarantee. The percentage of the gate may be a percentage of the gross revenue or net revenue. Gross revenue is all of the money paid for tickets, and net revenue is the amount left over after certain deductions have been taken. If the percentage is of net revenue, you need to know the deductions that are made by the club in determining net profits.

Performance Agreements

The performance agreement offers a short summary of the terms so that there will be no disagreements about how much the band is paid and how long

the band must play. Most promoters and club owners are legitimate, and they will honor the terms of these agreements. However, performance agreements (like all agreements) are only as reliable as the people making them. Therefore, don't assume that an agreement will protect your rights when dealing with an unsavory promoter. It's true that if a club owner disregards the terms of an agreement, your band can sue—but, realistically, most bands don't want to get involved in a lawsuit. Therefore, use common sense when booking. If you've been burned by a club before, you're likely to get burned again. Don't count on an agreement to protect you.

When Your Band Does Not Get Paid

After the applause dies down and the equipment is packed up, the band's manager (or someone from the band) walks into a funky office where the club owner is counting the evening's receipts. If all goes well, the owner reaches into the metal cash box and pays the band according to the agreed terms.

Sometimes, however, a club owner or concert promoter may refuse to pay your band, or pay only a portion of the fee, claiming that ticket sales were below expectations. It's often difficult to avoid being ripped off, particularly if your band is on tour. However, you can minimize the chances of getting stiffed by taking the time to do a little research. Before booking shows (especially out of town), talk to other bands who have played the same venues or dealt with the same promoters. If you have the bargaining power, request half or all of the guarantee before the gig (a common practice among union musicians and established acts). If you are a member of the musicians' union and have signed a union contract (known as a "Federation Contract"), you can file a dispute with your local union representative or with a union rep in the town of the performance. (The musicians' union is discussed below.)

Some bands obtain their shows through booking agents. These agents earn a fee for each performance they book for the band (see the sidebar "Booking Agents," below). If your band obtained the show through a booking agent and the band is stiffed, notify your agent immediately and ask the agent to pressure the club owner. After all, the booking agent got the gig and expects to earn a percentage of the fee.

If you are ripped off locally, you can consider filing a small claims case. However, most bands don't want to bother with this because they are afraid that if they assert legal rights, they will have trouble getting gigs in the future. Unfortunately, this can be a very real concern for bands who need exposure. If your band *does* intend to pursue legal rights, the limit for small claims cases ranges from $2,500 to $5,000 depending on the state. And remember: Winning

the case doesn't mean you will obtain the money. Enforcing the judgment can be difficult. (For more information about small claims court cases, see *Everybody's Guide to Small Claims Court,* by Ralph Warner (Nolo).)

To prove the amount you are owed or to increase your chances of victory in small claims court, it helps to have a written performance agreement. The next section discusses these agreements. Practically, however, many small clubs refuse to sign a written performance agreement. If you can't get a signed agreement, try to get any sort of documentation, such as a handwritten letter or a fax confirming the booking.

American Federation of Musicians

When you hear people talk about the musicians' union, they're talking about the American Federation of Musicians (AFM). The AFM is the union for U.S. and Canadian musicians, with 450 local offices throughout the U.S. and Canada. Most major labels require bands they sign to join the AFM. Even if you're not signed to a major label, it's a good idea to join the union if you tour a lot. The AFM guarantees minimum compensation for union contract shows and recording jobs. It also provides group insurance plans, including medical, liability, personal accident, term life, and equipment insurance. Another benefit for American musicians traveling to Canada is that they can avoid "work permit" hassles at the border through a union procedure that is arranged with their local union 30 days prior to the gig.

Keep in mind, however, that not all clubs have relationships with the AFM, and for that reason, many clubs do not sign union contracts or pay union wages. To join the AFM, a musician must complete a form and pay local and national dues (from $100 to $150 total). Union musicians also pay the union a percentage of income from union performance and recording jobs (usually 2% to 4%).

The U.S. AFM headquarters is located in New York; the Canadian headquarters is in Toronto. If you run into a problem while touring, the union has a special tour hotline to call for help: 800-ROADGIG in the U.S. and 800-INFOFED in Canada for union-related problems.

Performance Agreement

Many bands and venues use a one-page contract that lists the basic arrangements, such as the date of the show and payment. These may vary in appearance and content, but they usually contain the information provided in the sample performance agreement, below. Sometimes, however, a band or a venue may have more detailed requirements than payment and booking times. Requirements such as backstage food

and drinks, merchandise rights, lights and sound, or insurance are included in a document called a "rider" that is attached to the one-page contract. That is, the one-page contract establishes the essentials while the rider sets forth the detailed information about what color M&Ms are required backstage. If your band is looking for a simple agreement, then just use the one-page contract. But if your band has the bargaining power, you might include a detailed rider.

This section provides instructions on how to complete a performance agreement and rider and what the provisions mean. We've included a performance agreement on the accompanying forms disk, and a sample appears below.

It's possible that a venue may provide you with a performance agreement that differs from our version. If so, you can use our agreement for comparison purposes and to help you understand what the clauses mean. The agreements do not have to be identical. As long as you can understand the venue's agreement and it basically covers the same issues as our agreement, it's probably fine.

Finally, be aware that some club agreements require your band to post a bond, or to assume all liability for damages (if, for instance, someone is hurt during your show). Your band should approach these kinds of provisions carefully, as they have the potential for a heavy financial burden.

This agreement is included on the forms CD in the back of this book.

Basic Terms

The "Basic Terms" section is completed by simply filling in the requested information. Most of the basic terms are self-explanatory. The term "purchaser" is often used to refer to the promoter or club owner. A promoter is a person who organizes events and may or may not own the venue.

Enter the date and time of the gig. It may seem too obvious, but you wouldn't be the first band to show up on the wrong day, or show up on the right day to find another band booked. Also be sure to insert the number of sets and their length (for example: "One 25-30 minute set at 9 p.m."), as this will determine your work schedule at the venue. The requirements regarding load-in and sound check are usually furnished by the venue.

Under "Total compensation," insert the method of payment and the amount. Bands are usually paid in one of four ways: a percentage of the gate; a flat fee with no percentage; a guaranteed fee or a percentage of the gate, whichever is higher; or a guaranteed fee plus a percentage of revenues above the guarantee. Enter any deposit paid or due before the show, and when it was paid or is due.

If the band has a partnership tax number or EIN (see Chapter 16), insert that number. Otherwise, insert one of the band member's Social Security numbers.

Names of Musicians and Tax Information

Some venues may require the names and Social Security numbers of each musician. This is most likely if the venue plans to pay any of the musicians directly rather than through a manager of some sort. Fill in any information that the venue requires. If a musician will receive pay directly, enter the amount under "Direct Pay" and enter that musician's social security number. The space marked "Local" is a reference to the number of the local musicians' union.

Artist's Right to Terminate

This allows the Artist to terminate the agreement if the deposit has not been paid as promised. It's possible that if a venue furnishes the performance agreement, this provision will not be in it. Even without this provision, however, your band would have a legal right to cancel if you don't receive the deposit on time and the venue fails to respond to your written requests for the deposit.

Rider and Attachments

This provision is simply a statement that the rider and any other attachments to the agreement are legally binding.

General

The following provisions are standard contractual provisions referred to as boilerplate. Boilerplate provisions are explained in Chapter 2.

In the blank space, insert the state (or province, in the case of Canadian bands) of residence for the Band Partners. In the event of a dispute, this determines which state law will govern the arbitration or lawsuit. Like the "termination" provision, these general or boilerplate provisions are often missing from performance agreements furnished by a venue.

Signatures

The band's manager or one of the band members should sign. Indicate the name and title of the person signing for the Band under "Artist Name and Title." Also enter the band's mailing address. The Purchaser signature should be made by a person authorized to sign, such as the club's owner or an authorized booker. To help ensure that the person signing for the purchaser is actually authorized to sign, have the person signing for the purchaser indicate his title (for example, "Miguel Corrigan, Owner," or "Dana Burgy, Booking Agent").

The rest of the provisions are optional rider provisions. If your band has the bargaining power (for example, you're a popular headlining act), you may be able to obtain most of the provisions in the rider. However, most bands lack the clout to obtain many of these provisions. Include as many of them as you can. Provisions that you don't want to (or can't) include should be struck out and initialed by both parties signing the agreement, or deleted altogether.

Merchandise Rider Provision

Venues usually want to receive 15% to 40% of gross sales from merchandise. Enter the amount your band and the venue agree on. Some riders state that the venue will handle the sales, in which case you will deliver the merchandise and have the venue sign a receipt indicating the count for all merchandise before sales begin. At the end, the band inventories the remaining merchandise and is owed money for the number of items sold or missing.

Merchandise and Performance

Many bands lose money on tour or when performing locally. Selling merchandise such as compact discs, cassettes, T-shirts, hats, posters, and stickers can help minimize these losses. According to industry estimates, successful rock bands often earn $5 per concert fan in merchandise sales (punk and metal bands often earn $8 per person).

Many venues demand a cut—anywhere from 15% to 40%—of your total merchandise sales. When booking, find out each venue's merchandise policy and whether the club will provide personnel to handle sales. Arrange with your T-shirt manufacturer or CD duplicator to ship your merchandise to a venue or hotel so that you can obtain additional products on the road. Some bands even take silk-screening materials with them and make T-shirts on the road. Also find out from the venue about any requirements for local taxes or fees for merchandise sales.

Tickets and Ticket Sales Rider Provision

While major label headliners often travel with tour accountants who audit all ticket sales, many bands lack the resources to do so. This provision guarantees the band some basic oversight of ticket sales. Enter the ticket prices, and the maximum number of free admissions that may be allowed as a percentage of total ticket sales. The purpose of limiting free admissions is to prevent unscrupulous concert promoters from taking free tickets themselves, then selling or bartering them and keeping the money.

Dressing Room Rider Provision

This is a basic "clean and safe" dressing room provision. (Depending on how much clout they have, some bands make more elaborate requests such as green ceilings, floor lamps, and carpeted floors.) Enter the number of locked dressing rooms you will get. Enter any special arrangements the venue agrees to make for you, or enter "none."

Complimentary Tickets Rider Provision

Enter the number of free tickets per band member that will be allowed, and the maximum total number for the band. Most venues allow one or two free tickets per band member up to a maximum of 20 for the whole band.

Security Rider Provision

This provision guarantees basic security measures to protect your band and the audience. Your security request can be more specific, depending on your needs and what the club will agree to. For instance, you might request a specific number of security persons or indicate where you want them stationed. If you have no special requests, enter "none."

Hospitality Rider Provision

Hospitality refers to the food and drinks provided backstage. This is a bare-bones hospitality provision. Some artists may make more elaborate requests: Michael Bolton includes a special requirement that backstage coffee be fresh and from a local independent coffee shop. If you don't have any special requests, enter "none."

Background Music Rider Provision

For some bands, the choice of introductory background music is very important. Headlining bands usually have an easy time of getting the background music they want. These bands supply a cassette or CD to the sound man. This provision establishes that the music must meet your approval.

Clippings and Posters Rider Provision

This allows your band to review the press generated before and after your show. It may be a measure of how well the club promoted the show.

Insurance Rider Provision

Most legitimate venues have adequate insurance. That is, the club pays an insurance company, and if someone is injured, the insurance company pays for the damage. Therefore, most clubs will permit a national touring band to include this provision in the rider. The real benefit to the band of including this provision is that if the club does not have insurance and signs the agreement, and there is a disaster, the band has a basis to sue the club because it relied on the club owner's promise of insurance.

Cancellation Rider Provision

If you have the bargaining power, you can still get paid for your gig even if the venue cancels the show. The closer the cancellation is to the show date, the larger the payment. Popular groups ask for 50% at four weeks away and 100% at two weeks. Enter the percentage of the payment that you and the venue agree you will be paid in the event of cancellation.

Sound System Rider Provision

Some bands attach a separate "Sound Reinforcement Rider" that includes all the details of the band's public address, speaker, mixer, and personnel requirements. This is done to guarantee that the venue's sound system meets the band's requirements. Enter any requirements about your sound system here.

Pyrotechnic Devices Rider Provision

For obvious reasons, venues are wary of pyrotechnics, and most require a provision such as this to limit damages and to comply with local laws.

Video and Audio Taping Rider Provision

This is your band's anti-bootlegging provision.

Performance Agreement

Basic Terms

Name of band ("Artist") _____

Name of venue _____

Person booking performance ("Purchaser") _____

Date(s) and time(s) of performance _____

Number of sets and duration _____

Time for load-in _____

Time for sound check _____

Total compensation _____

Deposit payment _____

Date deposit payment to be paid _____

Band's SS # or Fed. Tax ID # _____

Names of Musicians and Tax Information (optional)

Name of Musician	Direct Pay	Soc. Sec. #	Local Musicians' Union #

Artist's Right to Terminate

If Artist is entitled to a deposit payment as provided in the Payment section of this Agreement, and the deposit has not been paid within the time specified, Artist shall have the right to terminate this Agreement without any further obligation.

Rider and Attachments

Any attached Performance Agreement Rider (the "Rider") and any other attachments or exhibits to this Agreement are incorporated in this Agreement by reference.

General

Nothing contained in this Agreement or the accompanying Rider constitutes either Purchaser or Artist a partner or employee of the other party. This Agreement and the accompanying Rider and exhibits express the complete understanding of the parties and may not be amended except in a writing signed by both parties. If a court finds any provision of this Agreement or the accompanying rider invalid or unenforceable, the remainder of this Agreement will be interpreted so as best to effect the intent of the parties. This Agreement shall be governed by and interpreted in accordance with the laws of _____. In the event of any dispute arising from or related to this Agreement, the prevailing party is entitled to attorney's fees.

Artist Name and Title _____

Artist Signature _____

Address _____

_____

Date _____

Purchaser Name and Title _____

Purchaser Signature _____

Address _____

_____

Date _____

[Optional] Performance Agreement Rider

Additional Terms and Conditions

Merchandise

A fee of _____ percent of gross sales will be paid to Purchaser by Artist for all merchandise sold before, during, or after the performance at the Venue. This fee will be paid to Purchaser on completion of selling.

Purchaser will not permit any other sale or distribution of merchandise bearing Artist's trademarks or image. Purchaser will provide:

❍ a six-foot table and two chairs and two people for merchandise sales in a prominent area of the foyer or lounge leading to the performance area, or

❍ _____.

Tickets and Ticket Sales

Purchaser agrees that tickets will be consecutively numbered and shall be available at the following prices: _____. Artist's representative has the right to inspect all ticket records and to be present in the box office prior to and during the performance. Free admission will not exceed _____ percent of total tickets.

Dressing Room

Purchaser will provide _____ safe, clean dressing room(s) with lock(s). Purchaser will provide backstage security to prevent unauthorized personnel from having access to the dressing area. Special arrangements include: _____.

Complimentary Tickets

Unless otherwise agreed, Purchaser will allow _____ guests per band member, with a maximum of _____ tickets.

Security

Purchaser will provide adequate security so as to guarantee the safety of the audience and the Artist. Special arrangements include _____

_____.

Hospitality

Unless otherwise indicated, Purchaser will provide an allowance of hot and cold beverages in the dressing rooms for the sole use of band and crew members. Special arrangements include: _____

Background Music

Artist will approve all background music played before and after the Artist's performance.

Clippings and Posters

Purchaser will forward copies of all clippings, reviews, and posters to Artist.

Insurance

Purchaser will obtain and maintain, at its own expense, adequate personal injury and property damage liability insurance coverage. This coverage will extend to all activities related to Artist's engagement and performance. Except for claims arising from Artist's willful or intentional acts, Purchaser will indemnify Artist for any third-party claims.

Cancellation

If Purchaser cancels the performance fewer than four weeks before the performance, Purchaser will pay Artist ____% of the guaranteed fee for the performance. If Purchaser cancels the performance fewer than two weeks before the performance, Purchaser will pay Artist ____% of the guaranteed fee for the performance. The parties agree that such payments are reasonable in light of anticipated or actual harm caused by the cancellation and the difficulties of proving the actual damages to Artist.

Sound System

Purchaser agrees to provide a sound system meeting the following requirements:

_____

Pyrotechnic Devices

Artist will get Purchaser's approval for any pyrotechnic device used by Artist. Any such device is subject to applicable fire laws and will be administered by a person with professional experience in pyrotechnics.

Video and Audio Taping

Purchaser will not arrange for video or audio taping or live broadcast without first receiving written approval from Artist.

Touring

Touring can be exciting, but it's also expensive. If your band has never traveled beyond your hometown, then get ready for sticker shock. Successful bands know how to travel light and cut costs in order to stay on the road. We'll help you do the same by highlighting common touring expenses and showing you ways to stretch your dollars.

Common Touring Expenses

Below are explanations for some of the common touring expenses.

Salaries

The road manager (sometimes referred to as a "tour manager") handles the day-to-day tour details; some road managers also drive the van and operate the P.A. Expect to pay a road manager $1,000 to $2,000 a week. A tech is a professional roadie who manages band equipment and directs the set up and breakdown. Some techs also drive the van. Expect to pay a tech $500 to $1,500 a week. If you hire someone as a driver, expect to pay $500 to $1,000 a week. Hired musicians usually want a salary of $750 to $2,000 a week. If you are hiring a union musician, you may be required to sign a special union contract and pay minimum wages established by the national headquarters. If possible, the rest of the band should be paid a salary as well.

Unfortunately, there is often not enough tour income to pay band members a salary on the road. However, if there are profits from merchandise, band members often split them at the end of each week.

Per Diems

Per diems (which means "by the day") are payments to the band and crew for daily living expenses such as food. Expect to pay at least $35-$50 a day for per diems for each person.

Van Expenses

Expect to pay $60 to $90 a day for a passenger van rental (a van with seats) and $70 to $100 a day for a two-seater cargo van. (You will need a credit card to rent a van.) To determine gas expenses, calculate your total mileage and divide it by the van's estimated miles per gallon (usually 15 to 30 cents a mile).

In this budget, insurance is included in the price of the rental. However, you may be entitled to more insurance if you pay with certain credit cards or if your personal auto insurance also covers rentals. Some states such as New York and California charge sales tax on rentals, often as high as 8% or 10%. Estimate $20 to $30 a week for tolls. Many tour managers recommend obtaining road service coverage (for flat tires and towing) from AAA or other insurance companies.

Airfare and Air Freight

If you are flying, you have two additional expenses: the cost of the airfare for band and crew, and the cost of airfreighting your equipment. As you are probably aware, you can obtain excellent airline prices using online services such as Expedia (www.expedia.com) and Orbitz (www.orbitz.com). Travel agents, especially those that specialize in planning tours for musicians, can also aid in finding excellent rates. Air freight rates for your equipment vary, and you can expect to pay 60 cents to $1.00 per pound. If you are using air freight there may be additional costs related to delivering and picking up the equipment at the airport.

Hotels

If your band plans to stay in hotels, we recommend using a travel agent, particularly someone who has experience with bands. You will usually get better rates at musician-friendly hotels. Expect to pay $75 to $125 a night for a double room. Most hotels also charge a special hotel tax, so estimate an additional 5% over the room costs. Pay hotel bills with credit cards, as your credit card contract may provide a method for resolving problems in the event of a dispute.

Equipment Rental

If your band chooses to rent equipment, the expenses vary depending on the equipment and the region. Check the Yellow Pages for musical equipment rental companies in the cities in which you are touring. Expect to pay at least $150 or more per week for amplifier rentals.

Carnets: When Touring Outside the U.S. and Canada

If your band is traveling out of the country, you may want to use an ATA Carnet, which is the equivalent of a passport for your equipment. The ATA Carnet system is accepted in 50 countries and facilitates movement of equipment through customs and avoids the payment of value added taxes (VATs) and duties that are charged by some foreign customs agents. You must complete an application, post a bond (a payment that will be refunded after the tour), and pay a fee based upon the value of your equipment. All of this must be completed several weeks prior to your departure.

For more information—and to apply for a Carnet online—visit the U.S. Council for International Business website (www.uscib .org) and click "ATA Carnet Export Service." You can also call 1-800-Carnets or use one of the Carnet application services available online, for example www. ATAcarnet.com.

Other Insurance

In addition to auto insurance (see above), some bands carry liability insurance (in case someone is injured) and equipment insurance (see Chapter 5).

Sound and Light Expenses

If you are taking sound and light personnel or equipment, you will need to estimate those costs. If you're not taking sound and lights, be aware that some venues charge for supplying these services.

Booking Agent Commissions

Expect to pay 10% or more of your tour income if you use the services of a booking agent (see sidebar, below).

Booking Agents

A booking agent arranges the tour and negotiates payments with the venues. A list of booking agents can be found in standard industry sourcebooks such as *The Recording Industry Sourcebook*. A booking agent usually receives 10% of your income from live performances (referred to as "concert grosses"). In some states, booking agents are regulated and in California, they must be licensed. Normally, a band signs an exclusive arrangement with a booking agent. That is, only *that* booking agent can book the band as long as that agent represents the band. We recommend limiting the arrangement to five years or fewer.

Miscellaneous

Estimate your phone and fax charges for planning the tour and while on the road. These costs depend on the length and location of the tour. Your band should set aside $100 per week for batteries, strings, drum heads, and other miscellaneous items. Some bands also budget for tips, laundry, and photocopying.

5% Contingency

Most tour managers recommend including a 5% contingency fee for overruns. That is, estimate your total tour expenses and then add an additional 5% for breathing room in case your estimates are low or there is an emergency.

Touring Expenses: Some Tips for Balancing the Budget

If your band is facing losing money on tour—referred to as a tour shortfall—you've got a couple of options. If you are signed to a record label or a music publisher, you may be able to get tour support, which is financial help from the company to supplement the tour shortfall. Any money you get is deducted from future royalties. Sometimes, tour support payments are part of the recording or publishing agreement. That is, the contract provides for specific tour support payments. Sometimes, however, the record company may simply decide, after discussions with the band or manager, that the company will advance some support for a specific tour.

Without tour support, you'll need to cut expenses. Most bands start with salaries, cutting the road manager, the tech, or both. The second cut is usually hotel costs. The band either sleeps in the van, shares one motel room, or stays with friends. The third cut is probably van rental. If they have them, the band members will use their own vehicles.

Unfortunately, the problem with cutting the road manager, tech, and hotel is that the band can suffer from overwork and sleep deprivation. When you cut van rental, your transportation may be less reliable. Despite these dangers,

cost-cutting may be your only option if you want your tour to go forward. Lots of bands have successfully toured this way through the U.S. and Canada.

Frank Gallagher, who has worked as tour manager for many rock and pop bands, offers a few simple money-saving tour tips. "Travel with as little crew as possible. It's ideal to have your own soundman, but usually it's the most expensive item," says Gallagher. He advises working with the local sound person. "A lot of them do a good job and they know the room, so try to defer to the house soundman's advice. If one of your roadies knows how to do monitors, then use that person to handle your monitor mix."

As for your food budget, you can save money as an opening act on a big tour because "they feed you every day and you get the bare minimum of refreshments in your dressing room," says Gallagher. For bands on club tours, George Earth, a prominent touring guitarist, offers a simple tip: "Buy a cooler and use it to save the backstage refreshments you don't drink at night. You'll be glad you had them on the road the next day."

Sample Tour Budget

In order to survive on tour, you should prepare a tour budget. We have provided two sample tour budgets below. One is for a fictional band and demonstrates how the budget is completed. The other is a blank form for you to use with your band.

Fictional Tour Budget

The following sample tour budget is for a fictional band. Imagine this as a first draft of the budget. The fictional band has booked 14 shows. The band has four members, and they want to hire a road manager and tech. The band also wants to rent a van and stay in hotels. The band will need three hotel rooms a night. The estimate for the band's total expenses is approximately $13,000.

If the band were earning $1,000 a night for the 14 shows, they could break even. However, the band expects to earn $300 a night. Therefore, the total band income (not counting merchandise sales) is $4,200—creating a loss of $8,000. What will the band do? Like most bands on a shoestring touring budget, they will forget about the road manager and tech and consider borrowing a van, rather than renting.

Sample Budget Blank Form

The following blank form is for your band to use.

 The following form is included on the forms CD in the back of this book.

Tour Budget
17 Days/14 Shows/16 Nights

		Amount
Salaries	Road mgr 17 days @ $1,250 per week..	$3,035.00
	Backline tech 17 days @ $800 per week	$1,942.00
	Salaries Total	**$4,977.00**
Per Diems	Road mgr 17 days @ $25 per day	$425.00
	Backline tech 17 days @ $25 per day	$425.00
	Band member #1...	$425.00
	Band member #2...	$425.00
	Band member #3...	$425.00
	Band member #4...	$425.00
	Per Diems Total	**$2,550.00**
Van	Van rental (17 days)	$700.00
	Insurance ($1,000 deductible w/rental)..	$00.00
	State tax	$56.00
	Transport fees...	$35.00
	Gas (2,200 miles)	$185.00
	Total Transportation	**$976.00**
Hotel	Road mgr/tech double rm 16 nights @ $60..	$960.00
	2 band double rms 16 nights @ $60	$1,920.00
	Hotel tax, etc.	$300.00
	Total Hotel	**$3,180.00**
Misc.	Supplies (drum heads, strings, etc.)..	$200.00
	Parking and tolls	$200.00
	Printing/copying (itinerary)	$20.00
	Tips	$50.00
	Laundry...	$50.00
	Advance phone and fax charges..	$30.00
	Road phone and fax	$50.00
	Misc. Total	**$600.00**
	Total Tour Expenses	**$12,283.00**
	5% Contingency	**$614.15**
	TOTAL ESTIMATED TOUR BUDGET	**$12,897.15**

Tour Budget
_____ Days _____ Shows _____ Nights

		Amount
Salaries	Road mgr _____ days @ $_____ per week.............................	_____
	Tech _____ days @ $_____ per week......................................	_____
	Salaries Total	_____
Per Diems	Road mgr _____ days @ $_____ per day.................................	_____
	Tech _____ days @ $_____ per day..	_____
	Band member #1 _____ days @ $_____ per day	_____
	Band member #2 _____ days @ $_____ per day	_____
	Band member #3 _____ days @ $_____ per day	_____
	Band member #4 _____ days @ $_____ per day	_____
	Per Diems Total	_____
Van	Van rental _____ days @ $_____ per day	_____
	Insurance..	_____
	State tax...	_____
	Transport fees	_____
	Gas (_____ miles, _____ mpg @ $_____ per gallon)...............	_____
	Transportation Total	_____
Hotel	Road mgr/tech double rm _____ days @ $_____ per day.......	_____
	2 band double rms _____ days @ $_____ per day	_____
	Hotel tax, etc.	_____
	Total Hotel	_____
Misc.	Supplies (drum heads, strings, etc.)	_____
	Parking and tolls..	_____
	Printing/copying (itinerary)	_____
	Tips..	_____
	Laundry	_____
	Advance phone and fax charges	_____
	Road phone and fax..	_____
	Misc. Total	_____
	Total Tour Expenses	_____
	5% Contingency	_____
	TOTAL ESTIMATED TOUR BUDGET	_____

Chapter 7

Copyright and Song Ownership

This chapter and the next (Chapter 8) both deal with songwriting. This chapter discusses song ownership—essentially, who owns the rights to a song. Ownership is important because it directly affects *who* earns money from the song. Chapter 8 is about music publishing, which is the method by which songs earn money through record sales, motion pictures, or radio or TV play.

It's easy to determine song ownership if one person writes a song. However, if more than one person contributes to writing a song, as in many band situations, there may be confusion as to ownership. In this chapter, we'll explain the principles of cowriting songs and evaluating songwriter contributions. We'll also talk about what happens when someone claims that you ripped off their song (that is, "infringed" their copyright), or if you believe someone infringed your copyright. Finally, we'll explain how to complete a copyright application and register your song.

Copyright Basics

You may have heard a musician say he or she has "copyright" in a song. This means the musician, as the author of the song, is protected under federal copyright laws. These laws protect the creators of music, literature, visual arts, or other art forms. The creator of a song is the original copyright owner. However, over time the copyright may be bought or sold, which transfers ownership of the rights to the song to other people. For example, Michael Jackson bought and currently owns copyright in many Beatles songs.

⚠ **Canadian and American copyright laws are not identical.** We'll alert you to the major differences between the two countries' laws. Otherwise, you can apply most of the principles in this chapter to songs written by Canadian citizens.

Copyright Ownership

Copyright literally refers to the "right to copy." The owner of a song controls this right (as well as a number of other rights, discussed below). The owner grants others permission to use the song and can sue anyone who uses the song without permission.

With one important exception (addressed in the sidebar below), the first owner of a song is the songwriter (the "author" under copyright law). The songwriter may then sell the copyright to a music publisher in return for cash payments and continuing royalties. In this way, a song copyright is like other forms of property: It can be bought and sold. When there is more than one writer, there are special rules regarding dividing income and selling song copyrights. These "joint ownership" rules are discussed below.

An Exception to the First Owner Rule

There is one situation where the writer of a song is not the first owner. This is when a person is employed as a songwriter. In that case, the employer owns the song. Under copyright law, an employee who creates a work such as a song or a magazine article in the course of their employment does not own copyright in the work; the employer does. If a member of your band is employed to write music or has signed an agreement to write a song (or songs) for payment, you should review the "work made for hire" rules in *The Copyright Handbook*, by Stephen Fishman (Nolo), or visit the Copyright Office website (www.copyright.gov) and download Circular 9 (Work-Made-For-Hire Under the 1976 Copyright Act).

A Copyright Is a Bundle of Rights

In addition to preventing unauthorized copying of the song, the owner controls the sale, use, or public performance of the song. This means that unless the song owner gives permission (referred to as a "license") or unless a law permits the use, no other person can record, sell, copy, or publicly perform the song. The owner of the song also controls the right to modify or make "derivative" versions of the song. Derivative versions may include parodies, translations, or abbreviated versions of the song.

To Perform a Song

A song is publicly performed whenever it is heard by the public, whether at a live show, on a television broadcast, over the radio, or on a supermarket loudspeaker. For purposes of defining public performance, it doesn't matter if the performance is free (for example, an open concert in the park) or nonprofit (for example, a charity benefit). In the next chapter, we explain how songwriters are compensated when their song is performed.

How Do You Obtain a Copyright?

Musicians often believe that you can't have a copyright without obtaining a copyright registration. However, for most countries, including the U.S. and Canada, no registration is necessary. All that is required to copyright your song is that it be original and fixed. "Original" means that the song is original to the writer and that it was not copied from another source. A work is "fixed" when it exists in some tangible manner such as sheet music or a tape recording, or saved onto a computer disk. A work is *not* fixed if it is sung live and never put into sheet music or otherwise recorded. For example, many great American blues artists who only performed live would not have copyright protection for their songs. Lucky for many of these artists, they were recorded by bluesaholic Alan Lomax, who captured legends such as Leadbelly and Muddy Waters on tape. If it weren't for these recordings, these songs would be free for anyone to copy—and sell.

Despite the fact that registration isn't technically necessary, we recommend registering your works. Why? Because registering your song will strengthen the rights you would otherwise have under copyright law and will give you additional rights. Later in this chapter we discuss some of the advantages of registration, and we explain how to file a copyright application for registration.

⚠ Canadian copyright includes moral rights. One major difference between U.S. and Canadian copyright laws is a principle known as "moral rights." Under the law of moral rights, the author of a song is considered to have some "moral" claim to what happens to the song. That is, in Canada, even if you sell your song to a music publisher, you can still prevent anyone from distorting or modifying your song or prevent anyone from using your song in connection with a product or service that is prejudicial to your honor or reputation. In other words, if you sold your song, you could still prevent the new owner from using the song in a beer commercial if that commercial would make your fans think less of you. This rule does not apply to American songwriters under American copyright law, but it is an important standard that is also common in Europe.

Licenses and Sales: Transferring Rights

Song owners earn money when people pay for the right to use the song, such as including a song in a movie or recording a cover version of the song. In exchange for a payment, song owners give permission in the form of a written agreement known as a "license." Licenses are generally made by negotiating with the owner. For example, if a movie company wants to use a song, the company would negotiate a license with the song owner.

There is a special license called a compulsory license that applies when you want to cover a copyrighted song for a recording. In that case, you don't need permission for the license. Congress has established a uniform price for the license, and you do not have to negotiate with the song owner. All you have to do is to pay the amounts required under law and follow a few other rules. For example, if your band wants to sell its cover version of "Knocking on Heaven's Door," you would have to pay about 9 cents per CD to the owners of the song. Compulsory licenses apply only in the case of covering someone else's song for a recording. (The rules governing compulsory licenses are discussed in more detail in Chapter 8.)

A license is a temporary grant of permission. The owner of the song keeps all copyright ownership. In this way, a license is different than a sale of the copyright. In a sale (sometimes referred to as an "assignment"), the seller permanently gives up some or all of the ownership rights to another. Generally, the assignment is considered a permanent transfer of rights, although copyright law provides a method for the author or the author's heirs to reclaim rights after a period of 35 years.

Many songwriters sell their songs to music publishing companies. Music publishers are companies that exploit songs and collect revenues. Selling to a music publisher doesn't mean that the songwriter stops earning money from the song. Usually the songwriter continues to receive royalties under the terms of a music publishing contract. For example, "Walk on the Wild Side" is owned by a music publishing company, not by the author, Lou Reed. However, if the song is downloaded, played on the radio, or used in a commercial or movie, Lou Reed receives a share of the royalties. In the next chapter we discuss the basics of these publishing deals.

What Can't You Copy?

The purpose of copyright law is to prevent copying—but what exactly does "copying" mean? After all, nobody writes in a vacuum, and every songwriter borrows something from others. How do you know if you borrowed too much? Unfortunately, there's no fixed standard for what is "too much" copying. This can

be very frustrating for a musician who wants to borrow from another song, because determining whether there is an infringement is a subjective decision.

Courts sometimes rely on a "lay observer" approach that asks whether an average listener (not a musical expert) hearing both songs would believe that the similarities could result only from copying, not from coincidence. Another rule of thumb is that you can't just borrow well-known parts of music if the result could fairly be said to compete with the original. A good way to approach this as a songwriter is to ask yourself, if you were the *other* songwriter, would you feel ripped off? If the answer is yes, then you shouldn't be surprised if you get a nasty letter from the other band's lawyers when you go ahead with your song.

Avoid Infringement Disputes

When trying to determine whether your song infringes somebody else's copyrighted material, keep in mind that your goal should be to avoid a lawsuit altogether—not to win or lose in court. If you think that the two songs are close enough to spark a lawsuit but you're convinced you would win the case, don't take that as a sign that you should proceed. Copyright infringement lawsuits are expensive to defend and can easily bankrupt your band. It's much better to play it safe and stay out of the courtroom.

When Copying Is Okay

Not all copying is prohibited. Generally speaking, you're allowed to copy anything in the public domain, and you can make limited use of copying under rules of fair use.

The Public Domain

Music that isn't protected by copyright is said to be in the "public domain" and is free for anyone to copy. All songs published before 1923 (and some published after 1923) are in the public domain and can thus be copied freely. For example, the music for "Love Me Tender" was taken from a public domain song called "Aura Lee."

Under a similar principle, you are also free to copy familiar chord progressions or drum or bass patterns. These common elements (for example, a boogie-woogie piano riff) are considered to be the "language" of music and are free for all to use. Think of these elements in the way that words are used in books. By themselves, words or common phrases are not protectible. Everyone is free to use them. But the unique way that these elements are combined (or expressed) is what makes the song protectible.

For example, in a songwriting lawsuit, John Fogerty successfully proved he did not infringe a copyright by demonstrating that the only similarities between the two songs were elements common to all rock and roll songs—simple and common riffs

and arrangements. The same rules would apply for common lyric lines such as "got my mojo working" or "baby, be mine."

Note, however, these rules may not apply when sampling a distinctive drumbeat or distinctive vocal rendition—for example, the opening drum line of "Love to Love You Baby" or James Brown singing "Give It Up." In that case, you may be infringing a second type of copyright known as a sound recording copyright. Sound recording copyrights follow many of the same principles that we discuss in this chapter, but have special rules specific to sound recordings. We discuss sampling and sound recording copyrights in Chapter 11.

Song titles are also not protected under copyright law. That is, anyone is free to use a similar song title—and in fact, many hit songs have identical titles, such as "Wild Thing." The only exception would be if a title for a song is extremely unique, such as "Does Your Chewing Gum Lose Its Flavor on the Bed Post Overnight?" Beware, however, that using identical titles might raise trademark issues. Trademark law is discussed in Chapter 9.

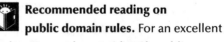 **Recommended reading on public domain rules.** For an excellent explanation on how to identify public domain music, see *The Public Domain*, by Stephen Fishman (Nolo).

From Public Domain to Public Domain

Musician Dave Alvin and his brother used to collect old blues, folk, rhythm and blues, and country recordings, including many long-out-of-print reissue albums on obscure labels. When looking for material for a solo album in 2000, Alvin decided to use many of these public domain songs. The result is Public Domain, a recording released by Oakland's Hightone Records (www.hightone. com). Among the songs recorded by Alvin were "Shenandoah," "Walk Right In," "Short Life of Trouble," "What Did the Deep Sea Say," "Engine 143," "Delia," and "The Murder of the Lawson Family." Because the songs were in the public domain, Hightone Records didn't have to pay any mechanical royalties to use them.

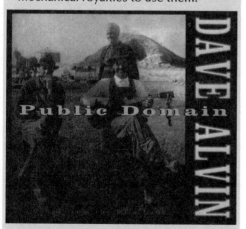

Public Domain, Dave Alvin, ℗ © copyright Hightone Records

Fair Use

You are also free to copy a portion of a copyrighted work if your copying qualifies as a fair use. Fair use of copyrighted works includes commenting on, criticizing, or parodying the works. For example, a newspaper can freely copy a portion of your song lyrics in a music review. Fair use can apply in songwriting when a writer borrows a phrase or riff from another source. For example, the rap group 2 Live Crew borrowed the opening bass riff of the song "Pretty Woman" and the words (but not the melody) from the first line of the song ("Oh pretty woman walking down the street"). The rest of the lyrics and the music were different. The U.S. Supreme Court permitted it as a fair use because the 2 Live Crew song was a parody, holding the original song up to ridicule.

The difficulty of applying fair use is that the standard is often subjective. That is, you can't guarantee that your band's use is a fair use until a judge makes a determination in a lawsuit—at which point your band may be bankrupt from legal fees. As with other copyright issues, the problem with suing people about fair use claims is that you can't tell ahead of time whether you'll win, and astronomical legal bills often make "winning" not even worth it.

⚠️ **Fair use principles differ in the U.S. and Canada.** The standards for the American principle of fair use are defined in the federal copyright law. In Canada, a related principle known as "fair dealing" is used, although it is not explicitly defined in the Canadian law. U.S. rules of fair use may not be the same as Canadian fair dealing principles. Contact the Canadian Intellectual Property Office for more detailed information on fair dealing principles. (Contact information is below and in Chapter 17.)

For More Information About Canadian Copyright Law

Copyright Office
Canadian Intellectual Property Office (CIPO)
Industry Canada
50 Victoria Street
Place du Portage, Phase I
Hull, Quebec,
K1A 0C9
819-997-1936
Fax 819-953-7620

The CIPO website (http://cipo.gc.ca) is also extremely helpful, because you can download circulars about various copyright subjects as well as copyright applications and forms. Circular 2, *Musical Works and Mechanical Contrivances*, is particularly helpful.

Coauthorship and Co-Ownership of Songs

When a song or other creative work is created by more than one person, the issue of copyright ownership becomes more complex. This section will discuss how to figure out who owns copyright to a song written by more than one person.

Cowriters Are Co-Owners

When a song has more than one writer, the writers are known as co-owners. This is true whether the songwriters made equal or unequal contributions to the song. (Respective shares of contributions are discussed below.)

The co-owners share the legal rights to the song in the absence of an agreement to the contrary. Joint copyright owners can separately grant permission (a license) for someone to use the song in a movie, provided you share the income with the other. Similarly, either one of you could sue someone who illegally copied your song, provided that you share the financial recovery with your fellow writer.

When it comes to assignment (selling) of copyright, co-owners must jointly agree to sell rights to the whole song, or they can sell their individual share of the ownership. Before a song can be recorded for the first time, we recommend that you obtain the consent of all co-writers. Although copyright law does not explicitly require all writers to consent to the first recording, we recommend this approach since, after the first recording, anyone can record the song as long as payments are made according to compulsory license rules (explained in Chapter 12).

Although each co-owner is entitled to receive money from the song, this doesn't mean that the two writers have to share money from the song equally. One writer may receive 30% of the income and the other may earn 70%. Each writer's share is usually based on the value of their contribution. This is a matter that is agreed on by the two writers. If the writers do not agree and the issue turns into a lawsuit, then a court will decide on the value of each writer's contribution. Courts often start with the presumption that all songwriters contributed equally.

Evaluating Songwriting Contributions

Sometimes, cowriters have a difficult time evaluating their relative contributions. Songwriting credit is one of the touchiest subjects among band members. The following scenario is a common one: The guitar player creates a song structure— some chord changes over a rhythm. The singer adds words and a melody. The bass player figures a bass part. The keyboard player improvises a solo. The problem begins when all four believe they should be listed as cowriters of the song. The internal dispute distracts the band from its music and disrupts band business.

Traditional Methods of Determining the Songwriter

Historically, the creators of the words, melody, and chord structure were considered the songwriters. That's because the words, music, and chord changes (along with the tempo) were traditionally the only elements necessary for sheet music. The creation of a solo or a supporting bass or drum part was usually *not* considered an element of songwriting for two reasons: 1) These parts, although they enhance the recorded performance, are not considered essential to the structure of the song; and 2) solos and rhythm parts are usually derived from a limited language of musical parts, and this limited language is not protected by copyright law. For many bands, the old rule still holds true: The creators of the words, melody, and chords are the songwriters.

Exceptions to the Traditional Approach

As songwriting has evolved, exceptions have developed to traditional rules. For example, in rock, pop, and dance music, it's possible that a bass or drum part is so integral to the song that it becomes as important as the melody—for example, the memorable bass riffs on "Come Together" or "White Lines," or the drum solo on "Wipeout." In that case, the members of the band may determine among themselves that the contributor of the riff be included as a songwriter.

How can you tell if a part is important enough to become an element of the song? One way is to ask yourself if another artist covered your song, would the other artist want to duplicate this part? Almost every artist who covers the song "Satisfaction" includes the opening guitar/bass riff. (Of course there are exceptions to this rule: Devo's popular cover of "Satisfaction" did not use this riff.) As a general rule, if the part is an indispensable element of the song, then the creator of the part should be considered a songwriter.

A Whiter Shade of Pale An interesting case of songwriter credit arose in the case of the song "A Whiter Shade of Pale" by the '60s group Procol Harum. For an analysis of the songwriting credits for the haunting organ part, see www.procolharum.com/awsopcomp.htm.

Sometimes Rules Don't Matter

It's possible that a band can ditch these evaluation rules and decide on its own method of evaluating songwriter contributions. It's even possible that a person who made no contribution to a song can be listed as a writer. For example, Elvis Presley's manager often demanded that songwriters give Elvis a cowriting credit if they wanted him to perform a song. Songwriters, eager to have a song on an Elvis recording, sometimes shared the credit and partial ownership interest.

It is also important to remember that a person can earn money from a song even if not listed as a songwriter. As we explain in the next chapter, a band member can earn money from a song even if not listed as a writer. If the band earns money from publishing songs, all band members can receive income from band songs if the band partnership agreement provides for sharing songwriting income.

EXAMPLE: *The Smokers Split Their Songwriting Income*

The Smokers is a group consisting of four members: songwriters Sasha and Gompers, as well as nonwriters Cherry and Ratgirl. The group has decided to share songwriting royalties. The songs written by Sasha and Gompers are published by their band publishing company. Under their band partnership agreement, the income from the published songs is split equally among the four members.

If You Don't Come Up With a System, Someone Else Will

If you do not have a system for allocating songwriting contributions and a dispute about distributing profits ends up in court, the court will presume that each songwriter contributed equally. For example, if three people wrote a song and there was no agreement among them, a court, unless faced with contrary evidence, would presume that each writer owned a one-third interest. If you want to make ownership decisions yourselves rather than letting a court decide, work out an agreement early on.

Partnership and Collaboration Agreements

Songwriting ownership among joint owners is usually addressed in two types of agreements. One is a collaboration or cowriter agreement; the other is the band partnership agreement. If your band does not have a partnership agreement or does not intend to address songwriting ownership in your partnership agreement, the songwriters should enter into a collaboration agreement.

The collaboration agreement is usually used when two or more people write together. The agreement can be used for one song or for many songs, and it sets forth the percentages and rights of the songwriters. A collaboration agreement can be as simple as a statement of the percentage interests and the name of the song, signed by all writers.

If songs are written jointly by band members, the ownership rights are expressed in the band's partnership agreement (BPA) rather than a collaboration agreement. As discussed in Chapter 2, you can use customized clauses in your BPA to establish exactly the division of songwriting rights and income among band members. For example, if there are four members in a band, but all songs

are written by two of the members, the partnership agreement can establish a system dividing up songwriting income as follows:
songwriting band members earn 60%, nonsongwriting band members earn 40%.

In Chapter 8 we offer several alternative systems for dividing up band songwriting income.

Copyright Infringement

Copyright infringement occurs when a song is copied, modified, or performed without authorization of the song owner(s). If the owner did not authorize the use, and if no legal principle such as fair use permitted it (discussed above), then the infringer can be sued for damages to the copyright owner.

Is There Damage?

There are various standards and tests for determining infringement. However, these tests and standards are often less important than a very basic issue: Has the song owner been injured? That is, has the song owner suffered some financial damage because of the infringement? The purpose of an infringement lawsuit is to provide a remedy for the copyright owner's injury. Without a real injury (that is, lost revenue), the issue of infringement is academic and one for which judges have little patience. Even if the songwriter who is suing can claim a minimum amount of damages established by law, a judge will still fashion an award that reflects the true injury.

For example, in one famous case the composer of a song called "Dardanella" sued Jerome Kern, the composer of "Kahlua." The melodies of the songs were different, but the composer of "Dardanella" claimed Mr. Kern had copied part of the *ostinato,* an eight-note pattern that repeated within the background accompaniment. The *ostinato* was not a particularly important aspect of either work, and the owner of "Dardanella" could not prove any injury from the infringement. The judge presiding over the trial, the famous Judge Learned Hand, was annoyed. "This controversy is a mere point of honor of scarcely more than irritation, involving no substantial interest. Except that it raises an interesting point of law, it would be a waste of time for everyone concerned." Judge Hand awarded the plaintiff the minimum amount possible: $250. This case is a reminder that copyright claims should not be filed on principle, but only if actual damages exist. Similarity of works is important, but only if it is closely related to proving an injury.

A large damage payment was justified in a 1994 case involving the singer Michael Bolton. The court in this case ruled that one of Bolton's biggest hits, "Love Is a Wonderful Thing," infringed a song by the Isley Brothers. A jury awarded the Isley Brothers $5.4 million. The verdict was upheld on appeal.

Of course, many copyright infringement lawsuits are brought out of spite or revenge, or just on principle. When copyright cases are brought for reasons other than money, it's usually because the participants can afford to slug it out in court.

Substantial Similarity

The standard for copyright infringement is whether the songs are "substantially similar." For purposes of determining infringement, unprotectible similarities such as similar tempos or use of common song forms are generally disregarded. Other similarities may be evaluated by themselves, but the final decision is always based on comparing the complete songs.

There is a common myth among musicians that four bars of music may be copied without infringing copyright. Like most myths, this one's not true. The criteria to determine whether infringement has occurred is not the *amount* taken, but the *importance* of the portion taken. If the copied portion of a song is quantitatively small, the court will determine the importance of that portion to the original song. For example, the copying of two bars of music in one song was held to be an infringement, while the copying of six bars of music in another song was not an infringement. Unfortunately, there is no formula that establishes how much taking equals substantial similarity. Below, we briefly discuss some of the common issues that arise regarding song infringement.

Pursuing an Infringer

If you think someone is stealing your song, you will have to prove that the other artist had access to your song (see "All Access: Proving an Infringer Heard Your Song," below) and copied it (or a portion of it), and that the portion that was copied is protected under copyright. If you win your lawsuit, you are entitled to money damages: either the infringer's profits or the fair market value of the use of the song (or special statutory damages; see below). That is, you are entitled to the amount of money that the infringer received for sales of the record, or to the amount you would have received for licensing the song *minus* gross expenses.

If you registered your song prior to the infringement, you may choose to receive special damages, known as statutory damages, instead. These can range up to $150,000 for willful infringements. The actual amount is determined by a judge. Regardless of whether you registered the song prior to the infringement, you can also stop the infringer from any further uses of the infringing song. You should also note that songs are ripped off in many ways. Several advertising companies have been sued for using popular songs in TV commercials without a license.

When considering the strength of your case and deciding whether or not to pursue it, an equally important issue is whether it's worth it even if you win. If the infringing song has not earned money or if the person you are suing has no assets (or

if they declare bankruptcy), you will have spent a lot of money for an empty victory. And few copyright infringement cases are assured of victory; they're notoriously difficult to predict. The only general rule is that the more successful your band, the better your chances.

EXAMPLE: *John Fogerty and "The Old Man Down the Road"*

Can an author infringe his own work? This may seem like an academic question, but it had a very real application for songwriter John Fogerty when he was sued in 1985. Many of the songs written by Fogerty and popularized by his group Creedence Clearwater Revival are now owned by Fantasy Records, a California company. Fantasy sued Fogerty, claiming that one of his newer songs, "The Old Man Down the Road," infringed a 1970 song, "Run Through the Jungle," also written by Fogerty and owned by Fantasy. Fogerty brought his guitar into court, sang both songs for the jury and demonstrated that the elements common to both songs were unprotectible and common to many rock and roll songs. Fogerty won this novel lawsuit (*Fantasy, Inc. v. Fogerty*, 510 U.S. 517 (1994)) and in the process established that a person defending an infringement lawsuit, like the person bringing the suit, is also entitled to the awarding of attorney fees.

All Access: Proving an Infringer Heard Your Song

If you're trying to prove that your song was copied, you won't be able to make that claim unless there is evidence that the alleged infringer listened to your tune (known as "access").

If there is no access, there is no infringement. For example, in a case involving the Britney Spears song, "What U See is What U Get," two men alleged that they had sent their version of a song to a talent scout representing Spears. However, the court ruled for Spears because the evidence at trial showed that she had recorded her version several months before the two men had even submitted their composition. (*Cottrill v. Spears*, 2003 U.S. Dist. LEXIS 8823 (E.D. Pa 2003).)

The more popular your song is, the easier it is for you to prove access. For example, the copyright owner of the hit song "He's So Fine" sued the late George Harrison, alleging that Harrison's song "My Sweet Lord" infringed copyright. It was proven that Harrison had access to "He's So Fine," since the song was on the British pop charts in 1963 (while a song by the Beatles was also on the British charts). The court concluded Harrison

had access—that is, a reasonable opportunity to hear the plaintiff's song.

Conversely, if a song was never released, the copyright owner has a much harder time proving access. For example, an unknown songwriter mailed a demo copy of his song to publishers and record companies listed in an industry songwriter book. Later, the songwriter claimed that two songs performed by Celine Dion infringed his song. The evidence demonstrated that the songwriter's demo never made it past the corporate mailrooms of the companies being sued. The court concluded that "bare corporate receipt" of a song generated by an unsolicited mass mailing, was inadequate, by itself, to show access. (*Jorgensen v. Epic/Sony Records*, 351 F.3d 46 (S.D. NY 2002).)

When two songs in question are identical, access may be presumed and does not need to be proven. That's because in cases of verbatim copying, it is virtually impossible that two songs could have been independently created. In situations such as this, the burden is on the defendant, the alleged infringer, to disprove access.

Defending Against an Infringement Claim

There are two common reasons why someone may threaten to sue your band over a song:

- A songwriter claims that your song (or a portion of your song) is taken from his copyrighted song.
- A songwriter claims that your song uses a sample from his copyrighted recording. (A "sample" is a portion of a recording that is digitally copied and mixed into your song.)

In the first situation—a songwriter claims you have stolen a song—you will be subject to the copyright infringement standards expressed previously in this chapter. That is, did your band have access to the song, and are the two songs substantially similar? The second situation—sampling—is more complex. We discuss sampling issues in Chapter 11.

As in the case of pursuing an infringer, you need to ask yourself: Regardless of whether any copyright law has actually been violated, how much will it cost to fight? The unfortunate fact is that most working bands can't spare the money necessary to defend a lawsuit. They usually settle the dispute in the cheapest manner possible. Sometimes this means that the band changes the song or stops using the song altogether. For the sake of your band's business, you need to carefully evaluate your course of action with an attorney.

When Your Song Insults Someone

Occasionally, songwriters are sued if a song makes disparaging remarks about a person, character, or product. For example, John Fogerty wrote a song critical of a record company owner and got sued. (He eventually changed the lyrics.) This type of lawsuit is not based on infringement of copyright. Instead it is based on libel and slander law, which may prohibit you from making untrue statements that cause the public to think less of someone or some product. The standards for libel and slander vary considerably from situation to situation. If you are threatened with such a lawsuit, you should consult an attorney or someone knowledgeable as to the libel laws in your state.

How to Avoid Getting Screwed in Conflicts Over Songs

There are several ways in which bands get into conflicts over band songs. With a basic understanding of copyright law and a willingness to deal with it, these types of disputes can usually be avoided.

Situation #1:
There is a dispute among your band members as to who wrote a song.

Many bands neglect to hammer out song ownership shares before they begin to perform or record a song. If the song becomes popular and the band has not established who will receive songwriting credit, a nasty dispute can ensue, which can seriously harm the band's business.

How to avoid getting screwed:
The best way to deal with a songwriting dispute within your band is to avoid it in the first place. Besides educating yourself about how songs can be jointly owned (see above), it's important to be up front about what each band member wants and expects. If the songwriters in the band do not want to share income from songs with nonsongwriters, they need to clearly say so. It's an understandable and common position among songwriters; after all, songwriting is a special talent that can catapult a good band into a best-selling band. The songwriters, like star athletes on a team, may want to receive a reward for their special talents. If this is the case in your band, it's important to deal with it before releasing a record or preparing to sign a record deal. Band discussions about songwriting can become heated, but don't let that dissuade you from having the discussion if it's time. Avoiding the issue can only cause problems later.

Situation #2:
Your band is sued on an infringement claim.

Bands get screwed in two ways when they are sued over songwriting: 1) A band is pressured into giving up rights because it can't afford to fight the lawsuit; or 2) a band spends too much money and time fighting a lawsuit, even if it ultimately wins.

How to avoid getting screwed:
If your band is threatened with a lawsuit over a song, you need to first evaluate your band's song. Determine whether the song is important enough for your band that it's worth fighting over. For example, if you created a song that borrows a great deal from "Communication Breakdown," and the owners of the Led Zeppelin song threaten to sue your band, your first decision is whether you care enough about your song to fight over it. If you don't, it's easiest (and cheapest) to agree to stop using and selling the song. We are not recommending that you always give up when threatened. We are suggesting, however, always to keep in mind that lawsuits do not always resolve "who is right?" but rather, "who has more money?"

If you *do* care about the song and it is important to your band, then you should seek professional help *pronto!* Take your dispute to an attorney (see Chapter 4 for information on dealing with attorneys) and get an assessment of your chances of success in the lawsuit. Do this *immediately* after receiving the threat of the lawsuit—any delay may affect your ability to settle the suit. No lawyer can guarantee whether you'll win or lose, but an experienced copyright attorney can assess your chances of success.

Only if your odds are better than 75% should your band think about fighting. It's possible in some cases that an attorney can deal with the matter inexpensively (between $200 to $500) and you won't have to be bullied into a settlement. It's also possible that if the claim against your band is completely worthless (referred to as a frivolous claim), a court may award you an amount to cover your attorney fees. However, don't count on this, as attorney fees awards are rare.

Situation #3:
Your band wants to sue another band for infringement.

A band hears a song on the radio that contains some chords and riffs that are somewhat similar to one of its songs. The band gets angry and hires an attorney. If it loses the case, it gets buried in legal fees. It may even be required to pay the other side's legal fees. Or, worse, it may win the case but fail to recover any money from the other band (which has no real assets) and still end up buried in legal fees.

How to avoid getting screwed:

It's a mistake to hire an attorney and go after a potential infringer without thoroughly reviewing the case and determining whether any money can be recovered. In order to avoid getting screwed, your band needs the opinion of a copyright attorney. If an attorney doesn't believe that your band will win a lawsuit or recover any money, then it's probably a good idea to give up on the matter. You may feel that you have been cheated, but don't confuse your moral outrage with your legal rights.

If your attorney feels you have a good case of copyright infringement and that money can be recovered, you need to figure out how you will pay your lawyer. Perhaps your attorney will take the case on a contingency basis, in which case the attorney usually receives one-quarter to one-third of any money recovered. If you lose, you don't have to pay any attorney fees. Note, however, that even if you use a contingency arrangement, your band will probably have to pay nonattorney legal costs such as document fees or court costs, which can quickly add up to hundreds (or thousands) of dollars. (See Chapter 4 for information about hiring attorneys.)

What About Song Parodies?

In order to parody or satirize a song, it's necessary to borrow a portion of the song. For example, Weird Al Yankovic's "Like a Surgeon" wouldn't be an effective parody of "Like a Virgin" if the melody was not borrowed from the original. Therefore, all parodies borrow or modify the original songs. Since only the copyright owner is allowed to modify the song without authorization, the makers of parodies must either get permission or prove that their parody is excused under the principle of fair use.

Judges understand that, by its nature, parody demands some taking from an original work, and a more extensive use of a copyrighted work is permitted, therefore, in order to "conjure up" the original. At issue is often the effect on the potential market—or as it is sometimes phrased in legalese, whether the parodist's result had the intent or the effect of fulfilling a demand for the original work.

This determination is often tricky. For example, in the case of *Fisher v. Dees*, 794 F. 2d 432 (9th Cir. 1986), the composers of the song "When Sunny Gets Blue" claimed that their song was infringed by "When Sonny Sniffs Glue," a 29-second parody that altered the original lyric line and borrowed six bars of the plaintiff's music. The copyright owner argued that the parody reflected negatively on the original song and therefore affected its marketability. The court responded that: "[T]he economic effect of a parody with which we are concerned is not its potential to destroy or diminish the market for the original—any bad review can have that effect—but whether it *fulfills the demand* for the original." In other words, the important factor is whether the market for the original will be reduced due to people buying the parody instead of the original. The court permitted "When Sonny Sniffs Glue" as a fair use.

A similar result was reached in a case involving a rap song entitled "The Forest." The rap song borrowed the first three lines of "What a Wonderful World" ("I see trees of green, red roses too/I see them bloom for me and you/And I think to myself, what a wonderful world") and ridiculed the description of beauty and optimism by changing the lyrics into an invitation to get high on marijuana ("I see buds that are green, red roses too/I see blunts for me and you/And I say to myself, what a wonderful world").

The lyrics in the rap song borrowed three lines from "Wonderful World," used them once at the beginning of the song, and did not borrow any other music or lyrics or sample the original recording. On that basis a court determined that the use was a parody and permitted under fair use principles. (*Abilene Music, Inc. v. Sony Music Entertainment, Inc.* 67 USPQ.2d 1356 (S.D. NY 2003).)

Borrowing a complete song (not merely 29 seconds or the first three lines) and modifying the lyrics is, however, unlikely to be excused as fair use or parody. Performers such as Weird Al Yankovic who earn a living by humorously modifying hit songs seek permission of the songwriters before recording their parodies.

What If Your Song Parodies a Doll?

What if your song isn't a parody of another song, but instead parodies a famous brand name such as the Barbie doll? In 1997, the Danish group Aqua had a hit with their song "Barbie Girl," in which a singer impersonating Barbie in a high-pitched, doll-like voice chanted, "Life in plastic, it's fantastic." The band did not take any copyrighted material—that is, they did not copy words, music, or images owned by Mattel, the maker of Barbie Doll. Instead, the band only borrowed the famous "Barbie" trademarked name. Mattel sued for trademark infringement and for trademark dilution, a claim that someone is blurring or tarnishing a famous trademark (see Chapter 9). This type of lawsuit differs from copyright infringement because it raises the issue of how the parody affects consumers. For example, would consumers be confused that Mattel sponsored or supported the song? Fortunately, a federal judge stepped in to protect the free speech rights of the band and its label, declaring that consumers were not likely to be confused by the band's use of "Barbie." Demonstrating the resilience of the Barbie trademark to such uses, the judge (referring to Mattel as "Speech-Zilla") declared, "Over the years ... Barbie has been labeled both the ideal American woman and a bimbo. She has survived attacks both psychic (from feminists critical of her fictitious figure) and physical (more than 500 professional makeovers)." (*Mattel v. MCA Records*, 296 F.3d 894 (9th Cir. 2002).)

Before your band rushes out to parody famous trademarks, keep in mind that Aqua had the legal resources of one of the world's largest record labels, MCA, to fight Mattel. Most bands faced with a lawsuit from the owner of an internationally known trademark will have a difficult time battling—even if legally in the right—against corporate suits. This isn't to say that you should shy away from using your free speech rights, but choose your parodies carefully and, when in doubt, seek the advice of an entertainment lawyer.

Copyright Registration

As we explained earlier in this chapter, copyright registration is not necessary to protect your songs—but it can help. There are three strong arguments in favor of copyright registration:

- The registration creates a presumption of ownership and validity. That is, if you register the song within five years of releasing it to the public, it is presumed that you are the owner of the song and that copyright is valid.
- If a work has been registered prior to an infringement or within three months of publication, the copyright owner may be entitled to special payments known as "statutory damages" in the case of a successful lawsuit against an infringer. You may also be entitled to receive your attorney fees from the person you sued.
- A registration is required to file a copyright infringement lawsuit. That is, if you sue someone over infringement of your song, you will have to register before filing your lawsuit. If you wish to accomplish registration within a week, there is a method for expediting it. For a special handling fee of $685 (including the $45 filing fee), the Copyright Office will process an application within five working days. However, this service is not for convenience; it is allowed only in urgent cases. The Copyright Office has prepared a form for Request for Special Handling (see Circular 10 at www.copyright.gov).

Completing a copyright application is not difficult. If you need help, the Copyright Office provides guides for filling out the application.

Copyright Preregistration

Starting in 2006, copyright law permits songwriters (and other copyright owners) the ability to preregister their works. This was done in order to deal with a digital-age problem: prerelease infringement. Songwriters or musicians whose works are prone to infringement before release may preregister their work by filling out an online application at the Copyright Office website. A copy of the unpublished work need not be provided.

The copyright owner of an unpublished work that has been preregistered may file a copyright infringement suit without having to register the work with the Copyright Office. This allows a lawsuit to be filed quickly and may help the owner obtain court action to prevent distribution of the work.

Even more important, the copyright owner may obtain statutory damages and attorney fees in a successful infringement suit against anyone who pirated the unfinished work after the preregistration was made, provided that the work is fully registered with the Copyright Office during the earlier of the following times:

- three months after the first publication of the work, or
- one month after the copyright owner learned of the infringement.

For the vast majority of musicians, preregistration is a waste of money. Few songs or recordings are infringed before they are published or otherwise distributed. This type of thing usually occurs with popular songs recorded by superstar artists. However, you may benefit by pre-registering your work if you think it's likely someone may infringe your unfinished song or recording before it is released.

You can preregister your song only if:

- it is unpublished
- its creation has begun, and
- it is being prepared for commercial distribution.

You preregister by completing an online application at the Copyright Office website (www.copyright.gov). You must provide the following information:

- the work's title (a working title may be used)
- the names of the author and copyright claimant
- the date the actual writing of the book began and the date you anticipate completing it, and
- a description of the work—for example, that it is a song and any other details that may help identify the work in published form.

You need not provide the Copyright Office with a copy of your unpublished song or make any other deposit. The non-refundable filing fee for preregistration is $100.

If you fill out the application correctly, the Copyright Office will email you a notification of preregistration, which will include a preregistration number and date. This is the only notice you will receive that preregistration has been made. The Copyright Office does not issue a paper certificate of preregistration.

Choosing the Right Copyright Form: Form PA

Registering a song is done by submitting Form PA to the Copyright Office. A sample appears below and on the CD at the back of this book. You can also obtain copies of this form by writing to the Copyright Office or downloading a copy from the Copyright Office website at www.copyright.gov.

Contacting the Copyright Office

You can contact the Copyright Office by writing to Copyright Office, Library of Congress, Washington, DC 20559-6000. On the Web, you can find the Copyright Office at www.copyright. gov. You can call the Forms Hotline 24 hours a day at 202-707-9100. Copyright Circulars are special publications that explain copyright laws and rules in plain language, and you can obtain them at the Copyright Office website or by calling Fax on Demand at 202-707-2600.

I have posted an instructional video on how to fill out a Form PA at YouTube. com. To locate it, type "How to Register a Song Copyright" into the search engine at YouTube.

Registering Multiple Songs

Each registration is $30, so you can save money by registering a group of songs. Registering a collection can also be done on Form PA. We'll explain the procedure below. However, you may register a group of songs in only two situations: 1) All of the songs were written by one songwriter, or 2) if the songs were written by more than one writer, one of the writers wrote part of each song in the collection.

> **EXAMPLE:** Your band has ten songs. Nine were written by Joan and Tom, and one was written by Joan. You can register all ten songs in one Form PA.

> **EXAMPLE:** Your band has ten songs. Seven were written by Joan and Tom, two were written by Joan, and one was written by Bob. You can register the nine songs on which Joan is a songwriter on one Form PA. A separate Form PA will have to be used for Bob's song.

Filling Out Form PA

We will walk you through Form PA by referencing each of the numbered spaces on the form. You should be aware that some of the numbered spaces require more than one piece of information. Special instructions are included for registering collections of songs.

SPACE ❶: Title of This Work

Every song must have a title in order to be registered. The title is used to index the work in Copyright Office records. If your title is in a foreign language, do not use a foreign alphabet to write it; use the Roman alphabet.

If Registering a Collection of Songs.

Instead of listing the titles of all the songs in the collection, create a collective title such as *Ten Tunes by the Spyders, Songs From Our New Album,* or *Songs We Wrote While Drinking Beer.* We'll explain a procedure for supplying each separate song title below.

SPACE ❶: Previous or Alternative Titles

The alternative or previous title is any additional title under which someone searching for the song might look. For example, the song, "Everybody's Talkin'" is also known by an alternate title, "Theme From *Midnight Cowboy.*"

SPACE ❶: Nature of This Work

Space 1 of Form PA also requires information about the "nature of the work." You should state "words and music" unless there are no lyrics, in which case simply write "music."

SPACE ❷: Name of Author

In this space, you must identify all songwriters and their contributions. For example: "Gary Wilson, words and music." If songwriters in your band are known by a nickname such as Slash or Flea, you may use the nickname, although when it comes to matters of song ownership and payments it's usually wiser to use your legal name. Among other things, there will be fewer hassles when cashing royalty checks

at the bank. If a songwriter wants to be listed by a pseudonym, give the pseudonym and identify it as such (for example, Flea, pseudonym); or reveal the author's name, making it clear that it is a pseudonym (for example, Robert Zimmerman, whose pseudonym is Bob Dylan.) You should also note that, in certain cases, using a pseudonym may shorten the period of copyright protection.

SPACE ❷: Works Made for Hire

A work made for hire is a song prepared by an employee hired to write songs or a song that is commissioned and meets certain legal requirements. Most likely, your song is not a work made for hire and you should check the "No" box. If your band hired people to write songs (for example, if the bandleader employed a songwriter), check the "Yes" box. If in doubt, refer to Copyright Circular 9.

SPACE ❷: Nature of Authorship

Provide a short statement of the nature of each writer's contribution. For example, if Bob wrote the words and music to a song, the nature of authorship would be "words and music." If Bob wrote the music and Sally wrote the words, the nature of Bob's authorship would be "music" and the nature of Sally's authorship would be "words" or "lyrics."

If Registering a Collection of Songs.

For a collection of songs, list the names of each songwriter and complete each section as described above. Under

"Nature of Authorship," list each writer's contribution.

SPACE ❷: Dates of Birth and Death

The date of birth of each author should be provided. If one of the songwriters has died, the year of death should be provided.

SPACE ❷: Nationality or Domicile

State each author's nationality.

SPACE ❸: Creation and Publication

Creation and publication have two very different meanings under copyright law. A work is created when a final version of it is fixed for the first time in sheet music or on a recording. So, as a general rule, the date of creation is when the work is completed and recorded or put into sheet music. For example, if you've been working on a song for months but finally finish it and record it in December 1998, then that is the date of creation.

A work is published if it is distributed to the public—for example, offered for sale or given away at shows. If you've made some demo recordings and sent them to music publishers or record companies, that is *not* considered a publication of the work—it hasn't been distributed to the public.

If Registering a Collection of Songs.

For purposes of registering a group of songs, all of the songs in the collection should have the same status, either published or unpublished.

SPACE ❸: Date and Nation of First Publication

If you have not published your song (that is, pressed it on recordings and distributed it to the public), leave this section blank. If you have published the song, give the full date (that is, month, day, and year) when the work was published. If you're unsure, it is okay to state "approximately" (that is, "approximately June 4, 1998"). If the work was first published in the United States, the initials "U.S.A." may be used. If the work was simultaneously published (within 30 days) in two countries, for example, the U.S. and Canada, it is acceptable to state "U.S.A." If the work was first published in a foreign country, the foreign edition constitutes the first publication.

If Registering a Collection of Songs.

List the creation and publication dates of the last song that was completed on the collection.

SPACE ❹: Copyright Claimants

The copyright "claimant" is either the author of the work or a person or company to whom the song has been sold or transferred. For example, if all the songwriters transferred their rights to a band publishing company, the name (and address) of the band publishing company would be listed here. If the song hasn't been transferred, list the names of the writers. You can list each of their addresses or one address for all of them. If the song is a work made for hire, the

Copyright Office fees are subject to change. For current fees, check the Copyright Office website at *www.copyright.gov*, write the Copyright Office, or call (202) 707-3000.

FORM PA

For a Work of the Performing Arts
UNITED STATES COPYRIGHT OFFICE

REGISTRATION NUMBER

_____

PA   PAU

EFFECTIVE DATE OF REGISTRATION

_____

Month   Day   Year

DO NOT WRITE ABOVE THIS LINE. IF YOU NEED MORE SPACE, USE A SEPARATE CONTINUATION SHEET.

1

TITLE OF THIS WORK ▼

_____

PREVIOUS OR ALTERNATIVE TITLES ▼

_____

NATURE OF THIS WORK ▼ See instructions

2

a

NAME OF AUTHOR ▼

DATES OF BIRTH AND DEATH
Year Born ▼   Year Died ▼

Was this contribution to the work a "work made for hire"?
☐ Yes
☐ No

AUTHOR'S NATIONALITY OR DOMICILE
Name of Country
OR { Citizen of _____
Domiciled in _____

WAS THIS AUTHOR'S CONTRIBUTION TO THE WORK
Anonymous?   ☐ Yes ☐ No
Pseudonymous? ☐ Yes ☐ No

If the answer to either of these questions is "Yes," see detailed instructions.

NATURE OF AUTHORSHIP Briefly describe nature of material created by this author in which copyright is claimed. ▼

NOTE

Under the law, the "author" of a "work made for hire" is generally the employer, not the employee (see instructions). For any part of this work that was "made for hire" check "Yes" in the space provided, give the employer (or other person for whom the work was prepared) as "Author" of that part, and leave the space for dates of birth and death blank.

b

NAME OF AUTHOR ▼

DATES OF BIRTH AND DEATH
Year Born ▼   Year Died ▼

Was this contribution to the work a "work made for hire"?
☐ Yes
☐ No

AUTHOR'S NATIONALITY OR DOMICILE
Name of Country
OR { Citizen of _____
Domiciled in _____

WAS THIS AUTHOR'S CONTRIBUTION TO THE WORK
Anonymous?   ☐ Yes ☐ No
Pseudonymous? ☐ Yes ☐ No

If the answer to either of these questions is "Yes," see detailed instructions.

NATURE OF AUTHORSHIP Briefly describe nature of material created by this author in which copyright is claimed. ▼

c

NAME OF AUTHOR ▼

DATES OF BIRTH AND DEATH
Year Born ▼   Year Died ▼

Was this contribution to the work a "work made for hire"?
☐ Yes
☐ No

AUTHOR'S NATIONALITY OR DOMICILE
Name of Country
OR { Citizen of _____
Domiciled in _____

WAS THIS AUTHOR'S CONTRIBUTION TO THE WORK
Anonymous?   ☐ Yes ☐ No
Pseudonymous? ☐ Yes ☐ No

If the answer to either of these questions is "Yes," see detailed instructions.

NATURE OF AUTHORSHIP Briefly describe nature of material created by this author in which copyright is claimed. ▼

3

a **YEAR IN WHICH CREATION OF THIS WORK WAS COMPLETED** This information must be given Year in all cases.

b **DATE AND NATION OF FIRST PUBLICATION OF THIS PARTICULAR WORK** Complete this information ONLY if this work has been published. Month _____ Day _____ Year _____ Nation

4

See instructions before completing this space.

COPYRIGHT CLAIMANT(S) Name and address must be given even if the claimant is the same as the author given in space 2. ▼

TRANSFER If the claimant(s) named here in space 4 is (are) different from the author(s) named in space 2, give a brief statement of how the claimant(s) obtained ownership of the copyright. ▼

DO NOT WRITE HERE OFFICE USE ONLY

APPLICATION RECEIVED

ONE DEPOSIT RECEIVED

TWO DEPOSITS RECEIVED

FUNDS RECEIVED

MORE ON BACK ▶ • Complete all applicable spaces (numbers 5-9) on the reverse side of this page.
• See detailed instructions.   • Sign the form at line 8.

DO NOT WRITE HERE
Page 1 of _____ pages

EXAMINED BY	**FORM PA**
CHECKED BY	
☐ CORRESPONDENCE Yes	FOR COPYRIGHT OFFICE USE ONLY

DO NOT WRITE ABOVE THIS LINE. IF YOU NEED MORE SPACE, USE A SEPARATE CONTINUATION SHEET.

PREVIOUS REGISTRATION Has registration for this work, or for an earlier version of this work, already been made in the Copyright Office?

☐ **Yes** ☐ **No** If your answer is "Yes," why is another registration being sought? (Check appropriate box.) ▼ If your answer is No, do **not** check box A, B, or C.

a. ☐ This is the first published edition of a work previously registered in unpublished form.

b. ☐ This is the first application submitted by this author as copyright claimant.

c. ☐ This is a changed version of the work, as shown by space 6 on this application.

If your answer is "Yes," give: **Previous Registration Number** ▼   **Year of Registration** ▼

5

DERIVATIVE WORK OR COMPILATION Complete both space 6a and 6b for a derivative work; complete only 6b for a compilation.

Preexisting Material Identify any preexisting work or works that this work is based on or incorporates. ▼

a

6

See instructions before completing this space.

Material Added to This Work Give a brief, general statement of the material that has been added to this work and in which copyright is claimed. ▼

b

DEPOSIT ACCOUNT If the registration fee is to be charged to a Deposit Account established in the Copyright Office, give name and number of Account.

Name ▼   **Account Number** ▼

a

7

CORRESPONDENCE Give name and address to which correspondence about this application should be sent. Name/Address/Apt/City/State/ZIP ▼

b

Area code and daytime telephone number   (   )   Fax number   (   )

Email

CERTIFICATION* I, the undersigned, hereby certify that I am the

Check only one ▶
☐ author
☐ other copyright claimant
☐ owner of exclusive right(s)
☐ authorized agent of

8

Name of author or other copyright claimant, or owner of exclusive right(s) ▲

of the work identified in this application and that the statements made by me in this application are correct to the best of my knowledge.

Typed or printed name and date ▼ If this application gives a date of publication in space 3, do not sign and submit it before that date.

                                                                    Date

Handwritten signature (X) ▼

☞   X _____

Certificate will be mailed in window envelope to this address:	Name ▼	YOU MUST: • Complete all necessary spaces • Sign your application in space 8	**9**
	Number/Street/Apt ▼	SEND ALL 3 ELEMENTS IN THE SAME PACKAGE: 1. Application form 2. Nonrefundable filing fee in check or money order payable to *Register of Copyrights* 3. Deposit material	
	City/State/ZIP ▼	MAIL TO: Library of Congress Copyright Office 101 Independence Avenue, S.E. Washington, D.C. 20559-6000	Fees are subject to change. For current fees, check the Copyright Office website at www.copyright.gov, write the Copyright Office, or call (202) 707-3000.

*17 U.S.C. § 506(e): Any person who knowingly makes a false representation of a material fact in the application for copyright registration provided for by section 409, or in any written statement filed in connection with the application, shall be fined not more than $2,500.

Rev: June 2002—20,000   Web Rev: June 2002   ♲ Printed on recycled paper   U.S. Government Printing Office: 2000-461-113/20,021 claimant is the person who hired or employed the songwriter.

If Registering a Collection of Songs.

You should not register a collection of songs if some of the songs have been transferred and others have not. All of the songs should have the same claimants.

SPACE ❹: Transfer

If the claimant is not the same as the person in Space 2 (the "Author"), you must provide a brief statement of how the claimant acquired copyright. For example, if you sold your song rights to a music publisher or transferred them to a band publishing company, you can insert the statement "by written contract." Do *not* attach the contract to the application.

SPACE ❺: Previous Registration

You should check the "No" box unless you have earlier filed a registration for the song.

SPACE ❻: Derivative Work or Compilation

This section deals with songs that are derived from other sources. For example, if you used several lyric lines from the Bible (such as the song "Turn, Turn, Turn"), you would complete Section 6 as follows:

- ❻a (preexisting material): selected lyrics from the Bible
- ❻b (material added): additional original lyrics and original music

If you revised a melody from an old folk song and wrote new lyrics, complete Section 6 as follows:

- ❻a (preexisting material): music from folk song "Froggy Went a' Courtin'"
- ❻b (material added): original words and revision of music

If you revised your own song, complete Section 6 as follows:

- ❻a (preexisting material): music and lyrics from song "The Rat #1"
- ❻b (material added): new words and revision of music

SPACE ❼: Deposit Account and Correspondence

The Copyright Office maintains deposit accounts for applicants who register works on a regular basis. If the applicant maintains a deposit account, the registration fee can be charged against the balance. Information about establishing a deposit account is provided in Copyright Circular 5. Space 7 also requires the name, address, area code, and telephone number of the person to be contacted if there is a question about the application.

SPACE ❽: Certification

The person preparing the application must check one of the four boxes in Space 8 as either the author, other copyright claimant, owner of exclusive rights, or authorized agent. If you are one of the songwriters, check the box marked "Author." If you are filling out the application on behalf of the songwriters, check the box marked "Authorized Agent" and insert the names of the songwriters.

After checking the appropriate box, you should type or print your name and date, and sign it where marked. You are certifying to the Copyright Office that the information contained in the application is correct to the best of your knowledge. **NOTE:** An application for registration of a published work will not be accepted if the date in the certification box is earlier than the date of publication given in Space 3 of the application.

SPACE ❾: Mailing Information
Space 9 becomes the mailing label when the certified registration is mailed back to the applicant. That is, after the application has been processed, it will be mailed back in a window envelope, and Space 9 (Mailing Information) is the mailing address.

The Fee

Along with the copyright application, a filing fee and deposit material are also required. The fee is currently $45 per application. A check or money order, made payable to "Register of Copyrights," should be enclosed with the application. If the application is rejected or if the applicant withdraws it, the fee will not be refunded. If the check bounces, the Copyright Office will not proceed with registration.

Deposit Materials

In addition to the application and fee, you must furnish the Copyright Office with a copy of your song. If the song has not been published, you must furnish only one copy. If it's been published, you should furnish two copies. These copies may be sheet music or a recording. The Copyright Office requests the best version available of your song. In other words, if a compact disc is available, it is preferable to a cassette recording of the song.

If Registering a Collection of Songs.
Prepare a cassette or CD that contains all of the songs you plan to register, or furnish a bound (or fastened) collection of sheet music for the songs.

Processing the Application

You should mail a package to the Copyright Office containing:

- the completed Form PA
- deposit materials (one copy of an unpublished song; two copies of a published song)
- the fee ($45 per application in check or money order made payable to the Register of Copyrights), and
- a cover letter detailing the contents of the package and referencing the name of the work and the applicant.

You can mail your package to the Register of Copyrights, Library of Congress, Washington, DC 20559-6000.

Copyright Office fees are subject to change. For current fees, check the Copyright Office website at *www.copyright.gov*, write the Copyright Office, or call (202) 707-3000.

Form CA
For Supplementary Registration
UNITED STATES COPYRIGHT OFFICE

REGISTRATION NUMBER

| TX | TXU | PA | PAU | VA | VAU | SR | SRU | RE |

EFFECTIVE DATE OF SUPPLEMENTARY REGISTRATION

Month   Day   Year

DO NOT WRITE ABOVE THIS LINE. IF YOU NEED MORE SPACE, USE A SEPARATE CONTINUATION SHEET.

A

Title of Work ▼

Registration Number of the Basic Registration ▼

Year of Basic Registration ▼

Name(s) of Author(s) ▼

Name(s) of Copyright Claimant(s) ▼

B

Location and Nature of Incorrect Information in Basic Registration ▼

Line Number _____ Line Heading or Description _____

Incorrect Information as It Appears in Basic Registration ▼

Corrected Information ▼

Explanation of Correction ▼

C

Location and Nature of Information in Basic Registration to be Amplified ▼

Line Number _____ Line Heading or Description _____

Amplified Information and Explanation of Information ▼

MORE ON BACK ▶ • Complete all applicable spaces (D-G) on the reverse side of this page.
• See detailed instructions.   • Sign the form at Space F.

DO NOT WRITE HERE
Page 1 of_____ pages

FORM CA RECEIVED

FORM CA

FUNDS RECEIVED DATE

EXAMINED BY

CORRESPONDENCE ❑

REFERENCE TO THIS REGISTRATION ADDED TO
BASIC REGISTRATION   ❑ YES ❑ NO

FOR
COPYRIGHT
OFFICE
USE
ONLY

DO NOT WRITE ABOVE THIS LINE. IF YOU NEED MORE SPACE, USE A SEPARATE CONTINUATION SHEET.

Continuation of: ❑ Part B *or* ❑ Part C

D

Correspondence: Give name and address to which correspondence about this application should be sent.

E

Phone (_____)_____   Fax (_____)_____   Email _____

Deposit Account: If the registration fee is to be charged to a Deposit Account established in the Copyright Office, give name and number of Account.

Name _____

Account Number _____

Certification* I, the undersigned, hereby certify that I am the: (Check only one)

❑ author   ❑ owner of exclusive right(s)
❑ other copyright claimant   ❑ duly authorized agent of _____

Name of author or other copyright claimant, or owner of exclusive right(s) ▲

of the work identified in this application and that the statements made by me in this application are correct to the best of my knowledge.

Typed or printed name ▼ _____   **Date ▼** _____

Handwritten signature (X) ▼ _____

F

**Certificate
will be
mailed in
window
envelope
to this
address:**

Name ▼ _____

Number/Street/Apt ▼ _____

City/State/ZIP ▼ _____

YOU MUST:
• Complete all necessary spaces
• Sign your application in Space F

SEND ALL ELEMENTS
IN THE SAME PACKAGE:

1. Application form
2. Nonrefundable filing fee in check or
   money order payable to *Register of
   Copyrights*

MAIL TO:
Library of Congress
Copyright Office
101 Independence Avenue, S.E.
Washington, D.C. 20559-6000

Fees are subject to
change. For current
fees, check the
Copyright Office
website at
www.copyright.gov,
write the Copyright
Office, or call
(202) 707-3000.

G

*17 U.S.C. § 506(e): Any person who knowingly makes a false representation of a material fact in the application for copyright registration provided for by section 409, or in any written statement filed in connection
with the application, shall be fined not more than $2,500.

Rev: July 2002—20,000   Web Rev: July 2002   Printed on recycled paper

U.S. Government Printing Office: 2002-491-423/60,009

However, we advise that you send your application (or anything else) to the Copyright Office via a commercial carrier such as UPS, FedEx, DHL, or Airborne Express.

Also, if you send your application by UPS, FedEx, DHL, Airborne Express, or another commercial carrier (which is advisable), you'll be able to track when the package is received by the Copyright Office through the carrier's website. You can also request that the carrier provide you with delivery confirmation. The Copyright Office does not provide any confirmation for applications sent by standard delivery U.S. mail.

It takes six months or more for your copyright registration to be processed. If you are involved in a songwriting dispute, there is a method to speed the registration process. Obtain Circular 10 (Special Handling) from the Copyright Office.

Registering a Group of Songs

If you are registering a group of songs, you have one more task to complete the process. After you receive your registration, you must then file a second copyright form, Form CA, a copy of which is on the CD at the back of this book. A sample of Form CA appears earlier in this chapter.

On Form CA, enter the title of your collection and copy all of the other relevant information from the PA registration (songwriter names, copyright

claimants, and so on). You will see a section entitled "Amplified Information." That's where you should write the individual song titles. Once this is filed with the Copyright Office, all of the song titles will be listed with the Copyright Office.

Canadian Copyright Applications

In many ways, the Canadian copyright application process is easier than the U.S. system. For one thing, the Canadian "Application for Registration of Copyright" is simpler and shorter. It's so simple that you may not even need any instructions. If you do need assistance, you can obtain instructions from the Canadian Copyright Office, the address of which is provided at the beginning of this chapter and in Chapter 17. You can also download the instructions from the CIPO website (http://cipo.gc.ca). The website will also provide you with the current fees for filing an application. Unlike in the U.S., you can pay your Canadian copyright application fee with your Visa or MasterCard. Also unlike the U.S. process, you are not required to send copies of your song with your application.

Obtaining Copyright Forms

There are three methods of acquiring copyright application forms:

- by mail
- online, or
- via special software.

Copyright Forms by Mail

Forms PA and CA can be obtained by writing to the Publications Section (LM-455) of the Copyright Office. Delivery takes approximately two to four weeks. Only one copy of each form will be furnished. You may use photocopies of the forms, as long as the copies conform to the Copyright Office requirements:

- on paper measuring 8.5 x 11 inches
- printed back to back (that is, double-sided), and
- not shrunk or scaled to a smaller size on the page.

Copyright Forms From the Web

Copyright application forms can be downloaded from the Copyright Office website (www.copyright.gov). These application forms are in Portable Document format, or PDF, which can be viewed and printed with Adobe Acrobat Reader. You can download this software for free from Adobe's website (www.adobe.com).

The downloaded forms are now interactive, so you can use your computer to enter information into the form. The forms should be printed head to head (top of page 2 is directly behind the top of page 1) using both sides of a single sheet of paper. Short forms are one-sided. Dot-matrix printer copies of the forms are not acceptable, and inkjet printer copies of the forms may require enlarging (if using the "shrink to fit page" option). To achieve the best quality copies of the application forms, the Copyright Office recommends a laser printer. ■

Chapter 8

Publishing Your Band's Music

Making money from publishing songs is different from earning money from sales of recordings, though the two sources of income are closely related. In this chapter we'll explain the quirky world of music publishing, and show you how to earn money by publishing your band's songs. Basically, your band's songs can be published by an outside music publishing company, or your band can be its own publisher. One reason that bands often act as their own publishers is that it gives them more freedom to divide the income from published songs. When a song is published, the publisher receives royalties whenever the song is played or manufactured into a recording.

In this chapter, we'll explain your options for publishing your music, and the kinds of royalties you can earn. We'll also discuss different ways for your band to divide song income. We'll look at how to work with music publishers—companies that own songs and collect money on behalf of songwriters. And we'll go through the factors you should consider in determining whether you should create your own music publishing company, and explain how to create one.

Music Publishing Glossary

Here are some basic terms used in music publishing. These terms are discussed in more depth throughout the chapter.

Mechanical royalties: Each time a song is reproduced on a recording, the song owner receives a payment from a record company called a mechanical royalty. It's called a mechanical royalty because it's paid each time the song is mechanically reproduced, as opposed to being performed. Federal law has established a uniform mechanical royalty, which is 9.1 cents per copy of the song. Therefore, if 100 copies are pressed of a song, the record company would pay the song owner approximately $9.10.

Music publisher: A music publisher is a company that owns song copyrights. A music publisher will control how a song is used and collect money from people who sell, perform, or modify the song. A songwriter either sells the songs to an established music publisher or creates his or her own music publishing company. We will explain the advantages and disadvantages of each system in this chapter.

Music publishing agreement: A music publisher acquires ownership of a song copyright by signing a music publishing agreement with the songwriter. Usually the music publishing agreement provides for the songwriter to continue receiving income as the song earns money. The songwriter's portion usually ranges from 60% to 75% of the total song income

Performance royalties: Every time a song is played on the radio, in live concert, in a business establishment, on television, or on a website, the party playing the song must pay for the performance.

Performance rights organization: An organization that monitors radio and television stations, nightclubs, websites, and other entities that play music collects royalties from these places, and pays the royalties to the appropriate music publishers. The main performance rights organizations are BMI and ASCAP. All music publishers must register with a performance rights organization so that the performance rights organization knows which songs are published by its affiliated publishers, and thus knows who should receive royalties it collects.

Sync licenses: A song earns money if it is used in a movie or television commercial. The copyright law provides for a special payment when the song is synchronized (or linked) with a moving image. There are no fixed fees for this synchronization right, and usually the music publisher negotiates a fee and signs an agreement known as a "sync license."

Digital licenses: A song can earn money in digital configurations such as MP3s and AACs. In addition, a digital version of a song can be licensed for streaming radio, on-demand streaming, and CD burning. These new licenses—for full-length digital permanent downloads (or DPDs)—are sanctioned by Section 115 of the U.S. Copyright Act. Digital licensing of DPDs is handled by the Harry Fox Agency (www.harryfox.com). The rates are similar to mechanical royalties—currently 9.1 cents per download.

How Songs Earn Money

Before jumping into music publishing and song revenue, you may find it helpful to look at an example of how a song earns money (and lots of it).

"Have Yourself a Merry Little Christmas": How a Decades-Old Song Earned $2 Million in One Year

EMI Publishing, the music publishing company that owns the copyright for the song "Have Yourself a Merry Little Christmas," collected over $2 million in revenue from the song in one year, in the late '90s. Not bad for a tune that was written in 1944! The largest source of revenue was probably performance royalties earned from radio and TV play. When versions of the song are played on the radio, the stations must pay for each play—usually a few cents. The song was also played on television shows such as "ABC World News Tonight" and "General Hospital." A TV network must pay several dollars each time the song is played.

The song also earned money from mechanical royalties when recordings were sold. Many artists released recorded versions of the song that year, including Natalie Cole, Melissa Manchester, Amy Grant, Vince Gill, Shawn Colvin, Dave Koz, and Grover Washington. For example, using the mechanical royalty rate noted in the glossary above, if Shawn Colvin's version sold a million copies, the music publisher would receive over $75,000 from Colvin's record company.

"Have Yourself a Merry Little Christmas" has been used in several movies, and each of these uses was negotiated between the music publisher and movie company. The movie companies often pay $25,000 or more for the "sync right" (see glossary, above). Additional mechanical royalties are paid by the record company that releases the movie soundtrack. If the movie is shown on TV, the TV station must pay a performance fee when the movie is broadcast. If the song is used in a commercial, the company using the song must pay the music publisher. Finally, the song also earns money if sheet music of the song is sold.

Wow! Five decades after two songwriters composed "Have Yourself a Merry Little Christmas," it is still generating an amazing annual income. You should be aware, however, that one of the reasons that the song remains a classic and continues to earn money is that the song owner (in this case, the music publisher EMI) aggressively pushes for its use in different ways. We will see that not all publishers are the same, and that some music publishers work harder than others to make and maintain a hit. Below we will discuss each of the methods by which a song earns money.

Canadian Performance Royalties

Most of the rules discussed in this chapter apply for Canadian bands. Canadian copyright law, like the U.S. law, establishes various sources of song revenue, including payments for performance and for mechanical reproductions on records. Canadian performance royalties are collected by a collective known as SOCAN, whose rates are regulated indirectly by the Canadian Copyright Board. There is no fee for a songwriter to apply to SOCAN online. There is a $25 fee if applying on paper. However, the writer must either have a song published by a music publisher or have a song recorded by a record company or performed on the radio. Publishers must pay a one-time fee of $50. Like its American equivalents, SOCAN does not monitor every radio broadcast, but instead uses a survey system. SOCAN is affiliated internationally and can collect for performances of Canadian music in other countries. SOCAN refers to its clearance form as a "Work Registration Form," and each new song created by your Canadian band should be registered with the collective. For more information, contact SOCAN (www.socan.ca).

Performance Royalties

Radio and television stations must pay for the right to play a song. How much is paid? As a general rule, FM or AM radio performances result in payments between five cents and 15 cents per play per song, depending on the station's signal power (how far it broadcasts), advertising revenues, and audience size. When a song is played on a national television program such as "Saturday Night Live," a songwriter receives between $5 and $9 per individual television station broadcasting the song (again depending on the broadcast signal and size of the audience).

The music publisher does not collect this money directly. It's collected by the performing rights organizations, who pass it on to the music publisher and songwriter. For this reason, every music publisher and songwriter must affiliate with a performing rights organization, so that the performing rights organization knows what songs to collect royalties for and who should receive those royalties.

Performance Rights Organizations

The two major performance rights organizations are BMI and ASCAP. (There is also a third company, SESAC, that accounts for a small fraction of the performance rights business.) An explanation of the differences between BMI and ASCAP is provided later in this chapter. These nonprofit organizations collect fees from U.S. radio and TV stations, as well as other establishments where music is played, such as concert halls, clubs, clothing stores, taverns, and restaurants. The money is then distributed to songwriters and music publishers who have registered with these organizations. A songwriter can affiliate with only one of these organizations.

One of the many quirky rules of music publishing is that performance royalties are not paid in full to music publishers. BMI and ASCAP generally divide performance royalties earned by a song in half and pay half to the music publisher and half to the songwriter. This system ensures that songwriters will receive income directly from performances and not have to wait while it is filtered through the music publisher.

Just Because It's Played Doesn't Mean You Get Paid

Just because your song is played on the radio or in a club doesn't mean a check will be issued from a performance rights organization. BMI and ASCAP do not review every hour of radio play. Instead, they periodically survey the stations and base payments on an average. By way of example, ASCAP currently surveys less than 10% of all American radio broadcasts. Therefore, if your song is played infrequently, these performances may not show up on a survey, and as a result there will be no performance royalty check. This doesn't mean that the

radio stations pay only for the 10% of the music that is surveyed. The stations pay a fee that covers *all* songs played. However, this fee is then divided up and proportionally paid to the songs within the 10% survey sample. There is talk that these systems may someday change to a program that uses a digital coding for each song.

Doesn't the Performance Royalty System Favor Hit Songs?

Yes! Since radio payments are pennies per play and only a small amount of radio time is surveyed, a songwriter can earn real money only if the song is a hit. A hit song will show up on surveys, and the radio play will quickly add up to thousands (or hundreds of thousands) of dollars. Not only that, BMI rewards frequently played songs with higher payment rates. Like the rest of the U.S. music business, the performance royalty system is geared towards hit songs, and if your song is not popular, don't expect much in performance royalties.

What If the Song Is Played
in a Foreign Country?

What If the Song Is Played in a Foreign Country?

BMI and ASCAP are affiliated with foreign performance royalty organizations and will collect fees when your song is played in foreign countries. As a general rule, songs earn more per play when played in foreign countries than when played on stations in the U.S. This is because many foreign stations (for example, the BBC in Britain) are national stations and broadcast to the entire populace of the country. For example, one play on the BBC in Britain may result in a payment of several dollars (versus several pennies in the U.S.). In addition, the surveying techniques on these stations may be more precise.

Mechanical Royalties

The second way that a song earns money is when it is reproduced on compact discs or tapes.

Pennies From the Record Company

Under federal law, a record company must pay the copyright owner a mechanical royalty—currently 9.1 cents per copy per song—for the right to manufacture or "press" the song. For example, if your band writes and records a song and 1,000 copies of the song are pressed, the record company would owe the copyright owner a mechanical royalty of approximately $91.00 (1,000 times $.091).

As we indicated in the glossary above, however, few record companies actually pay the full mechanical royalty rate but instead negotiate for a reduced payment, usually 75% of the current rate (sometimes referred to as a "three-quarter" rate). In addition, federal law requires that the mechanical royalty be paid for every copy manufactured. Record companies often negotiate to pay for every copy sold (not manufactured). Why would a songwriter accept less than what the law provides? Because the record company may refuse to make a deal unless the songwriter accepts the lower rate.

Collecting Mechanical Royalties

Many record labels pay the mechanical royalties for compact discs and digital phonorecord deliveries (also known as "digital permanent downloads" or DPDs) directly to the owner of the copyright, usually the music publisher. However, there is an organization, the Harry Fox Agency, that will collect mechanical royalties for a song owner and will also negotiate with record labels who may want to record new versions of the song. In Canada, the Canadian Music Reproduction Rights Agency (CMRRA) performs the same function as the Harry Fox Agency. Contact information for these organizations is in Chapter 17.

Determining the Proper Rate

The mechanical royalty rate is set by Congress. The royalty rate for records made and distributed between January 1, 2006 and January 1, 2008 is 9.1 cents per song (or 1.75 cents per playing time), whichever is larger. To verify the current rate, check the copyright office website (www. copyright.gov). On the home page, click on Copyright Arbitration Panel (CARP) and scroll down to Mechanical Royalty Rates.

Sync Payments From Movies and TV Commercials

Another way that your song can earn money is if it is used in a movie or television commercial. There are no fixed fees for this synchronization right, and usually the music publisher negotiates what is known as a sync license. Sync licenses can range from several thousand dollars for independent films to $25,000 or more for major Hollywood films. Sync license fees for using a song in a national TV commercial can range from $15,000 for spot ads to $75,000 for a six-month advertising campaign.

Other Ways Songs Earn Money

Songs also earn money from the sales of sheet music, foreign record sales,

webcasting, or adaptation for use in another format such as a video game. Conceivably, songwriters and music publishers may also earn money under a law passed in 1992 which taxes sales of digital audio tape and then allocates the revenue to the music industry. However, revenues from digital audio tape are currently very small, and the distribution is based on record sales. So unless you've had a big hit, you won't see any of this money, anyway.

The Music Publishing System

While publishing your songs may seem simple in theory, in reality it's a strange and rather complicated process. The reason for this is that the music industry has clung to an old music publishing system even though many aspects of it are antiquated and confusing. If you want to publish songs, you'll need to use both an external publisher and a publishing company created by your band. In a nutshell, the publishing system used by the music industry allows only music publishers to collect money for the use of copyrighted songs and requires that a certain share of the money collected goes to the songwriters, while a certain share goes to the publisher. As we'll explain below, for songwriters to collect their full share of royalties, they need to create their own publishing company—even if they already use an external music publisher.

Music Publishers

Although organizations like BMI, ASCAP, and Harry Fox collect various forms of song royalties, they do so on behalf of music publishers. A music publisher is a company that owns and profits from song copyrights. Some music publishers are also known as administrators, because they "administer" copyrights. They may not own the copyright, but they earn revenue by handling business tasks for the songwriter. Some bands publish their music under their own music publishing company rather than using an external company. In that case, the songwriters in the band simply transfer their song copyrights to the publishing company, which then publishes the music. Sometimes, a manager or record label will ask you to give up your publishing rights. As explained below, be extra careful in such situations.

Some music publishers are large multinational companies, while others may be nothing more than a name on stationery. The only thing that all music publishers have in common is that they own and/or administer song copyrights.

How the System Works

The music industry has established a system that, although illogical, has become the accepted method of collecting and dividing songwriting income. At its foundation is a basic (though irrational) principle that any income from songs should be divided roughly equally between the publisher and the songwriter. For example, if a song earns $1,000, $500 is supposed to go to the songwriter and $500 to the publisher.

This half-and-half idea was born back when most recording artists weren't writing their own music but were recording tunes that were written by songwriters hired by publishers. In other words, in the old days (pre-Beatles), the real players in music publishing were publishers and songwriters, not bands. It made more sense back then to split the proceeds between the publisher and songwriter, because they often worked as a team.

But in today's world, bands are usually composing their own music. Much more than in the old days, the creators of the music are now also the performers. Since most of today's bands generally both write and perform the music they release, the industry recognizes that the old traditional division of the publishing pie isn't fair anymore. It's now accepted that external music publishers no longer deserve half of the income from publishing a song.

But rather than simply change the allocation of music publishing income to give the publisher less, the industry has adopted a strange system in which the publisher still gets half and the songwriter still gets half the money—but if a band who's already signed with a publisher sets up its own publishing company, then the external publishing company will split its "half" with the band publishing company. The final result of this convoluted system is that the external publishing company gets 25%, the band's publishing company gets 25%, and the band songwriters get the same 50% they've gotten all along.

In other words, the music publishing system slates half for publishers and half for songwriters, even though the publishers know they don't really deserve half. To even things out, they split their publishing half with the band—but since it's a "publisher's" half, the band has to create a publishing company to get it. That's why bands who want to publish music find themselves creating publishing companies, even though they'd just as soon go with an outside company altogether.

Since they have to create a publishing company anyway to get their full share of the publishing income, some bands don't bother working with an external company at all. That way, the band gets all the money: The publishing half goes to the band publishing company, and the other half goes to the band songwriters.

EXAMPLE: Your band signs a publishing deal with Megaglom Publishing, and a song earns $1,000. The writers' share of the payment—$500—goes to the writers. Megaglom would get $250, which is half of the publishing portion of the pie. The

other $250 (or remaining half of the publishing portion) goes to the publishing company set up by the band.

Do You Need a Music Publisher?

Your band will need a music publishing company—either internal or external—only if some or all of the band members are writing original songs that you want to publish. If you do want to publish songs, your main decision is whether to go it alone with your band's own publishing company or to go with an external company. You may wonder: "Why should we go with an external company if we have to create our own company anyway to get our full share of song income?" The main reason to sign with an external company is that some of them offer large cash advances and other perks for your band, such as marketing and publicity power. If your band is in doubt about what to do regarding a music publisher, compare your situation with the following scenarios:

- **Your band is unsigned and has no recordings.** If there's no song income to think about—that is, your band is not signed to a record company and your songs are not presently recorded for distribution—then your band does not need to create its own publishing company. However, your band may benefit from an affiliation with an established music publisher who can promote your band (see the sidebar "How Can a Music Publisher Promote a Band?," below).

- **Your band is releasing its own recordings or is signed to an independent label.** If your band is putting out its own recordings or is signed to an independent record label, your band should create its own music publishing company in order to get your full share of song income. An explanation of what this means and how to do so is provided later in this chapter. But whether you need an outside publisher is a trickier question. Generally speaking, it doesn't make much sense to transfer any rights to a music publisher at this point unless that publisher can give you decent advances or can help promote your band's songs in some significant way.

- **Your band is selling a lot of independent records or is signed to a major label.** If your band is: 1) selling a sizable amount of records (more than 10,000 units total); 2) getting substantial radio play, in heavy rotation on major radio stations; or 3) signed to a major label, you will probably be contacted by an established publisher, and your band will need to decide whether to sell music publishing rights to one of these publishers. A publishing

deal will usually result in an advance payment of $50,000 or more. The publisher may be able to assist in the promotion of your songs on radio or television or in the movies. Your attorney and manager can help you sort through the decision.

- **Your band is signing a management or record deal, and the manager or record company insists on acquiring your music publishing.** If a manager is pressuring you to give up your publishing rights, review Chapter 3. Be *very* wary of giving up a publishing interest to a manager who does not have a proven track record. If a record label is pressuring you into giving up publishing rights, then review Chapter 14. There may be financial reasons to give up your publishing rights to a record company, and your band will need to review the arrangement with a music business attorney.

How Can a Music Publisher Promote a Band?

"Music publishers can act as development companies for bands," Andy Olyphant, a former A&R representative for Rondor Publishing told us. "Most record companies simply don't have the time or desire to develop bands, and so publishers are taking on the role." For example, Olyphant signed Everclear to a publishing contract with Rondor and helped promote the band to CMJ (a music trade magazine). Rondor also helped the band buy new equipment and offered tour support. Rondor's interest in Everclear eventually paid off when the band signed a record deal and had a hit single, "Santa Monica."

How do you attract the interest of an A&R rep from a publishing company? "There are no rules," says Olyphant. "Sending in unsolicited demos may work, but it is usually not very effective. It's more effective to create a buzz in whatever way you can. Generally, if the word is out about a band, then the A&R people will find them." As for whether to sign with a publisher, Olyphant cautions, "The band and the publisher have to trust each other. The publisher is going to make suggestions, and the band has to be prepared for that and have an open mind."

These development deals for bands, as a general rule, apply only to larger music publishers such as Warner-Chappell, EMI, MCA, BMG, Jobete, Famous Music, or any publisher directly affiliated with one of these companies or with a major record label. Smaller publishers will probably not be able to offer these benefits. You can find lists of publishers at the ASCAP, BMI, and Harry Fox websites.

What About the Horror Stories?

In the early days of rock and roll, there were many music publisher rip-offs. For example, in 1956, Richard Berry, the composer of the song "Louie, Louie," sold all rights to his song for $750. The song went on to earn millions and was recorded by over 1,200 artists. Unlike modern publishing deals, Berry did not have an agreement that continued to pay him as the song earned money.

Songwriters are better protected today. For example, Sting, not his publisher, receives the lion's share of the song income earned by "Every Breath You Take." Songwriters have become more knowledgeable and are better protected by attorneys and songwriter organizations. Lawyers are also willing to fight on behalf of songwriters, sometimes in return for a cut of the recovery. For example, in 1986, Richard Berry won a court battle over "Louie, Louie" and was awarded over $2 million.

Dividing Up Song Income Within the Band

After the music publisher has taken its cut, the income that goes to the songwriters must be divided up however the band agrees. Dividing song income within a band is often a touchier issue than dividing it with the music publisher.

Bands can easily get screwed over song income when the band cannot determine how to divide it up. How songwriting income is allocated in a band can have a huge effect on the members long after the group breaks up.

For example, in 1983, Gordon Sumner (a.k.a. Sting) wrote "Every Breath You Take" and recorded it with his band, The Police. The song was a worldwide hit. Fourteen years later, Sean "Puffy" Combs (a.k.a. Puff Daddy and P. Diddy) rerecorded the song with new lyrics as "I'll Be Missing You," and it was again a worldwide hit. Sting, not the members of the Police, earned between $2 and $5 million for the Combs recording.

There is no standard as to how to divide up song income. In order to avoid getting screwed, your band needs to work out a system for dividing the income. There are two steps:

1) At some point soon after a song is recorded, the band must decide who the songwriter or songwriters are (that is, who should get credit for writing the song) and what their relative contributions are (generally a percentage, such as 30% or 50%). If you are unsure what it means to be a songwriter, review Chapter 7.

2) After you have decided on the songwriters and their contributions, you'll need to decide how to divide the income from the song. Remember, nonwriters can still receive song income if the band agrees on such a division—and many do.

Below we have provided examples of four systems that have been adopted by other bands. In addition, we have provided the language you should add to your band partnership agreement (BPA) if you want to adopt one of the systems. (BPAs are covered generally in Chapter 2.)

Credited Songwriters Always Earn More Performance Royalties

If publishing already seems confusing, then be prepared for another wrinkle. Although you can set up a system whereby everyone (songwriters and nonwriters) share equally in song income, it's still possible that a credited songwriter will receive more money from performance royalties. That's because in the case of performance royalties, BMI and ASCAP split the revenue for each song and make separate payments to music publishers and songwriters. In other words, with performance royalties the songwriter's portion is paid *directly* to the songwriter and does not pass through the band's publishing company. Therefore, if a song is a big hit on the radio or in a TV show, a credited songwriter will probably receive more money than a nonsongwriter. It is possible that the agreement among the band or between the band and the publisher could deal with this share, but usually it's not addressed and the writer's portion of performance royalties is paid directly to the credited songwriters.

System #1: Songwriters Take All

Under this first system, only the songwriters receive song income. That is, the writer gets the songwriting credit, and the writer usually has a separate publishing company. Under a "songwriter takes all" system, there probably is no need for a band to create its own publishing company (unless a record company requires it as part of a record deal). For information on independent record deals, see Chapter 14.

What Type of Band Is System #1 Most Suitable For?

System #1 works best for a band that is centered around a songwriter who is usually the bandleader (for example, Nine Inch Nails). It can also work for a band in which two members write most or all of the songs (for example, the Rolling Stones or Oasis). It should also be considered if the band members (other than the songwriters) are constantly changing.

How Much Does Each Band Member Get?

Unless agreed otherwise, the songwriters take equal shares of the song income after the publishing company (if there is one) has taken its cut. The rest of the band would not receive any publishing proceeds.

EXAMPLE: The Centipedes are a four-member band, and two members, Phil and Ernie, write all of the songs. A publishing company pays a $50,000 advance for the songs. Phil and Ernie each get $25,000. The other two members do not receive any money.

Language to Use in Your Band Agreement

Under this system, there would not be a band-created music publishing company, and you would not need to add any language to your band agreement.

System #2: Band Splits Songwriting Money Equally

Under this system, all of the song income is divided equally among all band members. To use this system, a band must create its own music publishing company in order to get its cut of the publishing portion.

What Type of Band Is System #2 Most Suitable For?

System #2 would work best for a "jam" band in which songs evolve at performances or at practice (for example, the Grateful Dead or Phish). This system might also work for a techno, acid-jazz, or dance band in which the members build songs around grooves (for example, Jamiroquai). This system could also work for a band that believes in "band democracy" and considers songwriting as just another band task. The members believe all money should be divided equally (for example, Rage Against the Machine). Note: Many bands, such as Nirvana, started with a system like this, only to change later when the key songwriters realize the cash cow they'd given up.

How Much Does Each Band Member Get?

All band members take an equal share of publishing proceeds.

> **EXAMPLE:** The Fleas are a four-member band, and two members (Lindsay and Avi) write all of the songs. A song they publish through their own company earns $50,000 in royalties. Each band member gets $12,500.

Language to Use In Your Band Agreement

In your BPA, choose the following language in the Division of Publishing Revenue section:

"All music publishing income derived from Recorded Compositions, including both writer's and publisher's shares, will be divided equally among the band members."

System #3: Band Splits "Publishing Income" Equally; Songwriters Split "Songwriter Income" Proportionately

Under this system, the band divides the publishing half equally, and the songwriters divide the songwriting half based upon their contributions.

What Type of Band Is System #3 Most Suitable For?

Many rock and pop groups use this system. It is a compromise approach in which all band members receive some song income, yet the songwriters still receive the bulk of the money. Note, however, if your band later signs with a large publisher, then the publisher will probably take half of the publishing income. As a result, band members no longer share *half* of the song income; they share a *quarter* of it.

How Much Does Each Band Member Get?

Consider the following examples.

> **EXAMPLE:** The Waterbugs are a four-member band, and two members (George and Tommi) write all of the songs.
>
> **Scenario #1:** The Waterbugs do not use an external publisher. If a song earns $50,000, half ($25,000) is divided equally among the band, giving $6,250 to everybody. The

other half would be divided equally between the songwriters, giving George and Tommi an additional $12,500 each.

Scenario #2: The Waterbugs use an external publisher, and the song earns $50,000. The external publishing company would keep half of the publishing portion ($12,500) and give the other half to the band's publishing company. The band's publishing company would distribute its half equally among all members, giving each one $3,125. The songwriting half ($25,000) would go to George and Tommi, the songwriters. They would divide it in half for an additional $12,500 each.

Language to Use in Your Band Agreement

In your BPA, choose the following language in the Division of Publishing Revenue section:

"The Band Partners will share equally in the publishing income from all Recorded Compositions. The writers of each Recorded Composition will receive an equal pro-rata share of the songwriters' income with respect to each Recorded Composition. By way of example, if two Band Partners write a Recorded Composition, each will share equally in the songwriters' income from that song. The publishing income from that song will be distributed equally to all Band Partners."

System #4: One Credit for Performing on a Song; Two Credits for Writing and Performing on a Song

This is a unique compromise system (and it may give your band ideas for creating other methods of dividing song income). Take a band song. How many people played on it? How many people wrote it? Add up these totals (for example, if there were four players and two writers, that's six). That becomes the denominator (the bottom number of a fraction). If a person is a writer and performer of the song they get two credits, for 2/6 of the song income. If they only perform, they get one credit, for 1/6 of the song income. All of the song income is pooled (regardless of its source), and the money is divided according to these fractions.

What Type of Band Is System #4 Most Suitable For?

This compromise system works well for a band in which songwriting and performing are equally important tasks (for example, a jazz band in which the members improvise on each song).

How Much Does Each Band Member Get?

Consider the following example.

> **EXAMPLE:** The Termites are a four-member band, and two members (Chet and Max) write all of the

songs. The Termites use their own publishing company, and it receives $50,000 in income from the songs. Since four people played on the songs and two wrote them, the denominator in the Termites' formula for dividing song income is six. Chet and Max both wrote and performed on each song, so they each get two credits, giving each of them a third of song income, which totals $16,666.60 for each of them. The other two band members get one credit each for performing on the songs. That gives each of them one-sixth of the song income, or $8,333.33 each.

Language to Use in Your Band Agreement

In your BPA, choose the following language in the Division of Publishing Revenue section:

"All revenue derived from Recorded Compositions will be pooled (whether it is characterized as publishing or songwriter revenue). Each Band Partner will receive one credit for performing on each Recorded Composition. The writers of each Recorded Composition will receive one credit for writing. Each Band Partner's total number of credits equals the numerator (top number of a fraction). The total number of credits equals the denominator or bottom number of a fraction. Each Band Partner then receives this fraction of the song income.

By way of example, if four Band Partners perform on a song and one Band Partner has written that song, the songwriter Band Partner would receive 2/5 of the revenue and the other three band members would each receive 1/5 of the revenue."

It's possible that a band member may not perform on a song because of the song's arrangement (for example, a guitar is not needed). This can influence the amount of money earned by a band member. If the band agrees, this can be altered by modifying the second sentence to read: "Each Band Partner who is a member of the Partnership at the time of the recording will receive one credit for each Recorded Composition."

Create Your Own System

You can create any system you want to divide song income. After you have devised your system, write it out and include it in your band agreement. If possible, provide a short, written example of how the system works, as well.

How to Form Your Own Music Publishing Company

Forming your own music publishing company will take a few hours and may cost anywhere between $25 to $100. The major cost is for filing a fictitious business statement at the local county clerk's office.

Don't Bother Creating a Music Publishing Company If ...

Don't bother forming a music publishing company unless a song has been released on a recording or in a movie, or you know a song will be released in the near future. Otherwise, there won't be any song income to be collected or divided up, which eliminates the need for a music publishing company.

Affiliate With Either BMI or ASCAP

The first step in creating a music publishing company is to affiliate with BMI or ASCAP.

- **Songwriter Affiliations.** A music publisher represents the interest of its songwriters. Each songwriter usually registers with a performing rights organization, because the writer is guaranteed to get songwriter payments directly from the organization (BMI or ASCAP). A songwriter can affiliate with only one performing rights organization. It would be helpful if the songwriters in your band all affiliate with the same performing rights organization. Otherwise, it gets confusing when forming a music publishing company.

- **Request the Application and Contract.** In order to create a music publishing company, contact either BMI or ASCAP at the addresses listed in Chapter 17 or online (www.bmi.com or www.ascap.com). You can request that an application for a music publisher be sent to you by mail, or you can apply online. There is a one-time fee of $100 for a publisher to join BMI (with no subsequent fees). There is no fee to join ASCAP, but there are dues of $50 a year for a publisher.

- **Pick a Name and Complete the Forms.** You will need to furnish a name for your music publishing company. Since many names are already in use, your band will have to furnish alternate titles with the application. Now that BMI and ASCAP have websites, it is possible to search these sites to find out if a name is already being used. If possible, try to use your band name or band partnership name for your music publishing company, as it may make it easier for you to cash checks (see below).

- **Clearance Forms.** Your band registers its songs with BMI and ASCAP by completing a clearance form, which can be done online. If you don't submit a clearance form for each song that is being released, you will not get paid! (Songwriters can complete separate writer's clearance forms.) The publisher's clearance form asks for each writer's "share." As we discussed earlier in the chapter, your band needs to decide on each songwriter's percentage contribution to the song.

- **Writers' Shares.** The writers' shares on the clearance form should total 100% (for example, Tom 75% and Nancy 25%). This section is concerned *only* with credited songwriters. It's possible that nonwriting band members will receive song income under your band system as discussed above, but their names should *not* be listed on the clearance form.
- **Publisher Shares.** The clearance form also asks for the names of all publishers and their shares. If your music publishing company is the only publisher of the song, indicate 100% for the publisher's share. If you are splitting the song between two publishers, list each and give the appropriate percentage of ownership.

EXAMPLE: Spyder has formed a publishing company called SpyderBiter Music and is registering a song that is written by two of its members, Tom and Nancy. For purposes of the clearance form, Tom and Nancy each have a 50% songwriter share. SpyderBiter Music has a 100% publisher share.

Is There a Difference Between BMI and ASCAP?

A common question among musicians is whether there is any difference between BMI and ASCAP. Generally, both organizations offer similar payment rates and follow similar rules. If you have a hit song, you'll probably receive the same income from either organization. Some differences are as follows:

- ASCAP charges annual dues ($50 for publishers); BMI does not charge annual dues but charges publishers a one-time fee of $100.
- BMI surveys various "low-wattage" college and public access stations.
- BMI offers bonuses for songs that have a cumulative history in excess of 25,000 performances.
- ASCAP and BMI both offer instrument insurance, and medical and dental insurance.
- ASCAP has a credit union that offers financial benefits.

To fully explore the differences between these two groups, contact each one and ask for information. Contact information is in Chapter 17.

File a DBA/FBN and Set Up a Bank Account

After you have registered as a music publisher with BMI or ASCAP, you need to set up a bank account so that you can deposit and cash checks. For example, if your band Spyder creates a music publishing company called SpyderBiter Music, a bank will not allow you to deposit checks written to SpyderBiter Music into an account with a different name (such as your personal account), or to cash that check without proof that you are in fact an authorized representative of SpyderBiter Music. The only accepted proof is usually a certified fictitious business name statement (FBN), also known as a DBA statement, for "doing business as." The statement basically asks you to give the names and addresses of the people who are doing business under a name different from their legal names. You file this statement with the clerk of the county in which your band resides.

Usually the procedure is as follows: You fill out a form furnished by the county clerk, pay a fee and then arrange to have the contents of the form published in a local newspaper. (The county clerk will be able to walk you though the procedure.) After publication in the local newspaper, your band will receive a certificate that will enable you to cash checks or to start a bank account. In some places, when you file a DBA, you must also pay a local business tax.

Setting up a business bank account can be an expensive proposition, with monthly fees and check-printing charges, so shop around if you intend to create an account. Some banks may also require a federal tax ID or social security number. See Chapter 16 for information about obtaining a federal tax ID. See Chapter 9 for information regarding the relationship between DBAs and protecting your band name.

Take Care of the Administration

A music publisher administers the songs. So as your own music publisher, you need to take care of some paperwork. One of the most important jobs is to register copyrights for the songs (see Chapter 7). In addition, you should file clearance forms for any new songs that will be released. Six to eight weeks after submitting a clearance form, you should also review the BMI or ASCAP website to make sure that the song has been registered properly. If there is an error, contact the indexing department for that performing rights organization.

SongTracker Pro Software

For managing songwriter/publisher details, many songwriters recommend SongTracker Pro software (www.bizbasics.net), a set of integrated templates that, in conjunction with FileMaker Pro software provides an automated publishing/song shopping system for songwriters and music publishers. A demo version is available.

Band Names

This chapter deals with disputes between bands over the right to use a name. Disputes about band names can have disastrous effects. For example, the country band Shenandoah was sued by bands with similar names from Kentucky, Nevada, and Massachusetts. Shenandoah got to keep its name, but the cost of the lawsuits eventually landed the group in bankruptcy court.

In this chapter, we provide some basic information about trademark law—the legal specialty that deals with band names—and explain how to avoid the two common name problems: when your band chooses a name similar to another band or another band chooses a name similar to yours. We also show you some inexpensive ways to research band names and explain how to prepare a federal trademark application. (For information on who owns your band name or who can use the name if the band breaks up, review Chapter 2.)

In this chapter, we discuss the difference between domain names and trademarks. In Chapter 15, we discuss how to obtain a domain name and how to deal with conflicts with other domain name owners.

Trademark Basics for Bands

Your band name is protected under trademark law—an altogether different body of law from the copyright laws that protect your songs and recordings. This section discusses the basic rules of trademark law that your band should know.

It's Easy to Get a Trademark; the Trick Is Protecting It

A common misconception is that owning a trademark allows you to prevent anyone else from using it. Contrary to what many believe, owning a trademark doesn't give the owner a specific set of rights (like copyright or patent), and it doesn't necessarily mean you can prevent another band from using it. A trademark is nothing more than a word, phrase, or other symbol used in commerce to identify your business—in your case, your band. The real question is not whether the trademark is yours, but whether or not you can protect it. In very broad terms, the first user of a band name can prevent another band from using their trademark if it's likely that people would be confused by the use of the name by both bands. The "likelihood of confusion" rule is discussed below.

Trade-Mark Rules for Canadian Bands

Trademark laws in the U.S. and Canada are both derived from British trademark laws, and thus are based on the same principles. That is, the first user within a geographic area has superior rights. However, there are some minor differences between the U.S. and Canada. For example, in Canada it is "Trade-Mark" with a hyphen, not "Trademark." The registration process is also different (see the sidebar "Canadian Trade-Mark Registration," below).

For more information, go to the Canadian Intellectual Property Office website (http://cipo.gc.ca). It offers all of the basic information necessary for protecting a trademark and filing a trademark application in Canada. Or contact the Canadian Intellectual Property Office at:

Place du Portage I
50 Victoria St., Room C-114
Gatineau, Quebec K1A 0C9
(819) 997-1936
Fax: (819) 953-7620

First to Use; Others Lose

It doesn't matter who is the first to create a band name. What matters is which band is the first to use it in public commerce—on posters, in newspaper advertisements, online, or on recordings. As soon as you publicly use the word or symbol—and assuming no one else has already used it for music purposes—it is your trademark. Public use of your name doesn't include using it only among yourselves or on a demo submitted to a club or record company. It must be used in public to identify yourselves to your potential audience who may buy your CD or tickets to your show.

Likelihood of Confusion

If you are the first to use a name and another band starts using the same or a similar name, you have the legal right to stop them if it's likely that people will be confused by the dual uses of the name. The "likelihood of confusion" rule is the bottom-line question for trademark disputes. That is, is a consumer of music likely to buy the other group's records or attend its shows, thinking it was your band?

In a legal dispute over a band name, a court will look at a number of factors to determine whether customer confusion is likely. Two of the most important factors are:

- how distinctive the name is, and
- to what degree you and the other band are actually competitors in the same geographic area.

If a different band already has the same name that you want to use, don't be tempted to get around trademark law by changing the name slightly. Names that sound alike or have the same meaning—even if they're spelled differently or are in a different language—are often likely to cause customer confusion. The name "Le Band," for instance, might be confused with the trademarked name "The Band," even though part of the name is translated into French. Similarly, the name "Lead Zeppelin" would likely get confused with "Led Zeppelin," even though the names were spelled differently. (Also see the sidebar "What If the Band Names Are Not Identical?," below.)

Distinctiveness of Name

A band's name is distinctive if it is unique or if it is so well-known that music buyers can distinguish it from other bands. For example, the name "The Beatles" is clever and immediately distinctive. Band names that are not distinctive are referred to as "descriptive." For example, "The Hard-Rocking Salsa Band" is a descriptive name—not distinctive—because it simply describes a hard-rocking salsa band.

A descriptive name can, over time, become a distinctive name. That's because the most important factor affecting distinctiveness is how well-known the name has become. For example, the name "The Band" is a perfect example of a descriptive, undistinctive band name. However, through extensive performing, large record sales, and substantial radio play, the 1960s group The Band has made their name distinctive and protectible. Since distinctiveness is based on how

well-known your mark has become, the more you use the name, the stronger your trademark rights. That is, the longer you use the name, the more show posters you paste up, and the more records you sell, the greater your legal rights to your band name.

Whether the Bands Actually Compete in the Same Area

Band names (like all trademarks) are limited by geographic areas. That is, the use of a trademark in one country does not automatically mean that the owner can stop the use of a similar mark in another country. For example, a U.S. singer/songwriter had been using the name "Suede" for many years. When a British band with a similar name began competing in the U.S., the singer/songwriter sued and made the band change its name to "London Suede." However, this name change was necessary only in the United States. In the rest of the world, the British band retained its name "Suede." Why? Because the singer/songwriter had not established superior rights to the name outside of the U.S.

With the increasing popularity of the Internet, the geographic impact of a band's name has grown much larger. For example, if your band maintains or is featured at a website, this would expand your band's usage of the name across the United States, rather than limit the usage to the one state where you may perform.

Sometimes, a court may also be influenced by the style of music performed. That is, if different bands are marketed to different types of listeners (for example, a barbershop quartet and a hard-core punk band), there is not much likelihood of confusion among their respective fans, and both bands could exist with a similar name. For example, in one case a court reviewed evidence as to whether two genres of music—heavy metal and rap—competed for the same consumers and determined that there was not much overlap. Generally, when measuring confusion, a court will consider not only record buyers but also whether there is confusion among radio stations and record distributors.

Registration Helps

You don't have to register your name with the state or federal government to get trademark protection—but it helps. A trademark is automatically created when you use the name in connection with your shows and records. However, registration will give you additional rights, and we recommend that you register if your band is signing a record deal or if you are earning over $10,000 a year. We explain how to file a federal trademark registration later in this chapter.

Your Logo, Design, and Slogan Can Also Be Protected

Your band's name isn't the only thing protected by trademark: logos, designs, slogans, packaging features, and more can also be protected by trademark. The same principles of trademark protection that protect names apply to these other features.

Give a Hoot—Don't Dilute

Your band can run into hassles if you use a band name based on a famous trademark, even if there is barely any likelihood of customer confusion. That's because federal trademark law was modified in 1995 to allow owners of famous marks to prevent someone from tarnishing or diluting their trademark's distinctive quality. This is based on different principles from ordinary claims of trademark infringement. In most infringement cases, one band sues another because record buyers or concertgoers are confused by similar band names. In a dilution case, the issue is not whether consumers are confused, but whether the famous mark's reputation is being degraded or tarnished. A "famous mark" is determined by various factors, including the distinction the mark has achieved within its channel of trade. Examples of famous marks would be Nike, Intel, McDonald's, or Pepsi-Cola.

EXAMPLE: Toys "Я" Us is a famous mark because it is well-known as a retail source for toys. A rap group using adult lyrics names itself Boys "Я" Us. The retail store chain sues the band, claiming that the use of the band name tarnishes the toy store's reputation.

Service Marks Versus Trademarks

Throughout this chapter we have referred to band names as trademarks. When registering your band name, however, you will refer to it as a service mark. What's the difference? A trademark is used on goods or products; a service mark is used in connection with services. When your band sells merchandise under the band name, the name is used as a trademark. When your band gives a show, the name is used as a service mark, because you are providing entertainment services. Except for some minor differences, the rules of trademark law are applied the same for both types of marks, and the term "trademark" is used interchangeably for both types of marks.

When applying to register the band name, we recommend that you apply for a service mark. (The application form we describe below is for a service mark.) By doing this, you will secure the necessary rights to use your name in performance and stop other bands from using a similar name.

One reason to seek a service mark registration is because it is more difficult to acquire trademark registration for a band name. The Trademark Office traditionally views the name of the record company, not the band, as the appropriate trademark for recordings, and is unlikely to grant a trademark registration to a band name unless certain criteria are met. If your band is achieving widespread success and sales, it may justify your proceeding with filing of trademark applications for recordings and merchandise. Until then, the filing of a service mark application will suffice.

Can You Trademark a Song Title?

You will have a hard time getting a trademark for one of your band's song titles unless you can demonstrate that the song has been a *big* hit. For example, it may be possible to trademark a song such as "Stand By Your Man," which has been publicly performed over two million times. But a trademark is not available in the case of a country song, "Better Class of Losers" which has been publicly performed 47,000 times. *(Tree Publishing Co. v. Warner Bros. Records,* 785 F. Supp. 1272 (M.D. Tenn 1991).)

A song title that achieved trademark protection is "Sing, Sing, Sing" by Benny Goodman, which according to a poll introduced in court, was one the 100 most important musical works of the 20th Century. *(EMI Catalogue Partnership v. Hill Holliday, Connors,* 2000 U.S.App. LEXIS 30761 (2d Cir. 2000).)* In summary, it's unlikely that one of your band's songs will have attained the level of popularity required to create trademark rights.

Domain Names Versus Trademarks

Registration of a domain name is not the same thing as registering a trademark, but it is affected by trademark law. If you register a domain name that is similar to a famous registered trademark, you may later discover that you've infringed someone else's trademark (see the discussion of trademark dilution, above). For example, if your band's name was Candyland and you created a website, www.candyland.com, you would likely soon hear from Milton Bradley, the company that owns the children's game Candyland. Keep in mind that trademark disputes can involve complex issues—particularly for conflicts over domain names and other Internet-related claims. (There are dispute resolution procedures for people who claim rights to the same domain name, and we discuss these in Chapter 15.)

If you use a domain that is different from your band's name—for example, one of your band's song titles—that domain name may also function as a trademark. And in that case, the domain name would be subject to the same rules as your band's name trademark. For example, you would want to avoid using a domain name that is similar to another band's name or that dilutes a famous trademark.

 If you want to perform a trademark search of your domain name, don't use the ".com" in your search. While it may seem logical to search for "thesmokers. com" in the USPTO databases, such a search would likely overlook many important marks that you should know about. It's better to focus on the "smokers" part of the name. That's the part of the name that may create confusion with other bands.

Registering Your Fictitious Business Name Is Not the Same as Trademark Registration

In most places, when you conduct business under a fictitious business name you must register a fictitious business name (FBN) statement (also called a DBA statement for "doing business as") with your local government. This is because the band name that you're doing business under (for example, "Giant Sand" or "Ween") is not the same as your real names (for example, Joe Smith and Joanna Jones). Registering your fictitious business name generally involves filing a form with the name you're using and the names and addresses of all owners of the business. Before registering, you're usually required to check a database of other business names in that area to make sure no one else is doing business under that name.

It's important to understand that the process of registering a fictitious business name does not grant any form of trademark rights. Your local fictitious business name requirements are totally separate from federal and state trademark laws. In other words, you still must follow the trademark rules in this chapter even if you have filed a DBA.

Researching Band Names

The best way to deal with trademark disputes is to avoid them in the first place. And the single most effective method of avoiding a dispute is to research your band name before using it. Although there is no foolproof way to determine if another band has a similar name, below are some common methods of checking.

Searching the Internet

Searching the Internet is an inexpensive method of researching band names. There are many search engines and different databases of information that you can research.

In addition to search engines such as Google, you should also try the following online resources:

- **Band Directories.** There are several band directories on the Net, and new ones continue to appear. These directories, such as the Band Register (www.bandreg.com) or Artist Direct's Ultimate Band List (http://ubl.artistdirect.com), include lists of names of existing bands and an email address or website for each group. You can use these directories in two ways: to research for similar names, and to register your own band's name in order to provide notice of your use. To find band directories, do an Internet search using keywords such as "band names," "band directory," or "band register."

- **Online Record Stores.** Check online record stores such as Amazon (www. amazon.com) or CDNoW (www. cdnow.com). These stores allow you to search by the name of the recording artist. Type in your band name to see if there are any recordings by artists with a similar name.

- **Domain Names.** You should check whether another band is using the same name as its domain name. To check on the availability of a name, go to any approved domain registry and look for the search feature. For an alphabetical list of approved registrars, go to www. icann.org. If you want to learn the name of the individual who owns it, use the Whois tool (www.whois. net). If a band is using your name in its domain name for its website, it should appear in this database. Of course, if a band doesn't have a Web page it won't appear in this directory.

When searching for certain words or phrases, always consider simple variations on the spelling or pronunciation (for example, Beatles and Beetles). Also be sure to include music-related search terms such as "band" or "music." For example, if you're searching for another band with the name "The Spyders," you should search for not only the word "spyders" but also the word "band" or "music." This will keep your search results in the music world and avoid pulling up websites dealing with arachnids.

Federal Trademark Database on the Internet

Since it's free, start your trademark search by reviewing the database of registered marks in the U.S. Trademark Office (www.uspto.gov).

Hitting the Books

Besides online resources, there are a number of publications that contain information about existing bands. *Phonolog* is a loose-leaf guide to existing recordings and recording artists that is available at most record stores. *Billboard International Talent and Touring Directory* is in many libraries and has a listing of touring bands.

Using a Trademark Searching Company

When a record label wants to be sure that a name is safe, the label hires a professional searching service to prepare a report. These professional searching companies check band names that are registered with the state and federal government. They also check some unregistered band names. An extensive written report is provided showing any potential conflicts. Type "trademark searching" into your search engine to obtain a list. Since these searches are fairly expensive ($200 to $500), your band probably doesn't need to pay for one unless you are preparing to sign a major label recording deal where you have to make a contractual promise that the name is safe, or if your band has been sued by another band and you need to research the facts.

EXAMPLE: Your band begins to use the name Spyders in 2005 in Kansas. Unknown to you, another band was using the name The Spyders in 2000, toured the West Coast, and released independent albums that were distributed throughout the U.S. in 2002 and 2004. The other band can stop you from using the name, because they had nationwide use of the name prior to your band's use.

Dealing With Trademark Disputes

Unfortunately, disputes over band names are fairly common in the music industry. In this section we will address three common types of disputes: Your band wants to stop another band with a similar name; another band wants to stop your band; or your group is battling over which members of your band are allowed to use the band name.

Your Band Chooses a Name That Is Already Being Used by Another Band

As a general rule, if another band has been using the same name longer than your band, then the other band can stop your band from using the name. Other factors, such as the amount of record sales or the geographic area in which the bands perform, may influence the result.

The best way to avoid this type of dispute is to research your band's name before adopting it. If you have already adopted a name and suspect a problem, don't manufacture large quantities of recordings or merchandise. If you have to change your name, try to keep some aspect of your former name in order to retain familiarity with your fans. For example, the other band may agree to let you use Spyders & Snakes or The Kansas City Spiders. If you've adopted a name and received a "cease and desist" letter (a letter telling you to stop using the name), consult a trademark attorney. (Methods for locating legal help are provided in Chapters 4 and 17.)

What If the Band Names Are Not Identical?

Can one band stop another from using a similar but not identical name—for example, The Spiders and Spyder? The answer again depends on the likelihood of confusion. Is it likely that music fans or music business people will confuse one band with the other? If people are likely to be confused by the sound or meaning of the two names, then one band will have to stop. For example, a band named Far Side is likely to be confused with the pop band Pharcyde, because both names sound alike even though they are not spelled alike.

If fans and business people are not likely to be confused—that is, it's easy enough to understand these are two different bands—then both bands can continue without a name change. This might be the case if the bands play radically different kinds of music. Because this issue is often difficult to resolve, you should either consult with a trademark attorney or review *Trademark: Legal Care for Your Business & Product Name*, by Stephen Elias (Nolo).

Another Band Chooses the Same Name as Yours

Generally, if you have used a name for a longer period than a new band, your band has the legal right to stop the other band from using the similar name.

For example, say your band has been touring and releasing records in the U.S. under the name "Crystal" for seven years. You learn that a U.S. record company is releasing a recording by a new band with an identical name. Assuming that you are the first user of the band name, you have superior rights and can stop the other band.

Remember, however, that even though you have a superior right (that is, you have been using the name longer), it's tough to enforce your rights unless you hire an attorney. Unfortunately, the other band or its record company may not take you seriously unless you file a lawsuit. In reality, *both* bands usually get screwed by a legal dispute over the name. For most bands, the expense (from $10,000 to $100,000 in legal fees) outweighs any benefit.

Before filing, consider whether the other band is really going to cause your group a problem. Is there a chance that fans of your band will be confused? Will your group suffer any real damage? If not, then it may not be worthwhile to pursue the matter. Remember, many bands disappear within a year, and your group may be able to simply outlast your competition.

If you do have to confront the other band with a lawsuit, the usual solution is that either:

- **The newer group changes its name.** Many bands have modified their names to avoid a lawsuit. For example, Charlatans UK, the English Beat, and Wham UK adopted the "British" references in their name to avoid lawsuits from U.S. bands with similar names.

- **Your band changes its name in return for a money payment.** It may seem odd that your band would take money to change its name, especially when your band has the superior right to the name. However, some bands don't mind modifying or changing their name in return for some cash. Payments are commonly between $1,500 and $5,000.

In some cases, it's possible that you can handle at least some aspects of a name dispute without the aid of an attorney. Consult the self-help guide *Trademark: Legal Care for Your Business & Product Name*, by Stephen Elias (Nolo).

Other Confusing Uses of a Band Name

What happens if someone uses your band name for a purpose other than to name a band? For example, a band called Pump attempted to stop Aerosmith from naming its album *Pump*. A band named Aftermath tried to stop Dr. Dre from naming his new record company Aftermath. In both cases, the bands failed to stop these alternate uses. The courts did not feel that consumers would be confused. For example, the court did not believe that fans of the band Pump would think that the Aerosmith album was made by the group Pump. A similar result was reached in the Aftermath case. Therefore, as a general rule, you will probably be able to stop only similar use of your band name by other bands. If your band becomes very well known and sells a lot of records, the situation may change, and you may be able to stop alternate uses.

Registering Your Band Name With the Government

Once you've done some research and decided on a name that no one else appears to be using, one remaining concern is how adequately to protect the name. Being the first to use a trademark that no one else is using is enough to establish your rights to the name. Still, registering the name with the federal government will strengthen your rights. This section will discuss why you might want to formally register your name, and how to do so if you choose. (For information about state registration, see the sidebar "State or Federal Registration?," below.)

Canadian Trade-Mark Registration

The Canadian Trade-Mark application process is similar to the U.S.'s. An application is prepared, filed, and examined, and then, if there is no opposition, it is registered. There are some bureaucratic differences in Canada—for example, you must pay $250 when you file and an additional $200 on registration—but for the most part, the procedures are similar. You can obtain all of the necessary information and forms from the Canadian Intellectual Property Office website (http://cipo.ga.ca).

Should You Register Your Name?

As we have explained, your band has legal rights to its name without registering. That is, even without filing trademark papers with the government, you can still go to court and stop a newer band from using a confusingly similar name. In fact, you can even stop a newer band that has registered its name.

Since federal registration can cost $275 to $375, you may wonder: "Why should we bother to register?" For one thing, regardless of the legal benefits, federal trademark registration often has a deterrent effect on infringing bands and their attorneys, because it lets them know that you are serious about protecting and enforcing your rights. There are other benefits as well:

- **Nationwide Rights.** If you register, you can claim trademark rights in all regions of the country, not just where you perform or sell records.
- **Right to Use the ® Symbol.** As the owner of a federally registered mark, your band may use the symbol ® in conjunction with your shows and records. (Note: If a mark is not federally registered, it is illegal to use the ® symbol or to state that the mark is federally registered.)
- **Advantage in Website Disputes.** If a dispute arises as to who has the right to use a name for a website, the organization that oversees the award of website names (www.icann.org)

has indicated that it will award the name to the owner of a federally registered trademark.

State or Federal Registration?

If you are going to register, should you register your name with the federal or state government? If your band travels out of the state to perform, advertises out of the state, or uses a website to reach concertgoers and fans in other states, you should apply for a federal registration. If your band performs and advertises in only one state and has no Internet presence, state registration may be enough. This book covers only federal registration procedures. For information on state registrations, write to your state's Secretary of State. You should find contact information for your state's Secretary of State office in the state government pages of your phone book.

What If You Haven't Begun Using a Name But You Intend To?

If you haven't started using a name but plan to in the near future, you can file a special application with the federal Trademark Office that will in effect reserve the name for you. The form is called an Intent to Use Application, also known as an ITU. In order to file an ITU, your band must have a sincere intention to use the name within six months. That is, you can't reserve the name merely to prevent someone else from using it. The ITU is fairly simple, but it requires the filing of an additional form and an extra $100 payment when the mark is put into use. For more information on this type of filing, consult Trademark: Legal Care for Your Business & Product Name, by Stephen Elias (Nolo).

Filing for Trademark Registration

In this section, we explain how to complete a federal trademark application. Applicants can also obtain help from the instructions provided at the USPTO website (www.uspto.gov).

The USPTO site assists only in the preparation and processing of electronic applications. The fees have changed to reflect this new electronic bias. An electronic filing is $325 per class, a paper filing—should you prepare a paper application on your own—is $375. In another twist on the keep-it-electronic approach, the USPTO introduced a new version of the application for a Trademark/Servicemark, Principal Register in July 2005. The new "TEAS Plus" form has a lower filing fee of $275 per class of goods and/or services but has stricter requirements than the TEAS form. If you use the TEAS Plus version of the form, you must pay an additional fee of $50 per class if, at any time during the examination of the application, the USPTO decide your did not meet the requirements set forth.

Before you begin your federal application, you'll need to figure out what theory it's based on. Most federal trademark applications are based on either "use in commerce" or an applicant's intention to use the trademark (referred to as an "intent-to-use" or ITU application). The process for both "in use" and "intent-to-use" application involves three steps:

- **Preparation and filing of application.** A trademark application consists of a completed application form, a drawing of the mark, the filing fee, and a specimen of the mark. You can either mail the materials to the USPTO or file the application electronically and pay by credit card.
- **Examination by the USPTO.** Upon receipt, the trademark application is given a number and assigned to a USPTO examining attorney. If there is an error or inconsistency in the application, or if the examining

attorney believes that registration is inappropriate, the attorney will contact the applicant to discuss the objection. The applicant can respond to the objections or can abandon the application. The examining attorney will either approve the mark for publication or reject it. If it is rejected, the applicant may challenge the rejection.

- **Publication in the Official Gazette.** Once the examining attorney approves the mark, it is published in the Official Gazette. The public is given 30 days to object to the registration. If no one objects, a trademark registration will be issued (or in the case of an ITU application, the mark is allowed pending use in commerce.) If there is an objection from the public, the matter will be resolved through a proceeding at the USPTO.

The total time for an application to be processed may range from a year to several years, depending on the basis for filing and the legal issues that may arise in the course of examining the application. The registration expires ten years from the date of registration. You have certain obligations to maintain your trademark registration—for example, you must file a Section 8 Declaration of Continued Use between the fifth and sixth anniversary of the registration. Information about these maintenance requirements can be obtained at the USPTO website or by reviewing *Trademark: Legal Care for Your Business & Product Name*, by Stephen Elias (Nolo).

The Trademark Application: the TEAS System

The preferred method of preparing the federal trademark application is to use the online Trademark Electronic Application System (TEAS), located at the USPTO's website (www.uspto.gov/teas/index.html) TEAS is an interactive system in which the user is asked a series of questions. If a question is not answered or an essential element is not completed, the applicant is asked to correct the error. The system is remarkably easy to use and there's a low probability of error in preparing the form. (In addition to the electronic system, applicants can create their own application forms by typing the necessary information onto a sheet of paper and paying the higher fee.) The information provided below is intended for use on a standard TEAS application.

To get started, go to the PTO's website at (www.uspto.gov). Under Trademarks (on the left side) click File. Then click Apply for a New Mark. This gives you a choice of forms to fill in. Here we are talking about the Trademark/Servicemark Application for the Principal Register. You should be able to complete much of the form without assistance, but the following suggestions may help.

Name. If you are applying as partnership, insert the name of the partnership.

Entity Type. Since most bands are partnerships, you will probably click on the partnership box, insert the state where you are organized (usually the state where you reside), and insert each partner's name and citizenship. If only one person in the band owns the name, click on "Individual." If your band is a corporation, click on "corporation."

As you fill in the rest of this form, make sure that your specimen, mark information, and description of goods and services are all consistent with each other. That is, if your specimen shows a different band name from what you enter in the mark information box (or submit in a GIF or JPEG file), you'll have some explaining to do. Similarly, if your specimen shows a different band name from what you describe in the application, you'll have to submit another specimen or change your product/service description. If you are filing an intent-to-use application, you won't be worried about the specimen requirement at this stage in the process, but you will ultimately have to submit a specimen (once you begin using the mark) to complete your registration.

Mark Information: If your band name consists of unstylized words or numbers (or both), click the circle above the words "Standard Character Format." In the box just below the words "Enter the mark here," enter your band name in capital letters. Pay close attention to the rules regarding what punctuation is allowed. In general, we recommend you register your band name for the first time in a nonstylized format—for example, the word "KISS" instead of registering "KISS" in its stylized lightning bolt design. If you prefer to register the mark in a stylized or in design format (such as a logo or trade dress), read the help and attach a GIF or JPEG file showing the mark.

Basis for Filing and Goods or Services Information: The information required here varies depending on whether you are already using your band name in commerce or are filing on an intent-to-use basis. The top part of this box shows you which type of application you are filling out: Section 1(a) Use in Commerce or Section 1(b) Intent-to-use.

Specimen: If you're using the band name (and not filing an intent-to-use application), you'll need to provide a specimen image file in JPEG format as well as a description of the specimen in the next box. You must scan an advertisement or poster of one of your band's shows or some other evidence that you provide live entertainment services. The specimen must show your band's name in connection with a performance. For example, you can furnish a poster indicating that The Falcons will appear at Lindsay's Castle at 10 p.m. on March 31. However, a business card with name and address of The Falcons would

not be suitable, because there is no connection with a specific performance. As we indicated above, for purposes of this application, the Trademark Office is interested only in proof that you provide entertainment services (performances), not that you sell products (records). If you're an intent-to-use applicant, you will not have a specimen information section on your application and should go to the International Class step.

Description of Specimen: The next part of the specimen box asks you to describe the specimen. You will probably insert a statement such as "poster advertising live performance." See the help topic for what is required.

International Class: Enter Class 041 for entertainment services. Or, if you prefer, you can send in your application without specifying a class and let the trademark examiner help you.

Listing of Goods or Services: Here is where you describe the goods or services to which your mark is (or will be) attached. We recommend that you state "musical entertainment services." A trademark examiner who doesn't approve of your description, or is confused by it, will let you know and work with you to come up with an appropriate description.

If you are filing an intent-to-use application, the following two items about use will not appear. Skip to "Final Instructions for All Applicants."

Date of First Use of Mark Anywhere: Here you are asked to provide the date your band first started using the name in the marketplace. Insert the date you first used the name in an advertisement or poster. It's usually the date of your first show. If you're not sure of the exact date, estimate as accurately as possible. If necessary, use imprecise dates, such as "before March 25, 1998," "on or about January 16, 2005," "in 1998," or "in February 1984." Use the earliest possible date that you can reasonably assert as correct.

Date of First Use of the Mark in Commerce: Insert the date when your band first advertised its services in more than one state, for example, the date a newspaper or website ad about your performance reached concertgoers in Kansas and Missouri or the date when you did a show in a neighboring state. This date is often the same date as "Date of First Use of Mark Anywhere." Keep in mind, you should not use references to sales of recordings—use dates for performances and related advertising only. Again, if you're not sure of the exact date, estimate as accurately as possible.

Fee Information: There are three ways to pay the fees for your trademark application: credit card, automatic payment account and electronic funds transfer. Read the descriptions of these options by clicking the appropriate links.

Declaration: The declaration is a statement that the facts in the trademark application are true. Read it carefully. If there are statements in the declaration

that raise serious doubts or questions in your mind, do not file the application until you see a trademark lawyer.

Signature: The information box right above the signature section provides the surprising information that your electronic "signature" can be any combination of letters, numbers, or other characters. Each signature must begin and end with a forward slash (/). For example, /pat smith/, /ps/, and /268-3421/ are all acceptable signatures. There's no trick here. Entering your own name is the simplest option. Click the signature link just below the information box for the PTO's own words on this subject.

Validate: This process checks your application and alerts you if you forgot to include any information that is mandatory. You will then have a chance to go back and fill in the missing information. A warning message will also appear for nonmandatory missing information, but you are not required to go back and include that information. Once the validation is done, click Pay/Submit at the bottom of the Validation screen. Since you are using a credit card for payment, you will next be asked to enter payment information. If your transaction is successful, you will receive a confirmation screen.

Later, you will receive an email acknowledging the submission of your application. Hold on to that email, because it is the only proof you'll have that the PTO has your application. It is also proof of your filing date and contains the serial number assigned to your application.

Disclaimers: Many trademarks include words or phrases that, by themselves, cannot be protected under trademark law. For example, no band can claim an exclusive right to the word "blues" or "mambo." To allow one person an exclusive right to use such terms would decimate the English language. Therefore, the Trademark Office usually requires a disclaimer as to certain portions of trademarks. For example, if a band wanted to register the mark, Philly Dog Blues Band, the applicant would likely be required to disclaim "blues band." This means that apart from the use as a part of the trademark, the applicant claims no exclusive right to use the word "blues band."

Completing the Process

You complete the process by paying the fees, authorizing your electronic signature, and validating the application. After you click "Pay/Submit" and your transaction is successful, you will receive a confirmation.

Later, you will receive email acknowledging the submission of your application. Hold on to that email, because it is the only proof you'll have that the USPTO has your application. It is also proof of your filing date and contains the serial number assigned to your application.

After Filing

The USPTO filing receipt explains that you should not expect to hear anything about your application for approximately three months. If you have not heard anything in three and a half months, it is wise to call and inquire as to the status of your application. There are three ways to do this:

- Check TARR: The online Trademark Applications and Registrations Retrieval system page (http://tarr. uspto.gov) allows you to information about pending trademarks obtained from the USPTO's internal database by entering a valid trademark serial number.
- TRAM automated system: TRAM stands for trademark reporting and monitoring. From any touch-tone phone, Monday through Friday from 6:30 a.m. to midnight, eastern time, dial 703-305-8747. After the welcome message and tone, enter your mark's eight-digit serial number and the pound symbol. You should immediately hear the computer give you the current status of your mark along with the effective date of the status.
- If you want additional information or would prefer talking with a human, call the Trademark Assistance Center at 703-308-9400 and request a status check.

You will likely receive some communication from the USPTO within three to six months. If there is a problem with your application, you will receive what's called an "action letter." This is a letter from your examiner explaining what the problems are. Most problems can be resolved with a phone call to the examiner.

When the examiner approves your application for publication, you will receive a Notice of Publication in the mail. Your mark will then be published online in the Official Gazette. For 30 days following publication, anyone may oppose your registration. Only 3% of all published marks are opposed, so it is very unlikely you will run into trouble.

Once your mark has made it through the 30-day publication period, and you are filing on an actual use basis, you will receive a Certificate of Registration. The USPTO sometimes has a difficult time moving applications through this long process. As a result, it may take a year or more to process your application.

If you filed on an intent-to-use basis, your mark will not be placed on the trademark register until you file an additional document with the USPTO when you put it into actual use. This form, available on the TEAS system, is called "Statement of Use/Amendment to Allege Use for Intent-to-Use Application." It tells the USPTO the date you started using the mark and completes the registration process. You must also provide a specimen at that time, showing how you are using the mark.

Communicating With the USPTO

The chances are good that you will be communicating with the USPTO after you have filed your application. Few applications sail through completely unscathed.

You are required to be diligent in pursuing your application. If you are expecting some action from the USPTO (the ball is in their court) and more than six months have elapsed without your hearing from them, immediately check the TARR system or call the USPTO Status Line (the TRAM Automated System, described above). If you discover a problem, bring it to the USPTO's attention. If you fail to respond in a timely manner to a request from a USPTO examining attorney, your application may be considered abandoned. If that happens, you may petition the Commissioner for Trademarks within 60 days to reactivate your application.

If the examiner wants you to change your application, such as claiming a different description of services or goods, there is usually some room for negotiation.

An examiner with a brief question might call you and then issue and mail you an examiner's amendment. This is a form on which the examiner records in handwriting a phone conversation or meeting with the applicant. Read the amendment carefully to make sure it matches your understanding of the conversation. If you disagree or don't understand the amendment, first call the examiner and then, if necessary, write the examiner a letter with your concerns, explaining your point of view on the communication.

Scandalous or Celebrity Names: Two Bases for Refusal of Trademark Registration

Two situations that may cause problems for your band's registration of a trademark are if your band name consists of scandalous or immoral content or if you use the name of a living person without permission. Although the Trademark Office rarely exercises its right to stop the use of a scandalous or immoral mark, it has done so on occasion—for example, refusing drawings of nude men and women embracing, and refusing the name "Bullshit." Do not confuse your band's right to freedom of speech with trademark registration. The Trademark Office's standard for refusing an immoral trademark is lower (in other words, much easier for them) than the Constitutional standard for banning obscene speech.

So if you have a sexually explicit name for your band, be prepared for potential problems.

The Trademark Office will also not permit registration of a band name that consists of a living celebrity's name (such as "the Tori Spellings") without the consent of the celebrity. In addition, the use of a celebrity's name could trigger a lawsuit based on a claim known as a "right of publicity." This is different from trademark law, and is based on the principle that each person has a right to control the commercial use of his or her name. For these reasons, your band name should steer clear of the use of celebrity names unless one of you is already a celebrity.

Album Artwork

In this chapter, we'll walk you through the issues related to album artwork. For example, we'll advise when you need to obtain permission to use a photograph or to obtain a release from a model. We discuss the information that is legally required on the album, such as copyright and trademark notices, and suggest where it should be placed. We also provide sample agreements for acquiring rights to use artwork and for permitting your band to use a person's image on your album.

Copyright and Trademark Issues With Album Artwork

A good deal of the information we discuss in this chapter has to do with avoiding copyright and trademark trouble with your album artwork. For more detailed information about these areas of intellectual property law, see Chapter 7 on copyright issues and Chapter 9 on trademark.

Legal Issues With Album Artwork

Creating a cover for your recording can be fun, but you also have to take care of business. This section covers some legal issues related to preparing your artwork for albums and merchandise.

Album Titles

The trademark laws that we discussed in the previous chapter apply not only to your band's name, but also to the names of your albums. If you aren't careful when titling your albums, you could find yourself in serious hot water. Consider the following example.

In 1991, the group Negativland released an album entitled *U2/Negativland* which poked fun at the famous Irish rock band U2. U2's record label sued Negativland and its record label, SST. One of the major issues was the use of U2's name on the cover. As part of the settlement, SST agreed to stop using the name "U2" on the Negativland album cover, to destroy all existing copies, and to pay the attorneys' fees for U2's record company. Then, SST sued Negativland for over $90,000 to cover its costs from the lawsuit.

Was the use of "U2" in the Negativland title worth all that hassle? Perhaps it was for Negativland, which prides itself on rock and roll performance art. Most bands, however, don't want to be dragged into court over the use of an album title. Here are a couple of suggestions for choosing a title:

- **Don't Infringe.** You can use any phrase or wording for your title provided that it doesn't confuse consumers into thinking they're buying another group's music. For example, you should not title your album *Arrowsmith*, as fans of Aerosmith may be confused.

As a general rule, you may use the title of any book or a famous phrase. The band Oasis, for example, released an album called *Be Here Now*, which is the title of a spiritual book from the 1960s. Titles of movies are also not protected by copyright and trademark law and may be used as album titles. For example, the Ramones album title *It's Alive* is borrowed from the name of a horror movie. If you do use a title, however, avoid using books or movies that have become series (for example, *Die Hard*), blockbuster bestsellers (*Men Are From Mars, Women Are From Venus*), or classics (*Wizard of Oz, Star Wars,* or *Gone With the Wind*). Under trademark law, the owners of these works may have a right to prevent your title use. The reason for this is that if the title of the work or series is extremely well known, then consumers can be expected to associate this title with one particular source. Therefore, your band's use could be confusing to consumers. Avoid using a film title if the film has a well-known soundtrack, for the same reasons.

- **Don't Dilute.** You should avoid using corporate names or well-known trademarks such as Trump Towers or Mickey Mouse. Trademark law permits the owners of famous marks to prevent these marks from being "diluted." That means you can be

sued if you somehow diminish the way people perceive these marks, such as by using the McDonald's trademark "You Deserve a Break Today" for the title of a thrash recording with explicit lyrics. Regardless of your legal rights in these cases, your band probably can't afford the hassles.

Images in Album Artwork

An artist should be able to use whatever is necessary to make great artwork, right? Not exactly. Your album artwork cannot use another artist's copyrighted work unless you have permission. You cannot use a person's image (a picture of the person) on your artwork unless you have permission. We'll explain some of these principles below.

Avoiding Copyright Infringement

If you don't have the legal right to use something in your artwork, your band runs the risk of a lawsuit. If your band, for instance, uses a copyrighted picture from a newspaper without permission, your band might have to stop using the photo or even have to pay a financial settlement. Recalling compact discs, destroying artwork, and supplying new artwork is an expensive and time-consuming proposition.

How can you tell if artwork is protected by copyright? Unless it was published before 1923, you should assume the artwork is protected and the owner of the artwork controls the right to use it. For example, a graphic artist owns his or her images; a photographer owns the rights to his or her photos. These people can decide who may use the work. Also, don't assume that because artwork is included on a computer program or is included in a "stock" photography catalog, that it is free for use. For computer programs, check the accompanying "Read Me" files to determine if there is a licensing fee.

It is a violation of copyright law to use a work without permission from the owner. The reality is that you probably won't get sued if you sell only 500 to 1,000 compact discs at local shows, because the copyright owner won't be likely to find out about it. And besides, if your band has no money, the copyright owner probably wouldn't even bother to sue you. But if sales increase or if the record is featured in the press or is distributed by a record label, the chances for a lawsuit increase. That's why major labels and large independent labels insist on obtaining rights for all artwork on an album. A simple way to avoid artwork copyright problems is to obtain the rights for all artwork before having it printed. Sample agreements are provided later in this chapter.

Obtaining Permissions From Models

Imagine this scenario: The guitarist in your band takes a "personal" photo of his girlfriend clad in lingerie. The band (being all-male) determines it is the perfect cover photo. After the guitarist breaks up with his girlfriend, the album is released. The ex-girlfriend, who never consented to the use, sues the band. She wins the lawsuit, and all copies of the artwork must be destroyed. Oops!

In the previous section we indicated that you needed the photographer's permission to use a photograph. However, when a photo includes a person, your band must *also* obtain a release from the model (that is, the person in the photo). That's because under most state laws, a person can prevent the use of his or her image when it is used for commercial purposes. This is known as the "right of publicity." There are some exceptions: For example, you can usually use photos of people in large public gatherings, such as the crowd at an outdoor show. As with artwork copyright problems, the best solution to this problem is to avoid it in the first place: Obtain the permission of the model with a model release agreement. A sample agreement is provided in this chapter.

Objectionable Titles and Artwork

Some bands may want the controversy surrounding an indecent title or artwork; that's what makes rock and roll rebellious. John Lennon, Guns 'N' Roses and Jane's Addiction all dealt with public outcry over album artwork. In the case of these well-known artists, such controversies may actually help to sell records.

However, objectionable artwork or titles can often cause problems and delays for bands. That's because each community is permitted to establish its own standards of decency within Constitutional guidelines. In other words, if a district attorney in a town in Maryland wants to make an issue out of it, your record could be seized for having obscene artwork and your band (or record label) could be prosecuted for selling obscene materials.

This scenario is not that common, but it does happen. For example, albums by the Dead Kennedys were seized as obscene in California, even though the offensive artwork was not even visible from the outside. The band's record label eventually prevailed in court, but only after years of legal hassles.

Based on cases such as these, your band's decisions about artwork should be balanced by aesthetic and business realities. Offensive artwork or titles may keep your band's record from being distributed.

Information to Include in Your Artwork

Certain legal information such as copyright and trademark notices should be included on your artwork. Other information, though it does not have a legal significance, should be included for business purposes. This section discusses what information your artwork should include and where it should appear.

Legal Information

To enhance your legal protection under copyright and trademark laws, your band should include certain copyright and trademark notices on the artwork. This information places the world on notice that your band (or record label) owns the exclusive rights to the recordings, titles, and band names.

Copyright Notices

Copyright notice is not required, but it is strongly recommended. There are a number of different notices that you should use, including a copyright notice for the recording, for the songs, and for the artwork.

- **Recording Copyright Notice.** Your band should include a copyright notice for the recording. This notice has three parts: the symbol ℗ followed by the year of first publication of the recording and the owner of the record (probably your band or record label). The year of first publication is usually the year when the manufacturer first makes copies. If last year your band made 20 to 30 copies of the same recording and distributed them to friends or radio stations, that is not considered a "publication." Note: It's difficult to find the symbol ℗ on most computer programs. Sometimes it can be found in Hebrew lettering sets as the symbol for Kosher foods.

- **Artwork Copyright Notice.** Your band should also include a notice such as "© 2007 Spyders." Usually this notice is joined with the recording copyright notice—for example, "℗ and © 2007 Spyders." This notice protects the artwork and text on the cover, booklet, or label. This notice has three parts: the "C" in a circle followed by the year of first publication of the recording and the owner of the artwork rights (probably your band; see the artwork agreement at the end of this chapter). The year of first publication is the year when this artwork is first distributed to the public (usually the year when the manufacturer first makes copies).

- **Song Lyric Copyright Notice.** If you have included song lyrics, you should include a separate copyright notice such as "© 2004 SpyderBiter Music." This notice has three parts: the "C" in a circle followed by the year of first publication of the song and the name of the owner of the song (usually the music publisher; see Chapter 8). The year of first publication is the year when the lyrics or sheet music were first distributed to the public, which is

probably the year of the manufacture of the recording.

Song Copyrights and Recording Copyrights

You may wonder why there is a copyright notice for the songs and another notice for the recording. That's because there are two types of music copyrights: song copyrights (as discussed in Chapter 7) and recording copyrights, which protect the manner in which music is arranged and recorded (that is, the way the music is fixed on the recording). Usually the song copyright is owned by a music publisher and the sound recording copyright is owned by a record company. In Chapter 7 we explain how to register a song copyright with the Copyright Office. In Chapter 11 we explain how to register a recording copyright.

Trademark Notices

If you have received a federal registration for your band name, you should include the symbol ® near your name, for example Spyders®. *Do not* use the ® symbol if you have not received a federal trademark registration. You can, if you wish, use the symbols ™ or SM (trademark or service mark) by your name, but we do not recommend it as they do not guarantee trademark protection.

Compact Disc Logo

Although it is not required under law, many manufacturers and record companies insist on including the compact disc trademark. This is the word "disc" in small letters surrounded by the words "compact" and "digital audio." (Pick up any compact disc recording and you'll see it.) This is included because manufacturers and record companies have entered into legal agreements to include the industry trademark certifying the patented compact disc production system.

Suggested Information to Include

The following information is not required under law but is usually included on most artwork.

Basic Information

Album title; band name; song titles; song lengths (in minutes and seconds); total playing time; songwriters and music publisher (for example SpyderBiter Music); BMI or ASCAP; name, logo, and address of the record label; mail-order information; website and e-mail address; and credits for producers, engineers, musicians, art direction, photographers, recording studio, mastering, and manufacturer. Be careful if you are pressing both audio cassettes and compact discs; the compact discs may have bonus tracks, and the credits should reflect this.

Catalog Number

Catalog numbers are composed of six to eight letters or digits and are used to keep track of inventory. The first three or four digits indicate the record company or format, and the last three to four digits indicate the company's catalog number. If you're signed to a label, the label will furnish you with a catalog number, such as ARCD001 for compact discs or ARCS001 for cassettes. AR stands for the record company, CD stands for compact disc, CS stands for cassette, and 001 indicates that it is that label's first release. Record labels assign consecutive numbers to the records they release. If your band is acting as its own label, you will need to create a catalog number. Follow the formula above: initials for the label and configuration (CD or cassette), and number for the release.

Bar Codes

The Universal Product Code (UPC), also called a bar code, is a series of black lines that usually appears on the back of the compact disc. Distributors and retail stores use the bar code to keep track of inventory, and it is also used to monitor nationwide record sales. You probably don't need a bar code if you're planning to sell recordings only at concerts and local stores. However, if you are signed to a label or plan on selling your recordings through nationwide distributors or chain stores, or you want to offer your music through download services such as iTunes, you'll probably need the UPC code. Some manufacturers, distributors, or online stores (for example, CDBaby.com) will assist you in obtaining the bar code. For more information about UPC bar codes, contact the Uniform Code Council (www.uc-council.org).

Record Speed and Noise Reduction

If you're releasing a 7-inch or 12-inch vinyl recording, make sure to indicate the speed (33 or 45 rpm).

Recording, Mixing, and Mastering Symbols

Many bands and record companies like to include information about the recording process—specifically, whether the recording, mixing, and mastering process were digital or analog. Analog recording is the traditional method of recording in which the music is not converted into a digital signal. This information is presented by the use of three letters. The first letter stands for the recording process, the next letter for the mixing process, and the third letter for mastering. For example, if you see the letters AAD, that means the recording and mixing were analog and the mastering was digital.

Where Does the Information Go?

Before explaining where to place the required information on the compact disc, let's go through some album artwork terminology.

The plastic case that holds a compact disc is a **jewel box.** The artwork for a compact disc has three parts: The **booklet** is the pamphlet inserted in the front of the jewel box (which becomes the front of the compact disc); the **tray card** is the sheet that is inserted in the back of the jewel box (which becomes the back of the compact disc); and the **label** is the information printed directly onto the compact disc. The folded edge of the tray card (viewed from the side of the jewel box) is known as the **spine.**

Place your information as follows: the title of the album, the name of the band, and the catalog number always appear on the spine. The UPC bar code can be placed anywhere that is visible to consumers in the store (although it usually appears on the CD tray card). The trademarks for the record label usually appear on the CD label and tray card. The "compact disc" trademark is placed on the CD label. Copyright notices can be placed either on the booklet, tray card, or label.

Tagging MP3s

If you're distributing digital downloads either via your own website or through a download service, you will want to provide much of the same information on your CD but encoded within your MP3. This is done through a process known as "tagging". Most music encoding programs such as SoundForge, Wavelab, or Peak can tag—usually via popup window or dialog box—the title, album, and cover art so that it is available to those who download the MP3. Tagging can also be done within your music player program—for example in Musicmatch or iTunes—or by purchasing a tagging program such as MP3Tagger or TagEditor.

Getting the Artwork Done

As a general rule, your band will have an easier time if you entrust the job of artwork to an experienced graphic artist who can provide appealing and professional imagery. However, many bands cannot afford a graphic artist and instead rely on assistance from friends, local printers, or the manufacturer. (When we refer to manufacturers, we're talking about the companies that duplicate compact discs, vinyl records, and cassettes.)

Regardless of who prepares the imagery and layout, your band will share the responsibility of providing the basic information required for the artwork. That is, your band will have the responsibility to guarantee titles are spelled correctly, credits are accurate, and legal notices are proper. Below, we discuss the artwork process and your band's responsibilities.

Learn the Lingo

Graphic artists and manufacturers use special terms when dealing with album artwork. A **template** is a pattern or outline for each piece of artwork, including the measurements and specifications. For example, a CD manufacturer will provide you with template showing the dimensions of each piece of artwork (booklet, tray card, and so on). Each template usually includes extra space on all four sides of the artwork known as **bleed.** Your photos or artwork should "bleed" into these blank spaces so that when the artwork is finally cut, the artwork and any background color or images reach all the way to the edge.

If you are preparing artwork on a computer or if it will be converted into computer format, your photographs and artwork will have to be **scanned.** This process converts a two-dimensional image into a digital image. The typestyles used are called **fonts.** A full-color design is referred to as a **four-color** design, because it includes the three primary colors and black. When the artwork is completed, it is **camera-ready.** That is, your band's artwork needs no further modification and can be reproduced "as is" by the manufacturer. If you will be delivering your artwork to the manufacturer on computer disk, the manufacturer will need to know whether your disks are formatted for use in PC or Macintosh computers. If you don't have the necessary computer equipment, your band may need to use a **service bureau,** a company that provides computer-related services.

Working With a Professional Artist

You can follow many of the same rules for hiring an artist as you would for hiring any professional. That is, rely on referrals from others, ask to see examples of the work, and obtain a written estimate for the work.

Be sure to discuss ownership of the artwork and to make clear your band's intended purposes for it. Under copyright law, a freelance artist retains copyright ownership of the artwork. Generally, if you hire someone to create art for a purpose, you as the hiring party have an implied license to use the art for that purpose. For instance, if you hired a photographer to take a picture for an album, you can use the picture on your album without having to obtain a written license from the artist. But remember, that's *all* you can use it for, and the

photographer retains ownership of the picture and could even sell it to another band for use on their cover.

Since these ownership issues can be complicated, we recommend that you obtain written permission to use the work or that the artist assign *all* ownership to your band. The artwork agreement, below, covers these ownership issues.

Doing the Artwork Yourself

If your band can't afford the $250 to $1,000 to hire a graphic artist, it's possible for you to do some or all of it by using computer programs such as Freehand, Photoshop, InDesign, Quark Express, PageMaker, and Illustrator. Since not all computer graphic programs can produce the camera-ready artwork needed by manufacturers, talk to the manufacturers first about what type of graphic files must be furnished. They may send you templates or offer graphic assistance. For example, your band can create its cover photo using Photoshop and your band logo using Illustrator and then send these two items to the manufacturer, whose design department will assemble the art and make it camera-ready.

Most computer graphic programs come with tutorials that are quite helpful. If you cannot afford to buy these programs or your computer cannot run them, there are companies (such as Kinko's) that rent computer time.

If your band is creating the artwork on a computer, the colors on your computer screen may not accurately reflect the final print job. Once you have the final design, you should pay for a high-quality test print (also called a proof). It's always wise to review a proof before forwarding artwork to the manufacturer.

Some bands have their album artwork printed locally to save money and then ship the finished artwork to the manufacturer. Local printers are fine for J-cards and inserts, but beware when hiring a printer for compact disc work. If the printer is not familiar with the manufacturer's standards, the result can be a booklet that is cut too small or too large for insertion in the jewel box.

What to Do If the Artwork Is Wrong

Typos, misspellings, or poor image reproduction can make the product worthless, depending on how bad the mistake is. If your band's name is misspelled, for instance, you'll probably have to trash however many CD booklets were printed with the mistake. You might be willing to use artwork with minor typos, but your band's image and reputation might suffer.

Most artwork problems result from not reviewing credits and test prints carefully. In order to avoid errors, check and doublecheck the credits before submitting them. When you get the test prints of the artwork, check the credits again.

If the error is your fault (that is, you submitted incorrect information or failed to spot errors in test prints), then you'll have a hard time getting the printer or manufacturer to redo the work for free. Your best hope is to have the artwork done at a reduced rate. Larger manufacturers, because of the large volume of business they do, are often better suited to make this type of arrangement.

If the error is not your fault (that is, the manufacturer or printer used the wrong colors or never furnished you with a test print), then you should seek to have the work redone without charge. If you run into a serious dispute with a printer or manufacturer, you will have a better position if you paid with a credit card. For example, if your dispute is for more than $50 and with a manufacturer within your state or 100 miles from your home, your credit card company will not deduct the amount from your account until the dispute is resolved. This is far easier than dealing with small claims court. Your credit card carrier can provide you with the dispute resolution rules.

Shipping Artwork

When mailing original artwork, pack it carefully and, if possible, keep a good copy for yourself. Photos should be in heavy cardboard; disks in bubble wrap. Always use a trackable shipping system such as FedEx or UPS. Always place your name and phone number on the back of each item in case it is separated at the manufacturer or printer. If your artwork includes a unique computer font, remember to ship the font set (on disk) with the artwork. A manufacturer who does not have the identical font will use the closest approximation, which may not be acceptable.

Artwork Is Always Late

Don't bother booking the date for your record release party until the artwork is completed. Generally, the artwork is the item that holds up the manufacturing, either because it's late or must be corrected. If you are doing the artwork yourself, be prepared for it to take several weeks. Even if you go as fast as you can, you are often waiting for film to be shot, developed, or reproduced. Also, friends may be helpful in offering graphic services, but as a general rule, you're more likely to get what you want on time if you're paying for services or doing it yourself.

Abbreviated Artwork Agreement

If your band wants a simple artwork agreement that transfers all rights in the artwork to the band for one payment, then use this abbreviated artwork agreement. We'll walk you through the simple task of putting this agreement together. A sample appears below. If your band needs a more detailed agreement for an artist who is not willing to transfer all rights, use the agreement that follows this one.

 This agreement is included on the forms CD in the back of this book.

In the introductory section, insert the name of your band partnership if it owns your recordings. If you created a separate company for the release of your recordings (such as "Our Band's Records"), list that name. If the name doesn't make it clear what kind of business form it is (for example, "The Spyder Partnership"), indicate the business form (for example, "Centipede, a general partnership"). The artist can be a photographer, illustrator, or any type of graphic artist.

Services

Indicate the specific services. For example, "design camera-ready artwork and text for a four-panel booklet, tray card, and compact disc label and furnish that artwork in a digital format" or "photography services to create a suitable band photo for use in album artwork." You should also insert the date when the artwork or photography will be completed. If the artwork has already been completed, simply state "Completed."

Payment

Insert the total amount of the payment and the method for payment (for example, "Half at time of commencement of work and half on acceptance by Band").

Rights

Under this agreement, your band owns the artwork and can do whatever you wish without any further reimbursement (other than provided in the Payment section) to the artist.

Expenses

In this section your band agrees to pay for the artist's expenses incurred in the course of completing the artwork. It establishes that expenses must be itemized to be paid, and that your approval is necessary for expenses over $50.

Credit

Indicate the type of credit the artist will get in your album information. For example, "Graphic Design and Cover Artwork by Joan Smith."

Artist Warranties

Warranties are contractual promises. If the artist breaks this promise (for example, the artist infringes someone's photo), the band can seek money damages from the artist.

Mediation; Arbitration

This provision provides a less-expensive method of resolving disputes than filing a lawsuit. (See the sidebar in Chapter 2 for an explanation of mediation and arbitration.) We recommend that you use this provision in order to help avoid an expensive lawsuit.

We suggest that you choose the county, province, or city in which the band resides for arbitration. If all the members do not reside within one area, choose a place that is convenient. Enter your location of choice in the blank.

Signatures

Only one member of your band needs to sign the agreement, though, of course, it's best to make sure that everybody agrees about hiring the artist. Enter the business name of the band, the name of which band member is signing, and the band member's title (usually "Partner"). That band member should sign and date the form. Have the artist enter his or her address, and sign and date the form.

[Abbreviated] Artwork Agreement

This Artwork Agreement (the "Agreement") is made between _____

("Band") and _____ ("Artist").

Services

Artist agrees to perform the following services and create the following artwork (the "Art"):

_____

_____

_____

The Art will be completed by the following date: _____

During the process, Artist will keep the Band informed of work in progress and will furnish test prints of the Art prior to completion.

Payment

Band agrees to pay Artist $_____ as follows:

_____

_____

_____

for performance of the art services and acquisition of the rights provided below.

Rights

Artist assigns to the Band all copyright to the Art and agrees to cooperate in the preparation of any documents necessary to demonstrate this assignment of rights. Artist retains the right to display the work as part of Artist's portfolio and to reproduce the Art in connection with the promotion of Artist's services.

Expenses

Band agrees to reimburse Artist for all reasonable production expenses including halftones, stats, photography, disks, illustrations, or related costs. These expenses will be itemized on invoices, and in no event will any expense exceed $50 without approval from the Band.

Credit

Credit for Artist will be included on reproductions of the Art as follows:

_____

Artist Warranties

Artist warrants that the Art will not infringe any intellectual property rights or violate any laws.

Mediation; Arbitration

If a dispute arises under this Agreement, the parties agree to first try to resolve the dispute with the help of a mutually agreed-on mediator in _____. Any costs and fees other than attorney fees will be shared equally by the parties. If it is impossible to arrive at a mutually satisfactory solution within a reasonable time, the parties agree to submit the dispute to binding arbitration in the same city or region, conducted on a confidential basis pursuant to the Commercial Arbitration Rules of the American Arbitration Association, or the rules of _____.

Band Partnership Name _____

Band Partner Name & Title _____

Band Partner Signature _____

Address _____

_____

Date _____

Artist Name _____

Artist Signature _____

Address _____

_____

Date _____

Full-Length Artwork Agreement

If your band wants a full-length artwork agreement that offers more choices regarding ownership rights and more detailed protection for your band, then use this Full-Length Artwork Agreement. This section explains how to fill out this agreement. A sample appears below.

 This agreement is included on the forms CD in the back of this book.

In the introductory section, put the name of your band partnership if it owns your recordings. If you created a separate company for the release of your recordings (such as "Our Band's Records"), list that name. If the name doesn't make it clear what kind of business form it is (for example, "The Spyder Partnership"), then indicate the business form (for example, "Centipede, a general partnership"). The artist can be a photographer, illustrator, or any type of graphic artist.

Services

Indicate the specific services. For example, "design camera-ready artwork and text for a four-panel booklet, tray card, and compact disc label and furnish that artwork in a digital format" or "photography services to create a suitable band photo for use in album artwork." You should also insert the date when the artwork or photography will be completed. If the artwork has already been completed, simply state "Completed."

Payment

Insert the total amount of the payment and the method for payment (for example, "Half at time of commencement of work and half on acceptance by Band").

Rights (Includes Optional Provisions)

We have provided five different rights provisions to deal with five common situations. Check one of the provisions, or delete the unwanted provisions entirely.

Option #1: Under the first choice, your band owns the artwork and can do whatever you wish with it without any further reimbursement (other than the Payment section) to the artist. This is the provision that is preferable if you intend to furnish this artwork to a major record label, because major music companies prefer to own all rights.

Option #2: If the artist is willing to sell (assign) to your band all rights to the artwork but wants to be paid for merchandise sales, then use this selection. Merchandise sales include products other than recordings, such as T-shirts, stickers, hats, and so on. Check one of the two different ways to pay for merchandise. You can select a royalty payment for the artist (usually ranging from 2% to 10%), or you can make a lump sum payment per every 1,000 T-shirts or items sold.

Under all of the remaining choices, the artist retains copyright ownership and your band gets permission to use the artwork for different purposes. Think of it as a "rental" of the artwork rights. The primary difference is that under these choices, the artist retains all rights to the artwork that are not granted to the band. Therefore, for example, the artist could permit the use of the artwork on postcards.

You may find that some artists bristle at the thought of allowing modification of the artwork. You should explain that modification is often necessary for formatting and advertising purposes. If the artist is adamant about not permitting modification, strike the word "modify." (In the United States, you do not need to seek permission for modification if you have used one of the first two choices. However, in Canada, you may have to obtain permission under a principle known as "moral rights." (See Chapter 7.))

Option #3: Under the third choice, your band can use the artwork solely for use in connection with recordings, but not merchandise. That is, you can use the art on recordings and materials promoting those recordings such as your website, but if you want to sell merchandise such as T-shirts with the artwork, you'll need to go back to the artist and get permission.

Option #4: Under the fourth choice, your band can use the artwork in connection with recordings and merchandise without any further reimbursement (other than the Payment section) to the artist. That is, you have the right to use the art on recordings, ads and promos at your website, and you can sell merchandise with the artwork. Most savvy artists do not grant such rights without further reimbursement for the merchandise. In this case, you would use the last choice, described below.

Option #5: This final choice is the same as the previous one, except your band pays for merchandise rights as the money comes in from those sales. The theory behind these payments is that the artist's work, as well as the band's popularity, is triggering merchandise sales, and, therefore, the artist should receive a royalty. Check one of the two different ways to pay for merchandise. You can select a royalty payment for the artist (usually ranging from 2% to 10%), or you can make a lump sum payment per every 1,000 T-shirts or items sold.

Expenses

In this section your band agrees to pay for the artist's expenses incurred in the course of completing the artwork. It establishes that expenses must be itemized to be paid, and that your approval is necessary for expenses over $50.

Credit

Indicate the type of credit the artist will get in the album information. For example, "Graphic Design and Cover Artwork by Joan Smith."

Artist Warranties and Indemnification

Warranties and representations are contractual promises. If the artist breaks one of these promises (for example, the artist infringes someone's photo), the band can seek money damages from the artist. By "indemnifying" your band the artist agrees to pay for your damages that are caused by the artist. For example, if your band is sued because the art includes unauthorized images, the artist would have to pay for your band's legal expenses.

Assignment

This allows the band to grant its rights to another company. For example, if a label wanted to release your recording, your band could assign the rights to the artwork to the label.

Mediation; Arbitration

This provision provides a less-expensive method of resolving disputes than filing a lawsuit. (See the sidebar in Chapter 2 for an explanation of mediation and arbitration.) We recommend that you use this provision in order to help avoid an expensive lawsuit.

We suggest that you choose the county, province, or city in which the band resides for arbitration. If all the members do not live in one area, choose a place that is convenient. Enter your location of choice in the blank.

In some states there are organizations that specialize in arbitration for people in the arts, such as California Lawyers

for the Arts (CLA) and, in New York, Volunteer Lawyers for the Arts (VLA). You can substitute the rules of such an organization for those of the American Arbitration Association in your agreement. If your band is based in Canada, you can still use the AAA's rules, as they perform arbitration in all major Canadian cities. (For more information on the AAA, see Chapter 17.) Check one of the choices, or delete the unwanted alternative.

General

The following provisions are standard contract provisions referred to as boilerplate. Boilerplate provisions are explained in Chapter 2.

In the blank space, insert the state (or province, in the case of Canadian bands) of residence for the band partners. In the event of a dispute, this determines which state law will govern the arbitration or lawsuit. This provision also provides that the winner in any lawsuit between the band and the artist will receive attorney's fees.

Signatures

Only one member of your band needs to sign the agreement, though you should make sure that everybody agrees about hiring the artist. Enter the business name of the band, the name of the band member who is signing, and the band member's title (usually "Partner"). That band member should sign and date the form. Have the artist enter his or her address, and sign and date the form.

Artwork Agreement

This Artwork Agreement (the "Agreement") is made between _____ ("Band") and _____ ("Artist").

The Band wants Artist to create artwork to be used in conjunction with their musical recordings. The parties agree as follows:

Services

In consideration of the payments provided in this Agreement, Artist agrees to perform the following services and create the following artwork (the "Art"): _____

_____

The Art will be completed by the following date: _____

During the process, Artist will keep the Band informed of work in progress and shall furnish test prints of the Art prior to completion.

Payment

Band agrees to pay Artist $_____ as follows: _____ for performance of the art services and acquisition of the rights provided below.

Rights

The rights to the artwork will be as follows: (select one)

○ Artist assigns to the Band all copyright to the Art and agrees to cooperate in the preparation of any documents necessary to demonstrate this assignment of rights. Artist retains the right to display the work as part of Artist's portfolio and to reproduce the Art in connection with the promotion of Artist's services.

○ Artist assigns to the Band all copyright to the Art and agrees to cooperate in the preparation of any documents necessary to demonstrate this assignment of rights. Artist retains the right to display the work as part of Artist's portfolio and to reproduce the Art in connection with the promotion of Artist's services. In addition to any other payments provided under this agreement, if the Art is used on merchandise authorized by the Band that is sold to the public, Artist is entitled to the following payments, which will be paid twice a year at the end of June and December:

Complete one:	Amount
• Royalty on net profits from _____ sale of merchandise	_____%
• Lump sum payments for every 1,000_____ sold	$_____

(Net profits are all revenues received minus the costs of production, shipping, and any discounts or fees paid to distributors or retailers.)

Check one:

○ Artist grants to the Band for the length of copyright the exclusive worldwide right to use, sell, modify, and distribute the Art in connection with the sale of the Band's musical recordings and for purposes of advertising and promotion of the Band's musical recordings. All other rights are reserved to Artist.

○ Artist grants to the Band for the length of copyright the exclusive worldwide right to use, sell, modify, and distribute the Art in connection with the sale of the Band's musical recordings and for purposes of advertising and promotion of the Band's musical recordings and in connection with Band merchandise including upper body apparel, hats, and other items. All other rights are reserved to Artist.

○ Artist grants to the Band for the length of copyright the exclusive worldwide right to use, sell, modify, and distribute the Art in connection with the sale of the Band's musical recordings and for purposes of advertising and promotion of the Band's musical recordings and in connection with Band merchandise including upper body apparel, hats, and other items. All other rights are reserved to Artist. In addition to any other payments provided under this agreement, if the Art is used on merchandise authorized by the Band that is sold to the public, Artist is entitled to the following payments, which will be paid twice a year, at the end of June and December:

Complete one:	Amount
• Royalty on net profits from _____ sale of merchandise	_____%
• Lump sum payments for every 1,000_____ sold	$_____

(Net profits are all revenues received minus the costs of production, shipping, and any discounts or fees paid to distributors or retailers.)

Expenses

Band agrees to reimburse Artist for all reasonable production expenses including halftones, stats, photography, disks, illustrations, or related costs. These expenses will be itemized on invoices, and in no event will any expense exceed $50 without approval from the Band.

Credit

Credit for Artist will be included on reproductions of the Art as follows:

_____

_____

Artist Warranties and Indemnification

Artist warrants to Band that: (a) Artist has the power and authority to enter into this Agreement; (b) the Art will not infringe any intellectual property rights or violate any laws; and (c) Artist has or will obtain all necessary rights or licenses associated with any artwork, photos, or illustrations incorporated into the Art. Artist indemnifies Band and undertakes to defend Band against and hold Band harmless (including, without limitation, attorney fees and costs) from any claims and damage arising out of any breach of Artist's warranties, above.

Assignment

The Band has the right to assign its rights under this Agreement.

Mediation; Arbitration

If a dispute arises under this Agreement, the parties agree to first try to resolve the dispute with the help of a mutually agreed-on mediator in _____. Any costs and fees other than attorney fees will be shared equally by the parties. If it is impossible to arrive at a mutually satisfactory solution within a reasonable time, the parties agree to submit the dispute to binding arbitration in the same city or region, conducted on a confidential basis pursuant to:

❍ the Commercial Arbitration Rules of the American Arbitration Association, or

❍ the rules of _____.

Any decision or award as a result of any such arbitration proceeding will include the assessment of costs, expenses, and reasonable attorney's fees and include a written determination of the arbitrators. Absent an agreement to the contrary, any such arbitration will be conducted by an arbitrator experienced in music industry law. An award of arbitration is final and binding on the Band Partners and may be confirmed in a court of competent jurisdiction. The prevailing party has the right to collect from the other party its reasonable costs and attorney fees incurred in enforcing this agreement.

General

Nothing contained in this Agreement constitutes either Band or Artist a partner or employee of the other party. This Agreement expresses the complete understanding of the parties and may not be amended except in a writing signed by both parties. If a court finds any provision of this Agreement invalid or unenforceable, the remainder of this Agreement will be interpreted so as best to effect the intent of the parties. This Agreement is governed by and interpreted in accordance with the laws of _____ . Notices required under this agreement can be sent to parties at the addresses provided below.

Band Partnership Name _____

Band Partner Name & Title _____

Band Partner Signature _____

Address _____

_____

Date _____

Artist Name _____

Artist Signature _____

Address _____

_____

Date _____

Model Release Agreement

The Model Release Agreement is a simple agreement that allows your band to use a person's image on your artwork, such as a photograph of a friend or a professional model. Band members who may appear on album artwork would not need to sign this release. Although the term "model" is used, we're not necessarily talking about professional models. The term applies to any person whose image is used. Below is an explanation of how to put together this agreement. A sample appears below.

 This agreement is included on the forms CD in the back of this book.

In the introductory section, insert the name of your band partnership if it owns your recordings. If you created a separate company for the release of your recordings (such as "Our Band's Records"), list that name. If the name doesn't make it clear what kind of business form it is (for example, "The Spyder Partnership"), then indicate the business form (for example, "Centipede, a general partnership"). Insert the name of the model.

Rights

Describe the imagery your band is using for the artwork. For example, "outdoor photos of Model taken at Ocean Beach in May 2002." If possible, attach a photocopy of the image. Under this provision, your band gets the exclusive right to use the model's image for any purpose related to your music, such as recordings or merchandise. If the model does not want to give up the merchandise rights, or if the model wants to be paid an additional fee for merchandise rights, you will need to negotiate a merchandise royalty fee. We do not recommend paying royalties to models, especially if you are also paying royalties to the artwork artists.

Payment

Insert the amount of the payment. Even if the model is a friend, your band should make a nominal payment, such as $1. This payment will cover all of your uses. However, if the model insists on royalties or additional payments for use of the model image on merchandise, you will need to add an additional page (or exhibit) detailing this arrangement. Both parties should sign this exhibit.

Credit

Models often do not receive credit on artwork, and, for that reason, this provision is optional. If the model will receive credit, indicate the type of credit that will appear. For example, "Man on Back Cover: M. Polazzo."

Mediation; Arbitration

This provision provides a less expensive method of resolving disputes than filing a lawsuit. (See the sidebar in Chapter 2 for an explanation of mediation and arbitration.) We recommend that you use this provision in order to help avoid an expensive lawsuit.

We suggest that you choose the county, province, or city in which the band resides for arbitration. If all the members do not reside in one area, choose a place that is convenient. Enter your location of choice in the blank.

In some states there are organizations that specialize in arbitration for people in the arts, such as California Lawyers for the Arts (CLA) and, in New York, Volunteer Lawyers for the Arts (VLA). You can substitute the rules of such an organization for those of the American Arbitration Association in your Agreement. If your band is based in Canada, you can still use the AAA's rules, as they perform arbitration in all major Canadian cities. (For more information on the AAA, see Chapter 17.) Check one of the choices or delete the unwanted alternative.

General

The following provisions are standard contractual provisions referred to as boilerplate. Boilerplate provisions are explained in Chapter 2.

In the blank space, insert the state (or province, in the case of Canadian bands) of residence for the band partners. In the event of a dispute, this determines which state law will govern the arbitration or lawsuit.

Signatures

Only one member of your band needs to sign the agreement, though you should make sure that everybody agrees about hiring the model. Enter the business name of the band, the name of the band member who is signing, and the band member's title (usually "Partner"). That band member should sign and date the form. Have the model enter his or her address, and sign and date the form.

Model Release Agreement

This Model Release Agreement (the "Agreement") is made between _____ ("Band") and _____ ("Model").

Rights

The Band is using Model's image in conjunction with the artwork for their musical recordings. In consideration of the payments provided in this Agreement, Model grants to the Band and its assigns or licensees the right to use Model's picture as embodied on _____ in all forms and media and (including composite or modified representations) for use in connection with the sale of the Band's musical recordings, for purposes of advertising and promotion of the Band's musical recordings, and in connection with Band-related merchandise.

Payment

Band will pay Model as follows: $_____.

Credit

(Check and fill in blank if applicable.)

O Model is entitled to the following credit: _____

Mediation; Arbitration

If a dispute arises under this Agreement, the parties agree to first try to resolve the dispute with the help of a mutually agreed-on mediator in _____.
Any costs and fees other than attorney fees will be shared equally by the parties. If it proves impossible to arrive at a mutually satisfactory solution within a reasonable time, the parties agree to submit the dispute to binding arbitration in the same city or region, conducted on a confidential basis pursuant to:

O the Commercial Arbitration Rules of the American Arbitration Association, or

O the rules of _____.

Any decision or award as a result of any such arbitration proceeding will include the assessment of costs, expenses, and reasonable attorney's fees and a written determination of the arbitrators. Absent an agreement to the contrary, any such arbitration will be conducted by an arbitrator experienced in music industry law. An award of arbitration is final and binding on the Band Partners and may be confirmed in a court of competent jurisdiction. The prevailing party has the right to collect from the other party its reasonable costs and attorney fees incurred in enforcing this Agreement.

General

Nothing contained in this Agreement is deemed to constitute either Band or Model a partner or employee of the other party. This Agreement expresses the complete understanding of the parties and may not be amended except in a writing signed by both parties. If a court finds any provision of this Agreement invalid or unenforceable, the remainder of this Agreement be interpreted so as best to carry out the intent of the parties. This Agreement is governed by and interpreted in accordance with the laws of

_____.

Band Partnership Name _____

Band Partner Name & Title _____

Band Partner Signature _____

Address _____

_____

Date _____

Model Name _____

Model Signature _____

Address _____

_____

Date _____

Chapter 11

Recording

A recording studio is like a magnifying glass. Your band's music is placed under laboratory-like scrutiny. Suddenly, mistakes that may have been acceptable on stage are no longer tolerable when heard through studio monitors. In the same way, the recording studio places your band's business under scrutiny. Your band must produce a desired result within an expected time period and within a budget. Can you do it? How do you juggle financial limits with your artistic intentions?

This chapter deals with issues that tend to arise in the course of recording music. We will help you prepare a recording budget, and we will advise you on legal issues such as obtaining releases from musicians who perform on your recording or for using a digital sample of someone else's music. We will also offer advice on choosing a studio and how to save money while recording. At the end of the chapter we provide information about registering your copyright in the recording.

Legal Issues in the Recording Studio

When we discuss legal issues in the recording studio, we are concerned primarily with whether you are giving up (or risking) your rights in the recordings. That is, by using an outside musician or by sampling a recording, have you in

any way diluted your ownership of the recordings? Or, looking at it from a more practical perspective, are you risking a lawsuit over the rights to your music?

Recording Studios

Your relationship with a recording studio is a straightforward "service" arrangement. You either pay in advance for a block of time or you pay an hourly rate after each session. The studio, by recording your music, obtains no legal rights to the music. That is, the studio cannot claim an ownership in your music simply because the recording was made there. Beware, however, that this may not be true in two situations: a) Studio employees arrange your music or perform on your recordings; or b) the studio does the recording on "spec" in return for a percentage of any income.

Studio Employees

In cases of a performing studio employee, the situation is the same as if any nonband musician played on your recording. That musician may claim a coauthorship claim to the song or to the recording copyright based on their contribution. The claim may or may not be validated by a court—that depends on the quality of the contribution and other factors. However, any claim is enough to temporarily cloud your ownership.

You probably do not need to be concerned about such issues with studio employees, because studios usually do not want to claim rights in songs or recordings (it's bad for business). However, if you are signed to a record label, you can guarantee your rights are protected by having all musicians who assist in the making of the recording sign a musician's release.

Recording on Spec

If a studio does your recording on spec, that means the studio will allow you to record for free or at a reduced rate because the studio is speculating that your recording will be a success. If the record is a success, you will be required to repay the recording costs—and more. A studio may request a percentage of the record company advance or future royalty income. You should be cautious entering into spec deals, as the payout may far exceed the value of the recording services. If you enter into a spec arrangement, get it in writing and avoid transferring any ownership interest of the copyright in the songs or the recording.

Producers

If you are signed to a major label, you will have to use a producer—a professional who directs the recording and mixing sessions. Most producers are paid a fee for their work and receive a percentage of the income from the recording. Unlike an engineer, a producer will provide an impartial criticism of your performance, as well as an objective analysis of your songs. If you are signed to an independent label, the company may suggest (but not demand) that you work with a producer.

Usually a producer (or the producer's agent or attorney) provides a written agreement or deal memo establishing the producer's fee. These agreements also establish the record company's rights to the recording, thereby avoiding any potential claims of copyright ownership by the producer.

Some unsigned bands work with producers, often under an arrangement known as a producer-demo deal. In this arrangement, a recording is made at the producer's expense, often at the producer's studio. The producer then shops the band to a record label. Demo deals vary, and in some cases the producer is entitled to a cut of any money received from a band record deal regardless of whether the demo was responsible. The demo deal may also grant publishing rights to the producer.

Generally, bands have little negotiating ability in producer-demo deals. That is, you're usually told to take it or leave it. Since such deals are often extremely one-sided, you should review them carefully and research the producer to determine if he or she is trustworthy and well-connected. Since these deals have some of the features of management agreements, you should compare the provisions of any demo deal you're considering to those in the management agreement in Chapter 3. You can also compare it to the label-shopping agreement in Chapter 4. Finally, you might want to have the demo deal reviewed by an attorney.

Engineers

Generally, an unsigned band does not use a producer but instead relies on an experienced engineer to guide the band through the recording. Some engineers, eager for producing experience, may waive a portion of their hourly fee in return for a coproduction credit and a payment if the recording is released by a label.

Musician Releases

In the studio, your band may use other musicians, such as a cello player used on one song. Copyright law requires that your band obtain permission to use the performance on your recording. We have provided a sample release agreement, below. We advise getting a signed release, but, practically, if you're only making a demo or releasing your own record, your band can probably get by without it. However, all major labels and some independents will require a release.

If a musician is under an exclusive recording agreement with a record company, you will need to find out if the musician is permitted to perform on "outside" recordings. If so, there may be

a special credit required in your album information (for example, "Lindsay Hutton appears courtesy of NBT Records"). If a musician on your recording is a member of the American Federation of Musicians union, then the musician must be paid according to union rates. The musician will furnish your band with the AFM forms for each recording session. Every recording made for a major label must use union musicians.

Sampling

It's possible that you turned directly to this section because your band is planning to use a sample on your recording and you want to know your rights. Can you use the sample for free? If you have to pay, whom do you ask about it? Unfortunately, there are no one-size-fits-all solutions. We'll walk you through the legal side and then offer you some practical suggestions.

As you are probably aware, sampling is the process of copying a piece of recorded music—usually on a computer or sampler—and then reproducing it on your recording. Sometimes the sample is repeated to create a drum pattern or a chorus; sometimes the sample is used only once. If you sample your band's own musical recordings, that's never a problem (assuming you haven't sold the rights to the recording to a record company). But if you sample another recording, that raises legal issues.

(Note: There is another quite different legal definition of sampling. In the *Napster* case, the court defined the practice of making temporary copies of a recording before purchasing as "sampling." That definition is not applicable to our discussion here.)

Sampling is a violation of copyright law if it's done without the permission of the owner of the recording (usually the record company) and the owner of the song (usually the music publisher). There are some exceptions to this rule, discussed below.

Precleared Samples

Some samples have been "precleared." That means that it's okay with the owner for others to sample the recording. For example, if you use the ACID-brand loops sold by Sonic Foundry (www.sonicfoundry .com) in your band's compositions, you don't need to get permission to do so. This is also sometimes the case with other companies "DJ" recordings that include precleared drum beats and musical riffs, and it also may be true for digital sounds included on a computer disk. Consider these sampled sounds like audio clip art—free to use. But before freely using the sample, check the notice on the recording or disk package to make sure that the material is available for your use.

Sampling the Majors

Major publishers and labels are finally waking up to the sample clearance business. When the first edition of this book appeared in 1998, the only people who could acquire sampling rights were entertainment lawyers and sampling experts. Now, several companies are simplifying the process by offering online sample clearance. Check out Universal Music (www. universalmusicpublishing.com) and BMG Music (www.bmgmusicsearch. com), two major players now offering clearance request forms online.

To Sample or Not to Sample?

For musicians and songwriters there are many dangers involved in unauthorized sampling … but don't tell that to Brian Burton aka DJ Danger Mouse, whose career as a music producer was launched through illegal use of samples. In 2004 Burton created *The Grey Album*, a mash up of the Beatles *White Album* and Jay-Z's *Black Album*. He pressed 3000 copies of *The Grey Album* and distributed them to indie music sources.

EMI, the owner of rights to the Beatles album, learned of the project and quickly squelched it by sending a cease and desist letter. "EMI is absolutely in favor of music sampling," an EMI spokesperson told the press. "There's a very well established way to get sampling and [Burton] did not participate."

Burton complied with the EMI order and stopped distribution of the recording. But fans uploaded the album to the Internet where it became a worldwide sensation. Since EMI never pursued Burton after he agreed to stop, he suffered no serious legal consequences. And The Grey Album led to a slew of producing opportunities as well as recognition in *Rolling Stone* and the New York *Times*.

Sampling, however, has not been as kind to other artists. Consider the makers of the film "I Got the Hook-Up," who were sued because a two-second sample (a three-note riff) from George Clinton's "Get Off Your Ass and Jam," (sampled by N.W.A. in their song "100 Miles and Runnin'") appeared in the film. Although many listeners could not even discern the sample in the mix, a federal court ruled that any sampling from a recording amounts to copyright infringement and found the filmmakers liable for infringement and financial penalties. Ouch!

So should you make use of samples from someone else's copyrighted music? How does the average working musician decide what to do?

In a nutshell, you should always seek clearance for use of a recognizable sample when you are signed to a recording contract or when preparing music for a commercial client—for example, for a video game, advertisement, commercially released film, or the like.

If you don't get permission under these circumstances, you could get sued, your record label or client could get sued, and you might not be prevented from distributing your music to the public at all.

As a practical matter, if you're selling recordings only at shows and don't expect to press more than 1,000 copies of a record, you run less risk for uncleared samples, because it's unlikely that the owner of the source recording will ever learn of your samples—and if they do learn of it, they may not be inclined to pursue you unless they sense you have deep pockets (legal slang for people with substantial assets).

However, always keep in mind that if your recording becomes popular and becomes a staple of clubs, a radio hit, or a major download sensation, you'll likely have to deal with the issue of clearance. And unfortunately, using uncleared samples can be dangerous to your financial health. Artists have been forced to pay sums in the range of $100,000 as settlement for the uncleared use of samples (and often must give up substantial music publishing royalties).

You're also probably familiar with the Catch-22 of sample clearance: In order to get a signed sample clearance agreement, you'll have to provide the owners of the sample (a music publisher and record company) with a recording that shows how much of the source you intend to use, and how you intend to use it. So you'll likely be doing your recording first, with no permission. If you then find that you can't get permission, a lot of hard work will have gone to waste. (FYI, in the event that you intend to proceed without clearance, you should be familiar with some legal principles that we'll explain a little later.)

So what should you know about getting permission to use samples?

The process of getting permission from the owners of the sampled music is referred to as "sample clearance." When you sample music from a pop recording, you'll need two clearances: one from the copyright owner of the song, who is usually a music publisher, and the other from the copyright owner of the master tapes, which is usually a record company. In general, clearance is required only if you're planning to make copies of your music and distribute the copies to the public, not for sampling at home. If you're using samples only in your live performance, you probably don't need to bother with clearance unless your act is drawing the type of attention that would awaken a copyright owner as to your use. (In any case, most venues have blanket licenses with performing rights societies such as ASCAP and BMI, and these licenses may cover the sampled music as well.)

The costs for clearance are negotiable, and there are no standard fees. However, as a general rule the music publisher usually wants an up-front "advance"

payment (which, unfortunately, could be anywhere between $5,000 and $10,000) plus a percentage of the song income (anywhere between 15% and 50%). The owner of the master recording will also want an up-front payment (usually at least $1,000) plus a "rollover." A rollover is a payment made when a certain number of copies have been sold. Sometimes, instead of a rollover, the owner of the master may want a portion of future record royalties (although sampling consultants advise against this practice).

Sample rates have become so steep that it's often difficult for small independent labels to acquire clearance. An independent artist with a recording budget of $20,000 may, for example, have to pay $10,000 on up-front payments for two or three samples.

In some ways sample clearance has become easier than it was ten years ago, and in some ways it has become more difficult. Some labels and publishers have begun to make it easier for artists to acquire rights by providing online sample clearance procedures and by permitting the emailing of the proposed use. But a bigger issue—mergers and acquisitions within the music industry—has slowed down the licensing process.

"It's become harder to clear samples," says Cathy Carapella of Diamond Time, Ltd (www.diamondtime.net), a clearance service in New York, "because there are fewer people handling the same amount of requests. People are dropping like flies [in the music business] ... and often there's one person handling the clearances that two or three people used to do. Nowadays, it's just much more difficult to get the attention of a licensing executive."

Find the Copyright Owners

The first step in obtaining permission is to locate the copyright owner(s) of both the song and the master recording. The song and the master recording will often be owned by different entities, and you need permission from both of them. Since it's always easiest to find the music publisher, you should start there. The best way to locate a publisher is through performing rights organizations such as BMI, ASCAP, and SESAC. These groups collect money on behalf of songwriters for radio, TV, and other public performances of songs. (In Canada, the performing rights organization is SOCAN.) You may also be able to obtain similar information from the Harry Fox Agency.

You can locate the key information on the Internet by visiting the performing rights society websites and determining which organization controls rights for the source song. That will lead you to the music publisher.

Some detective work may be required. BMI's searchable database includes more than 20 entries, for instance, for songs titled "Yesterday." If you can't locate the song you're looking for online, try phoning

the performing rights organizations and ask for the song indexing department. Once you have the publisher's name and address, phone or write the publisher to determine if they will grant clearance for the source music. Many publishers, unfortunately, have a policy not to grant permission for sampling.

If the publisher can't lead you to the owner of the master recording, you can check online record stores or the Phonolog directory at your local record shop to find the record company that is currently releasing the source music. Major labels have special departments to handle sample clearance. For example, masters owned by Warner Bros., Elektra, and Atlantic are handled by Warner Special Products. Locating master owners may prove troublesome—record companies may fold or sell their copyrights to other companies. In addition, rights in masters may revert to the original artists after a number of years. In that case, you may have to use the assistance of a sampling consultant. Here are a few tips if you plan to sample:

- **Use a Clearance Expert.** For an hourly fee, sampling consultants can guide you through the clearance process. Consultants like Cathy Carapella of Diamond Time, Ltd. can save you time and money because they're familiar with the procedures, costs, and key people who license rights at the major music publishing and record companies.

- **Plan Ahead.** "The biggest mistakes [in sampling clearance] are not planning far enough ahead and not having enough alternatives if a sample is rejected," says a representative of EMI Music. "Sometimes it can take months to get all of the approvals." Remember, many copyright owners (for example, the Beatles) have a no-sampling policy. If the sample request isn't approved, be prepared to replace the sample with something else. You also need to plan ahead on your end, says Cathy Carapella. Carapella strongly recommends that before beginning the clearance process, "you get all your songwriting info upfront. Really think about who owns what percentage of the new work. I have a couple of deals that have been slowed down because the songwriters still haven't figured out their splits. You have to get that stuff straightened out upfront."

- **Re-Create the Sample.** Some artists have avoided paying part of the sampling clearance fee by re-recording the sampled section. How does this work? Let's say you want to use a six-second sample from "Green Onions." Instead of sampling the original recording, you play the parts yourself and rerecord the music to sound exactly like the original. In that case you have not infringed the master recording. (Due to a quirk

in copyright law, you can infringe a master recording only if you actually copy it—not if you imitate it). You will not need to seek permission from the master owner, and need pay no fees. You will, however, still need to seek permission from the music publisher of "Green Onions."

- **Show Them the Money.** If you're an independent or unsigned artist, you may be able to overcome the "never heard of you" syndrome by offering to make the payment up-front. If you show them that you can write the check to pay the advance, they'll be more inclined to deal with clearance.

- **Find Sample-Friendly Copyright Owners.** Some copyright owners are willing to clear samples—so much so that they encourage the process. Copyright owners of songs by the Average White Band and the Gap Band have in the past, proactively sought to promote their music for sampling.

- **Contact the Artist or Songwriter Directly.** If you run into problems with a music publisher or owner of a master, you may have better luck contacting the artist directly. This works if the artist still has some say or control in what gets cleared. For example, Shirley Manson of Garbage wanted to use the line, "You're the talk of the town," at the end of a song. Lawyers for the band ordered her to drop it, but Shirley called up Chrissie Hynde, who sent the following letter to Garbage's attorneys: "I, Chrissie Hynde, hereby allow the rock band Garbage to sample my songs, my words, and indeed my very ass." (Of course, this works only if the musician or songwriter controls the copyrights—not a third-party music publisher or label.)

- **Try the Creative Commons License.** A newer, more enlightened method of obtaining sampling clearance is available through the Creative Commons, an organization that proposes an alternative to traditional copyright thinking. Musicians can post their music under a Creative Commons license and permit others to take and transform pieces of the music for sampling purposes (but not for advertising). Check out their website (www.creativecommons.org) for more details.

Operating Without Clearance

If you are using an uncleared sample, you can lower your risks by making it unrecognizable, by not using the sample as the groove or hook, and by burying it in the mix. And of course, don't use the title of the source music in the title of your song. Under the copyright law, you may be in the clear in the following situations:

- **If your use of the sample doesn't infringe or is considered inconsequential.** Unfortunately the current state of sampling law is not so clear that we can chart a noninfringing course for you. As noted earlier, a federal court ruled that the use of any sampled recording—even as little as two seconds—was an infringement. Although many legal experts think the ruling went too far and was improper under copyright law (including the Recording Industry Association of America (RIAA), who stated in legal papers that the decision is "unprecedented and unsustainable"), this ruling is law … at least in Michigan, Tennessee, Ohio, and Kentucky where this court has jurisdiction. (In other states, it's not clear if this "zero-tolerance" policy applies.)

Certainly if the master recording clearance is not an issue, you may be permitted to use only certain elements of a song without permission. For example, when the Beastie Boys recorded the song "Pass the Mic," they repeated a six-second sample from a song entitled "Choir," from an album by the award-winning flautist James Newton, Jr. The sample consisted of a three-note pattern, C, D-flat, C. Newton simultaneously sang and played these notes, a method known as vocalization. The Beastie

Boys obtained permission to use the sample from ECM, the label that owned the sound recording copyright, but they did not get permission from Newton, the owner of the musical composition copyright. Newton sued and in 2002, a federal judge ruled that the three-note pattern from Choir was not, by itself, a protectible composition and that permission from Newton was not necessary. In other words, the three-note pattern, even though it included Newton's rare vocalization skills, was not original enough to merit a payment and it was labeled "de minimis" (too small to matter).

- **If your use of the sample qualifies as a fair use.** Fair use is the right to copy a portion of a copyrighted work without permission because your use is for a limited purpose, such as for educational use in a classroom or to comment upon, criticize, or parody the work being sampled. For example, the rap group 2 Live Crew's use of the musical tag and the opening lyric line from Roy Orbison's "Oh Pretty Woman" was considered to be a fair use because it was limited (they used the riff only once) and it was for purposes of parody. (Keep in mind that 2 Live Crew did not include a sample from the Orbison master recording.)

Also, there's a widespread myth in the sampling community that "less than two seconds is fair use." Don't believe it. What a judge and jury will feel is fair use depends on a number of factors other than the length of the sample. Generally, when reviewing fair use questions, courts are looking for three things: (1) that you did not take a substantial amount of the original work; (2) that you transformed the material in some way; and (3) that you did not cause significant financial harm to the copyright owner.

What kind of financial harm might sampling cause? It could cause the loss of income from other artists who might want to use the sample but were discouraged because you sampled it first. Or what you consider a "parody" might be so close to the original that substantial numbers of music lovers buy it *instead* of the original.

In principle, it's good to know these defenses, but the obvious difficulty with all of them is that they are *defenses*. The time you'll use them is when someone is coming after you. There is no predictable way to guarantee that you'll win your court case based on these defenses (assuming you can even afford to hire attorneys to fight the case). Of course, in some cases, this fact can give rise to a form of legal blackmail: The fear of a lawsuit may outweigh any benefits of winning the legal battle, so you may prefer not to use a sample even if the usage would have been ruled permissible.

You'll find yourself on safer legal ground if you seek permission. This is especially true if you're signed to a record label and your record contract puts the burden of sample clearance on your shoulders. Your contract probably contains an indemnity clause, which means that if you and the record company are sued, you must pay the record company's legal costs. Ouch!

Using Samples with Commercial Clients

There's an extra wrinkle if you use a sample for purposes of selling or endorsing a product (for example, in a Volkswagen ad) and the sampled artist is identifiable. In cases like this, your band will need to get the source artist's consent. That's because the ad creates the impression of an endorsement. Without the consent, the source artist could sue for what is known as the violation of the "right of publicity." (The same would be true if you imitated the source artist's voice without sampling it.) So when you use a sample for an advertising agency or other commercial client, be aware that a third type of clearance or "release" may be necessary.

Precleared Samples. What about sample CDs—recordings that contain sounds and riffs specifically sold to be used in samplers? Most sample discs are "precleared," which means that by buying the disc, you're automatically granted permission for music usage without the payment of any further fees. (Note: The permitted use of precleared samples may vary from one disc to another.

Don't assume you can use the sample in whatever way you like: Review the documentation that comes with the CD for any license information. If you find that your purchase of the disc doesn't grant the rights you need, contact the soundware manufacturer to see if you're eligible for a refund.)

Most companies that make sample discs grant the user a "nonexclusive license" to use the samples. A "license" is a grant of permission to do something (for example, use the sample in your composition). "Nonexclusive" means that you're not the only person who can use the samples. All buyers of these sample discs share the right to use them. You're not buying the right to redistribute the samples, however, only the right to use them in musical works.

The fact that the license is nonexclusive can make a difference if you're composing music on behalf of a client —for example, creating music for commercials. The issue is "ownability," says Rick Lyon of New York's Lyon Music, who has scored spots and TV themes for the likes of ABC, MCI, Volvo, and ESPN. "'Ownability' is the holy grail of advertising," says Lyon. "It helps ensure uniqueness in the marketplace. That's why brands work so hard to control the creative elements of their identities. Clients want to be sure that a riff featured in their new campaign isn't going to appear in another spot for someone else. We're talking about the sanctity of brand image, with millions of dollars at stake." Since the composer doesn't own exclusive rights to the precleared sample, he or she will probably be unable to sell the requested rights to the client.

Even with these legal issues aside, the greater concern is whether you're going to aggravate a client. So beware of using a precleared sample as an important element of an ad campaign. Anyone who buys the same sample disc has the potential to dilute your campaign and may raise legal and business risks for you.

Recording a Nonband Member's Songs

If your band is recording a song that is written by a nonband member (in other words, a cover—such as a new version of Michael Jackson's "Thriller"), the law requires that your band, or the company releasing your record, obtain what's known as a compulsory license. Under copyright law, you do not have to "ask" for a compulsory license to cover a song. Instead, you can obtain one simply by following certain procedures established in the Copyright Act. These procedures are discussed in detail in Chapter 12. If, on the other hand, the song you are covering has never been released (for example, it was written by a friend), there is a different licensing procedure. This is also discussed in Chapter 12.

Musician Release Agreement

In this section we'll explain how to put together a musician release agreement. A sample appears below. This is a simple release that permits you to use a nonband musician's performance on your recording. Band members would not need to sign this release.

 This agreement is included on the forms CD in the back of this book.

Below, we explain the provisions in the musician release agreement.

Introduction

In the introductory section, put the name of your band partnership if it owns your recordings. If you created a separate company for the release of your recordings (such as "Our Band's Records"), list that name. If the name doesn't make it clear what kind of business form it is (for example, "The Spyder Partnership"), then indicate the business form (for example, "Centipede, a general partnership"). Insert the name of the musician.

Rights

List the songs on which the musician played on your recording.

Payment

Insert the amount of the payment. If there is no payment, indicate $1.

Credit

Indicate the type of credit the musician will get on the album information. For example, "Saxophone: S. Murphy." If the musician is under an exclusive recording agreement with a record company, you will need to find out if the musician is permitted to perform on other people's recordings. If so, there may be a special credit required, such as "S. Murphy appears courtesy of Pretend Records."

Mediation; Arbitration

Under this clause, if a dispute arises the parties agree to try to resolve it through mediation or, if that fails, binding arbitration, rather than immediately going to court. Mediation can save money in legal fees and often produces better results than court verdicts. Enter the location where you agree to mediate and arbitrate (most likely the city where you all live).

General

Most of the following provisions are standard contractual provisions referred to as boilerplate. In the blank space, insert the state (or province, in the case of Canadian bands) of residence for the band partners. In the event of a dispute, this determines which state law will govern the arbitration or lawsuit.

Signatures

Only one member of your band needs to sign the agreement. Enter the band business name, the name of which band member is signing, and the band member's title (usually "Partner"). That band member should sign and date the form. Have the musician enter his or her address, and sign and date the form.

Musician Release Agreement

This Musician Release Agreement (the "Agreement") is made between _____
("Band") and _____ ("Musician").

Rights

The Band has recorded Musician's performance in conjunction with a Band recording
under the titles _____. In consideration of the
payments provided in this Agreement, Musician assigns all rights in the performance to the
Band and its assigns or licensees.

Payment

Band will pay Musician $_____.

Credit (*Check if applicable and fill in blank.*)

○ Musician is entitled to the following credit:

_____.

Mediation; Arbitration

If a dispute arises under this Agreement, the parties agree first to try to resolve the dispute
with the help of a mutually agreed-on mediator in _____. Any
costs and fees other than attorney fees will be shared equally by the parties. If it proves
impossible to arrive at a mutually satisfactory solution in a reasonable time, the parties
agree to submit the dispute to binding arbitration in the same city or region, conducted
on a confidential basis pursuant to the Commercial Arbitration Rules of the American
Arbitration Association.

General

Nothing contained in this Agreement is deemed to constitute either Band or Musician a
partner or employee of the other party. This Agreement is governed by and interpreted in
accordance with the laws of _____.

Band Partnership Name _____

Band Partner Name & Title _____

Band Partner Signature _____

Address _____

_____

Date _____

Musician Name _____

Musician Signature _____

Address _____

_____

Date _____

License for Use of Sampled Music From Record Company

As we explained above, the use of a recognizable digital sample can create legal problems for a band and its record company. Although the law is still evolving on this issue, you should presume that when you use a portion of someone's music without authorization, you have violated copyright law and may be subject to a lawsuit. For that reason, many bands and record companies have samples "cleared" by obtaining permission from the owners of the sample. This clearance is usually referred to as a license. The person who owns the rights is the licensor, and the person seeking to use the sample is the licensee.

We've provided two clearance agreements: one to give to the owner of the recorded music (the record company), and the other to give to the owner of the song (the music publisher). Sometimes the record company controls the publishing rights and you can clear everything with only one agreement. Below we provide an explanation of the various provisions of the agreement, titled "Agreement With Record Company for Use of Master Recording Sample." A sample appears below.

 This agreement is included on the forms CD in the back of this book.

Introduction

This section defines the parties. Insert the name of your band partnership, your record company, or whoever is responsible for paying for the sample usage. In the second blank, insert the name of the record company that owns the sample.

Master Recording and New Recording

These sections establish the parties' respective rights to the original recording and the new recording. Insert the name of the song or track that has been sampled in the first blank. In the next blank, insert the name of the artist who originally performed the version of the song that you want to sample. In the "New Recordings" section, insert the name of your band's song that uses the sample, and in the second blank insert the name of your band.

Approved Usage

This establishes that your band cannot create another version that uses more of the original sample than in the version you first furnished to the owner of the sample.

Grant of Rights

This provision is what allows you to use the sample on recordings and for promotional videos. The statement "This grant is binding on Licensee's assigns and sublicensees" means that if your band gets a record deal, you can still use the sample, but the record company will be bound to the terms of the license.

Territory

Insert the World, United States, or Canada, or whatever region you have agreed on. It would be best for your band to obtain worldwide rights. However, if the company you are dealing with only has rights in certain countries, then your agreement will be limited to that "territory," and if you intend to sell in other territories you will have to acquire rights there as well.

Payments

In the early days of sampling, many companies obtained worldwide rights for a flat fee. Today, payments for use of rights may range from $500 to $5,000 per 100,000 copies of your recording. These amounts often depend on the amount of the sample and its relative importance in your band's song.

Copyright Registration

This provision is optional, although many sample owners insist on it. It is not a burdensome request. When applying for copyright for your recording, you must indicate that you are using a sample.

Credit

This provision is optional, and not all companies insist on receiving a credit.

Warranties

This is simply a legal promise that the person you are dealing with owns the recording.

Commercial Release

Usually the record company wants a copy of your recording to verify the sample usage.

Mediation; Arbitration

This provision provides a less expensive method of resolving disputes than filing a lawsuit. (See the sidebar in Chapter 2 for an explanation of mediation and arbitration.) We recommend that you use this provision in order to help avoid an expensive lawsuit.

We suggest that you choose the county, province, or city in which the band resides for arbitration. If all the members do not reside in one area, choose a place that is convenient. Enter your location of choice in the blank.

In some states there are organizations that specialize in arbitration for people in the arts, such as California Lawyers for the Arts (CLA) and, in New York, Volunteer Lawyers for the Arts (VLA). You can substitute the rules of such an organization for those of the American Arbitration Association in your agreement. If your band is based in Canada, you can still use the AAA's rules, as they perform arbitration in all major Canadian cities. (For more information on the AAA, see Chapter 17.) Check one of the choices or delete the unwanted alternative.

General

The following provisions are standard contractual provisions referred to as boilerplate. Boilerplate provisions are explained in Chapter 2.

In the blank space, insert the state (or province, in the case of Canadian bands) of residence for the band partners. In the event of a dispute, this determines which state law will govern the arbitration or lawsuit.

Signatures

Only one member of your band needs to sign the agreement. Enter the band business name, the name of the band member who is signing, and the band member's title (usually "Partner"). That band member should sign and date the form. The record company representative should do the same.

Agreement With Record Company for Use of Master Recording Sample

Introduction

This Agreement is between_____ ("Licensee")
and _____ ("Licensor").

Master Recording

Licensor owns all rights in a recording entitled _____ (the
"Master Recording") as performed by _____.

New Recording

Licensee intends to use a portion of the Master Recording (the "Sample") in a recorded
composition entitled _____ (the "New Recording"), as performed by
_____.

Approved Usage

Licensee agrees that the amount of the Sample usage will not exceed that in the copy of
the New Recording furnished to Licensor ("the Approved Usage").

Grant of Rights

Licensor grants to Licensee the nonexclusive right to use, reproduce, and sell the Sample
as included in the New Recording. Licensee may remix, edit, or create new derivative
versions of the New Recording, but in no event will Licensee's usage exceed the Approved
Usage. This grant of rights is for the full length of copyright of the New Recording.
Licensor also grants to Licensee and its assigns the right to include and exploit the Sample
in the Approved Usage for digital Internet usage, video clips, and audiovisual uses, all
solely for advertising and promoting the sale of the New Recording. This grant is binding
on Licensee's assigns and sublicensees. Licensor retains all rights other than those granted
in this Agreement.

Territory

The rights granted in this Agreement are for use in _____ (the
"Territory").

Other Uses

In the event that the Licensee intends to use the Sample for any purposes other than those
stated in this Agreement, Licensor agrees to negotiate those licenses in good faith.

Payments

Licensee will pay Licensor as follows. Payments based on unit sales shall be due regardless of the configuration of the New Recording (that is, compact disc, cassette, and so on) or whether released by Licensee or Licensee's affiliates or sublicensees. Any payments provided in this Agreement are contingent on the embodiment of the Original Recording within the New Recording. That is, if the Original Recording is not included, no payment is due to Licensor.

(Choose one and fill in the blank.)

○ **Flat Fee.** Licensee will pay Licensor a flat fee of $_____ on execution of this Agreement as full payment for all rights granted.

○ **Flat Rate.** Licensee will pay Licensor a flat rate of $_____ per 100,000 units of the New Recording manufactured and distributed. Licensee agrees to pay Licensor a recoupable advance of $_____ for the first 100,000 units on execution of this Agreement.

○ **Royalties and Advance.** Licensee agrees to pay Licensor a royalty rate of $_____ per each copy of the New Recording manufactured and distributed. Licensee agrees to pay Licensor a recoupable mechanical royalty advance of $_____ on execution of this Agreement.

Licensee will pay Licensor within 30 days after the end of each quarter. Licensee will also furnish an accurate statement of sales of Records during that quarter. Licensor will have the right to inspect Licensee's books on reasonable notice.

Copyright Registration

If the New Recording is registered for a sound recording copyright, the Master Recording will be identified in space six of the Form SR as a preexisting work, and a copy of the application will be sent to Licensor.

Credit

(Check if applicable and fill in blanks.)

○ All releases of the Recording must contain the following statement: "Contains portions of _____ used by permission of _____. All rights reserved."

Warranties

Licensor warrants that it has the power to enter into and grant the rights in this Agreement.

Commercial Release

Licensee will furnish Licensor with two copies of any compact disc, single, or cassette (or any other configuration) of the New Recording within two weeks of its commercial release.

Mediation; Arbitration

If a dispute arises under this Agreement, the parties agree to first try to resolve the dispute with the help of a mutually agreed-on mediator in _____.
Any costs and fees other than attorney fees will be shared equally by the parties. If it is impossible to arrive at a mutually satisfactory solution within a reasonable time, the parties agree to submit the dispute to binding arbitration in the same city or region, conducted on a confidential basis under:

O the Commercial Arbitration Rules of the American Arbitration Association, or

O the rules of _____.

Any decision or award as a result of arbitration will include the assessment of costs, expenses, and reasonable attorney's fees and a written determination by the arbitrators. Absent an agreement to the contrary, arbitration will be conducted by an arbitrator experienced in music industry law. An award of arbitration is final and binding on the Band Partners and may be confirmed in a court of competent jurisdiction. The prevailing party has the right to collect from the other party its reasonable costs and attorney fees incurred in enforcing this agreement.

General

Nothing contained in this Agreement makes either Licensee or Licensor a partner or employee of the other party. This Agreement expresses the complete understanding of the parties and may not be amended except in a writing signed by both parties. If a court finds any provision of this Agreement invalid or unenforceable, the remainder of this Agreement will be interpreted to carry out the intent of the parties. This Agreement is governed by and interpreted in accordance with the laws of _____.
Notices required under this Agreement can be sent to Band at the address provided below.

Licensee

Name of Licensee _____

Licensee Representative Signature _____

Licensee Representative Name & Title _____

Address _____

Date _____

Licensor

Name of Licensor _____

Licensor Representative Signature _____

Licensor Representative Name & Title _____

Address _____

Date _____

License for Use of Sampled Music From Music Publisher

As we explained in Section C, above, if your band uses a sample, you must obtain the permission of the record company and the music publisher that owns the song. Below is an explanation for the provisions of an agreement with the music publisher. A sample appears below.

 This agreement is included on the forms CD in the back of this book.

Introduction

This section defines the parties. Insert the name of your band partnership, your record company, or whoever is responsible for paying for the sample usage. In the second blank, insert name of the music publisher that owns the sample.

Original Composition and New Composition

These sections establish the parties' respective rights to the original recording and the new recording. Insert the name of the song that has been sampled in the first blank. In the next blank, insert the name of the artist who originally performed the song being sampled. In the "New Composition" section, insert the name of your band's song that uses the sample and, in the second blank, insert the name of your band.

Approved Usage

This establishes that your band cannot create another version that uses more of the original sample than in the version you first furnished to the owner of the sample.

Grant of Rights

This provision is what allows you to use the sample on recordings and for promotional videos. The statement "This grant is binding on Licensee's assigns and sublicensees" means that if your band gets a record deal, you can still use the sample, but the record company will be bound to the terms of the license.

Territory

Insert the territory (for example, "the world"). It would be best for your band to obtain worldwide rights. However, if the publishing company you are dealing with has rights only in certain countries, then your agreement will be limited to that "territory," and if you intend to sell in other territories you will have to acquire publishing rights there, as well.

Mechanical Income

If you are unfamiliar with mechanical royalty payments, review Chapter 8. It is often preferable to acquire all rights for a flat fee, because there are no further payments to make. However, it may be a good thing to base the payments on a royalty, because that way you may have to pay more than the advance only if the song is a hit. Music publishers often seek anywhere from 15% to 50% of the music publishing income. That is, the owner of the sampled song receives 15% to 50% of all the money earned by the song. It is reported, for example, that Sting received at least half the royalties for the use of his sample at the end of the Dire Straits song "Money for Nothing," and the same percentage or more for the Puff Daddy song "I'll Be Missing You."

Performance Income

If you are unfamiliar with performance royalty payments, review Chapter 8. The percentage payments for performance royalties are always the same as for the mechanical income (above). That is, if the owner of the sampled song is getting 33% of the mechanical income, then the owner would get the same percentage of the publishing and writing income from the performance royalties.

EXAMPLE: Happy Publishing owns "You Conquered My World," written by Sasha and Andrea Rose. The publisher has negotiated for 25% of the mechanical income. The publisher has negotiated for the same performance royalty, and each writer would get 12.5% of the writer's share of the performance royalties.

Credit

This provision is optional, and not all companies insist on receiving a credit.

Copyright Registration

This provision is optional, although many sample owners insist on it. It is not a burdensome request. When applying for copyright for your song, you must indicate that you are using a sample.

Warranties

This is simply a legal promise that the person you are dealing with owns the recording.

Commercial Release

Usually the music publisher wants a copy of your recording to verify the sample usage.

Mediation; Arbitration

This provision provides a less expensive method of resolving disputes than filing a lawsuit. (See the sidebar in Chapter 2 for an explanation of mediation.) We recommend that you use this provision in order to help avoid an expensive lawsuit.

We suggest that you choose the county, province, or city in which the band resides for arbitration. If all the members do not reside in one area, choose a place that is convenient. Enter your location of choice in the blank.

In some states there are organizations that specialize in arbitration for people in the arts, such as California Lawyers for the Arts (CLA) and, in New York, Volunteer Lawyers for the Arts (VLA). You can substitute the rules of such an organization for those of the American Arbitration Association in your Agreement. If your band is based in Canada, you can still use the AAA's rules, as they perform arbitration in all major Canadian cities. (For more information on the AAA, see Chapter 17.) Check one of the choices, or delete the unwanted alternative.

General

The following provisions are standard contractual provisions referred to as boilerplate. Boilerplate provisions are explained in Chapter 2.

In the blank space, insert the state (or province, in the case of Canadian bands) of residence for the band partners. In the event of a dispute, this determines which state law will govern the arbitration or lawsuit.

Signatures

Only one member of your band needs to sign the agreement. Enter the band business name, the name of the band member who is signing, and the band member's title (usually "Partner"). That band member should sign and date the form. The music publishing company representative should do the same.

Agreement With Music Publisher for Use of Song Sample

Introduction

This Agreement is between _____
("Licensee") and _____ ("Licensor").

Original Composition

Licensor is the owner of an original composition _____
(the "Original Composition").

New Composition

Licensee intends to use a portion of the Original Composition in a new composition
entitled _____ the "New Composition"), as
performed by _____ (the "Artist"). The
New Composition will appear on Artist's recording (the "Recording").

Approved Usage

Licensee agrees that the amount of the Original Composition usage will not exceed that in
the copy of the New Composition furnished to Licensor ("Approved Usage").

Grant of Rights

Licensor grants to Licensee the nonexclusive right to use, reproduce, and sell the Original
Composition as included within the New Composition. Licensee may remix, edit, or
create new derivative versions of the New Composition, but Licensee's usage cannot
exceed the Approved Usage. This grant of rights lasts for the full length of copyright of
the New Composition. Licensor also grants to Licensee and its assigns the right to include
and exploit the Original Composition in the Approved Usage for Internet usage, video
clips, and audiovisual uses, all solely for advertising and promoting the sale of the New
Composition. This grant is binding on Licensee's assigns and sublicensees. Licensor retains
all rights other than those granted in this Agreement.

Territory

The rights granted under this Agreement cover _____ (the "Territory").

Other Uses

In the event that the Licensee intends to use portions of the Original Composition for any other purposes (other than those stated in this Agreement), Licensor agrees to negotiate those licenses in good faith.

Mechanical Income

Licensee will pay Licensor as follows. Payments based on unit sales will be due regardless of the configuration of the Recording (that is, compact disc, cassette, and so on) or whether released by Licensee or Licensee's affiliates or sublicensees. Any payments provided in this Agreement are contingent on the embodiment of the Original Composition within the New Composition. That is, if the Original Composition is not included within the Recording, no payment is due to Licensor. Licensee will pay Licensor as follows:

(Select one and fill in blanks.)

○ **Flat Fee.** Licensee will pay Licensor a flat fee of $_____ on execution of this Agreement as full payment for all rights granted.

○ **Royalties and Advance.** Licensee agrees to pay Licensor a reduced mechanical royalty rate of _____% of the statutory rate. Licensee agrees to pay Licensor a recoupable mechanical royalty advance of $_____ on execution of this Agreement. Licensee will pay Licensor within 30 days after the end of each quarter. Licensee will also furnish an accurate statement of sales of Records during that quarter. Licensor has the right to inspect Licensee's books on reasonable notice.

Performance Income

(Check and fill in blanks if applicable.)

○ The Recording must be cleared with the appropriate performance society (that is, BMI, ASCAP, SOCAN, and so on), and the clearances must state that the Recording includes the Original Composition. Licensor will be credited with _____% of the Licensor Income, and the writers of the Original Composition _____

_____

will be credited with a total of _____% of the Writer's Income.

Credit

(Check and fill in blanks if applicable.)

O All releases of the Recording will contain the following statement: "Contains portions of _____ used by permission of _____. All rights reserved."

Copyright Registration

In the event that the New Composition is registered for copyright, the Original Composition must be identified in space six of the Form PA as a preexisting work, and a copy of the application must be sent to Licensor.

Warranties

Licensor warrants that it has the power to enter into and grant the rights in this Agreement.

Commercial Release

Licensee will furnish Licensor with two copies of any compact disc, single, or cassette (or any other configuration) of the Recording within two weeks of its commercial release.

Mediation; Arbitration

If a dispute arises under this Agreement, the parties agree to first try to resolve the dispute with the help of a mutually agreed-on mediator in _____ .
Any costs and fees other than attorney fees will be shared equally by the parties. If it is impossible to arrive at a mutually satisfactory solution within a reasonable time, the parties agree to submit the dispute to binding arbitration in the same city or region, conducted on a confidential basis under:

O the Commercial Arbitration Rules of the American Arbitration Association, or

O the rules of _____ .

Any decision or award as a result of arbitration will include the assessment of costs, expenses, and reasonable attorney's fees and a written determination of the arbitrators. Absent an agreement to the contrary, arbitration will be conducted by an arbitrator experienced in music industry law. An award of arbitration is final and binding on the Band Partners and may be confirmed in a court of competent jurisdiction. The prevailing party has the right to collect from the other party its reasonable costs and attorney fees incurred in enforcing this Agreement.

General

Nothing contained in this Agreement makes either Licensee or Licensor a partner, joint venturer, or employee of the other party for any purpose. This Agreement may not be amended except in a writing signed by both parties. No waiver by either party of any right can be construed as a waiver of any other right. If a court finds any provision of this Agreement invalid or unenforceable as applied to any circumstance, the remainder of this Agreement will be interpreted to carry out the intent of the parties. This Agreement is governed by and interpreted under the laws of the State of _____.

This Agreement expresses the complete understanding of the parties and supersedes all prior proposals, agreements, representations, and understandings. Notices required under this Agreement can be sent to the parties at the addresses provided below. In the event of any dispute arising from or related to this Agreement, the prevailing party is entitled to attorney's fees.

Licensee

Licensee Name _____

Licensee Representative Name & Title _____

Licensee Representative Signature _____

Address _____

Date _____

Licensor

Name of Licensor _____

Licensor Representative Name & Title _____

Licensor Representative Signature _____

Address _____

Date _____

Budgeting for Recording

Bands run into problems in the recording studio because they do not budget realistically. Suddenly the money's run out, and the recording or mixing is incomplete. To avoid this "recording interruptus" syndrome, you need to prepare a budget (see below) and to follow some of the tips provided below.

To avoid financial problems in the studio, your band needs three things: a realistic budget, a person to watch the clock so that the budget is enforced, and techniques to get the most of each dollar spent in the studio.

- **Budget realistically.** If you're making a live recording with little or no overdubs, expect to spend two to three hours for setup and at least an hour per song for recording. Expect to spend at least an hour or more mixing each live song. If you're making a multitracked recording with overdubbing, expect to spend three to five hours per song and the same amount of time for mixing. As a general rule, recording and mixing always take longer than expected. As a buffer, many bands add an hour or two when budgeting. Automated mixing saves time, money, and aggravation. Apply these estimates to your budget.
- **Get a good rate.** Shop around for studios and recording deals. Ask other bands for recommendations.

If you're doing multitracking and overdubbing, consider using different studios for different tasks: for example, one for recording and another for mixing. Ask about block rates (a reduced rate when you buy a chunk of hours up front) and after-hours rates. Find out if the studio charges for setup time or charges for the use of pianos or other studio equipment.

- **Be prepared.** Make demos before your recording session and play them for the engineer. Know your tracks! Decide on the system for recording before your first session (for example, start with drums and bass). Try to do all of the recording of one instrument or all of the vocals at one session (it saves setup time). If you're using a click track (a metronome heard in headphones), have the drummer practice with a metronome ahead of time. Bring in printed lyric sheets, and write out each line of the chorus (don't simply state "chorus"). The engineer will use these in conjunction with the track sheets, so the clearer the sheets, the easier the recording and mixing. Pay attention to playback tracking numbers. That way, when you have a question, the engineer can quickly find the trouble spot instead of searching. Don't waste time making copies of each rough mix for every band member. Get one mix on CD and duplicate it at home. Make sure all of your band equipment is working.

- **Buy your own recording supplies.** Studios usually charge more than stores for blank tape, CD-Rs, DVDs, and other supplies. To save money, buy your supplies through national wholesalers such as Tapeonline (www.tapeonline.com), Amazon (www.amazon.com), or National Recording Supplies (www.tapes .com).

Sample Recording Budget

The recording budget will vary from project to project, but the experience of sitting down and estimating the costs is always the same. As realistically as possible, you need to determine how many hours your band will spend recording and mixing, and then you need to estimate all of the related costs (tape, other musician fees, and so on). This process prepares you for working with independent and major label record companies, who always establish financial limits on spending.

Below is a budget for a four-song demo done at a small production studio. In our sample budget, there will be no producer fee (the band is producing the recording with the help of the engineer). In addition, the band is bringing in a saxophone player (Musician #1) to overdub some parts. Below are explanations for each item. We have also included a blank form.

Preproduction/Rehearsal

Some studios have preproduction or rehearsal facilities. This budget includes ten hours of preproduction to prepare drum and sound samples that will be added into the mixes.

Recording

The band plans to spend 2.5 hours recording each song. Most of the recording will be live (that is, the band members will play at the same time). The band expects to overdub the vocals and some instruments.

Mixing

Most songs require as much time to mix as to record, and this band has budgeted accordingly.

Engineer

Many studios include the engineer's time within the studio rate. However, this studio bills the engineer separately.

Producer

There is no producer on this recording.

Musician

An outside musician (at $25 an hour) will add saxophone, flute, and clarinet.

Equipment Rental

A Leslie organ was rented for eight hours.

Two-Inch Tape

Two-inch tape is used at some 16- and 24-track studios. Expect to pay $100 to $150 per reel. One reel can hold 15 to 30 minutes of music depending on the speed of the tape machine.

External Hard Drive

Most recording studios accomplish some (or all) of their recording using computer software such as *ProTools* or *Digital Performer*. You may have to provide an external hard drive to store your recording at the studio. Expect to pay $150 to $250 depending on the size of the drive.

DAT Tape

DAT tape is sometimes used for mixdowns. Expect to pay $7 to $10 per DAT if you buy from a wholesaler.

CD-Rs

Band members want mixes on CD-Rs. Expect to pay approximately 40 cents per disc from a national wholesaler.

Gas

If the drive to the studio is more than an hour, you should consider budgeting gas money.

Hotels

Some budgets include hotel rooms for session musicians or producers.

Food

This budget won't include all of the food for three days of recording, but it does include four take-out meals (sandwiches and soda) at $20 apiece. Most bands don't serve food, but if you can afford it, providing a small spread has a positive effect on the band and engineer.

10% Overrun

No matter how accurately your band estimates its costs, the total often turns out to be higher than expected. The purpose of the "overrun" (usually 10% of the total) is to cover these additional costs.

Estimated Total

This is the final estimate. Now is a good time to also estimate additional costs such as duplication and mechanical royalty payments (see Chapter 12).

 The following form is included on the forms CD in the back of this book.

Estimated Recording Costs for Four-Song Demo

Hourly Costs	Hours	Rate	Amount
Preproduction/Rehearsal	10	$15	$150.00
Recording	10	35	350.00
Mixing	10	35	350.00
Engineer	20	10	200.00
Producer			
Musician #1	2	25	50.00
Musician #2			
Equipment/Inst. Rental #1	8	10	80.00
Equipment/Inst. Rental #2			
		Total Hourly Costs:	**$1,180.00**

Tape Costs	Units	Unit Cost	Amount
Two-inch Recording Tape			
External Hard Drive	1	$180	$180.00
DAT tape	4	8.00	32.00
CD-Rs	20	.50	10.00
		Total Tape Costs:	**$222.00**

Travel, Lodging & Food Costs			
Gas			
Hotels			
Food	4	$20	$80.00
		Total Travel, Lodging & Food Costs:	**$80.00**

	Subtotal	**$1,397.00**
	10% Overrun	**$139.70**
	Estimated TOTAL	**$1,536.70**

Recording Budget Form

Hourly Costs	Hours	Rate	Amount
Preproduction/Rehearsal			
Recording			
Mixing			
Engineer			
Producer			
Musician #1			
Musician #2			
Equipment/Inst. Rental #1			
Equipment/Inst. Rental #2			

Total Hourly Costs: $_____

Tape Costs	Units	Unit Cost	Amount
Two-inch Recording Tape			
External Hard Drive			
DAT tape			
CD-Rs			

Total Tape Costs: $_____

Travel, Loding & Food Costs			
Gas			
Hotels			
Food			

Total Travel, Lodging & Food Costs: $_____

Subtotal $_____

10% Overrun $_____

Estimated TOTAL $_____

Choosing a Recording Studio

If your band has not had much experience with recording, then you should review some of the following suggestions for choosing a studio and for saving time and money in the session.

Types of Studios

Below are some of the common types of recording studios:

- Project studios that are used primarily for preproduction (preparing drum and sequenced tracks) and for mixing electronic and sampled music. These studios usually do not have a recording room, just a control room. Expect to pay $25 to $100 an hour.
- Mid-sized studios that are suitable for bands who want more multitracking and overdubbing capability. Expect to pay $25 to $50 an hour.
- 24- to 64-track studios that feature extensive sound processing and editing gear. Expect to pay $75 to $200 an hour.
- "Mobile Direct to two-track" studios that will record your band in performance and simultaneously mix down to a master recording. Expect to pay $25 to $100 an hour.

What's Important When Choosing a Studio?

Here are some tips:

- **The "feel" of the studio.** According to Craig Leon (producer for the Ramones, Blondie, and Front 242), the most important factor is the feel of the studio. "Is the studio too sterile? Too posh? You have to make sure the rooms feel comfortable. This is where you'll be living while you make your music, whether it's for three hours or three months. If you are a loud band, there has to be enough space to carry the power and energy of your performance. If you work with a lot of samplers and sound modules, the control room has to be large enough for your equipment."
- **Choice of engineer.** An engineer manages the technical details of the recording such as mike placement, track sheets, and the mixing board. "A great engineer can get a good sound out of almost any equipment," says Leon. The studio manager can help your band choose an engineer best suited for your style and studio experience.
- **Lounge or kitchen.** A studio with a lounge or kitchen area is a priority, because it can relieve tension and boredom. "It's not important for everyone to be in the control room

all the time," says Leon, "and you'd be surprised how fresh something sounds if you step away from it for a few minutes." A kitchen can also save money on food if the band doesn't have to go out for lunch and dinner.

- **Quality of microphones.** A microphone is to recording like a camera is to filmmaking—the better the quality, the better the result. "Within the budget," says Leon, "the band should go to the studio that has the best mikes available."

- **Familiarity with software applications.** Almost all studios are now using some combination of software and hard-disk editing. Generally, transferring or converting audio files from the studio to your home recording situation is easy. However, there may be some instances—for example, when plug-ins work only with certain programs—that you may want to match the studio's software with software that your band uses.

- **Outboard gear.** Outboard gear is used to process the recording, adding effects such as reverb, delay, or equalization. It's usually not that important for bands who make live or "organic" recordings. "The important thing, especially on a demo," says Leon, "is to get the feel and sound of the song and the band

across. Usually, the more gloss on the recording, the more distracting."

- **Number of tracks.** Don't choose a studio solely based on the number of tracks. If your band is recording live, you can make a great demo using eight tracks. Multitracking and overdubbing can create great demos with 16 tracks.

What About DIY (Do It Yourself) Recording?

The process has become so inexpensive that it's led to the demise of many small studios across the country. A typical setup might include several computers, digital editing software, a digital-to-analog converter, a 16- or 24- track mixer, and microphones. Some DIY bands split the recording and mixing duties between home studio and professional studio, by recording tracks at home and mixing at a studio or vice versa. For more on home recording, check out publications such as *Electronic Musician* or *Mix Magazine*.

When Band Arguments Disrupt the Recording Session

If band members are arguing, the final recording will often reflect an "uptight" session. To avoid this problem, consider the following suggestions:

- **Avoid disputes while the meter is running.** If the band is having an argument, move to another song and resolve the dispute when you're not on studio time.

- **Fix it: Don't argue about it.** If one band member wants to rerecord something and another doesn't, it's usually faster to fix it than to discuss fixing it.

- **See the big picture, not just individual parts.** According to producer Craig Leon, one of the major sources of arguments is that band members are more concerned with their individual part or performance than with working together as a whole for the entire sound and feel of the record.

Somehow, you need to focus the band into the same team mentality that is exhibited on stage.

- **Don't bring friends into the studio.** Besides getting bored quickly, friends distract from the work and often lead to arguments.

- **Don't burn out.** Don't book an eight-hour session unless you're sure your ears can concentrate. If you do have long sessions, make sure you eat a decent meal. Overwork, hunger, and lack of concentration are leading causes of arguments. Book your sessions so that there is ample time in between for the band to listen to rough mixes. Avoid listening to playbacks at high volume; it will tire your ears and reduce concentration.

The Sound Recording Copyright

In Chapter 7, we discussed filing a copyright application (known as Form PA) to protect your songs. In this section, we discuss copyright protection for your sound recordings, which is different from your song copyrights. The primary purpose of a sound recording copyright is to protect against bootlegging (the unauthorized copying of your recording) and unauthorized sampling (using a portion of your recording). Generally, only record companies register sound recording copyrights, because they are concerned with bootlegging and sampling. If your band is selling its own recordings and pressing only 1,000 to 2,000 copies, you probably don't need to bother.

Sound recording copyright applications are made with Form SR. You can obtain copies of this form by writing to the Copyright Office or downloading a copy from the Copyright Office website. For more information about contacting the Copyright Office, see Chapter 17.

In addition to the Form SR and application fee ($45), you must furnish the Copyright Office with two copies of your recording. The Copyright Office requests the best version available (for example, a compact disc is preferable to a cassette recording).

If your band partnership owns the copyrights to all of the songs (see Chapter 8) and if the band partnership also owns the recording, there is a method to register both song copyrights and sound recording copyright at one time. You would use a Form SR and in Space 2 of the form (nature of authorship) indicate "music and performance" or "music, words, performance." Special instructions for this type of application are also available in Circulars 56 and 56a, which are available from the Copyright Office website.

Canadian Copyright Law: Registration of Musical Contrivances

The principles of U.S. copyright law are very similar to Canadian copyright law. For example, you do not need to register your sound recording to obtain copyright protection in Canada: It is granted on creation of the work. As a general rule, you can apply most of the principles in this chapter to recordings by Canadian citizens. One difference is in the terminology, however. In Canada, sound recordings are referred to as "musical contrivances."

In many ways, the Canadian copyright application process is easier than the U.S. system. For one thing, the Canadian Application for Registration of Copyright is simpler and shorter. It's so simple that you may not even need any instructions. If you do need assistance, you can obtain instructions from the Canadian Copyright Office, the address of which is provided below. Unlike U.S. copyright law, you can pay your application fee with your Visa or MasterCard.

For more information about Canadian copyright law, contact the Copyright Office at:

Canadian Intellectual Property Office (CIPO)
Industry Canada
50 Victoria Street
Place du Portage, Phase I
Hull, Quebec
K1A OC9
819-997-1936
Fax 819-953-7620

The CIPO website (http://cipo.gc.ca) is also extremely helpful, because you can download circulars about various copyright subjects as well as copyright applications and forms. Circular 2, Musical Works and Mechanical Contrivances, is particularly helpful.

Chapter 12

Duplication: Manufacturing Your Recordings

In the previous chapter, we provided information about recording your band's music. This chapter deals with the duplicating and manufacturing process that comes after you've finished recording your music. We are devoting a separate chapter to duplication because this process has its own legal and practical implications. For example, when you make copies of your recording (such as CDs or digital downloads), you are obligated under copyright law to pay a mechanical royalty to the owner of every song on the recording. Obviously, this won't be an issue if your band owns all the rights to the songs. But if you are covering another artist's material, you must obtain a compulsory license and pay the appropriate royalties. This chapter explains how to use a compulsory license and what royalties will be due. This chapter also reviews practical issues in the duplication process, such as how to deal with manufacturing problems and defective products.

Paying for the Right to Duplicate Songs

Under copyright law, when you duplicate recordings (that is, make compact discs, vinyl records, or digital downloads), you are making "copies" of the songs on those recordings. Unless you have permission of the owners of the song and you pay mechanical royalties, your duplication

is illegal. (For general information on copyright issues, including compulsory licenses and mechanical royalties, see Chapter 7.)

Compulsory Licenses

By law, a publisher *must* permit you to record any song that has previously been recorded and released to the public. In fact, there is a simple legal procedure for obtaining a license for this purpose—called a compulsory license— that doesn't even involve the publisher. In other words, you do not need to ask for permission for a compulsory license. You'll automatically get one when you send a Notice of Intention to Obtain Compulsory License to the copyright owner (usually the music publisher) at least 30 days prior to distributing the recordings, and then pay mechanical royalties to the publisher. A sample compulsory license notice appears below. It's also possible to acquire a compulsory license for limited duplication of CDs and digital phonorecord deliveries (DPDs) online via the Harry Fox website (www. harryfox.com).

Compulsory licenses apply only to songs that have already been released to the public on a sound recording such as a CD or record. You cannot use a compulsory license if your recording will be the first one to be sold to the public. In other words, if the songwriters never recorded their song, or if it was played on TV or in a movie but never released on a sound recording, you cannot use the compulsory license. Instead you'll have to seek authorization from the song owners. We provide a form for obtaining authorization for a first-time use.

Finally, your band cannot use a compulsory license if you change the basic melody or fundamental character of the song. For example, your singer cannot alter a song's lyrics without permission.

Mechanical Royalties

Mechanical royalties are payments to a song owner for the right to make copies of a song. These payments are made by your record company or, if you have no record company, by your band. The mechanical royalty rate is set by the government (which is why it is also called the "statutory rate"), and it rises every few years. At the time of printing of this book (September 2006), the statutory rate is $.091 per song. So if your band recorded a version of Alanis Morisette's "Ironic" and pressed 1,000 copies, you would have to pay the owner of the song (the music publisher) $91.00 for the 1,000 copies. The same rules would apply if your band provided digital downloads of a cover song via iTunes, MusicMatch, Rhapsody, or any of the other download services. Mechanical royalties are due only when songs are reproduced on digital downloads, compact discs, and records (collectively

called "phonorecords" or "sound recordings" under copyright law).

Many bands are surprised to learn that most large record companies do not pay the statutory rate of $.091 per song. These companies negotiate a lower rate—usually three-quarters of the statutory rate—with the music publisher. It is not a violation of the law to negotiate a rate lower than that provided in the Copyright Act. If both parties consent to the lower rate, it is legal and enforceable. You can attempt to negotiate a lower rate on behalf of your band, although for small pressings many music publishers may not reduce the rate.

Video, Film, and Internet Licenses

Compulsory licenses and mechanical royalty rates apply only when reproducing songs on vinyl records or compact discs (sound recordings). These rates do not apply if you are making copies for use on a website or for a video. In one case, a court ruled that the compulsory license did not apply for a song used on a sing-along laser disc recording in which lyrics were reproduced on a TV screen. Therefore, if you are reproducing a song for video, Internet, laser disc, movies, or any use that is not purely audio, then you must contact the music publisher or the Harry Fox Agency (www.harryfox.com) and negotiate a separate license for each use. There are no fixed statutory rates for such uses.

How Songs Are Used

Below are some scenarios regarding the use of songs on your recording.

 Covering someone else's song is not the same thing as sampling. Although the two situations have some copyright principles in common, there are important legal and practical differences between them. See the previous chapter for information on sampling and how to get permission to use a sample of someone else's recording.

Previously Released Songs

Say, for instance, your band records a version of "Smells Like Teen Spirit" by Nirvana. Since that song has already been released to the public, you can use a compulsory license to include your version of it on your recording. As long as you follow the compulsory license rules—sending a Notice of Intention to Obtain Compulsory License and paying the statutory mechanical royalty rate per copy—the owner of "Smells Like Teen Spirit" must allow you to record and distribute the song via CD or digital download. Most song owners are music publishing companies who have bought the rights from the songwriters. You can locate the music publisher by using the Internet and visiting the BMI and ASCAP websites. See Chapter 8 for information about searching for music publishers.

Unreleased Songs Written by Nonband Members

If a friend of the band or some other nonband member has written a song and your band is the first to record it, then you cannot use a compulsory license, because the song has not been previously released. In that case, you must have an authorization from the song owners to record the song for the first time and to duplicate the song. (A sample authorization is provided below.) In addition, your band would be required to pay mechanical royalties.

Sometimes, if you personally know the songwriter, you can ask to forgo the mechanical royalties on the first 1,000 or 2,000 copies. If there is grumbling about this, you can agree to pay the mechanical royalties at a later date, such as after the band has met its break-even point.

Songs Written by Your Band's Members

If the songs on your recording are all written by band members, you don't need to obtain permission to duplicate them. You do, however, still have to pay mechanical royalties to the owners of the song—either the songwriters or a music publisher. When the owners of the song are band members, some bands request that the songwriters forego mechanical royalties, at least for the first few thousand copies. Otherwise the band will have to pay the songwriters approximately $91 per song per 1,000 copies—for ten songs, that equals $910. If the songwriters aren't willing to agree to this, the band can agree to pay the mechanical royalties at a later date, for example, if the band acquires a recording or publishing deal.

What If You Don't Play by the Rules?

Many bands don't bother with obtaining compulsory licenses or paying mechanical royalties. They record songs and press them without asking permission or paying the publisher, because they don't believe they will get caught. For small pressings and limited digital downloads, this illegal activity often goes undetected, but if the copyright owner learns of the unauthorized use, the band may be forced to pay past due mechanical royalties, sometimes plus interest, or the band may be required to stop distributing the recording entirely. If the music publisher brings a lawsuit, there may be additional costs including attorney's fees.

Songfile: A Licensing Shortcut

If you're making and distributing 500 to 2,500 physical recordings (CDs, vinyl recordings, or cassettes) or 150 to 2,500 permanent downloads, you may be able to automate the mechanical licensing process at Songfile (www.songfile.com), an affiliate of the Harry Fox Agency (www.harryfox.com). After answering some simple questions, Songfile will inform you whether the song is available for licensing and will guide you through the licensing process. You pay the statutory rate for the number of copies plus a processing fee of $8 to $10.

Notice of Intention to Obtain Compulsory License

If your band is doing covers—songs that have already appeared on records—the Notice of Intention to Obtain Compulsory License should be sent to the copyright owner of the song. A sample appears below. We will walk you through the procedure for completing the notice.

 This agreement is included on the forms CD in the back of this book.

Introductory Paragraphs

In the first blank of the first paragraph, insert the name of the song owner (usually the music publisher of the song). In the next blank insert the name of the song and, in the final blank, the name or names of the songwriters, for example, "John Lennon and Paul McCartney."

In the second paragraph, you must again insert the name of the song.

Legal Name of Entity Seeking The Compulsory License

Insert the name of the company that owns your recording. If your band or band partnership owns the recording, insert that name.

Fictitious or Assumed Names

If your band is acting as its own label and has made up a name for the company releasing the recording, enter the name of the releasing company. For example, if your band Spyder calls its record company SpyderBite Records, insert "SpyderBite Records" in this space.

Address

Insert your band's mailing address.

Business Form

Check the appropriate choice: sole proprietor, partnership, limited liability company (LLC), or corporation. Your band is probably a partnership. If you're uncertain, review Chapter 2.

Names of Individuals Who Own 25% or More of the Band

If your band (rather than a separate record company) is releasing the record, insert the name of anyone who owns 25% or more of the band, or 25% or more of the shares if your band is a corporation. For example, if your band partnership owns the recording and has four partners who share equally in the band, list the names of the partners. If no one band member owns at least 25% of the band, leave this blank.

Names of Corporate Officers and Directors

If your band is a corporation, list the officers and directors. If your band is not a corporation, leave this blank.

Configuration(s) to Be Made Under the Compulsory License

Check all the configurations (types of technology) of the recording that you expect to release.

Catalog Number

List the catalog number for the recording. (If you don't know the catalog number, see Chapter 10 on album information.)

Label name

Insert the name of your record label. If your band is putting out the record, the label name is probably the same as the name entered under "Fictitious or Assumed Names," above.

Principal Recording Artists

Insert your band's name.

Anticipated Date of Initial Release

Insert the expected release date.

Final Paragraph

The final paragraph establishes that the statutory rate will be paid for the compulsory license.

Signature

This compulsory license is signed by your band (or your record label, if you have one). It does not need to be signed by the music publisher. That's because you do not need to obtain consent from the music publisher. You only need to notify the publisher and follow the payment rules. Whoever signs the agreement should sign in the space next to the word "By" and, below that, indicate that person's name, title, and company. The company will be either the record company or your band. For example, if Paul Dodd, a member of the band The Margaret Explosion, signs, the space by "Name and Title" would read: "Paul Dodd, a general partner in The Margaret Explosion Partnership." Enter the date the agreement was signed.

Notice of Intention to Obtain Compulsory License for Making and Distributing Sound Recordings

To _____,

the copyright owner of _____,

written by _____:

Pursuant to the compulsory license provisions of the U.S. Copyright Act (17 U.S.C. 1115), we apply for a license to make and distribute sound recordings of _____ and provide the following information:

Legal name of entity seeking the compulsory license: _____

Fictitious or assumed names used for making and distributing sound recordings:

_____

Address: _____

Business form (check one): ○ sole proprietor   ○ partnership
                          ○ corporation   ○ limited liability company (LLC)

Names of individuals who own a beneficial interest of 25% or more in the entity:

_____

_____

_____

If a corporation, names of the officers and directors:

_____

_____

_____

Configuration(s) to be made under the compulsory license (check all that apply):
○ 7- or 12-inch vinyl single   ○ 12-inch long-playing vinyl record   ○ cassette
○ compact disc   ○ minidisc   ○ digital cassette recording

Catalog number(s): _____

Label name(s): _____

Principal recording artists: _____

Anticipated date of initial release: _____

We agree to pay the copyright owner royalties at the statutory rate provided by the Copyright Act.

By: _____

Name and Title: _____

Date: _____

Mechanical License and Authorization for First-Time Recording of Song

If your band is pressing a song by a nonband member that has never been released to the public, you must obtain a special license from each song owner (usually, but not always, the songwriter) in order to record and release it for the first time. This license is called a "Mechanical License and Authorization for First-Time Recording of Song." Unlike a compulsory license, this must be signed by both the band (or its record label) and the song owners. In other words, permission to do a first-time recording of a song by a nonband songwriter is not automatic; the song owner must agree to the recording. This section provides a sample agreement and explains how to fill it out.

 This agreement is included on the forms CD in the back of this book.

Introductory Paragraph

In the first blank of the first paragraph, insert the name of the song owner (usually the songwriter, but sometimes the music publisher of the song). In the next blank insert the name of the song, and in the third blank enter the names of the songwriters, for example, "John Lennon and Paul McCartney." In the next blank after the word "authorizes," insert the name of the company that owns your recording. If your band or band partnership owns the recording, insert that name. Finally, in the last blank, again insert the name of the song.

Catalog Number

List the catalog number for the recording. (If you don't know the catalog number, see Chapter 10 on album information.)

Label Name

Insert the name of your record label. If your band is putting out the record, the label name is probably the same as the name entered in the first paragraph after "authorizes."

Principal Recording Artists

Insert your band's name.

Anticipated Date of Initial Release

Insert the expected release date.

Final Paragraph

In the first blank, insert the name of the company that owns your recording. If your band or band partnership owns the recording, insert that name. In the second blank, insert the mechanical royalty rate. Remember that a reduced royalty rate is possible if the songwriter agrees to it. Of course, you should not pay more than the statutory rate, which is $.091 per song pressed.

Signatures

This agreement should be signed by a representative of your band (or your record label, if you have one) and should be signed by all of the song owners. Everyone who signs should indicate the name, title, and company, for example, "Ricky Gebow, a general partner in the I Love Jenny Partnership." All who sign should also enter a mailing address.

Mechanical License and Authorization for First-Time Recording of Song

_____,

the copyright owner of _____,

written by _____,

authorizes _____

to record and distribute _____.

Catalog number(s): _____

Label name(s): _____

Principal recording artists: _____

Anticipated date of initial release: _____

_____ agrees to pay the mechanical royalty rate of $_____ and issue statements and pay royalties on a quarterly basis. The song owners acknowledge that they are the sole song owners and that they have the right to authorize this first recording. The song owners do not require that a notice of intention to obtain a compulsory license be served or filed.

We acknowledge receipt of this agreement and agree to its terms. We have been advised to seek legal review of this agreement.

Band or Record Company

Name of Company That Owns Recording _____

Representative Name and Title _____

Representative Signature _____

Address _____

Date _____

Song Owner

Name of Company That Owns Song _____

Song Owner Name and Title _____

_____

Song Owner Signature _____

Address _____

Date _____

Song Owner Name and Title _____

_____

Song Owner Signature _____

Address _____

Date _____

Song Owner Name and Title _____

_____

Song Owner Signature _____

Address _____

Date _____

Song Owner Name and Title _____

_____

Song Owner Signature _____

Address _____

Date _____

Canadian Mechanical Rights

Although Canada has a system for mechanical licenses, it is not exactly the same as the U.S. system. Canadian musicians deal directly with a collective that administers mechanical rights known as the Canadian Music Reproduction Rights Agency (CMRRA). The CMRRA provides sample Mechanical and Synchronization Licenses, a sample single-song publishing contract, and a sample subpublishing agreement checklist. The French Canadian equivalent is La Societe des Droits de Reproduction Mechanique Canada (SDRM), based in Montreal, which administers French music catalogues. For more information on CMRRA, contact the Canadian Intellectual Property Office (CIPO) at:

50 Victoria St., Room C-114
Gatineau, Quebec K1A 0C9
(819) 997-1936
Fax: (819) 953-7620

The CIPO website is http://cipo.gc.ca.

Manufacturers and Duplication

Forty years ago, an unsigned band would have had only one method of duplicating their music: vinyl reproduction. Nowadays, however, a band has a range of choices

for reproduction: 7-inch or 12-inch vinyl, compact discs, DVDs, DAT tape, or digital mini-discs. Even more important, the quality of the reproduction is at the same sonic quality as that produced by major labels. The prices for reproduction of 500 to 1,000 copies are also within most bands' budgets. We will discuss the various practical issues that may arise when manufacturing copies of your recording.

The Business of Duplication

A manufacturer reproduces compact discs, duplicates cassettes, or presses vinyl records. Some manufacturers are full-service companies with in-house marketing, mastering, and graphic offices. Other so-called manufacturers are actually brokers who contract with others for the artwork, mastering, printing, and duplication. From August through November, major labels monopolize duplicating facilities, and it may be difficult for some brokers or manufacturers to guarantee duplication of your band's recording within the time frame you want.

Compact Discs

The most popular form of duplication remains the compact disc. Fans prefer them, stores are more likely to stock them, they are favored for radio play, and they have the largest profit margin.

The most common compact disc packaging is a "jewel box" that contains the disc plus a full-color booklet and tray card. Some manufacturers offer cardboard sleeves (either single sleeves or four-panel fold-out sleeves) instead of the plastic jewel box. Besides eliminating plastic, cardboard packaging is cheaper and easier to ship (jewel boxes often crack during shipping). The price per unit for manufacturing compact discs goes down with larger pressings (2,000 units or more), primarily because the cost of printing the booklet and traycard decreases in larger lots. (For more information on artwork and packaging, see Chapter 10.)

The total cost of compact disc manufacturing usually includes a one-time setup fee for converting your DAT or CD master into a PMCD pre-master. Before placing an order, ask whether setup costs are included in the estimate. Some bands create the pre-master locally and send it to the manufacturer. Your recording engineer can advise you where it can be done.

You can shop the Internet for the best offer (type "CD duplication" into your search engine). Generally, you should be able to obtain 1,000 compact discs with full-color booklets and jewel boxes for approximately $1,250 to $1,500 (or $1.25 to $1.50 per unit).

Reproducing Small Quantities of CDs

Most bands that need small quantities of CDs simply make copies on CD burners. Bands who do many of these short-run productions might want to invest in small duplication machines that are now selling for approximately $2,000. These machines connect to computers and can duplicate CDs (approximately 25 at a time) *and* print and insert color labels. For an example, check out Primera Technology (www.primera.com).

Vinyl

Vinyl recordings are popular in two formats: 12-inch singles—mandatory if your band is performing rap, hip-hop, dance, or any form of club music—and 7-inch singles, which are still popular as collector's items, particularly in Europe. Radio stations rarely play vinyl recordings, and many stores don't stock them. Vinyl pressing requires several setup steps (referred to as masters, acetates, and master lacquers), and the setup charges are usually included in the manufacturer's price. Before placing an order, ask whether setup costs are included in the estimate.

Approximate costs for vinyl pressing:
1,000 12-inch singles with full-color sleeve—
approximately $1,800 (or $1.80 per unit).

1,000 12-inch singles with white sleeve—
approximately $1,300 (or $1.30 per unit).

500 12-inch singles with white sleeve—
approximately $1,000 (or $2.00 per unit).

1,000 7-inch singles with full-color sleeve—
approximately $1,400 (or $1.30 per unit).
(**Note:** It is becoming more difficult to find manufacturers who will print full-color 7-inch sleeves.)

1,000 7-inch singles with white sleeve—
approximately $700 (or 70 cents per unit).

500 7-inch singles with white sleeve—
approximately $550 (or $1.10 per unit).

How Many Copies Should Your Band Order?

Many major label recordings by new bands don't sell more than 1,000 copies. It may be unrealistic for your band to expect to sell more than 1,000 copies unless you have an extensive touring schedule and a rabid fan base. If you want to avoid having thousands of unsold compact discs in your basement, limit your first pressing to 500 to 1,000 copies.

Some labels press a small number of compact discs (500 each time) but print

larger runs of artwork (for example, 2,000 copies of the tray card and booklet). That will save on setup costs every time the artwork is reproduced (and the per-unit costs for artwork are much lower when printing 2,000 pieces). After the first 500 compact discs sell out, you can order another 500 discs and ship the artwork to the manufacturer, where it will be assembled.

How to Avoid Getting Screwed During the Duplication Process

What if your compact discs arrive from the manufacturer and they have a defect? This is often a depressing problem for a band eager to race to local radio stations with their newest project. In order to deal with this situation, your band must analyze the defects in the recordings and determine who is at fault. In some cases, you may be surprised to find that your band—not the manufacturer—is at fault. (Artwork errors are discussed in Chapter 10.)

Generally there are two categories of problems:

- The band failed to review the mastering properly and the music doesn't sound right.
- The manufacturer made an error during duplication.

Situation #1:
The copies don't sound right because the band failed to review the mastering.

If the overall sound of the copies doesn't seem right (for example, band members want more high end), then you're probably dealing with an error that occurred during mastering. This is especially true with compact discs, because the final master and the resulting compact discs contain the same digital information. Mastering is the last step in the recording process. During the mastering, the recording is prepared for duplication. Track numbers are digitally inserted, and all of the tracks are made to conform to certain volume and equalization levels. This way, none of the cuts are too quiet or too loud. If the band doesn't supervise the mastering, the resulting copies may not reflect your band's sound.

How to avoid getting screwed:
The easiest way to avoid mastering errors is for the band to master the recording before shipping it to the manufacturer. Your studio engineer can recommend someone who can master. (It is also possible to perform mastering tasks using home studio software such as Steinberg's *Wavelab* or *Sonic Solutions*.) If your band does not master the recording, then the manufacturer will handle this task. Be sure it furnishes you with a copy of the master

to listen to before duplication, and listen to it carefully.

The mastering process for vinyl recordings is more complex and results in an acetate (a fragile copy made from the master) and a test pressing, which is an initial copy from the press run. The run is halted until you approve. Every vinyl manufacturer will furnish an acetate for approval, but not every company will also furnish a test pressing, because it means holding up the production line. Before ordering, ask the manufacturer whether vinyl test pressings will be furnished.

It's best for your band to listen to each master recording with your recording engineer. If that is not possible, be sure to at least listen to the test on high-quality audio equipment.

Situation #2:
The recordings contain mechanical defects due to a manufacturing error.

An example of a manufacturing error would be a record that skips or a compact disc that won't play. Copies that sound distinctively different from the master also may be the result of a manufacturing error.

How to avoid getting screwed:
A reliable manufacturer will correct this kind of error at no additional charge.

Usually, the issue isn't *whether* the manufacturer will correct the defect, but *when*. Your band is in a better position with a large, established manufacturer with direct ties to pressing plants. Otherwise, a "correction pressing" may take a month or two if your manufacturer/broker is waiting for space at a pressing plant.

Before you complain about a defect, review any written contract you have with the manufacturer and determine if there is a method for resolving disputes. You will have to abide by the requirements of the contract. There may be a section such as "arbitration," "dispute resolution," or "error correction" that outlines the procedure for resolving the dispute. For example, if the manufacturer has 30 days to correct an error, then you will have to allow 30 days for correction.

When you contact the manufacturer, detail the problems, indicate the dates of activities (when you ordered, when the copies arrived, and so on), and suggest a course of action. Keep copies of your correspondence. If you return recordings to the manufacturer, do it by a traceable system such as UPS or FedEx. If you paid for the duplication with a credit card, you may be in a better bargaining position. For example, if your dispute is for more than $50 and the manufacturer is within your state (or within 100 miles of your home), your credit card company will not deduct the amount from your account until the dispute is resolved. This is often far easier than dealing with small claims court. Ask your credit card carrier about its dispute resolution rules.

Contract law provides that a manufacturer has a right to correct a problem within a reasonable period of time. If this does not happen, your band can sue for breach of the contract—an option your band would probably prefer not to deal with. A lawsuit, even in small claims court, requires a great deal of work and doesn't guarantee you can collect your money (or get your tapes back) even if you win. You may also have trouble suing an out-of-state manufacturer. (For more information on small claims court, see *Everybody's Guide to Small Claims Court*, by Ralph Warner (Nolo).)

If you're concerned about problems with defects, we recommend some of the following strategies:

- Never send your only copy of a master tape (or artwork) to a manufacturer.

- Seek recommendations from other bands about reliable manufacturers.

- Always pay with a credit card, and if possible order your copies from a manufacturer within your state.

- Beware of offers from companies who will undercut any competitor's price—it's probably a broker, who may have difficulty correcting errors.

■

Chapter 13

Selling Your Music

How do you get your band's recordings into the bins at a local record store? How do you sell them online? Sometimes, it's as easy as walking in with a handful of compact discs or signing on to a retail website. Sometimes, your band has to use a distributor to place the records. Sometimes (as in the case of large chain stores), it's simply impossible to place your record in a store. In this chapter we explain the different methods of selling compact discs—direct sale, consignment, through online retailers, and so on—and how to deal with the common problems that occur when consigning records to stores, offering them to distributors, or selling them online. We also provide a distribution agreement that you can use if an independent distributor will handle your band's recordings.

When We Say "Records" ...

Although compact discs have emerged as the most popular format for selling music, the term "records" is still used within the retail industry as a generic term for prerecorded music. Unless otherwise specified (for example, as vinyl records), assume that the term "records" refers to all forms of prerecorded music offered for sale.

How Do Records Get Into Stores?

Almost all of the compact discs in your local record stores are delivered by distributors. A distributor is a company that sells records to the record store on behalf of a record company. In other words, a distributor is an agent or "middleman." There are two categories of distributors: majors and independents. Major label distributors distribute *only* the music of the large record companies (that is, the major labels). Independent distributors handle everything else. In addition to distributors, there are two other ways to get your records into a record store: consignment sales (where the store holds the records on a speculative basis and returns them to your band if unsold) and direct sales (where the store buys the record directly from the company or band). Below we discuss all four methods.

Major Label Distribution

There are four major label record distributors (sometimes referred to as the "Big Four"): Universal Music Group (UMG), Sony BMG, EMI Group, and Warner Music Group (WEA). These major label distributors will handle recordings by major label artists only. In other words, if you're not signed to Capitol, Warner Brothers, RCA, Atlantic, or one of the other major record labels, these distributors do not want to hear from you.

Independent Distribution

Independent distributors handle records from independent (that is, *not* major label) record companies and unsigned bands. For example, independent record labels such as Ryko, Rhino, and Rounder all use independent distributors. Under an independent distribution arrangement, a distributor orders records from your band. You ship the records along with an invoice (a sample is provided in this chapter). The distributor consigns your records to stores. If the records don't sell, they are returned to the distributor, who returns them to you. If the records sell, you are paid by the distributor (within 60 to 90 days). A sample distribution agreement is provided below.

Direct Sales

Some independent record stores purchase records directly from local bands. Although it's more profitable (the distributor is not taking a cut), it's also much more difficult, because many stores are wary of buying a local recording unless there is some guarantee of sales. "You need to have a sales pitch" is the advice of Marc Weinstein, one of the owners of Amoeba Records, one of the largest sellers of local music in California. "The band has to realize that the store

is taking a chance when it buys a record from a band," says Weinstein, "so be prepared to explain why the record will sell. Is there an established audience? Documentation helps. That includes radio play lists, lists of upcoming gigs, or prominent local press."

Consignment

Local stores are more apt to take a recording on consignment than by direct sale. That's because there is less financial risk to the store. Under a consignment arrangement, you leave your records at the store, and, if they sell within 60 or 90 days, the store pays you a percentage of the sales price. If the records don't sell, the store returns the records to you. The next section discusses consignment sales in more detail, and includes a sample consignment form to keep track of your records.

The Click & Brick Approach

Online retailers—in particular, CD Baby—are now offering a combination online/physical retail option. CD Baby has entered into arrangements with Tower, Borders, Best Buy, Hot Topic, and Transworld, as well as a large number of independent retailers. This does not mean that all recordings placed at CD Baby will become available at these stores. But if an album becomes hot, it can be placed into retail distribution.

Sales Tax

Many states have sales tax laws that require the seller (your band) to collect and pay the appropriate tax for each sale. The laws differ from state to state, but generally the tax must be collected only for sales to final users (in other words, not someone who will resell the record) within the state. So if you sell compact discs to fans at a concert in your home state, you're technically required to collect and pay the sales tax. Since the rules differ from state to state, you may want to contact your state sales tax board to review the rules.

Consignments

Under a standard consignment arrangement, a store will hold records for 90 days. If the records sell, the store will keep 25% to 50% and pay you the rest. The records that don't sell will be returned to you. Under a consignment agreement, it is your responsibility to check back at the store.

How Not to Lose Money on Consignments

Consignments are time-consuming to manage. Many bands place their records on consignment and then fail to follow up, or, when they do follow up, they are not prepared to do business. It's your responsibility to keep track of the written consignment statement. Remember, the store is doing you a favor by stocking your records. Be professional! Calendar the date when to check back with the store. Get the name of the person at the store who took the consignment, and always call ahead to make sure the consignment person is there before you go (it's good to deal with the same person each time). Also, it's wise to see that your records are placed in the proper bins (for example, if it's rock, make sure it's not in the reggae section).

The Consignment Agreement

In the event that the store does not have a consignment agreement, you can use the agreement below. The form basically shows what records you left at a store, when you left them, when they should sell by, and what their price is. You don't need to leave a copy with the store unless the store requests one.

 The following form is included on the forms CD in the back of this book.

Under "Store" and "Salesperson," fill in the name of the record store and salesperson who assisted in the consignment. Insert the date you dropped off your records, and under "Due Date" indicate the number of days for the consignment (usually 60 to 90). Indicate the title of your recording under "Description." If you have more than one title, list each title separately. Indicate the number of units of each title that you are leaving under "Quantity."

Consignment Form

Name of Band or Company: _____

Address: _____

Phone/Fax: _____

Store	Salesperson	Date Dropped Off	Due Date
_____	_____	_____	_____ days

Quantity	Description (Title)	Unit Price	Amount
_____		$ _____	$ _____
_____		$ _____	$ _____
_____		$ _____	$ _____
_____		$ _____	$ _____
		Subtotal	$ _____
		TOTAL DUE	$ _____

Store Representative Signature: _____

Name and Title: _____

Under "Unit Price," indicate the amount you will get back for each record sold. Usually the band gets somewhere between $4 and $7 per CD. Sometimes a store will tell the band how much it will make. For example, the store may tell your band, "We charge $12 for each CD and we keep 50%." In other words, your band gets $6 per CD. Multiply the unit price by the number of records left and enter that number in the "Amount" column. If, when you return to the store, only some of your CDs have sold, you would deduct the unsold CDs from the total amount due.

Independent Distributors

Unsigned bands and independent record labels use independent distributors, who often specialize in certain genres of music or who concentrate in supplying certain geographical regions. For example, an indie distributor may specialize only in 12-inch dance music or in blues. Some independent record companies also have their own affiliated independent distributor. Leading distributors of independent rock/pop music are ADA and Caroline. A list of distributors is provided in the *Recording Industry Sourcebook*. (See Chapter 17 for music resources.)

If you have friends at local record stores, find out which independent distributors might carry your band's type of music. Independent distributors are often discriminating about which bands and labels they will carry. For example, some distributors refuse to carry a record label's product unless the label has been in business for at least six months. When talking to a distributor, you should be prepared to make a sales pitch on behalf of your band, and you may have to send a sample recording as well as press clippings or evidence of radio play.

Exclusive and Nonexclusive Distribution Agreements

Some independent distribution arrangements are nonexclusive, meaning that you can use more than one independent distributor. These arrangements are often informal, and no written agreement is required. In most nonexclusive distribution deals, a distributor calls with an order or faxes you a purchase order (P.O.). Your band furnishes the distributor with the records and an invoice, which is the written record of the transaction. Keep it professional and make three copies of the invoice: one to be enclosed with the shipment, one to be mailed to the distributor's billing office, and one for your records. A sample invoice is provided below.

Some indie distribution arrangements are exclusive. That is, only one distributor can handle your recordings. If the arrangement is exclusive and the distributor anticipates (or is) ordering hundreds of records, you should consider using a written agreement (see below). Under some exclusive independent distribution agreements (known as "P&D" deals for "press and distribute"), a distributor will agree to manufacture the records for a small label. The indie distribution agreement below can be modified to accommodate a P&D arrangement.

When the Distributor Goes Belly Up

A band may get stiffed by an independent distributor if the distributor is in bad financial shape. In the past decade, dozens of U.S. distributors have folded, and hundreds of thousands of records have disappeared.

The solution for distributor problems is:

- **Take it slow.** Start with small orders (under 50 copies), and don't fill new orders until you are paid for previous orders.
- **Don't put all your eggs in one basket.** Avoid exclusive deals unless the deal is very attractive. For example, an exclusive deal might be okay if the distributor has a good reputation, pays on time, can get your records into a variety of stores, will order large quantities of records, and will pay you a standard (or better) royalty. Otherwise, your band should use more than one distributor. That way you'll be less likely to be

burned if a distributor turns out to be a deadbeat.

- **Check 'em out. Research the distributor before shipping.** You can get an idea about the company's stability by finding out how long the distributor has been doing business. Five years or more is a sign of financial stability. Use the Internet to contact bands or small labels who are willing to share information. You should be very concerned about whether a distributor is prompt when making payments.

The Independent Distributor Invoice

Below is a sample invoice that you can use when supplying records to an independent distributor.

 The following form is included on the forms CD at the back of this book.

Under "Contact Person," fill in the name of the person with whom you deal at the Distributor company. If the distributor has given you a purchase order number, insert that in the column marked "P.O. Number" Indicate the date that the recordings were shipped ("Date Shipped") and the method of shipment ("Shipped Via"). The "Terms" column indicates when you will be paid. For example, "Net 30" means that you will be paid 30 days after receipt of the records.

Indicate the number of each title you are shipping ("Quantity"), and provide the title under "Description." Under "Unit Price," indicate the amount you will get back for each record sold. For distribution deals, a band usually gets $6 or $7 per CD. Multiply the unit price by the number of titles you're shipping, and enter that number in the "Amount" column. If there are returns, these unsold units will be deducted from the total amount due.

Invoice

Make all checks payable to:

Name of Band or Company: _____

Address: _____

Phone/Fax: _____

Bill to: (distributor's name & address)   Ship to: (distributor's shipping address)

_____   _____

_____   _____

_____   _____

_____   _____

CONTACT PERSON _____

P.O. NUMBER	DATE SHIPPED	SHIPPED VIA	TERMS

Quantity	Description (Title of CD)	Unit Price	Amount
_____	_____	$ _____	$ _____
_____	_____	$ _____	$ _____
_____	_____	$ _____	$ _____
_____	_____	$ _____	$ _____

Subtotal $ _____

Tax/shipping $ _____

TOTAL DUE $ _____

If you have any questions concerning this invoice, call _____

Independent Distribution Agreement

It's possible that you may not use a written agreement with a distributor. Many distributors simply order records and invoice the labels or bands. No agreement is signed. However, some distributors, particularly if the arrangement is exclusive, want a written agreement. This chapter offers a sample independent distribution agreement. However, most distributors who use a written agreement furnish their own contracts, so it's unlikely you will furnish an agreement such as the one presented in this chapter. Our primary purpose in providing the distribution agreement is to offer you an explanation for the common provisions and to provide a sample against which to compare any agreement you're asked to sign.

 This agreement is included on the forms CD in the back of this book.

Introduction

If your band or band partnership owns your records, insert that name in the first blank for "Owner." If you created a separate company for your records (such as "Our Band's Records"), list that name. If you have signed to a label and the label owns the recordings, then the label (not your band) should be executing the distribution agreement. Insert the name of the distributor in the second blank.

If you intend to limit the distribution to specific recordings, then list those recordings in the optional "Records" section.

Grant of Rights

Indicate whether the arrangement is exclusive (that is, only the distributor can distribute your records) or nonexclusive (more than one distributor can carry your records).

The optional provision would create what's known as a "press and distribute" or "P&D" deal. Although it is rare (and becoming rarer), some distributors agree to manufacture records on behalf of the band. This hybrid arrangement can be advantageous to the band, because the distributor can get a better rate for manufacturing compact discs. Usually a distributor will do a P&D deal only if the band owns its own label, has a substantial catalog of recordings and sells more than 5,000 copies of each record. If your distributor wants to do a P&D deal, check the optional manufacturing provision.

Territory

List the countries or region in which the distributor can sell the records. Most distributors will want worldwide rights. If the deal is exclusive, ask about your distributor's ability to reach foreign markets.

The Term

Insert the number of months or years the deal will last. Most distribution deals are from 24 to 48 months, with the standard being 36 months. We recommend that your band keep the number of years as short as possible in case your distributor is not "working" your records. After the term ends, the agreement can be renewed by the parties by signing a new agreement, or it can continue on a month-to-month basis.

Payments

Independent distributors usually pay between 70% and 85% of net revenue (wholesale price minus deductions) to the owner. Another method of paying your band is to set a fixed price for each unit sold. To draft your agreement in this manner, use the "per unit" option. Insert the amount to be paid for compact discs and cassettes (usually $5 to $7 for compact discs and $4 to $6 for cassettes).

Advance Payment

Some distributors may provide an advance in a P&D deal. The advance is usually nonrefundable (which means that you don't have to pay it back) and recoupable (which means that it can be deducted from future payments you're expected to receive from the distributor). This is set up so that the advance won't

be deducted from your royalties all at once. A portion of the advance is deducted every royalty period. If the advance is over $5,000, we recommend that 25% to 50% or less be deducted from each accounting period.

Deductions

A distributor may need to make certain deductions from the money that is due to you. It is normal to deduct advances. Reserves are a system by which the distributor gets to hold part of your payment until the distributor is convinced there are no returns from stores. The reserve is usually 25% to 35% of the money you are supposed to receive. For example, if the distributor owed you $4,000 for sales in one month, the distributor might hold a 25% reserve of $1,000 to cover any future returns from record stores. The distributor holds the reserve from 30 to 180 days (the "liquidation period") depending on your agreement. After the liquidation period, the distributor pays your band the reserve it had withheld. If you include this deduction, indicate the percentage that may be held and the length of time it may be held by the distributor.

Generally, "costs advanced" are applicable only in the case of a P&D deal (in which the distributor is manufacturing your records). Other deductions can also be made, for example, if the distributor advances funds to repackage your records.

If you include this deduction in your agreement, the specific costs should be listed. These deductions can cut into your band's profits, so review them carefully.

Accounting

This section indicates the number of days your band has to wait to be paid *after* the accounting period ends. We recommend 30 days, although most distributors demand 60 or 90 days. While most distributors pay four times a year, some pay monthly, which is ideal for your band.

Termination

Distributors need a period to sell off their records, and usually request six months to a year. Nine months is standard. We recommend as short a period as possible.

Mediation; Arbitration

This provision provides a less expensive method of resolving disputes than filing a lawsuit. (See the sidebar in Chapter 2 for an explanation of mediation and arbitration.) We recommend that you use this provision in order to help avoid an expensive lawsuit.

We suggest that you choose the county, province, or city in which the band resides for arbitration. If all the members do not reside in one area, choose a place that is convenient. Enter your location of choice in the blank.

In some states there are organizations that specialize in arbitration for people in the arts, such as California Lawyers for the Arts (CLA) and, in New York, Volunteer Lawyers for the Arts (VLA). You can substitute the rules of such an organization for those of the American Arbitration Association in your Agreement. If your band is based in Canada, you can still use the AAA's rules, as they perform arbitration in all major Canadian cities. (For more information on the AAA, see Chapter 17.) Check one of the choices, or delete the unwanted alternative.

General

The following provisions are standard contractual provisions referred to as boilerplate. Boilerplate provisions are explained in Chapter 2.

In the blank space, insert the state (or province, in the case of Canadian bands) of residence for the band partners. In the event of a dispute, this determines which state law will govern the arbitration or lawsuit.

Warranties

We have not included a warranty section, but it is possible that you will see one in an agreement from a distributor. Warranties (also sometimes referred to as "representations" or "covenants") are contractual promises. If your band breaks one of these promises, the distributor can seek money damages from your band. For example, you may see warranties as follows:

(a) Owner has the power and authority to enter into this Agreement.

(b) Records and accompanying artwork for any Title or any related promotional material will not infringe any intellectual property rights or statutory right.

(c) Owner has or will obtain all necessary rights and licenses associated with the Records.

(d) Owner is responsible for paying all royalties or other required payments related to the music and artwork associated with the Records.

(e) Owner will maintain an enforceable agreement with each person having rights in the Records or related artwork.

Usually, your band will have no problem making these warranties. However, to assure your rights as the owner of the records, you should have a written agreement with all of the performers and artists who contributed to the recordings. For example, you would need a release (see Chapter 11) from any hired musicians or from a photographer who took the album cover photo (see Chapter 10).

Indemnification

We have not included an indemnity section, but it is possible that you will see one in an agreement from the distributor. When you provide indemnity (that is, "indemnify" someone), you agree to pay for their damages if you cause any. For example, if the distributor is sued because your records contain unauthorized samples, you would have to pay for those legal expenses if you had indemnified the distributor. The situation is reversed if the distributor agreed to provide indemnification for your band. A typical indemnity provision looks as follows: **Indemnification by Owner.** Owner indemnifies Distributor and undertakes to defend Distributor against and hold Distributor harmless (including, without limitation, attorney fees and costs) from any claims and damage arising out of any breach of Owner's warranties, above.

Your band can also seek indemnity from the distributor in the following form: **Indemnification by Distributor.** Distributor indemnifies Owner and undertakes to defend Owner and hold Owner harmless (including, without limitation, attorney fees and costs) from any claims and damage arising out of any of Distributor's advertising, distribution, or marketing of the Records.

Signatures

This agreement should be signed by a representative of your band and the distributor. Everyone who signs should indicate the name, title, and company (if a company exists), for example, "Ricky Gebow, a general partner in the I Love Jenny Partnership." All who sign should also enter a mailing address and the date they signed the agreement.

Independent Distribution Agreement

Introduction

This Distribution Agreement is between _____ ("Owner") and _____ ("Distributor"). Distributor agrees to distribute Owner's sound recordings (the "Records") in compact discs, cassettes, vinyl, or any other sound recording formats.

Records (Check if applicable and fill in blank.)

❍ The Records to be distributed are as follows:

_____

Grant of Rights

Owner grants to Distributor the (check one) ❍ exclusive ❍ nonexclusive right to distribute and sell the Records.

P&D Deal (Check if applicable.)

❍ Owner grants to Distributor the right to manufacture and reproduce the Records. Distributor may deduct manufacturing costs from the Owner's Share. However, all pressing and manufacturing costs must be approved in writing by Owner.

Territory

The rights granted under this Agreement shall be for: _____

_____ (the "Territory").

The Term

This Agreement shall be for _____. It shall be renewed (check one):

❍ on Owner and Distributor executing a new agreement.

❍ automatically on a month-to-month basis until Owner or Distributor gives a 30-day notice of termination.

Payments

Distributor will pay Owner as follows (select one and fill in applicable blanks):

○ **Net Revenue.** Distributor will pay Owner _____% of the net revenue derived from sales of the Records (the "Owner's Share").

○ **Per Unit.** Distributor will pay Owner $_____ for each compact disc and $_____ for each cassette.

Advance Payment (Check and fill in blank if applicable.)

○ As a nonrefundable advance against the Owner's Share, Distributor agrees to pay to Owner $_____ (the "Advance") on execution of this Agreement. The Advance is recoupable from Owner's payments at a rate not to exceed _____% of the Advance per accounting period.

Deductions

Distributor may deduct the following from payments due to Owner (check all that apply and fill in appropriate blanks):

○ Advance(s), if any, as provided in this Agreement.

○ Reasonable reserves against returns, not to exceed _____ % of the Owner's Share payable for that accounting period. Any reserve held by Distributor may be held for a period of _____ days.

○ Distributor costs advanced for the Records (if approved by Owner) for

_____

Accounting

Distributor will pay Owner the Owner's Share within _____ days after the end of each (select one) ○ quarter ○ month. Distributor will also furnish an accurate statement of sales of Records during that period. Owner has the right on reasonable written notice to audit Distributor's books relating to the Records.

Termination

Unless this Agreement is terminated because of Distributor's failure to pay or accurately report Owner's Share, Distributor may sell off the remaining inventory for a period of _____ months after termination (the "Sell-Off Period"). At the end of the Sell-Off Period, Distributor will furnish a final report of sales and final payment of Owner's Share. At the close of the Sell-Off Period, Distributor will deliver to Owner all remaining inventory and, if applicable, any original master tapes, artwork, or related materials.

Mediation; Arbitration

If a dispute arises under this Agreement, the parties agree to first try to resolve the dispute with the help of a mutually agreed-on mediator in _____ .
Any costs and fees other than attorney fees will be shared equally by the parties. If it is impossible to arrive at a mutually satisfactory solution within a reasonable time, the parties agree to submit the dispute to binding arbitration in the same city or region, conducted on a confidential basis pursuant to:

○ the Commercial Arbitration Rules of the American Arbitration Association, or

○ the rules of _____ .

Any decision or award as a result of arbitration will include the assessment of costs, expenses, and reasonable attorney's fees and a written determination of the arbitrators. Absent an agreement to the contrary, arbitration will be conducted by an arbitrator experienced in music industry law. An award of arbitration is final and binding on the Owner and may be confirmed in a court of competent jurisdiction. The prevailing party has the right to collect from the other party its reasonable costs and attorney fees incurred in enforcing this agreement.

General

Nothing contained in this Agreement makes either Distributor or Owner a partner, joint venturer, or employee of the other party for any purpose. This Agreement may not be amended except in a writing signed by both parties. No waiver by either party of any right is a waiver of any other right. If a court finds any provision of this Agreement invalid or unenforceable as applied to any circumstance, the remainder of this Agreement will be interpreted to carry out the intent of the parties. This Agreement is governed by and interpreted in accordance with the laws of the State of _____. This Agreement expresses the complete understanding of the parties about its subject matter and supersedes all prior proposals, agreements, representations, and understandings. Notices required under this Agreement can be sent to the parties at the addresses provided below. In the event of any dispute arising from or related to this Agreement, the prevailing party is entitled to attorney's fees.

Name of Company That Owns Recording _____

Owner Representative Name and Title _____

_____

Owner Representative Signature _____

Address _____

Date _____

Distributor Company Name _____

Distributor Representative Name and Title _____

_____

Distributor Representative Signature _____

Address _____

Date _____

Selling Your Music Online

There are two common methods of selling recorded music online: You can sell compact discs directly through your band website, or you can sell recorded music through an online retailer.

Selling From Your Website

Establishing a band website that sells directly to consumers takes time and money. If you want to provide this retail service, you'll need some information on credit card processing and mail order sales.

Shopping Carts and Credit Cards

How your band sells compact discs depends on your website hosting agreement and how your site is constructed (see Chapter 15). Keep in mind that setting up your website to accept credit cards can be complicated.

Monthly costs for maintaining a site with shopping carts and credit card processing can run from $75 to $200 a month. These fees can seriously cut into your profit margin. If you are committed to providing customers with credit card processing, here are some ways to save money:

- Look into PayPal if your site is handling fewer than 100 transactions a month. For a fee, the folks at PayPal (www.paypal.com) can handle all the details of getting

paid, and you won't need to set up a credit card merchant account. PayPal will accept your customers' credit card payments and transfer the money to your band's bank account. The process isn't quite as smooth as some large commercial websites— the Amazon.com shopping cart, for example—but many bands with modest sales find it suitable.

- There are two general types of credit card processing methods: an automatic system in which the card is processed in real time as the order is made, or a manual system in which you enter the credit card information by typing it into your computer and sending it to the processor. If your site expects fewer than 100 transactions per month and you want a typical shopping cart system, you can save money by using a credit transaction processing method where you manually enter the credit card information required for authorization.
- Consider offering your music for sale at sites that take credit cards, such as CD Baby. You can link directly from your website to the CD Baby site.

Shipments, Taxes, and Refunds

Once your band starts selling directly to consumers, you're in the mail order business, so you should be familiar with mail order rules regarding shipping, taxes, and refunds.

- You do not have to provide a shipment date to your website customers. If you do give the consumer a shipping date, you must state it clearly and prominently and have a good reason to believe you can meet that deadline. And if you don't state a shipping date, you still must have a reasonable expectation that you can ship any product you advertise within 30 days of taking the order.
- If you can't ship within the time promised on your website or within 30 days, you must notify the customer of the delay, provide a revised shipment date, and explain that the order can be cancelled for a full and prompt refund.
- You always have the right to cancel an order that you can't fill on time. If you decide to cancel, you must promptly notify the customer and refund the payment.

⚠️ State sales taxes apply to online sales if the customer is a resident of the state where your band is based. In other words, you must follow your state's sales tax rules in any transactions with in-state customers.

Once a sale is complete, you are not required to give refunds. This is based on traditional contract law, which treats a sale as a completed contract. If you do decide to offer refunds, post your rules conspicuously at your site.

Selling Through an Online Retailer

If you would like to sell your band's recordings at a large online retailer such as CDNow.com or Amazon.com, you will have to enter into an arrangement with a distributor who supplies these e-stores. These companies will not distribute the recordings directly from the band. For example, all of the recordings at CDNow are supplied by Valley Record Distributors. So, in order for your band's recordings to appear at CDNow, Valley or one its subdistributors (such as Navarre, City Hall, Caroline, RED, or MS Distributing) must carry the recordings. Information about these distributors can often be found at each online retailer's website.

Another breed of online retailer, exemplified by CD Baby (www.cdbaby. com), caters to the needs of independent or unsigned bands. At CD Baby, your band can obtain an artist page and sell its CDs for a one-time fee of $35 per title. The company keeps $4 from each sale and sends the band the remainder. CD Baby saves the band the hassle of setting up a shopping cart. The band can simply link from its band website to its CD Baby artist page, where customers can buy its CDs. For more information on the process, check out the CD Baby website.

In addition, you can license CD Baby to handle digital downloads of your music. The company will rip MP3s and distribute them to over 35 online music delivery services such as iTunes and Rhapsody.

Other online retailers have also followed the CD Baby success. Backstage Commerce (www.backstagecommerce .com), formerly CDStreet, offers retail services. The Orchard (www.theorchard .com) has achieved considerable success as an online retailer and digital distributor (including ringtones). TuneCore (www.tunecore.com) claims to offer the highest rates for digital download distribution, and through their relationship with IndieMerchandising (www.indiemerchandising.com) they also offer merchandise production services.

EXAMPLE: The Smokers are signed to an indie label and earn a 50% royalty rate from all sales. If the Smokers participate in an affiliate program with Amazon, they will earn 15% of each sale they refer. Since Amazon pays their label a wholesale price of $6, the Smokers earn a total of $5.25 per sale at Amazon—that is, $3 from record royalties and $2.25 for affiliate fees (15% of the list price of $15). If the Smokers' CD referred fans to their record label's website, they would earn $7.50 per sale (50% of the direct sale price). If the Smokers referred their fans to CD Baby, they would earn $5.50 per sale (50% of $15 minus $4 fee). There is, of course, one

instance when an affiliate agreement would make more sense for the Smokers—if their label was unethical and failed to pay them royalties.

Affiliate Programs: Are They Worth It?

Under an affiliate program, your band earns money every time a visitor to your website clicks on a link to buy your CD from an online store such as Amazon.com, CDNow, or TowerRecords.com. By sending the website user to the retailer, your band earns a fee as an "affiliate." Each online retailer has its own affiliate program, and you must register in order to collect your fee—which ranges from 7% to 15% of the sale. Such programs seem appealing because your band earns money twice: once from the sale of the record, and again from the affiliate fee.

Your band might earn more money, however, by bypassing the affiliate program and directing your fans to your record label or a site such as CD Baby. While these sites don't provide affiliate fees, they generally pay the artists more from each CD sale. When major online retailers such as CDNow sell your record, they've paid you or your record label a wholesale price of approximately $6 per disc. Even with an affiliate fee, the total is often less than what the record label or CD Baby would pay.

Chapter 14

Independent Record Agreements

Several years ago, *Musician Magazine* ran an article entitled "Getting Signed: The Day After." The story featured musicians who had signed recording agreements only to discover that once signed, they were faced with insurmountable problems and no money. "The worst part was definitely after we got signed," said the guitarist from Edie Brickell and the New Bohemians, a Top Ten band that has since broken up.

Legal and business knowledge will help your band prepare for the problems that often occur during and after signing a record agreement. In this chapter we provide information (and some tips) on record agreements. Although we focus on independent record company agreements, many of the contract principles apply to major label agreements as well. We concentrate on some of the problem issues that arise when entering into a record deal—for example, the infamous "controlled composition" clause and the money-losing principle known as "cross-collateralization." At the end of the chapter we provide some examples of record agreements, and we also walk you through an interpretation of a typical royalty statement.

No Deal May Be Better Than an Awful Deal

According to legend, a record company executive was once negotiating a recording contract with a famous artist. The two men could not agree on the royalty rate—whether to pay the artist 4% to 6%. After an hour of angry arguing the executive shouted, "Okay, I'll put six in the contract, but I'm only going to pay you four."

The moral: It doesn't matter what it says in your contract if you can't trust the record company. Review the company as well as the contract. If the owners and executives at the label are untrustworthy or incompetent, then your band will be in for a lot of headaches. It may be better to pass on the deal and wait for something else. Not *all* recording agreements are worth signing.

Majors and Independents

There are two classes of record companies: major label and independent. Most people think independent means "small" and major label means "big," and to some extent that's true. Majors are corporately owned, have bigger budgets, and sell tons more records (or "units") than indies. However, there are some large and powerful independent labels that sell a lot of recordings. In addition, there are some hybrids: independents, such as Matador, that have some of their recordings distributed by majors. There are also "majorettes"—labels such as Work that lack marketing, promotion, and art departments but that are affiliated with major labels. Below we have provided a chart that highlights some of the differences between majors and independents.

Record Agreements: Key Elements

Record companies, like most businesses, are guided by two principles: Reduce the company's risk and maximize the company's profits. These two principles are evident when you examine record agreements. In most deals, the band, not the record company, is actually taking the biggest risk with the smallest potential return. This isn't to say that your band can't earn a profit under a recording agreement. It's just that the record companies often make it as hard as possible to do so.

Record companies commonly enter into two types of "record contracts" with bands: record agreements, where a band agrees to make one or more recordings exclusively for a company; and licensing deals, where a label acquires the rights to release something that a band has already recorded. There are a lot of similarities between the two types of record deals,

and samples of both types are at the end of this chapter.

A record agreement commonly has several key elements. These are:

- the length of time for the agreement (called the "term")
- the number of recordings you must deliver
- the amount of advance for each recording
- the amount of royalty for each recording
- the deductions from your income
- related rights such as merchandising and videos
- whether all band members are locked into the agreement even if the band breaks up
- the presence or absence of a controlled composition clause, and
- whether the band must sign a co-publishing deal.

Options and Term

A record company usually wants to sign a band for as long as possible and to make as many recordings as possible. Assume, for example, that the company wants to sign your band to make six albums. Each album will typically be referred to in the recording agreement as an "option," because it will be at the record company's option whether you will make each recording. If the company wants to drop you after one album, that's it. But if they want to keep you for all six, you're locked into the arrangement. By doing this, the record company lowers its already low risk and increases its chances of profits. Independent record companies usually seek options to make one to three albums; majors typically seek four to seven. A band is screwed if it is forced to stay with a company it hates.

Remember, it may be tempting to sign a deal providing for several albums, even if they are only options. However, you must remember that because they are options, the band is not guaranteed anything. In other words, the promise of future recordings is truly an illusion.

Therefore, as a general rule, it benefits your band to keep all time periods as short as possible. We recommend that you limit the agreement to two recordings and learn as much as you can about the record company before signing the agreement. Talk to other bands signed to the record company, search for online information, or review trade publications.

Advances

When your band is signed to a record deal, you receive an advance to pay for the recording. In other words, the company is lending you money to make your recording. The advance is eventually deducted from money that is earned by the band. In other words, if you had a $10,000 advance and earned $10,000 in royalties, your band would not receive

any money. For that reason, some savvy musicians recommend keeping the advance (and recording costs) as low as possible. This enables your band to turn a profit sooner.

Royalties

When recordings are sold, your band receives a percentage of the sales, known as a royalty. A royalty is based on a rate of payment (a percentage). There are three common royalty rate arrangements:

- a percentage of the suggested retail list price (or SRLP—see the sidebar "What Is the Suggested Retail List Price?," below);
- a percentage of the wholesale price, or
- a fixed amount (for example, $1.79 per compact disc).

The royalty rate is negotiated and included in the payment portion of your contract. For example, your band may negotiate a royalty rate of 12% of the SRLP. This royalty rate is multiplied against the SRLP, and that determines your actual royalty. For example, say the SRLP for a compact disc is $16 and your royalty rate is 12%. Your royalty would be $1.92 per compact disc. In other words, your band earns $1.92 every time a compact disc is sold.

Many independents don't bother with the SRLP. They just pay a fixed sum per recording. For example, the contract may simply provide for a fixed royalty of $1.80

Recording Agreement

	Major Label	Independent
Examples	Sony, Capitol, Warner Bros., BMG, Epic, and Mercury.	Rounder, TVT, Touch & Go, and Mute.
Advantages	A bigger distribution channel (more places to sell your record). Bigger recording budgets. More promotional and marketing power.	More creative freedom. Less likelihood of being dropped, because it's easier to achieve a profit.
Disadvantages	More pressure. If the band is not quick to achieve a hit, the group is dropped and the album is discontinued.	Less marketing power and narrower distribution. It may be difficult for label to sell more than 20,000 records.
Recording contract	Major label recording agreements are 50 to 100 pages and contain archaic language and confusing rules unique to the record business. Your band will have to obtain professional help (such as an attorney or manager) to create an even playing field.	Independent recording agreements are usually less intimidating (commonly five to 20 pages in length) and faster to negotiate than major label deals.
How many records does the label have to sell before breaking even?	In a typical major label deal, a record company spends $100,000 or more on a new band and therefore would probably have to sell at least 40,000 records (or "units") before the record company broke even.	In a typical independent label deal, a record company spends $5,000 to $10,000 on a new band. Usually, an independent record company can earn a profit by selling 3,000 to 5,000 records.
Is it enough just to make a profit?	No. Most major labels are not satisfied just making a profit with a band. They are looking for a large profit—that is, a big hit.	Independent labels would like to have hits, but they are usually happy to make a profit.
Distribution	Major labels are distributed by one of the four major distributors: Universal Music Group (UMG), Sony BMG, EMI Group, and Warner Music Group (WEA).	An independent distributor is any distributor not in the Big Four. Examples are ADA and Caroline.
Relationship between label and distributor	Major labels usually share an ownership interest in the distributor or vice versa. For example, the same company owns both the Sony distribution company and the Epic and Columbia record companies.	Independent distributors may own (or share an ownership interest) with an independent label. However most independent labels are just that: independently owned.
What stores will sell your records?	All major chains and retail outlets.	Independent record stores and some chains (depending on the distributor).

per compact disc. In that case, the fixed royalty is multiplied against the number of units sold.

Below is an example of how an SRLP royalty rate and an advance affect the amount paid to a band.

EXAMPLE: *The Gordos Earn $9,200*

The Gordos receive an advance payment of $10,000, and their contract provides for a royalty of 12% of the SRLP of the units sold. The Gordos sell 10,000 units, and the SRLP for compact discs is $16. The Gordos are owed $9,200. This is calculated as follows:

Compact disc (SRLP)	$16
Royalty rate	x12%
Royalty	$1.92
Units sold	x10,000
	$19,200
Minus advance	-$10,000
TOTAL	$9,200

What Is the Suggested Retail List Price?

The suggested retail list price (SRLP) is the record company's suggested price for the recording. It is not related to the actual price paid by the consumer, and it is not tied to the wholesale price paid by distributors. It's a fictitious number dreamed up by the record companies for accounting purposes. The compact disc SRLP hovers at $16. Most consumers don't pay the SRLP; instead they pay the lowest price advertised at the local record store.

Deductions: Less Is More

Deductions are categories of expenses and payments that the record company can subtract from your income. For example, one band was surprised to find that the beer and chips that a label executive supplied at a recording session were deducted from their record royalties. As a general rule, when it comes to deductions in your recording contract, less is more. That is, the less that the record company deducts, the more that the band earns.

It may be difficult to avoid deductions. Major labels and some independents are often unwilling to make changes. Fortunately, some indies don't bother with many of these deductions. Below are some of the common ones:

- **Packaging deductions.** Some record companies deduct 15% to 25% of the suggested retail price for "packaging" costs. In other words, they sometimes take one-quarter of a band's potential royalty base to pay for the plastic case, artwork, and shrink-wrap (never mind that it actually costs only a fraction of this amount). If your band has any bargaining power in the record contract dealings, attempt to negotiate it to 15% or lower.

EXAMPLE: *The Grenadiers Lose $3,800 in Packaging Deductions*

The Grenadiers sell 10,000 units at $16. Their contract provides for a 20% packaging deduction. They received a $10,000 advance, and the Grenadiers royalty rate is 12%.

Compact disc (suggested price)	$16.00
Minus packaging costs (20%)	-$ 3.20
	$12.80
Royalty rate	x 12%
Royalty	$1.54
Units sold	x10,000
	$15,400
Minus advance	-$10,000
TOTAL	$5,400

If there were no packaging deduction, the Grenadiers would have earned $9,200. Therefore, the packaging deduction cost the band $3,800.

- **90% of net sales.** Another common (but unjustified) deduction is "Rule 90," under which a record company pays royalties on only 90% of the units sold because the remaining 10% is supposed to cover "breakage" (a remnant of the 1940s, when shellac recordings often cracked). Fortunately, most independents don't bother with this concept. If it is in your agreement and you have some bargaining power, negotiate to strike it.
- **Returns and reserves.** If a store returns your records, the record company deducts the returns from your next invoice. That's reasonable. However, most record companies use a system called "reserves" in which the record company, anticipating returns, holds a percentage of your payment (usually 25% to 35%) until the company can verify whether there are returns. For example, if your agreement provided for a reserve of 25% and the record company owed you $4,000, the company could withhold $1,000 for months or years (the "liquidation period"). If your agreement provides for reserves, attempt to lower the percentage to less than 25% and negotiate a "liquidation period" for as short as possible (we recommend three to six months).
- **Real free goods and promos.** It is acceptable for a record company to

exclude promotional copies from your total units sold. "Promos" are free copies distributed to radio stations and reviewers. "Real free goods" is a term used to describe copies that are "given" to distributors and stores as promotion. (This is a concept that is usually seen in major label agreements, but can also be found in some indie deals.)

- **Manufacturing, shipping, promotional, and marketing costs.** Some record companies deduct manufacturing, artwork design, shipping, independent promotion, or marketing costs from money that is earned by the band. If a record company is deducting items such as manufacturing costs from your royalties, you may want to think twice about entering into the recording agreement. Why? *The record company is charging you for the cost of manufacturing the recordings!* It's bad enough you were charged for recording it; you should not have to pay for the company's overhead expenses.

Merchandising and Video Rights

Perhaps you're hoping that your band can make a video. Often, videos cost as much (or more) than the making of an entire album. This cost is usually shared by the band and the label. If a video costs $100,000, your band must pay $50,000. Of course, your band doesn't have $50,000, so the record company lends you the money as part of your advance. Since videos rarely earn money (they're almost solely used for promotional purposes), which means you have to pay back the advance from record sales. In the event that the video is sold directly to consumers, your band will probably receive a reduced royalty (that is, a royalty lower than your record royalty) for video sales.

Many labels also seek a percentage of merchandise sales. Merchandise sales refers to sales of band T-shirts and paraphernalia. Usually this is a new band's only source of income because they're so heavily in debt to the record company already. If you give up part of your merchandise sales to the label, then you further reduce the chances of your band having enough money to stay on the road and promote the record. If your band has the bargaining power, we recommend holding on to your merchandising rights.

Leaving Members

A "leaving member" provision often requires that if a band member leaves, the record company can pick up the member for future recording under the same terms as the original deal. This rule can apply if the band breaks up as well. The label can choose who it will keep under contract. Worse, the members that must stay with the record company are sometimes saddled with the debts of the group. In other words, if the band breaks up and the label requires that you, the lead singer, must keep recording for them, it's possible that your solo career income will be held by the label until all of your band debts are paid off. Ouch!

Controlled Composition

A controlled composition is any song written by your band or any song in which your band has an ownership interest (for example, your band co-wrote it with an outside songwriter). As we explained in Chapter 8, the record company must pay a special songwriting royalty known as mechanical royalty each time a song is duplicated (or pressed) on a recording. This is a separate payment from your record royalties. The "controlled composition clause" limits how much mechanical royalties the record company will pay for your songs.

Most record companies pay 75% of the statutory mechanical royalty rate (sometimes referred to as the three-quarter rate) for controlled compositions. In addition, it is not uncommon for a record company to limit the total payment to ten songs. In other words, the record company will pay only ten times 75% of the statutory rate per album (approximately 50 cents per album). Even if you include 12 songs, the record company will pay you for only ten. Many record companies set this limit for *all* songs on your album, even if they

are not all controlled compositions (that is, some were written by nonband members). Bands are screwed, because they do not receive a full mechanical rate and do not get paid for more than ten songs. In some cases, the band may record a song written by another songwriter. If the band cannot obtain a 75% rate from the other songwriter, the difference (the remaining 25%) is deducted from the band's mechanical royalty income.

If you can negotiate at all, try either of the following:

- If there is a limit to the number of original songs you can include on your recording, attempt to increase the number of songs (to 11 or 12). This is especially important for compact discs, which often feature bonus tracks.

- Attempt to strike any deductions for noncontrolled compositions (written by nonband members.) If you don't, your band will have to pay the difference. How does this work? Let's say you agreed that the label will have to pay only a six-cent mechanical royalty (instead of 8.5 cents) for every song. Your band has recorded a song by a nonband songwriter who demands the full 8.5 cents rate from the label. Since you agreed on six cents, your band must pay the difference of two cents per record. These pennies can add up quickly as your band sells records.

Copublishing

Under a copublishing deal, the record company becomes a part owner in the band's songs. That is, it's not enough that the label has sunk its fangs into your recordings and merchandise. Now they want income from your songs. For example, if you copublish with your label, and a famous singer such as Mariah Carey covers your song, you and the label will share the income from the cover. Some record companies may seek copublishing deals. Depending on the copublishing agreement, the band may find itself losing control of songs to an ineffective copublisher.

If you have the bargaining power, avoid copublishing with an independent label. If you cannot strike the copublishing deal, consider the following suggestions:

- Limit the arrangement to the songs on the recordings *released* by the record company. That is, if the record company hasn't released the song, it cannot claim copublishing rights.
- Limit the copublisher's song royalties to your band's versions of the songs—not someone else's cover of the song.
- Get an advance for publishing.
- Avoid reducing the mechanical royalty rate for controlled compositions.

- Don't allow the record company to establish a long-term publishing deal separate from the recording deal. The two must be tied together.
- Don't allow the record company to cross-collateralize publishing and record royalties. (Cross-collateralization is covered below.)

Reversionary Rights: Reclaiming Rights to Recordings

Some record companies want ownership rights forever ("in perpetuity"); some companies return the rights ("reversion") after a period of years (usually five to ten). Bands get screwed if they lose all rights.

Always attempt to get a reversion of rights. Insist on it if the record company has not paid you any advances and you have self-financed your recording. If you have the bargaining power, make the reversion period as short as possible—five years is reasonable. Bands have benefited by their ability to later license the selections for compilations or reissues.

Perpetuity and Beyond

If the record company wants to own *all* rights in your work forever (or perpetuity), then you would retain no copyright control. That's referred to as an assignment. We recommend against making an assignment of your recording unless you believe in the record company, and the terms of the agreement, such as royalties and advances, are very good. (Compare the terms to the suggested royalties in the sample agreement in this chapter.) Although under copyright law it's possible to reclaim rights in an assignment after 35 years, you should view an assignment as if you are saying goodbye to the recording forever.

A Record Company Can Turn a Profit on a Recording Even Though the Band Still Owes Money

When negotiating a record company agreement, you should be aware that there are two points of profitability: the point when the record company profits, and the point when the band profits (or recoups). The record company generally earns a profit much earlier than the band. For example, if a record company advanced your band $5,000 to make a recording that subsequently sold 3,000 compact discs, chances are good that the record company has turned a profit of $3,000 or more. However, even with a 12% royalty, your band is still probably in debt. This explains how many record companies can afford to release recordings by bands that do not recoup their advances.

What About Creative Control?

Some bands want a provision in their recording agreements allowing them creative control over the album's content and its artwork. Rarely does a record company permit this provision. Usually, record companies want to have control over the albums and artwork for consistency and marketing purposes. The clause is not of much value anyway, because the only way to enforce it is to sue the record company. Such lawsuits are expensive to initiate and difficult to win. If you are concerned about creative control, talk to other bands signed by the record company and find out how the company treats them. In addition, take the initiative to control as much as you can. For example, oversee any mastering and furnish camera-ready artwork if possible.

EXAMPLE: Snappy's first album is in the red for $5,000. (The album cost $10,000 to make and earned only $5,000 in royalties.) Snappy has assigned some merchandising rights to its record company, and, under that arrangement, Snappy has earned $15,000 in merchandise royalties. The record company will cross-collateralize the debt for the first album with the income from the merchandise. As a result, Snappy will not receive all of its merchandising income and will get a payment of only $10,000.

Cross-Collateralization

Cross-collateralization is a process by which a record company uses band income from one source to pay off a band debt from another source. For example, let's say the record company controls the band's merchandising. The record company may withhold the merchandise royalties until the record royalties are paid off.

What If the Record Company Doesn't Release Your Band's Album?

Most record companies will agree to release a recording within six months of receipt of the masters. When an album isn't released, the band loses momentum and money. There are usually two reasons why a record company won't release a recording: financial problems or marketing problems. For example, the record company might have run out of cash and can't afford to release your album for 12 months, or it may refuse to release your recording because it contains obscene language or uncleared samples.

Here are some suggestions for avoiding these problems:

- **Delays caused by record company problems.** Your band should try for a "guaranteed release" provision requiring the record company to release your album within a period of three to six months of receipt of the master recording. If the label does not meet this deadline, your band can furnish a notice to the record company that they have an additional 30 days to release the album, after which time the agreement is terminated and you can sign with a different record company. If your band paid for the recording, then all rights should revert to your band so you can release the album elsewhere. If the record company paid for the recording, you are usually permitted to buy back the recording at the record company's cost.

- **Delays caused by content of your album.** Every record agreement requires that your band deliver an album that is lawsuit-free. Your band's recording cannot infringe rights or defame someone. Otherwise, the record company has a right to withhold release. Your band can either remove the offensive material or, in the case of samples or other copyrights, seek permission to use it. Your band may have to pay for sample clearances. (For more information on sampling, see Chapter 11.)

Some record agreements contain a requirement that the recording be "commercially satisfactory." Commercially satisfactory means that the record company concludes that your recording is marketable. Most independents don't require "commercially satisfactory" recordings. If that provision is included, attempt to change it to "technically satisfactory," which means only that the recording is professionally made.

It is standard for record companies to cross-collateralize debts and income from subsequent albums. However, some record companies cross-collateralize merchandise and mechanical royalty income against record royalties. That is, the record company does not have to pay mechanical royalties or merchandise income until all album debts are recouped. This is particularly unfair when the album may have already achieved profitability for the record company. Your band should make it a priority to attempt to negotiate out any attempts at cross-collateralization for songwriting payments (mechanical royalties) or merchandising. Why? Because otherwise, your band will receive little or no songwriting or T-shirt income—money that many bands rely on for living expenses.

Independent Record and License Agreements

This section deals with recording and license agreements: how to analyze them and how to modify them. If you have turned directly to this section without reviewing any other material in this book, you may have some difficulty deciphering the contracts. In order to evaluate an agreement, you will need some familiarity with the principles discussed in this book, particularly the information earlier in this chapter and the information regarding

publishing in Chapter 8. We suggest you review that before you begin.

It's very unlikely that your band will draft or furnish the recording or licensing agreement. Instead, you will be handed an agreement and asked to sign it. That's because every record company uses its own agreement, usually prepared by the company's lawyer. The sample agreements below are provided to give you an idea of what to expect in recording agreements and to give you a chance to learn what typical provisions mean. You can use the samples below to compare to any agreements you're given by your record company.

Do You Need an Attorney?

Can your band negotiate the agreement without an attorney? If it is an independent label agreement, you can probably do it yourself. If it's a major label agreement, you'll need an attorney's or manager's assistance. See Chapters 3 and 4 on managers and attorneys, and Chapter 17 on other resources for musicians.

In order to analyze an agreement, we suggest the following strategies:

- *Don't freak out!* Be prepared to spend several hours making your analysis.
- Make a photocopy of the agreement.

- Locate the major provisions (as discussed below) and label them in the margin.
- Compare each provision with the language in the sample agreements in this chapter.
- Underline everything you don't like or don't understand.
- List the number of the provision and write down your concerns about that section.
- Review the list with your band and decide which changes are the most important. List your changes in order of importance.
- Don't expect that every change you request will be made by the company. Most of your changes will not be granted. Instead, focus on those changes that are most important to your band.

Below, we explain the typical provisions of recording and license agreements. The explanation for each provision applies whether the provision appears in a recording agreement or a licensing agreement. We explain each provision only once, because the provisions are essentially the same between the two agreements. But keep in mind that the two agreements are not the same. Recording agreements are used when a record company wants to buy the rights to a new recording of your band. License agreements, on the other hand, are used when a record company wants to acquire rights to an album your band

has already cut. For example, say you recorded 12 songs, and an indie label heard them and wants to release them as an album. A license agreement would be used for this purpose, not a recording agreement.

Ready to begin? You'll need a clean (unmarked) photocopy of the agreement, and a pen and a ruler for underlining. Read the explanations for the provisions, and then review the provisions in the agreement furnished by your record company. Unfortunately, there are no rules for the ordering and placement of provisions in recording and license agreements. Many agreements seem haphazardly organized. We've included keywords to help you identify specific provisions in your agreement.

The following two agreements are included on the forms CD that comes with this book.

Introduction

Keywords: Whereas, Introduction

The introduction usually takes up the first few paragraphs of the agreement and often includes the term "Whereas" (as in, "Whereas the parties agree to enter into a recording agreement"). The introduction generally sets out the names of the record company, the band, and the band's individual members. Note that the phrase "collectively and individually" means that each individual member is individually liable under the agreement.

Exclusive Recording Services

Keyword: Exclusive

An exclusive recording services clause establishes that the recording agreement is exclusive and that you can record only for the record company, not for another company. Sometimes this exclusivity requirement is placed in another section of the agreement, such as in the Grant of Rights section, below.

Master Recordings

Keywords: Masters, Recordings, Commercially Satisfactory, Technically Satisfactory

This section defines "Master Recordings" and the standards under which the label must accept the recordings. One standard used is "technically satisfactory," which means that the recording must be accepted as long as it is professionally made and meets traditional recording standards. Some record companies prefer a different standard called "commercially satisfactory." In that case, the company won't release the recording unless the company thinks it is marketable. Labels generally want studio albums, not live albums, and, in that case, the label may insert a statement to that effect. Sometimes the "master recordings"

definition is included in a special section titled "Definitions."

Term

Keywords: Term, Length

After you submit a master recording to the record company, you may still be prohibited from recording for any other company. Most recording agreements require that a band grant what are known as "options" to the record company, which allow the company to take some time to decide whether it wants another recording from you. The maximum number of records your band will have to cut (besides the first one) is known as the number of options you grant the company. After you submit a recording, the company will decide whether or not to exercise its option to have you cut another record. While you wait for the company's decision, you are not allowed to record for anyone else, since you're still under the exclusive recording contract. If the label does not exercise its option to make another recording during this period, then your agreement is over and you may record for another company.

This period of time, after you submit your first master recording, during which the label can decide whether to keep you or drop you is called the term. We recommend a nine-month term. The term will be extended by a specified period if the label exercises an option, called the option term. For option terms, we also recommend nine months. As for the number of options, try to keep them down to one or two if possible, though some labels may insist on more.

In some agreements, this provision is buried at the end near the termination section.

This provision *does not* affect how long the record company can sell the recordings. That is controlled by the section entitled "Ownership of Recordings."

Grant of Rights

Keywords: Rights, Copyright, Ownership

This provision lists the rights that the label is acquiring from your band. In our sample agreement, the first part of the provision determines how long the label owns your band's recording, or what we refer to as the Ownership Period. You have two choices: a fixed period of years, or "in perpetuity" (forever).

We recommend a fixed period of years (commonly between three and ten). The shorter the better, because your band will reacquire rights sooner. *We recommend against granting rights in perpetuity,* especially if you have self-financed your recording (paid for it yourselves without an advance).

If you give up rights in perpetuity, then you will not be able to release the recording with another company later. *The company will always own the rights, or at least own them for 35 years!*

Right to Use Artist's Name and Likeness

Keywords: Artist's Name, Likeness, Image

Under this provision, the company acquires the right to use your band's name and image as necessary to set up promotional photo shoots and interviews. This is common, and every label must acquire these rights.

Side-Artist Recording

Keywords: Side-Artist, Outside Recording

Since you have signed an exclusive recording agreement, then technically you cannot record in any capacity for any other record company or even a friend's recording. This provision gets around this by allowing individual band members to perform on other recordings. If the company requires you to obtain permission before doing a side recording, you would use a provision similar to the first choice in the sample agreement.

Professional Name

*Keywords: Professional Name, Band
        Name, Service Mark,
        Trademark*

Unless the band breaks up or members
leave (as described in the section entitled
"Leaving Members"), the company wants
you to perform under your band name.

Trademark Search

*Keywords: Search, Trademark,
        Service Mark*

This section, often omitted from
independent deals, protects the label
against claims of trademark infringement
if another band has a similar name. See
Chapter 9 for information on band names.

Production of Master Recordings

Keywords: Recording, Advance

Under this provision, you are responsible
for the cost of recording the record.
Generally, this is okay, because the label
is lending you money (the advance), and
your band is responsible for using that
to pay recording costs. In some deals,
the label may pay the recording costs
directly to the recording studio. Even if
the label directly pays for the recording,
the amount is still deducted against
your band's future royalties. Often this
provision is included within the Payment
provision.

Subsequent Recording of Compositions

*Keywords: Subsequent, Compositions,
        Songs*

This is the period of time during which
your band is restricted from recording
any of the band songs released by the
label. We recommend two to three years,
although most labels insist on five years.

Advances and Recoupable Costs

Keywords: Advances, Recoupable

This provision is usually part of the
"Payment" section of the agreement. It
provides the amount of your advance
and establishes when you receive it.
Independent record companies usually
pay advances of $3,000 to $10,000.
Some labels do not pay any advances.
Some recording contracts are actually
just glorified license agreements. The
band pays for the recording out of its
own pocket, and the label releases the
recording. The advantage is that there
is no advance to deduct against future
royalties. The obvious disadvantage is that
your band has to finance the recording. If
you self-finance your recording, you will
not need this provision. However, if you
are self-financing and don't receive an
advance payment, you should be sure to
avoid giving up rights in perpetuity (see
Grant of Rights section, above).

   If you are getting an advance, we
recommend getting it when you sign the

contract (insert the words "execution of this agreement" where it asks for the date). Some labels pay an advance on delivery of the album. In that case, insert the words "delivery of the Master Recording."

Advance for Option Term

Keywords: Advances, Recoupable

This optional provision is the advance for the subsequent recordings. You should use this if you have included option periods. That is, if the label can require additional recordings, you should establish the amount of each advance for those future recordings. (See the Term section of your agreement.) Generally, the advances increase for each subsequent album.

Royalties

Keywords: Royalties, Percentage, Wholesale, SRLP

The royalty section describes how much your band is paid, and it usually permits the company to make certain deductions. The provision in the sample agreement uses the most common royalty system: The band earns a percentage of the suggested retail list price (SRLP). Independent labels usually pay 9% to 13%; majors pay 10% to 15%. Instead of using an SRLP, some independents pay 20% to 30% of the wholesale price or pay the band 25% to 50% of the total sales

income. A deal may also include sliding (or "escalating") royalties. That is, your royalty rate increases as you sell more albums (9% to 13% for independents, 10% to 20% for majors). We recommend a royalty of 12% or more of SRLP. If your label is paying a royalty on wholesale, we recommend a royalty of 25% or more.

The most common deduction is packaging costs. We recommend that you fight for the minimum possible packaging cost—15% or lower.

Singles

Keyword: Singles

Sometimes this provision is not included, because the label does not intend to release singles. The royalty rate for singles is often half of the royalty rate for an album. We recommend 5% to 6% of SRLP or 10% to 12% of wholesale.

Downloads; Electronic Transmissions

Keywords: Downloads, Electronic, New Media, MP3

When a label offers downloads via the Internet—for example, MP3s—we recommend splitting all revenues equally. That is, your band gets 50% (or more if you can negotiate it) of all income from the downloads.

Nickels for Downloads?

Beware of record company deals in which the label attempts to apply the 9% to 13% CD royalty rate when paying your band for MP3s. Under these arrangements, the label often reduces the royalty (sometimes by one-half) *and* applies packaging deductions (usually 15%) even though there is no packaging for MP3s. Under that arrangement, if the label received $1.00 per downloaded song, and the artist's royalty was 6%, the artist would receive approximately six cents per download. Under the arrangement provided for in our agreement, the band gets half the income from the download.

Foreign Licenses

Keywords: License, Sublicense, Foreign

Usually, the label sublicenses the rights to a foreign label and pays the band a percentage (we recommend 50%).

Reserves

Keyword: Reserves

Under this optional provision, the record company, anticipating returns, holds a percentage of your payment (usually 25% to 35% of the money you are supposed to receive) until the company is convinced

there are no returns from stores. The percentage that is not paid to your band is called a "reserve." Attempt to cap the reserves at 25% or less. Some labels hold the reserves for years. We recommend that you ask the label to hold the reserve for two accounting periods or less.

Compilations

Keywords: Compilation, Numerator, Denominator

This is a standard system for dividing up the royalties in case a track from your recording is used on a company compilation. Sometimes, the agreement refers to this calculation as a fraction and uses the terms "numerator" and "denominator."

Flat Fee

Keywords: License, Flat Fee

If part or all of your recording is licensed (that is, rented by your record company to some other company), your band is paid a percentage of a flat fee license. Fifty percent is common. An example of this would be if a cosmetic company wanted to include your song in a radio commercial. (Note: The cosmetic company would also need to obtain permission from your song publisher, as well.)

Promotional Recordings and Cutouts

Keywords: Promotional, Free, Cutouts

Record companies do not pay royalties on copies of the recordings that are distributed for free or for promotional purposes or that are scrapped (that is, where the record is thrown out).

Statements; Audit

Keywords: Audit, Statement

This provision details the company's obligations to pay you, and it also explains your rights in the event of an audit. These sections often differ drastically from agreement to agreement. Generally, you want to get paid as soon as possible. We recommend that the company pay within 30 days at the end of the accounting period, although many labels prefer 90 days. Although we endorse the terms of our audit provision, as a general rule, if you have a right to audit, don't get hung up on negotiating the related details such as how often or the amount of the underpayment.

Video

Keywords: Video, Audiovisual, Synchronization

This optional provision permits the company to create a video to promote your recording. If you have a record

contract in which the company owns the recordings for a limited number of years (not forever), then this section should have the same length of time as in the "Grant of Rights" section. If the grant is forever (in perpetuity), then insert "in perpetuity." We recommend a video royalty of 50% or more.

Commercial Release of Records

Keywords: Release, Guaranteed Release Date

A guaranteed release date protects your band. We recommend six months from the date you submit the master recording. The first provision in our sample agreement allows the band to acquire rights to the recording if the album is not released in a timely manner. Many labels will want to have any advances returned before allowing the band to reacquire ownership. If that's what you agree on with the record company, you would use something similar to the second choice in the sample agreement.

Artist Promotional Records

Keywords: Promos, Free Copies

Labels commonly provide at least five promotional copies per band member. Make sure this provision is in your agreement, as otherwise you will have to pay for copies of your own recording.

Album Artwork

Keywords: Artwork, Specifications

This provision in the model agreement establishes the band's right to prepare its own artwork at its own expense. You may be able to obtain an artwork advance from an independent label (usually between $300 and $500). Not all agreements will include such a provision.

Artist Warranties

Keywords: Indemnification, Warrant, Covenant, Represent

Warranties are contractual promises. If your band breaks one of these promises, the label can seek money damages from your band. If your agreement does not contain any warranties, that's fine. Don't bring it up. If your agreement does contain warranties, compare them to the ones in the model agreement. To protect yourself with regard to warranties, you should have a written agreement with all of the performers and artists who contributed to the recordings. For example, you would need a release (see Chapter 11) from a hired musician or from a photographer who took the album cover photo.

When you provide indemnity (that is, "indemnify" someone), you agree to pay for their damages that you caused. In other words, if the record company is sued because of your album art, you would have to pay for the label's legal

expenses. If this section is not present in your recording agreement, that's fine. Don't bring it up.

Controlled Compositions License

Keywords: Controlled Compositions, Songs, Copyright, Mechanical License

Controlled compositions are songs written or owned by your band. We discussed controlled compositions earlier in this chapter.

Mechanical Royalties

Keywords: (same as above)

The principles of mechanical royalties are explained in detail in Chapter 8. This provision permits the label to pay full rate (100%) or to pay less than the statutory rate. Seventy-five percent is standard for mechanical royalties, but try for a higher percentage if possible. The second option is provided in the event that the company insists on restricting the total number of songs on which they must pay mechanical royalties. In that case, we recommend at least 12 compositions, although some labels insist on ten compositions.

Leaving Members

Keywords: Leaving Member, Departing Member

This provision allows the label to obtain recording contracts with any band members who leave the group during the term of the recording agreement. Some labels may modify this provision in order to recoup what the band owes from the leaving member. Under that modification, the leaving member who is engaged by the label is stuck with the band's debts. We recommend against that arrangement.

Termination

Keywords: Termination, Breach, End
This provides the basis for either party to terminate. Under the provision in the sample agreement, if the company fails to pay royalties and does not correct it within 30 days of your notification, you can terminate the agreement and reacquire rights to your recordings. If possible, see if you can get this language into your recording agreement.

Termination in the Event of Leaving Member

Keywords: Leaving Members, Departing Members
This provision is related to the other Leaving Member provision, above. This allows the label to terminate the agreement if a key band member leaves the group. That is, the company has the option to terminate the agreement as to the whole band.

Mediation; Arbitration

Keywords: Mediation, Arbitration, Dispute Resolution
This provision provides a less expensive method of resolving disputes than filing a lawsuit. (See the sidebar in Chapter 2 for an explanation of mediation and arbitration.) We recommend that you use this provision in order to help avoid an expensive lawsuit.

General

Keywords: Miscellaneous, Govern, State, Controlling Law
The following provisions are standard contract provisions referred to as boilerplate. Boilerplate provisions are also explained in Chapter 2.

Signatures

Each party must sign the agreement in relation to the business that is represented, and each party must have the authority to sign the agreement. Use the following rules when determining who should sign:

- **Sole Proprietorship:** If the band or the record company is a sole proprietorship, the sole proprietor can simply sign his or her own name.
- **Partnership:** If the band or record company is a general or limited partnership, then the only person authorized to sign the agreement is

a general partner or someone who has written authority (usually in the form a partnership resolution) from a general partner.

- **Corporation or LLC:** If the company is a corporation or limited liability company (LLC), then only a person authorized by the corporation can sign the agreement. The president or chief executive officer (CEO) usually has such power, but not every officer of a corporation has the authority to bind the corporation.

If in doubt, ask for written proof of the authority. This proof is usually in the form of a corporate resolution. The name of the corporation should be mentioned above the signature line or the corporation may not be bound, only the person signing the agreement.

If you have doubts about the person's authority, don't proceed until you are satisfied that the person has full authority to represent the company.

Independent Label Recording Agreement

Introduction

This agreement (the "Agreement") is entered into between _____ ("Company") and _____ , known collectively as _____ and performing under the name_____ (referred to as "Artist.")

All references to "Artist" include all members of the group collectively and individually unless otherwise specified.

The parties agree as follows:

Exclusive Recording Services

During the Term (as described below), Artist will render recording services only for the Company and will not, unless otherwise permitted under this Agreement, render recording services for any other party.

Master Recordings

Artist will deliver to Company technically satisfactory recordings containing not less than forty (40) minutes of playing time (the "Master Recording"). Company will release a commercial product embodying the material contained on the Master Recordings (the "Records").

Term

The Artist's obligation to perform exclusive recording services begins on the latest signature date of this Agreement (the "Effective Date") and continues for _____ months after delivery of the first Master Recording (the "Term"). If Artist grants one or more options to Company as part of this Agreement, any time prior to the end of the Term, the Company may extend the Term by exercising its option. If an option is exercised, the term will continue for _____ months after the delivery of the previous Master Recording ("Option Term"). If Company ever chooses not to exercise an option, the agreement will terminate regardless of how many options remain.

Artist grants to Company (check if applicable):

O one option   O two options   O three options   O four options   O _____ options

Grant of Rights

(Select one and fill in appropriate blanks.)

○ Beginning on the date when a Master Recording is delivered to Company, Company will be the exclusive owner of rights to all Master Recordings for the period of time: _____ (the "Ownership Period").

○ Artist assigns to Company all rights to the Master Recording in perpetuity.

After the Ownership Period, all rights in the Master Recordings revert to Artist. During the Ownership Period, Artist grants to Company all right, title, and interest in the sound recording copyright (as provided under the U.S. Copyright Act of 1976 and international copyright treaties) to the Master Recordings, including:

- the exclusive right to manufacture copies of all or any portion of the Master Recordings

- the exclusive right to import, export, sell, transfer, release, license, publicly perform, rent, and otherwise exploit or dispose of the Master Recordings, and

- the exclusive right to edit, adapt, or conform the Master Recordings to technological or commercial requirements in various formats now known or later developed.

Territory

The rights granted to Company are limited to _____ (the "Territory").

Right to Use Artist's Name and Likeness

Company has the right to reproduce or distribute, in any medium, Artist's names, portraits, pictures, and likeness for purposes of advertising, promotion, or trade in connection with Artist or the exploitation of the Master Recordings. Artist will be available from time to time to appear for photography, video performance, or the like, under the reasonable direction of Company. Artist is not entitled to any compensation for such services except for reimbursement of travel expenses.

Side-Artist Recording

(Select one.)

○ During the Term, Artist may perform as part of another artist's recording project (a "side-artist" performance) provided that: (a) the side-artist recording does not interfere with obligations under this Agreement; (b) only one member of Artist performs on the side-artist project; and (c) the following credit is included on the side-artist recording: "[Name of Artist] appears courtesy of [Company Name]."

○ Artist may perform as part of another artist's recording project (a "side-artist" performance) provided that Company has furnished written consent for such performance. Consent must not be unreasonably withheld. In the event of such performance, the following credit is included on the side-artist recording: "[Name of Artist] appears courtesy of [Company Name]."

Professional Name

With the exception of the Leaving Member sections of this Agreement, Artist will perform and record under the professional name _____. Artist will not use a different name in connection with the Master Recordings unless Artist and Company mutually agree in writing.

Trademark Search *(Check if applicable.)*

○ Company, at its discretion, may institute a search to determine whether there are any third-party uses for Artist's name. If the search indicates that the name cannot be used, Company and Artist will mutually agree on a substitute name. Any amounts up to but not exceeding six hundred dollars ($600.00) may be expended for the purposes of the trademark search and will be considered as a recoupable advance.

Production of Master Recordings

Artist is responsible for payment of all expenses incurred in the production of the Master Recordings and will obtain the appropriate permission, clearance, or release from any person or union who renders services in the production of the Master Recordings.

Subsequent Recording of Compositions

Artist represents and warrants that Artist will not record any composition contained on a Master Recording for a period of _____ years from the date of first release of a Company recording containing such composition.

Advances and Recoupable Costs

All money paid by Company to Artist, other than royalties paid under this Agreement, will be considered an advance against royalties ("Advances"). All Advances will be set off against future royalties. In connection with the initial Master Recording delivered, Company will pay Artist an Advance of _____ on the date of _____.

Advance for Option Term *(Check and fill in blank if applicable.)*

O In connection with the Master Recording delivered under the Option Terms, Company will pay Artist an Advance of _____.

Royalties

Company will pay Artist a percentage (the "Royalty") of the Company's sales for all Records sold, less the actual container costs (not to exceed _____% of SRLP), plus excise, sales, and similar taxes.

Company will pay Artist _____% of (select one):

O suggested retail list price (SRLP) or O wholesale price.

Singles

In the event that Company releases singles, Company will pay Artist _____% of (select one):

O suggested retail list price (SRLP) or O wholesale price.

Downloads; Electronic Transmissions

In the event that Company offers a composition from the Master Recording for sale in electronic form via Internet, wireless, or other electronic transmission, Company will pay Artist _____% of the net receipts paid to Company for such transmissions.

Foreign Licenses

Company will pay Artist _____% of the net receipts paid to Company under any foreign license.

Reserves *(Check if applicable and fill in blanks.)*

O In computing the Records sold, only Records for which Company has been paid or credited shall be considered sold. Company has the right to deduct returns and credits and to make reasonable reserves, not to exceed _____% of sales in any one accounting period, provided that such reserves must be liquidated within _____ accounting period(s).

Compilations

If a composition from the Master Recording is used on a compilation or recording in which other artists are included, the Artist's royalty will be prorated. For example, if a composition from the Master Recording is included on a compilation containing nine selections from other artists, Artist shall be entitled to one-tenth (1/10th) of the royalty rate.

Flat Fee

Company will pay Artist _____% of the net receipts paid to Company under any flat fee license of the Master Recordings or any portion of the Master Recordings.

Promotional Recordings and Cutouts

No royalties will be due on Records furnished on a promotional basis. Nor will any royalty be due for Records sold by Company as cutouts or for scrap or otherwise on deletion from Company's catalog.

Statements; Audit

Company will pay Artist the Artist's Royalties within _____ days after the end of each quarter. Company will also furnish an accurate statement of sales of Records during that month. Company will pay interest on any late payment from the due date until paid. The acceptance by Artist of any statement or payment does not prevent Artist's later questioning its accuracy. Company will keep accurate books of account covering all transactions relating to this Agreement. Artist or its representatives have the right on reasonable written notice to audit Company's books relating to the Records. If the audit indicates an underpayment greater than $500 for any six-month period, Company will pay for the audit.

Video *(Check if applicable and fill in blanks.)*

○ If Company decides during the term of this Agreement to produce one or more recordings combining the audio performance of Artist with a visual image (the "Video"), Company and Artist will mutually agree on the budget and production costs (the "Production Budget") for such Video or Videos. All sums paid by Company as part of the Production Budget will be considered as an Advance against royalties. Company is the sole owner of all worldwide rights to each Video, including the worldwide copyrights. Company has the right to use and allow others to use each Video for advertising and promotional purposes with no payment to Artist. "Advertising and promotional purposes" means all uses for which Company receives no money in excess of incidental fees such as tape stock and duplication and shipping. Artist is entitled to a royalty as established in the Royalty Section for all revenue derived from commercial exploitation of the Videos. Artist will issue a worldwide synchronization license for any Controlled Compositions embodied on a Video. For a period of _____ years from the date of first release of any Video, Company has the right to allow others to use that Video for commercial purposes. If Company licenses or commercially exploits the Video(s), Company will pay, after deducting all costs advanced for production, a royalty of _____% of the net revenues from any license or sale of that Video. Artist grants to Company the right to synchronize the Master Recordings with visual images to create Videos.

Commercial Release of Records

○ Company will release the Records within _____ months of delivery of the Master Recordings (the "Guaranteed Release Date"). Artist will provide written notice if Company fails to release the recording by the Guaranteed Release Date. If, after 30 days from notification, Company has not released the recording, Artist may terminate this agreement. All rights in the Master Recordings will revert to Artist, and Company will have no further rights to the recording, or

○ Company will release the Records within _____ months of delivery of the Master Recordings (the "Guaranteed Release Date"). Artist will provide written notice if Company fails to release the recording by the Guaranteed Release Date. If, after 30 days from notification, Company has not released the recording, Artist may terminate this agreement and Artist may acquire the unreleased Master Recording and all related rights by paying to Company the sum of any advance for such Master Recording.

Artist Promotional Records

Company will furnish to Artist a total of _____ promotional Records at no charge. Artist may obtain further Records from Company at Company's then-wholesale cost.

Album Artwork (Check if applicable and fill in blank.)

○ Artist, at its own expense, may furnish camera-ready artwork for the Records at the time of delivery of the Master Recording. Such artwork may be delivered in electronic format. Company has the right to modify or conform the artwork to meet Company specifications and standards. However, Company will consult with Artist before making any modification. If Artist elects not to furnish artwork, Company will prepare the artwork and consult with Artist regarding the design. Company will advance the sum of $_____ for artwork preparation. This payment is an advance against future royalties.

Artist Warranties

Artist warrants to Company that Artist has the power and authority to enter into this Agreement, is the Artist and copyright holder of the Master Recordings, or has or will obtain all necessary and appropriate rights and licenses to grant the license in this Agreement with respect to the Master Recordings. Artist warrants that the Master Recordings are original to Artist except for material in the public domain and such excerpts from other works that may be included with the written permission of the copyright owners, and that proper clearances or permission have been obtained from the artists of any copyrighted material, including but not limited to any digitally reprocessed samples of material incorporated in the Master Recordings. Artist warrants that Artist's use of any name or moniker will not infringe on the rights of others and that Artist's use of any musical composition or arrangement will not infringe on the rights of others.

(Check if applicable.)

❍ Artist further warrants that the Master Recordings do not:

- contain any libelous material

- infringe any trade name, trademark, trade secret, or copyright, or

- invade or violate any right of privacy, personal or proprietary right, or other common law or statutory right.

(Check if applicable.)

❍ Artist hereby indemnifies Company and undertakes to defend Company against and hold Company harmless (including, without limitation, attorney fees and costs) from any claims and damage arising out of a breach of Artist's Warranties as provided above. Artist agrees to reimburse Company for any payment made by Company with respect to this Section, provided that the claim has been settled or has resulted in a final judgment against Company or its licensees. Artist will notify Company in writing of any infringements or imitations by others of the Master Recording that may come to Artist's attention.

Controlled Compositions License

Artist grants to Company an irrevocable worldwide license to reproduce all compositions wholly or partly written, owned or controlled by Artist (the "Controlled Compositions"). Artist grants to Company a first mechanical license for all Controlled Compositions.

Mechanical Royalties

Artist acknowledges and agrees that Company will pay a royalty for the mechanical license on all Records manufactured for sale or commercial distribution at __% of the minimum compulsory license rate (the "Company Mechanical Rate") applicable in the country of manufacture. The applicable minimum statutory rate will be determined as of the date of the commencement of the recording of the applicable Master Recording. Mechanical Royalties are not payable for musical compositions of one minute or less in duration.

(Check if applicable.)

❍ For each Master Recording, Company will pay only a sum equivalent to the Company Mechanical Royalty Rate multiplied by _____.

Leaving Members *(Check if applicable.)*

O If any member of Artist ceases to perform as a member of the group ("Leaving Member"), Artist will promptly give Company written notice. If the group disbands, each member of the group is considered to be a Leaving Member. Artist grants to Company an irrevocable option to engage the exclusive services of any Leaving Member as a recording artist. In the event of Company's exercise of this option, the Leaving Member will be considered to have entered into an agreement with Company on all the terms and conditions of this Agreement, including the initial term, the first option term, payments, royalties and all other applicable terms. The Leaving Member will not, however, be responsible for any outstanding Artist debts, including unrecouped advances.

Termination

Company may terminate this Agreement within thirty (30) days of the expiration of the Term or any Option Period. Artist can terminate this Agreement if Company fails to pay Artist's Royalties when due or to accurately report Net Sales, if the failure is not corrected within 30 days after notice from Artist. If this Agreement is breached because of a failure to pay or accurately report royalties, all rights granted under this agreement revert to Artist, and Company will have no further rights regarding Artist or the Master Recordings.

If this Agreement is terminated for a reason other than Company's failure to pay or accurately report Artist's Royalties, the termination will not terminate the underlying license and copyrights granted to Company by Artist, nor Company's obligations to pay Royalties under this Agreement.

Termination in the Event of Leaving Member

Within ninety (90) days of receipt of notice of any Leaving Member, as defined in the Leaving Members section, Company will have the right to terminate the Agreement as to the remaining members of Artist. If that happens, all members of Artist will be deemed to be Leaving Members.

Mediation; Arbitration

If a dispute arises under this Agreement, the parties agree to first try to resolve the dispute with the help of a mutually agreed-on mediator in _____. Any costs and fees other than attorney fees will be shared equally by the parties. If it is impossible to arrive at a mutually satisfactory solution within a reasonable time, the parties agree to submit the dispute to binding arbitration in the same city or region, conducted on a confidential basis under:

○ the Commercial Arbitration Rules of the American Arbitration Association, or

○ the rules of _____.

Any decision or award as a result of arbitration will include the assessment of costs, expenses, and reasonable attorney's fees and a written determination of the arbitrators. Absent an agreement to the contrary, arbitration will be conducted by an arbitrator experienced in music industry law. An award of arbitration is final and binding on the Artist and may be confirmed in a court of competent jurisdiction. The prevailing party has the right to collect from the other party its reasonable costs and attorney fees incurred in enforcing this agreement.

General

Nothing contained in this Agreement makes either Company or Artist a partner, joint venturer, or employee of the other party for any purpose. This Agreement may not be amended except in a writing signed by both parties. No waiver by either party of any right is a waiver of any other right. If a court finds any provision of this Agreement invalid or unenforceable as applied to any circumstance, the remainder of this Agreement will be interpreted to carry out the intent of the parties. This Agreement is governed by and interpreted in accordance with the laws of the State of _____. This Agreement expresses the complete understanding of the parties on the subject matter and supersedes all prior proposals, agreements, representations, and understandings. Notices required under this Agreement can be sent to the parties at the addresses provided below. In the event of any dispute arising from or related to this Agreement, the prevailing party is entitled to attorney's fees.

Artist Business Name _____

Artist Representative Name and Title _____

Artist Representative Signature _____

Artist Address _____

Date _____

Company Name _____

Company Representative Name and Title _____

Company Representative Signature _____

Company Address _____

Date _____

Independent Label License Agreement

Introduction

This agreement (the "Agreement") is entered into between _____ ("Company") and _____, known collectively as _____ and performing under the name _____ (referred to as "Artist.")

All references to "Artist" include all members of the group collectively and individually unless otherwise specified. The parties agree as follows:

Recordings and Records

Company wants to license rights to a sound recording entitled _____ (the "Master Recording") consisting of the following songs:

_____

_____

_____

_____

_____

Company will release a commercial product embodying the material contained on the Master Recordings (the "Records").

Grant of Rights

Company will be the exclusive licensee of all rights to the Master Recording for _____ years from the date of receipt of each Master Recording (the "Ownership Period"). After the Ownership Period, all rights granted under this Agreement will revert to Artist. Artist grants to Company the following rights to the Master Recording:

- the exclusive right to manufacture copies of all or any portion of the Master Recording
- the exclusive right to sell, transfer, release, license, publicly perform, rent, and otherwise exploit or dispose of the Master Recording, and
- the exclusive right to edit, adapt, or conform the Master Recording to technological or commercial requirements in various formats now known or later developed.

Territory

The rights granted to Company are limited to _____ (the "Territory").

Right to Use Artist's Name and Likeness

Company has the right to reproduce or distribute, in any medium, Artist's names, portraits, pictures, and likeness for purposes of advertising, promotion, or trade in connection with Artist or the exploitation of the Master Recording. Artist will be available from time to time to appear for photography, video performance, or the like, under the reasonable direction of Company. Artist is not entitled to any compensation for these services except for reimbursement of travel expenses.

Delivery of Master Recording

Within _____ months of the Effective Date, Artist will deliver to Company the Master Recording.

Production of Master Recording

Artist will be responsible for payment of all expenses incurred in the production of the Master Recording and will get the appropriate permission, clearance, or release from any person or union who renders services in the production of the Master Recording.

Advances (Check if applicable and fill in blanks.)

○ All monies paid by Company to Artist, other than royalties paid pursuant to this Agreement, will be considered an advance against royalties ("Advances"). All Advances will be set off against future royalties. In connection with the initial Recording delivered, Company will pay Artist an Advance of $_____ on the date of _____.

Royalties

Company will pay Artist a percentage (the "Royalty") of the Company's sales for all Records sold less the actual container costs (not to exceed _____% of SRLP) and excise, sales, and similar taxes.

Company will pay Artist _____% of (select one):

○ suggested retail list price (SRLP) or ○ wholesale price.

Singles

If Company releases singles, Company will pay Artist _____% of (select one):

○ suggested retail list price (SRLP) or ○ wholesale price.

Downloads; Electronic Transmissions

In the event that Company offers a composition from the Master Recording for sale in electronic form via Internet, wireless, or other electronic transmission, Company will pay Artist _____% of the net receipts paid to Company for such transmissions.

Reserves *(Check and fill in blanks if applicable.)*

○ In computing the recordings sold, only recordings for which Company has been paid or credited will be considered sold. Company has the right to deduct returns and credits and to make reasonable reserves, not to exceed _____% of sales in any one accounting period, provided that such reserves must be liquidated within _____ accounting period(s).

Compilations

If a composition from the Master Recording is used on a compilation or recording in which other artists are included, the Artist's royalty will be prorated. For example, if a composition from the Master Recording is included on a compilation containing nine selections from other artists, Artist will be entitled to one-tenth (1/10th) of the royalty rate.

Promotional Recordings and Cutouts

No royalties will be due on Records furnished on a promotional basis. No royalty will be due for Records sold by Company as cutouts or for scrap or otherwise upon deletion from Company's catalog.

Statements; Audit

Company will pay Artist the Artist's Royalties within _____ days after the end of each quarter. Company will furnish an accurate statement of sales of Records during that month. If late in any payment, Company will pay interest from the due date until paid. The acceptance by Artist of any statement or payment does not prevent Artist later questioning its accuracy. Company will keep accurate books of account covering all transactions relating to this Agreement. Artist or its representatives have the right on reasonable written notice to audit Company's books relating to the Records. If the audit indicates an underpayment greater than $500 for any six-month period, Company will pay for the audit.

Video *(Check and fill in blanks if applicable.)*

○ If Company decides, during the term of this Agreement, to produce a recording combining the audio performance of Artist with a visual image (the "Video"), Company and Artist will mutually agree on the budget and production costs (the "Production Budget") for such Video. All sums paid by Company as part of the Production Budget will be considered as an Advance against royalties. Company will be the sole owner of all worldwide rights to each Video, including the worldwide copyrights. Company will have the right to use and allow others to use each Video for advertising and promotional purposes with no payment to Artist. "Advertising and promotional purposes" means all uses for which Company receives no money in excess of incidental fees such as tape stock and duplication and shipping. Artist is entitled to a royalty as established in the Royalty Section for all revenue derived from commercial exploitation of the Videos. Artist will issue a worldwide synchronization license for any Controlled Compositions embodied on a Video. For a period of _____ years from the date of release of any Video, Company will have the right to allow others to use the Videos for commercial purposes. If Company licenses or commercially exploits the Videos, Company will pay, after deducting all costs advanced for production, a royalty of _____% of the net revenues from any license or sale of the Video. Artist grants to Company the right to synchronize the Master Recordings with visual images to create Videos.

Commercial Release of Records

(Select one and fill in blanks.)

○ Company will release the Records within _____ months of delivery of the Master Recordings (the "Guaranteed Release Date"). Artist will give written notice if Company fails to release the recording by the Guaranteed Release Date, and if, after thirty (30) days from notification, the Company has not released the recording, Artist may terminate this agreement, and all rights in the Master Recordings will revert to Artist and Company will have no further rights to the recording.

○ Company will release the Records within _____ months of delivery of the Master Recordings (the "Guaranteed Release Date"). Artist will give written notice if Company fails to release the recording by the Guaranteed Release Date, and if, after 30 days from notification, the Company has not released the recording, Artist may terminate this agreement and acquire the unreleased Master Recording and all related rights by paying to Company the sum of any advance for the Master Recording.

Artist Promotional Records

Company will furnish to Artist a total of _____ promotional Records at no charge. Artist may obtain further Records from Company at Company's then-wholesale cost.

Album Artwork

(Check if applicable and fill in blank.)

O Artist, at its own expense, may furnish camera-ready artwork for the Records at the time of delivery of the Master Recording. Such artwork may be delivered in electronic format. Company has the right to modify or conform the artwork to meet Company specifications and standards. However, Company will consult with Artist before making any modification. If Artist elects not to furnish artwork, Company will prepare the artwork and consult with Artist regarding the design. Company will advance the sum of $_____ for artwork preparation. This payment is an advance against future royalties.

Artist Warranties

Artist warrants to Company that Artist has the power and authority to enter into this Agreement, is the Artist and copyright holder of the Master Recordings, or has or will obtain all necessary and appropriate rights and licenses to grant the license in this Agreement with respect to the Master Recordings. Artist represents and warrants that the Master Recordings are original to Artist except for material in the public domain and such excerpts from other works as may be included with the written permission of the copyright owners and that proper clearances or permission have been obtained from the Artists of any copyrighted material, including but not limited to any digitally reprocessed samples of material incorporated in the Master Recordings. Artist warrants that Artist's use of any name or moniker will not infringe on the rights of others and that Artist's use of any musical composition or arrangement will not infringe on the rights of others.

Artist further warrants that the Master Recordings do not:

• contain any libelous material

• infringe any trade name, trademark, trade secret, or copyright, or

• invade or violate any right of privacy, personal or proprietary right, or other common law or statutory right.

Artist indemnifies Company and will defend Company against and hold Company harmless (including, without limitation, attorney fees and costs) from any claims and damage arising out of a breach of Artist's Warranties as provided above. Artist agrees to reimburse Company for any payment made by Company with respect to this Section, provided that the claim has been settled or has resulted in a final judgment against Company or its licensees. Artist will notify Company in writing of any infringements or imitations by others of the Master Recording that may come to Artist's attention.

Controlled Compositions License

Artist grants to Company an irrevocable worldwide license to reproduce all compositions wholly or partly written, owned or controlled by Artist (the "Controlled Compositions"). Artist grants to Company a first mechanical license with respect to all Controlled Compositions.

Mechanical Royalties

Artist acknowledges and agrees that Company will pay a royalty for the mechanical license on all Records manufactured for sale or commercial distribution at _____% of the minimum compulsory license rate (the "Company Mechanical Rate") applicable in the country of manufacture. The applicable minimum statutory rate will be determined as of the date of the commencement of the recording of the applicable Master Recording. Mechanical Royalties are not payable with respect to musical compositions of one minute or less in duration.

Termination

Artist can terminate this Agreement if Company fails to pay Artist's Royalties when due or to accurately report Net Sales and the failure is not corrected within 30 days after written notice from Artist. If this Agreement is terminated because of a failure to pay or accurately report royalties, all rights granted under this agreement will revert to Artist and Company will have no further rights regarding Artist or the Master Recording.

If this Agreement is terminated for a reason other than Company's failure to pay or accurately report Artist's Royalties, the termination will not terminate the underlying license and copyrights granted to Company by Artist or Company's obligations to pay Royalties under this Agreement.

Mediation; Arbitration

If a dispute arises under this Agreement, the parties agree to first try to resolve the dispute with the help of a mutually agreed-on mediator in _____. Any costs and fees other than attorney fees will be shared equally by the parties. If it is impossible to arrive at a mutually satisfactory solution within a reasonable time, the parties agree to submit the dispute to binding arbitration in the same city or region, conducted on a confidential basis under:

○ the Commercial Arbitration Rules of the American Arbitration Association, or

○ the rules of _____.

Any decision or award as a result of any such arbitration proceeding will include the assessment of costs, expenses, and reasonable attorney's fees and a written determination of the arbitrators. Absent an agreement to the contrary, arbitration will be conducted by an arbitrator experienced in music industry law. An award of arbitration is final and binding on the Artist and may be confirmed in a court of competent jurisdiction. The prevailing party has the right to collect from the other party its reasonable costs and attorney fees incurred in enforcing this agreement.

General

Nothing contained in this Agreement makes either Company or Artist a partner, joint venturer, or employee of the other party for any purpose. This Agreement may not be amended except in a writing signed by both parties. No waiver by either party of any right shall be construed as a waiver of any other right. If a court finds any provision of this Agreement invalid or unenforceable as applied to any circumstance, the remainder of this Agreement will be interpreted to carry out the intent of the parties. This Agreement is governed by and interpreted in accordance with the laws of the State of _____. This Agreement expresses the complete understanding of the parties with respect to the subject matter and supersedes all prior proposals, agreements, representations, and understandings. Notices required under this agreement can be sent to the parties at the addresses provided below. In the event of any dispute arising from or related to this Agreement, the prevailing party is entitled to attorney's fees.

Artist Business Name _____

Artist Representative Name and Title _____

Artist Representative Signature _____

Artist Address _____

_____

Date _____

Company Name _____

Company Representative Name and Title _____

Company Representative Signature _____

Company Address _____

_____

Date _____

Reviewing Royalty Statements

The record company's royalty statement may be confusing. To simplify your review of the statement, we have provided an example of an independent label royalty statement. In the statement below for the group the Bird Feeders, signed with Figment Records, the band has sold about 2,000 copies of its debut CD in the first six months. The group's deductions are fairly small because they recorded at their home studio and did not take an advance payment from the label. Fortunately, the Bird Feeder's contract did not provide for deductions such as packaging, breakage, and manufacturing.

The statement shows the total units shipped, followed by the units returned by two distributors. (The parentheses in financial reports indicate negative figures or numbers being subtracted.) The returned units are deducted from the shipped units. The result is the Total Units Sold. This amount is then multiplied by the band's royalty rate. When you review your band's statement, make sure that the royalty rate is accurate.

In the next section, the label lists deductions. You will see that the label and the band split the costs for a cooperative advertisement in a newspaper. In addition, the label fronted the band some CDs for sale at a show. These expenses are all included in the deductions. When you review your band's statement, make sure that the label has the right to make all of the deductions. That is, check the list of deductions against those permitted under the agreement.

The total deductions are subtracted from the royalties to arrive at the Total Due. This is the amount to be paid to the band, and it should be enclosed with the statement to the band. Not all statements will resemble this form, but the contents should be similar: a statement of sales, royalty rates, deductions, and earnings (or losses).

Figment Records—Sample Royalty Statement

Artist: The Bird Feeders

Title: Feeding Red-Beaked Seagulls

Cat # FG67CD   UPC#7-35286-19672

FORMAT CD

Units shipped	2,448
Units returned	(448)
Units sold	2,000
Royalty per compact disc (12% x $15.98= $1.92)	x $1.92

Total Royalty Amount   **$3,840**

Deductions

Mastering	($310.00)
Fed Ex costs	(51.00)
Co-op ad for show (50-50 split)	(150.00)
Artwork design proofs	(170.00)
Inventory for show	(93.15)

Total Deductions   **($774.15)**

TOTAL DUE (Royalty—Deductions)   **$3,065.85**

Chapter 15

Taking Your Band Online

Taking your band online is probably the most efficient way to reach fans, sell merchandise and music, and publicize the group. The cost of taking your band online is reasonable (a few hundred dollars, or, in some cases, free), and creating a basic website can be accomplished by even the most tech-challenged musician. In this chapter we'll discuss how to get your band on the Internet and how to avoid some common pitfalls in the process.

Developing Your Site

Developing a website is the most important part of taking your band online. Your site must be functional and must accurately reflect your band's persona. Thankfully, creating a band website is not rocket science.

There are plenty of great off-the-shelf programs such as Adobe *PageMill*, Microsoft *FrontPage*, and Macromedia *Dreamweaver* to help you create a decent site. In addition, there are many self-help books and websites that explain the process.

Before creating your site, here are some things to consider:

- **If you have to have only four things on your website,** Chris Knab (www .4frontmusic.com) recommends a well-written bio, several free rotating songs on MP3, a tour itinerary, and band CDs for sale.
- **Don't let important messages about upcoming shows or new recordings get lost in a cluttered sea of information.** Often, as the saying goes, less is more. Figure out what you want to say. Then make sure it comes through loud and clear on the user's computer screen.

Glossary of Website Terms

Downloading. The process of obtaining a copy of a file from the Internet. When downloading, the user obtains a file such as a song or document from the Internet and copies it onto the user's computer. The most popular downloading formats for music are MP3s, AAC (the standard used at iTunes), and WMAs (Windows Media files).

Internet Service Provider (ISP). An ISP such as Earthlink or Yahoo! allows users to connect to the Internet through various methods such as dialing in or connecting via a digital subscriber line (DSL) or a cable modem.

Server. Servers are high-capacity, fast-processing computers on which websites are stored. They are connected to the Internet with high-bandwidth connections, and run around the clock so that the websites on them are always accessible to Internet users.

Streaming. Streaming, also sometimes known as netcasting and webcasting, allows compressed audio and video to be broadcast in real time over the Internet.

Website Developer. A person or company that designs (and sometimes hosts) websites.

Website Host. A company that leases space on its servers to host third-party websites.

- **Many users don't like to scroll down a page to get to information.** You're usually better off to link users to another page for additional information.
- **Be old-fashioned if it saves time for users.** Flash animation and multimedia add-ons that require plug-ins are fun to create—but many users click right past these items to get to the real information.
- **You can't do everything on your home page.** You need different pages for different purposes: upcoming shows, reviews, discography, merchandise, taking orders, and soliciting email.

Whether you create the site yourself or use a developer, you must have some notion of what you'd like your website to do and what it should look like. The easiest approach is to use the graphic and stylistic preferences seen in your logo, album artwork, and show posters, and adapt them for your website. This provides continuity and uniformity for your band's public image.

You'll also need to know some of the functions your site will perform. The more functions—message boards, shopping carts, streaming audio—you have, the more you may need a developer's assistance, and the more you may have to pay to host the site (see below). Review these questions before starting your design:

- **Will you use the site mainly to provide information for your fans?** If your site is primarily a place to post notices of upcoming shows and recordings, you should be able to accomplish the design by yourself.

- **Will you encourage fans to communicate with you by email?** Providing an email response form is a fairly simple design task, and most off-the-shelf programs offer this feature. If you pay for your website host, you can get mailboxes for use with your site.

- **Will you take orders online?** Will you provide a shopping cart system? Providing a shopping cart is a complex design feature and may require the help of a developer or Web host. You will probably have to pay more to host the site if you offer shopping cart features.

- **Will you provide downloadable music or video?** It's not particularly difficult to post downloadable music for your site, but it will require more space on the website host's server. The more space you require, the more you will have to pay for website hosting.

- **Will you provide streaming music or video?** If you're technically savvy, you can probably post streaming music without assistance. You will, however, need to find a host with a server that is capable of streaming. As with downloadable music, the more you post for streaming media, the more space you will need.

- **Will you provide message boards or chat rooms?** You will need to consult with your website host if you want to provide message boards or chat rooms where fans can communicate with each other. A website host may charge more to host these features.

 Don't be rigid in dealing with the developer of your website. Working with a developer is like working with a music producer. You need to provide as much insight as you can into what you're looking for. Even though you're the ultimate arbiter of what the site should look like and do, keep an open mind when the website developer makes suggestions. After all, the developer is presumably a pro who can offer helpful ideas in addition to technical expertise.

The Website Development Contract

If you're paying someone to perform website development, be sure to get the agreement in writing. There are too many legal issues involved to leave it to a handshake. Chances are that the developer will provide you with his or her company's standard written contract. Below are some key issues that should be included in the agreement:

- **Specifications and timelines.** You'll need to reach an agreement with the developer as to the details of the website and dates when work should be completed.

- **Warranties and indemnity.** You should seek a promise that no copyrights or trademarks were infringed and that no one was libeled by any content created by the developer.
- **Ownership of the site.** You should obtain an assurance that your band claims copyright ownership of the site's design and appearance.
- **Contract assignability.** If you don't want the developer farming out the work to someone else, you'll need a clause that prevents assignment of the agreement.
- **Objections and approvals.** You'll want a simple system for approving or objecting to the developer's work—for example, an approval system that has several stages.
- **Termination.** You'll want an escape hatch in case things go sour during the development process—for example, a right to terminate the agreement, provided you pay for work completed.

Look into PayPal for handling fewer than 100 transactions a month. For a fee, the folks at PayPal (www.paypal.com) can handle all the details of getting paid, and you won't need to set up a credit card merchant account. PayPal will accept your customers' credit card payments and transfer the money to your band's bank account.

Setting up your website to accept credit cards is complicated. For information on credit card processing, check MerchantWorkz (www. merchantworkz.com), a site that provides merchant bank fees and profiles, advice on card service providers, and other necessary information for setting up an online credit card account.

Securing Your Domain Name

A domain name is an online address that Web surfers type in to go to your site. Choosing a domain name that is easy to remember is important, but your main legal concern when choosing a domain name is that you do not violate the rights of someone who's already using that name. If someone else has already acquired trademark rights in the name and you use it anyway, you may find yourself embroiled in a costly and disruptive legal battle—plus, of course, you risk losing the domain name and any goodwill you've built up. Even if you win, you'll have spent large amounts of time, money, and energy staving off the challenger. So, before you use a domain name, make sure your usage is safe from legal attacks.

Domain name registration does not give you trademark rights. We discuss two types of registration in this book: domain name registration and trademark registration (see Chapter 9). Every domain name must be registered with an approved domain name registry before the name can be used as an Internet address. That's domain name registration. A band may also want to register its domain name as a trademark or service mark with the U.S. Patent and Trademark Office (USPTO). That's referred to as trademark registration. Not all domain names can be registered as trademarks; we discuss those details in Chapter 9.

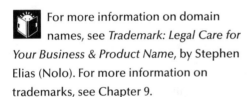 For more information on domain names, see *Trademark: Legal Care for Your Business & Product Name*, by Stephen Elias (Nolo). For more information on trademarks, see Chapter 9.

Registering Your Domain Name

You can secure your domain name by registering it with a domain name registry. For an alphabetical list of approved registries, visit the ICANN site (www. icann.org). Obtaining a domain name is easy and fairly automatic, provided someone else hasn't already acquired it. You just provide minimal information to the registry and pay a modest fee (never pay more than $35 per name). All of this can be done online, using a credit card. Fees can vary a bit among the registries, and some offer extra services such as email, website hosting, Web page design, or longer registration periods.

To check on the availability of a name, go to any domain name registry and look for the search feature. If the name is taken, you can learn who owns it by checking www.whois.net. This is helpful in case you want to offer to buy the name.

If your preferred domain name is available, you can register online using a credit card. To register the name, you'll need to provide some basic billing and band ownership information. The registry may also ask technical questions such as who is your Internet Service Provider (ISP) or which company will be physically maintaining (hosting) your website. If you do not know this information, you can leave it blank.

Once you register your domain name, it's yours. Normally, no one can stop you from using that domain name as your Internet address. But be aware that there are some exceptions to this general rule. The primary ones are:

- **You forget to pay your domain name fees.** You need to renew your domain name and pay a fee, either yearly or every two years. If you fail to pay, someone else can grab the name.
- **You're a cybersquatter.** You can lose the name if you registered it in bad faith—for example, with the intention of selling it to a company

with a similar domain name or trademark.

- **You're infringing on someone's trademark.** If customers will be confused because your domain name is too close to someone else's trademark, you may be forced to give up the name (see Chapter 9).
- **You're diluting a famous trademark.** You're not allowed to blur someone else's trademark or tarnish it (see Chapter 9).

If Your Preferred Domain Name Is Already Taken

It's always disappointing to discover that someone else got there first—but with 50 million registered domain names, it's likely most names have been taken. Take heart. All may not be lost. You have some options and strategies to consider.

Use .net, .org, .biz, or .info

If you're like most bands, you'll prefer to use .com in your domain name. But if the name you want is not available as a .com, it may be available as a .net, .org, .biz, or .info. The .biz and .info extensions are new suffixes that were put into use. Keep in mind that you do not need to be an organization to qualify for .org, a network to qualify for .net, or an information provider to obtain a .info domain name. Domain name registries do not verify the type or form of the businesses seeking domain names with these suffixes.

Regardless of the suffix, you should always check whether the domain name is someone else's trademark.

Get Creative

Many bands use a phrase from their lyrics or an album title as their domain name. For example, the band Luna was unable to obtain Luna.com, .net, or .org and instead opted for fuzzywuzzy.com, a reference to one of its song lyrics.

Buy the Name

If someone else owns the name you want but isn't using it, you could attempt to buy it. There are several ways to go about doing this. You can deal with the owner directly, make a bid on an auction website, or use an online broker such as GreatDomains.com (www.greatdomains. com). A broker can help track down the owner of a noninfringing domain name and negotiate a good price for you.

Assert Your Rights as a Senior User

If your band's name has been taken as a domain name by someone else—for example, another band—you can, under certain circumstances, assert your rights as a senior trademark user. Under trademark law, the first band to use a trademark for music services is considered the owner. If you used the name in commerce before the other registrant, you may be able to stop the registrant's use. (For more on trademark rights, see Chapter 9).

If someone registered your trademark as a domain name in a bad-faith attempt to profit from it, you can use the arbitration service offered by the international organization in charge of domain name registrations (ICANN). If you win, you'll get the domain name. Your other option is to sue under the federal cybersquatting law.

Of the two routes, we recommend the ICANN route for resolving domain name disputes, because it's relatively speedy and inexpensive. To learn more about the dispute resolution rules, visit the ICANN site (www.icann.org). Usually an ICANN dispute is resolved within 60 days—much faster than any court resolution would take. Based upon past ICANN arbitrations, the odds seem to be in favor of the person seeking to transfer the domain name—that is, the person who has or claims to have trademark rights.

Getting Permission to Use Content

Your band site will likely use lots of text, photos, and similar subject matter to attract and maintain fans. This content may be protected under copyright or trademark law. If you don't have the right to use it, you're courting trouble. The owner can sue to stop your use. You may have to remove the content from your site and pay damages for your wrongful use. To avoid problems, you can either buy

the rights or ask the copyright owner for permission to use the work.

Here are five tips for staying out of trouble:

- **Get it in writing.** When dealing with artists, models, photographers, independent contractors, and other outside sources who prepare content for your site, get your agreement in writing. In Chapter 10, we provide releases for models and agreements for acquiring rights in artwork.

- **Assume it's protected.** Just because an article or photograph doesn't carry a copyright notice doesn't mean it's safe to use it without permission. Find out who owns the copyright, and get permission in writing before using it on your website.

- **Don't rely on fair use exceptions.** Some website owners using works without permission rely on a legal defense known as fair use (see Chapter 7). This is a risky strategy, and we advise you to either get permission or create your own content.

- **Take infringement claims seriously.** If you receive a letter from someone who claims you are infringing a copyright, don't ignore it. Stop using it, temporarily at least, while you look into the facts and try to resolve the matter. If you leave the material on your website and a judge later finds you've infringed, the money damages you'll have to pay may be higher than if you had taken it down right away.

- **Be careful with links.** It's unlikely that you'll get into legal trouble by simply providing a link, but it's still considered good netiquette to obtain permission. The permission may be informal, such as an email from the distant site stating, "You have permission to link to our website's home page using the words [insert the words in the link]." We also recommend that you avoid linking to sites that you know contain infringing material.

MP3s and Streaming Audio

Just about everyone connected to the Internet knows that it is possible to download a song, or to copy and send a song from one destination to the other, with excellent sound clarity. And thanks to online music stores such as TowerRecords.com, everyone knows that it is possible to listen to a song without downloading it—a process known as streaming.

In this post-iTunes world, many new commercial subscription downloading sites are now available, for example, Rhapsody, MusicMatch, and the reinvigorated Napster. Streaming and downloads have created a new set of rules for bands that want to provide free

music for their fans. Below is a summary of these two common ways to transmit music over the Internet.

Downloads

To provide downloads (officially known as digital phonorecord delivery, or DPDs) at your site, you'll need to obtain permission from the owner of the song (music publisher) and owner of the sound recording (record company). For downloads of 150 to 2,500 copies, you can likely obtain permission (and pay compulsory licensing fees) via Songfile.com. Of course, if your band has self-produced the recording and owns the song, there's no problem and no permission needed. But if you are signed to a record label or are releasing a cover version of a song, you must get permission to permit downloads. Without permission, the owners can require that you remove the recording and perhaps make you pay financial damages. Below we discuss each type of permission.

 Selling CDs online. For information on selling your CDs online, see Chapter 13.

 The lower the MP3 compression, the faster the download. MP3 is a computer standard that enables a recording to be compressed so that it can be trans-mitted quickly online. Compression at a rate of 128 kbs is considered to be similar to a CD quality recording. A compression rate of 64 kbs is similar to FM radio broadcast quality. At a low compression rate, the sonic quality diminishes, but less file space is needed and the song downloads faster.

Music Publisher Permission

Before offering a song for downloading at your website, you'll need permission from the music publisher. The rules for how to pay the music publisher are still evolving; music publishers currently get paid in two ways (referred to as "double-dipping"): once for the reproduction of the MP3 file, and again for the transmission of the file over the Internet. Payments and permission are discussed below.

- **Payment to Music Publisher for Reproduction.** For songs previously recorded and released in the U.S., permission can be obtained by using a compulsory license, as described in Chapter 12. You may also be able to obtain such rights through the Harry Fox Agency (www.harryfox.com) and Songfile (www.songfile.com). In terms of payments, music publishers consider downloads the same as compact discs or cassette recordings. You must pay the compulsory rate per copy.
- **Payment to Music Publisher for Transmission.** A performance license and fee must be negotiated with the appropriate performing rights

societies (see Chapter 8) for the right to transmit a digital recording such as an MP3. These societies consider any transmission, whether streamed, or temporarily or permanently downloaded, to be a public performance. Fortunately, both BMI (www.bmi.com) and ASCAP (www.ascap.com) offer online agreements for licensing. Before entering into one of these licenses, you may want to contact either ASCAP or BMI directly and inquire whether such a license is necessary for your use. For information on determining whether BMI or ASCAP represents a music publisher, review Chapter 8.

MP3 Sound Recording Permission

If you're signed to a record label, your label probably owns the rights to your recordings. Therefore, you will need permission from the record company before posting your songs. Obviously, if you were posting another band's recording—for example, Blink 182—you would need permission from their record label as well.

EXAMPLE: The Burnt Siennas create a cover recording of the Robert Palmer song "Addicted to Love." They post their version and the original version on their website for downloading. The Siennas will need permission from the publisher of the song (for both downloads) and from the record company that owns the Robert Palmer classic in order to permit downloading of that version.

Of course, it's easy for us to tell you that you will need permission from a record label. Getting that permission is usually so difficult and expensive that most bands abandon the project or risk proceeding without authorization from the record company.

Webcasting and Audio Streaming

Webcasting and audio streaming are processes by which digital music is broadcast over the Internet, much like a radio station broadcasts music. The computer user hears the music simultaneously as it is being played by the website. Both webcasting and audio streaming are referred to as "digital audio transmissions." For bands webcasting songs, the rules for streaming are:

- If you own the rights to the song and the recording, no permission is needed for digital audio transmissions.
- If your band is covering someone else's song, you will need both performance and mechanical rights permissions from the music publisher.
- If your band is streaming a song that is owned by a music publisher and a record company, you will need permission from the performance

rights society—that is, ASCAP, BMI, or SESAC—and you must also pay a special fee for the sound recording rights. This fee is administered on behalf of the recording industry by SoundExchange (www.soundexchange.com). You can obtain more information on the permissions process at the SoundExchange website.

MP3.com, MySpace, and Taxi.com: Third-Party Downloads and Promotions

Several years ago, MP3.com (www.MP3.com) pioneered a new approach for marketing music. Bands can post their music to the site and earn rewards based on different systems, the most popular of which is frequency of downloads. Fans can also order any song from MP3.com. The company will burn it on a compact disc, ship it, and pay the artist a commission. Subsequently, other music sites have followed MP3.com and offer the potential of attracting new fans and earning money.

- **MySpace.com.** Many sites have proliferated since MP3.com, but none has exploded with the popularity of MySpace.com. At MySpace, your band can—for free—establish a website, create a blog, offer streaming music, downloads, videos, and get email. Fans can contact you and hear your music for free! That's a worthwhile proposition, especially if you don't have the ability to set up your own website. There's little downside to participating at MySpace.com, though there has been some grumbling by musicians regarding the MySpace User Agreement, which apparently gives the company the right to make and distribute copies of the media uploaded on to your website. It's not clear how or if the site's owner will ever exercise this provision in a manner that can harm musicians, but for now there's some concern about what rights are granted to the site's owners.

• **Taxi.com.** Sites such as Taxi.com (www.taxi.com) will review your music and shop it to appropriate record labels or film companies. Although Taxi.com does not take a cut of any subsequent deals, there is an annual subscription fee (approximately $500 a year) and a song submission fee ($5 per song). Unlike MP3.com, Taxi.com reviews each song submission before deciding whether to forward it to an A&R representative or agent. One experienced songwriter, Joanna Cazden, went undercover for *Electronic Musician* magazine and made several submissions to Taxi.com. She concluded: "For anyone serious about the songwriting business, Taxi.com provides a reality check and a cheering squad. I'd say it's worth the ride." Before paying Taxi.com's hefty fees, we suggest you investigate the site yourself and read about the services to make sure they will provide some benefit for your band. ∎

Taxes

Yuou may not want to think about taxes, but some of the tips in this chapter could save your band hundreds of dollars (or more) in tax payments. If you're one of the lucky bands that makes a healthy profit, you definitely should learn at least the basics on taxes. And if your band is losing money, you might be surprised to learn that you can use those losses to reduce your tax bill from any day job you might have. In other words, learning how tax laws affect your band and its individual members can save you money, whether or not your band is really making it (yet).

In preparing you for the taxman, this chapter will discuss how your business form can affect your taxes, and we'll describe the types of deductions that can save money. Deductions are an important element in the financial success of every band's business. We'll also help you understand principles of payroll taxes and how to obtain a federal employer identification number (called FEIN or EIN). When you become more successful, you will be glad that you learned these tax basics.

Taxing Situations: Understanding Your Band's Tax Responsibilities

There are three types of taxes that your band or individual band members may be responsible for paying:

- **Income Tax.** Each year, your band must declare all band income (minus deductions) to the federal, state, and maybe local tax agency. (See the sidebar "Local Business Taxes and Sales Taxes," below.) How you do this depends on your business form (partnership, corporation, sole proprietorship, and so on). For example, if your band is a partnership, one of the band partners would prepare a partnership tax form declaring the band's profit or loss, and each member would declare a portion of the profit or loss on his or her individual tax return. If the band is a sole proprietorship and you're the sole proprietor, you simply report the band income or loss on your personal tax return. This chapter discusses only federal taxes, though most state taxes have similar rules. Contact your state tax authority for specific instructions for your state. We provide more details on business forms and deductions below.

- **Self-Employment Tax.** Band members who operate as sole proprietorships, partnerships, and limited liability companies (LLCs) must all pay self-employment taxes if their net earnings from self-employment for the year are $400 or more. You pay self-employment taxes on your net band income, not your entire income. To determine your net self-employment income, you first figure the net income you've earned from your band. If you're a sole proprietor, use IRS Schedule C, Profit or Loss From Business, to determine your net business income. If your band is a partnership, your income will be indicated on your K-1 form. It's easy to compute the amount of your SE tax. First, determine your net self-employment income as described above. If your net self-employment income is below the social security tax ceiling—$94,200 in 2006—multiply it by 15.3% or .153. For example, if your net income from the band was $10,000, you would have to pay approximately $1,530 in self-employment taxes. If you have two jobs—for example, one as an employee of a photocopy shop and the other as self-employed musician—the self-employment tax would apply only to the income from your musician gigs. You pay self-employment taxes directly to the IRS during the year as part of your estimated taxes.

 For additional information on self-employment taxes, see IRS Publication 533, *Self-Employment Tax*. You can obtain this and all other IRS publications by calling the IRS at 800-TAX-FORM, by visiting your local IRS office, or at the IRS website (www.irs.gov).

- **Payroll Tax.** Whenever your band hires employees, your band is responsible for paying federal and state payroll taxes. If your band hires an independent contractor instead of an employee, you do not have to make these payments. Below, we discuss the differences between employees and independent contractors, and we provide more details about payroll tax payments.

Local Business Taxes and Sales Taxes

If you are registered to do business in your city or county, your band may have to pay a local business tax—either a fixed fee or a fee based on your annual income. If you sell recordings or merchandise directly to consumers (not to retail outlets or distributors), you may have to pay state or city sales tax. Check with your local sales tax office. (Note: Some states, such as California, have become very aggressive about going after sales tax revenue.)

Income Taxes: Different Rules for Different Businesses

Each business form—sole proprietorship, partnership, corporation, or LLC—has its own tax rules and procedures. As a general rule, taxes are much simpler for unincorporated businesses such as sole proprietorships and partnerships. That's because income from unincorporated businesses is simply treated as personal income to the owners. In other words, the business itself is not taxed. For example, if your four-person band is a partnership, any profits the band makes are divided among the four owners, who report them as personal income much like income from a job or investments. Corporations, on the other hand, are considered to be separate entities from their owners, and they pay their own taxes. This section will explain how taxes apply to each different business form and how to file them. For more information on business forms, see Chapter 2.

Flow-Through and Entity Taxation, Defined

In this section we use two common tax terms—flow-through (or pass-through) and entity taxation (which is related to double taxation).

Flow-through occurs when your band business profits and losses are reported on your individual tax return—that is, they pass through the business to you. Sole proprietorships, partnerships, and, in most cases, LLCs operate as flow-through businesses.

Entity taxation occurs when the IRS considers your band business as a separate tax-paying creature. (Corporations and some LLCs operate this way.) Under an entity-taxation business form, the corporation or LLC must pay taxes and file a tax return.

Reporting Band Income

The IRS has become sophisticated in sniffing out band income. For example, the IRS guide to auditing musicians advises examiners to contact booking agencies and unions for verification about musician income. Auditors are trained to search out income from record and merchandise sales and may even ask for copies of partnership or individual bank accounts.

It is a crime to deliberately fail to report income or to lie to the IRS. If you underreport your income, you could be subject to additional taxes and serious financial penalties—even jail time. In other words, *report your band income*. When in doubt about whether a payment is considered "income," speak to an accountant or tax expert for advice.

Partnership Taxes

Most bands are partnerships, because any business in which two or more persons are the owners is a partnership. A formal agreement is not necessary to create a partnership, although we recommend that your band use a written band partnership agreement to establish the details of how the partnership will operate. (A sample is provided in Chapter 2.)

Technically speaking, a partnership itself does not pay taxes. Instead, any profit or loss of the business is divided among the partners and reported with their personal income tax returns. Since income simply passes through the business to the owners, partnerships are called "pass-through" tax entities. (See the sidebar "Flow-Through and Entity Taxation, Defined," above.) Though a partnership does not owe taxes, it must complete and file a tax return to report any income or losses. Form 1065, U.S. Partnership Return of Income, is used. Since no taxes are ever due with Form 1065, it is called an "informational return."

Whoever files Form 1065 (a partner, an accountant, or a lawyer, for example) must also give each partner a report called Schedule K-1, which contains all the relevant profit or loss information about the partnership. Based on the information in the K-1 form, and based on the partnership agreement regarding each partner's share of profit or loss, each band partner declares a portion of the profit or loss on his or her individual tax returns. Each partner reports his or her share of band income or losses on Schedule E, which is submitted with that person's individual 1040 form. If a band partner has a day job and the band loses money, the partner can deduct his or her share of loss from the other income, which can reduce his or her tax bill.

EXAMPLE: Bob is a member of the El Niños, a band that lost money in 2006. According to Bob's K-1 Form,

Bob can deduct a $2,000 band loss from his total income, which includes wages from working at a music equipment store. By deducting the band loss, Bob pays less income tax for 2006.

In addition to income taxes, all band partners must pay self-employment tax on band profits. See the section above on self-employment taxes.

Your band will need a federal employer identification number (FEIN) to file a partnership tax return. Later in this chapter we explain how to get one. The FEIN will help your band to open a bank account and deposit checks under your band name.

In summary, if your band is classified as a partnership by the IRS, here are some rules to remember:

- Partnerships, though not taxed separately, must prepare and file a Form 1065, usually filed on April 15.
- The partnership must issue a K-1 form showing each partner's share of the income or loss. The K-1 is filed with each partner's individual return.
- Each partner must pay a tax based on his or her "distributive share," not on what the partner may have actually received. Unless a partnership agreement says otherwise, all partners are presumed to have an equal distributive share in the partnership.

- Even if the partnership leaves profits in the business, the partners must pay taxes on those profits. (If your partnership is able to retain profits each year, consider forming a corporation.)
- Partners must pay quarterly estimated income taxes, as well as self-employment tax for social security and Medicare contributions.

Sole Proprietorships

A sole proprietorship is a business that is run by just one person. Unlike a partnership, which must submit an informational return, sole proprietorships do not have to file any tax returns for the business. Only the owner reports the income with a personal return. Like partnerships, sole proprietorships are pass-through tax entities. Income from the sole proprietorship is reported on Schedule C, which is submitted with the individual 1040 form. If the sole proprietorship loses money, the sole proprietor can deduct that loss from income from other jobs, reducing the tax obligation.

Filing as a sole proprietorship is appropriate if the band is run by one person (the band leader) who hires musicians to perform in the band and pays each musician a fee or a salary. The paid musicians do not have an ownership interest in the band. In that situation, the sole proprietor/band leader may have

to file payroll taxes if the other band members were treated like employees. Keep in mind that having employees raises a host of legal issues that you may want to avoid. (See the section below on employees and independent contractors.)

An FEIN is not necessary for a sole proprietor to file taxes, because the personal social security number of the owner may be used. However, some tax experts suggest obtaining and using an FEIN for business taxes anyway, in order to keep business and personal tax records separate.

Sole proprietorships must pay self-employment taxes.

In summary, if the band business is owned by you and you haven't formed an LLC or corporation:

- You must report your business income or loss on a Schedule C, filed with your individual or joint tax return.
- You must pay quarterly estimated income taxes, as well as self-employment tax for social security and Medicare contributions.
- You are eligible for tax-sheltered retirement plans.

Preparing Taxes

Consider hiring a tax preparation expert or accountant knowledgeable in the music business when preparing your tax return. While you can expect to pay $100 to $500 for preparation of tax returns, a savvy tax professional will probably save your band the cost of this fee and more. You may not have to use a professional for each year you file, but it is sometimes helpful to have a professional tax preparer create your returns at least for the first year, so that you can see the form and style that will be suitable. You should also utilize an accounting software program such as Microsoft's *Money* or Intuit's *Quicken* to track your band's income and expenses.

Corporations

Unlike sole proprietorships and partnerships, corporations are considered to be separate legal entities from their owners (also called shareholders). In other words, when you incorporate your business you create a new legal being that is responsible for taxes and is subject to many state and federal laws. Corporations' profits do not pass through to the corporate owners for tax purposes, but instead are taxed at special corporate rates. Among other things, this means that corporate losses cannot be deducted from the shareholders' income on their individual tax returns. In some cases you can save tax money by operating as a corporation, but the fees and legal costs associated with running one often outweigh any financial benefit. In order to become a corporation (to "incorporate"), a band must file incorporation papers with its state's Secretary of State and pay a number of fees and minimum taxes.

If your band is a corporation, you will need the assistance of an accountant or other professional for tax preparation and planning. See Chapter 17, which suggests resources beyond this book.

Below we provide a basic summary of corporate tax principles:

- Bands that operate as corporations have more tax reporting responsibilities than any other business form. So, get ready for paperwork.
- Since corporations are separate tax entities, the owners must prepare a tax return for the corporation and pay corporate taxes, if any are owed.
- If you're an employee of the corporation or receive income from the corporation, you must report that on your individual tax return.

 You can avoid the burden of double taxation—for example, by paying higher salaries to shareholders, thereby reducing profits, or by reinvesting profits. An accountant can assist you in legally avoiding corporate income taxes.

Limited Liability Companies (LLCs)

A limited liability company (LLC) is a hybrid between a corporation and a partnership. Like a partnership, profits and losses are passed on to the owners of the LLC (your band), who then report them on individual tax returns. But, like a corporation, an LLC generally offers its owners protection from personal liability for business obligations. An LLC does not itself pay taxes but, like a partnership, it does have to file a tax return reporting income and expenses. LLCs are also subject to state fees that make them more expensive to run than partnerships.

All band owners in an LLC must pay self-employment tax on the band's net taxable income (that is, its profit). Below is a summary of rules regarding LLC taxation:

- The owners of a band LLC can choose either pass-through or entity taxation. (Most choose pass-through.) Your tax advisor can help you make that decision.
- If the owners choose pass-through taxation, the LLC operates like a general partnership and prepares and files a Form 1065. The LLC must also issue its members K-1 forms to be included with their individual returns.
- If the LLC has only one owner (and pass-through taxation has been chosen), the owner operates like a sole proprietorship and files

a Schedule C to report the LLC's income.
- Although no federal tax is paid for a pass-through LLC, some states such as California impose taxes on LLCs.

Paying Estimated Tax

Self-employed musicians do not have the luxury of waiting until April 15 to pay all their taxes for the previous year. The IRS wants to get its money a lot faster than that, so the self-employed are required to pay taxes on their estimated annual incomes in four payments spread out over each year. These are called estimated taxes and are used to pay both income taxes and self-employment taxes.

Because of estimated taxes, self-employed musicians need to carefully budget their money. If you fail to set aside enough of your earnings to pay your estimated taxes, you could face a huge tax bill on April 15—and have a tough time coming up with the money to cover it.

Who Must Pay

You must pay estimated taxes if you are a sole proprietor, partner in a partnership, or member of an LLC and you expect to owe at least $1,000 in federal tax for the year. If you've formed a C corporation, it may also have to pay estimated taxes.

However, if you paid no taxes last year—for example, because your business made no profit or you weren't working—

you don't have to pay any estimated tax this year no matter what your tax tally for the year. But this is true only if you were a U.S. citizen or resident for the year and your tax return for the previous year covered the whole 12 months.

Most States Have Estimated Taxes, Too

If your state has income taxes, it probably requires the self-employed to pay estimated taxes. The due dates are generally the same as for federal estimated tax. State income tax rates are lower than federal income taxes. The exact rate depends on the state in which you live. Contact your state tax office for information and the required forms.

How Much You Must Pay

You should normally determine how much estimated tax to pay after completing your tax return for the previous year. Most people want to pay as little estimated tax as possible during the year so they can earn interest on their money instead of handing it over to the IRS. However, the IRS imposes penalties if you don't pay enough estimated tax. There's no need to get excessively concerned about these penalties. They aren't terribly large in the first place, and it's easy to avoid having to pay them. All you have to do is pay at least the smaller of:

- 90% of your total tax due for the current year, or
- 100% of the tax you paid the previous year.

You normally make four estimated tax payments each year. There are three different ways you can calculate your payments. You can use any one of the three methods, and you won't have to pay a penalty as long as you pay the minimum total the IRS requires as explained above. One of the methods—basing your payments on last year's tax—is extremely easy to use. The other two are more complex, but might permit you to make smaller payments.

IRS Form 1040-ES contains a worksheet to use to calculate your estimated tax. You can obtain the form by calling the IRS at 800-TAX-FORM, visiting your local IRS office, or downloading it at www.irs.gov. Or, if you have a tax preparation computer program, it can help you with the calculations. If you have your taxes prepared by an accountant, he or she should determine what estimated tax to pay. If your income changes greatly during the year, ask your accountant to help you prepare a revised estimated tax payment schedule.

See IRS Publication 505, *Tax Withholding and Estimated Tax*, for a detailed explanation of the annualized income method. You can obtain the form by calling the IRS at 800-TAX-FORM, visiting your local IRS office, or downloading it at www.irs.gov.

When to Pay Estimated Tax

Estimated tax must ordinarily be paid in four installments, with the first one due on April 15. However, you don't have to start making payments until you actually earn income. If you don't receive any income by March 31, you can skip the April 15 payment. In this event, you'd ordinarily make three payments for the year starting on June 15. If you don't receive any income by May 31, you can skip the June 15 payment as well and so on.

The following chart shows the due dates and the periods each installment covers.

Your estimated tax payment must be postmarked by the dates noted below, but the IRS need not actually receive them then. If any of these days falls on a weekend or legal holiday, the due date is the next business day.

How to Pay

The IRS wants to make it easy for you to send in your money, so the mechanics of paying estimated taxes are very simple. If you made estimated tax payments last year, you should receive a copy of the current year's Form 1040-ES in the mail. It will have payment vouchers preprinted with your name, address, and social security number.

If you did not pay estimated taxes last year, get a copy of Form 1040-ES from the IRS. Do so by calling the IRS at 800-TAX-FORM, visiting your local IRS office, or downloading it at www.irs.gov. After you make your first payment, the IRS should mail you a Form 1040-ES package with the preprinted vouchers.

Paying the Wrong Amount

The IRS imposes a money penalty if you underpay your estimated taxes. Fortunately, the penalty is not very onerous. You have to pay the taxes

Estimated Tax Due

Income received for the period	Estimated tax due
January 1 through March 31	April 15
April 1 through May 31	June 15
June 1 through August 31	September 15
September 1 through December 31	January 15 of next year

due plus a percentage penalty for each day your estimated tax payments were unpaid. The percentage is set by the IRS each year. The penalty was 7% in early 2006.

The penalty has ranged between 6% and 8% in recent years. This is the mildest of all IRS interest penalties. Even if you paid no estimated tax at all during the year, the underpayment penalty you'd have to pay would be no more than 5% to 6% of your total taxes due for the year.

 You can find out what the current penalty is in the most recent version of IRS Publication 505, *Tax Withholding and Estimated Tax*. You can obtain the form by calling the IRS at 800-TAX-FORM, visiting your local IRS office, or downloading it at www.irs.gov.

The penalty is comparable to the interest you'd pay on borrowed money. Many self-employed people decide to pay the penalty at the end of the tax year rather than take money out of their businesses during the year to pay estimated taxes. If you do this, though, make sure you pay all the taxes you owe for the year by April 15 of the following year. If you don't, the IRS will tack on additional interest and penalties. The IRS usually adds a penalty of 1/2% to 1% per month to a tax bill that's not paid when due.

Tax Deductions: Secrets for Saving on Taxes

One easy way to reduce your tax obligation is for your band to take, or "declare," every permissible deduction. The IRS lets musicians deduct "ordinary and necessary" business expenses, such as practice studio rental, equipment, and touring expenses. Deducting these expenses from taxable income will reduce the net amount that is subject to taxes. Despite this opportunity to save money on taxes, IRS examiners routinely find that musicians fail to claim expenses. In other words, musicians often pay more taxes than necessary because they don't deduct their costs.

A deduction is an expense or the value of an item that you can subtract from your gross income to determine your taxable income—that is, the amount you earn that is subject to taxation. The more deductions you have, the less income tax you pay. Let's say your band earned $10,000 in one year. If your band deducted its expenses of $10,000, that would wipe out all your income, so you would owe no taxes. This simple principle—reducing taxable income through deductions—is a mantra of most businesses, and you should use it in your band's business as well.

If your band loses money—that is, the deductions are more than the income—then you may be able to deduct this loss against your income from another job. That is, you can apply your band's loss against income from your day job, thereby lowering your personal taxes.

Keeping Receipts and Records

The trick to saving money with business deductions is to create a system to keep track of financial information. Save your receipts, canceled checks, and credit card statements. Your system doesn't need to be complex; simply place your receipts in a box and tally them up at the end of each month using a ledger or software program. "It's not just for taxes," says one tax practitioner who specializes in the arts. "If you want something left over at the end, you have to see where the money is going. You have to keep track of finances." When you pay for services such as a hired musician or a roadie, ask for a receipt with the person's social security number and address—you may need it at tax time.

When to Deduct

Some expenses can be deducted all at once; others have to be deducted over a number of years. It all depends on how long the item you purchase can reasonably be expected to last—what the IRS calls its "useful life."

Current Expenses

The cost of anything your band buys for its business that has a useful life of less than one year must be fully deducted in the year it is purchased. This includes, for example, studio rent, telephone and utility bills, photocopying and promotional costs, and postage and other ordinary business operating costs. Such items are called "current expenses."

Capital Expenses

Certain types of costs are considered to be part of your investment in your business—the major costs of setting it up as opposed to the costs of operating it day to day. These are called "capital expenses." Subject to an important exception for a certain amount of personal property, you cannot deduct the full value of such expenses in the year you incur them. Instead, you must spread the cost over several years and deduct part of it each year.

There are two main categories of capital expenses. They include:

- the cost of any asset you will use in your business that has a useful life of more than one year—for example, sound equipment, vehicles, books, and machinery, and
- business start-up costs such as fees for an attorney and accounting fees paid to set up your business.

If the money you spend on your band business exceeds your band's income for the year, your business incurs a loss. This isn't as bad as it sounds, tax-wise. You can use a business loss to offset other income you may have.

If you fall into a pattern of incurring losses year after year, you risk running afoul of the hobby loss rule. This is no small risk—it could cost you a small fortune in additional income taxes.

For detailed information on deducting business losses, see IRS Publication 536, *Net Operating Losses*. You can obtain this and all other IRS publications by calling the IRS at 800-TAX-FORM, visiting your local IRS office, or downloading the publications at www.irs.gov.

Deducting the Cost of Business Assets

You can deduct from your band's income taxes what you spend for things you use to help produce income.

If you qualify for the Section 179 deduction discussed below, your band can deduct the entire cost of these items in the year you pay for them. Otherwise, you have to deduct the cost over a period of years—a process called depreciation.

The rules for deducting business assets can be complex, but it's worth spending the time to understand them. After all, the U.S. government is in effect offering to help you pay for your equipment and other business assets. All you have to do is take advantage of the offer.

Section 179 Deduction

If you learn only one section number in the tax code, it should be Section 179. It is one of the greatest tax boons for bands (and other small businesses). Section 179 permits the band members to deduct a large amount of your business purchases in the year you make them, rather than having to depreciate them over several years. This is called first-year expensing or Section 179 expensing. It allows you to get a big tax deduction all at once, rather than having to mete it out a little at a time.

> **EXAMPLE:** The band GingerTea buys a $4,000 sound system. The band can use Section 179 to deduct the entire $4,000 expense from its income for the year.

It's up to you to decide whether to use Section 179. It may not always be in your best interest to do so. If you do use it, you can't change your mind later and decide to use depreciation instead.

Property That Can Be Deducted

You can use Section 179 to deduct the cost of any tangible property you use for your business that the IRS has determined will last more than one year—for example, computers, musical equipment, and studio furniture. Special rules apply to cars. You can't use Section 179 for land, buildings, or intangible property such as patents, copyrights, and trademarks.

If you use property both for business and personal purposes, you may deduct under Section 179 only if you use it for business purposes more than half the time. The amount of your deduction is reduced by the percentage of personal use. You'll need to keep records showing your business use of such property. If you use an item for business less than half the time, you must depreciate it.

Deduction Limit

There is a limit on the total amount of business expenses you can deduct each year using Section 179. The deduction is currently (2006) $108,000.

If you purchase more than one item of Section 179 property during the year, you can divide the deduction among all the items in any way, as long as the total deduction is not more than the Section 179 limit. It's usually best to apply Section 179 to property that has the longest useful life and therefore the longest depreciation period. This reduces the total time you have to wait to get your deductions.

⚠️ **Limit on Section 179 deduction.** You can't use Section 179 to deduct more in one year than your total profit from all of your businesses and your salary if you have a job in addition to your business. That is, you can't use Section 179 to reduce your taxable income below zero.

What's Deductible: A Musician's Summary

As mentioned above, business expenses may be deducted from your band's income. The following band-related expenses may be deducted:

- **Amplifiers, guitars, keyboards, drums, and P.A.s**
- **Batteries, guitar strings, cords, reeds, and drumsticks**
- **Business banking and credit card fees**
- **Accounting and tax preparation expenses**
- **Flyers, mailers, and ads**
- **Telephone calls**
- **Legal services**
- **Website maintenance and computers**
- **Hired musicians, roadies, drivers, and techs.** (See the sidebar "The Employee/ Independent Contractor Distinction Can Be Tricky," below) Note: If you paid an independent contractor more than $600, your band must issue a 1099 form.
- **Practice space rental**
- **Auto expenses**
- **Hotels**
- **Food**
- **Airfare**
- **Recording equipment, microphones, and outboard gear**
- **Compact discs and concerts.** For most musicians, listening to music and going to a concert is a legitimate research and development expense and is deductible. However, note that the IRS is increasingly taking the view that these items are for personal pleasure, not business.
- **Home studios or home practice space**

Depreciation

Because it provides a big tax deduction immediately, most band businesses look first to Section 179 to deduct asset costs.

However, your band must use depreciation instead if you:

- don't qualify to use Section 179—for example, you want to deduct the cost of a building or a copyright—or
- use up your Section 179 deduction for the year.

Depreciation involves deducting the cost of a business asset a little at a time over a period of years. This means it will take you much longer to get your full deduction than under Section 179. Depreciable equipment is deducted on the partnership tax return (Form 4562, Depreciation and Amortization). If the band members individually own equipment, it is deducted on Schedule C of the individual 1040 return.

⚠️ The amounts that can be depreciated may change if tax laws are overhauled. Check the IRS website (www.irs.gov) for current limitations on depreciation of business equipment.

What Must Be Depreciated

Depreciation is used to deduct the cost of any asset you buy for your business that has a useful life of more than one year—for example, buildings, equipment, machinery, patents, trademarks, copyrights, and furniture. The IRS, not you, decides the useful life of your assets.

You can also depreciate the cost of major repairs that increase the value or extend the life of an asset—for example, the cost of a major upgrade to make your computer run faster. However, you deduct normal repairs or maintenance in the year they're incurred as a business expense.

EXAMPLE: Your band purchases a vintage drum set that costs $2,800 in the summer of 2006. According to the IRS rules, a drum set (new or vintage) depreciates over seven years, so each year you could deduct $400. Since you bought the set in July, however, you can deduct $200 only during the 2006 tax year, because you had it for only half of the year. You continue to deduct a portion in later years until the full cost has been deducted.

Mixed-Use Property

If you use property both for band business and personal purposes, you can take depreciation only for the business use of the asset. Unlike for the Section 179 deduction, you don't have to use an item over half the time for business to depreciate it.

EXAMPLE: Carl uses his photocopier 75% of the time for personal reasons and 25% for his band business. He can depreciate 25% of the cost of the copier.

Keep a diary or log with the dates, times, and reason the property was used to distinguish between the two uses.

Depreciation Period

The depreciation period—called the recovery period by the IRS—begins when you start using the asset, and lasts for the entire estimated useful life of the asset. The tax code has assigned an estimated useful life for all types of business assets, ranging from three to 39 years. Most of the assets you buy for your business will probably have an estimated useful life of five or seven years. You can't deduct any more depreciation after the property's estimated useful life expires.

If you need to know the depreciation period for an asset not included in this table, see IRS Publication 534, *Depreciation*, for a complete listing. You can obtain this and all other IRS publications by calling the IRS at 800-TAX-FORM, visiting your local IRS office, or downloading the publications at www.irs.gov.

Even though your equipment may become more valuable over time (such as a vintage guitar), it still is considered to depreciate like any other property in its category.

Calculating Depreciation

You can use three different methods to calculate the depreciation deduction: straight-line or one of two accelerated depreciation methods. A brief introduction is provided here. (Review the IRS publications for more details.) Once you choose your method, you're stuck with it for the entire life of the asset.

In addition, you must use the same method for all property of the same kind purchased during the year. For example, if you use the straight-line method to depreciate a computer, you must use that method to depreciate all other computers you purchase during the year for your business.

The straight-line method requires you to deduct an equal amount each year over the useful life of an asset. However, you ordinarily deduct only a half-year's worth of depreciation in the first year. You make up for this by adding an extra year of depreciation at the end.

Most small businesses use one of two types of accelerated depreciation: the double-declining balance method or the 150% declining balance method. The advantage to these methods is that they provide larger depreciation deductions in the earlier years and smaller ones later on. The double-declining balance method starts out by giving you double the deduction you'd get for the first full year with the straight-line method. The 150% declining balance method gives you

Depreciable Periods for Commonly Used Band Business Property

Type of Property	Recovery Period
Computer software (software that comes with your computer is not separately depreciable unless you're separately billed for it)	three years
Computers and peripherals, calculators, copiers, typewriters, and other office-related equipment	five years
Autos and light trucks	five years
Any property—including musical instruments and amplifiers—that does not have an established IRS classlife and has not been designated by laws as being in any other class	seven years

one and one-half times the straight-line deduction.

In the wake of the 9/11 tragedy and the ensuing recession, Congress revised the depreciation rules to give businesses an additional depreciation deduction. Under these rules, taxpayers get an additional "bonus" 30% depreciation deduction for property purchased between September 11, 2001 and September 10, 2004 and placed into service (used in business) before 2005. The 30% is deducted from the "adjusted basis" (usually the cost) of the property and is in addition to normal depreciation.

 If you'd rather be making MP3s instead of calculating depreciation, then invest in a tax software program such as TurboTax (the Home & Business version). Tax programs can help you calculate the depreciation and offer you tax solutions.

For more information, see IRS Publication 534, *Depreciation*, and Publication 946, *How to Depreciate Property*. You can obtain this and all other IRS publications by calling the IRS at 800-TAX-FORM, visiting your local IRS office, or downloading the publications at www.irs.gov.

Car Expenses

Most band members use their cars or vans to do some driving related to band business—for example, to performances or trade shows, to pick up or deliver work, or to obtain musical supplies. Of course, driving costs money—and you are allowed to deduct your driving expenses when you use your car, van, pickup, or panel truck for business.

Cars, Computers, and Cell Phones

There are special rules when claiming deductions for certain items that can be used for personal as well as business purposes. These are called listed property and include:

- cars, boats, airplanes, and other vehicles (see below, for rules on mileage and vehicle expenses)
- computers
- cellular phones, and
- any other property generally used for entertainment, recreation, or amusement—for example, VCRs, cameras, and camcorders.

The IRS fears that taxpayers might use listed property items such as computers for personal reasons but claim business deductions for them. For this reason, you're required to document your business use of listed property. You can satisfy this requirement by keeping a logbook showing when and how the property is used.

There are two ways to calculate the car expense deduction. You can:

- use the standard mileage rate, which requires relatively little recordkeeping, or
- deduct your actual-expenses, which requires much more recordkeeping but might give you a larger deduction.

If you own a late model car worth more than $15,000, you'll usually get a larger deduction by using the actual-expense method, because the standard mileage rate doesn't include enough for depreciation of new cars. On the other hand, the standard mileage rate will be better if you have an inexpensive or old car and put in a lot of business mileage.

Either way, you'll need to have records showing how many miles you drive your car for business during the year—also called business miles. Keep a mileage logbook for this purpose.

Standard Mileage Rate

The easiest way to deduct car expenses is to take the standard mileage rate. When you use this method, you need to keep track of only how many business miles you drive, not the actual expenses for your car such as gas or repairs.

You can use the standard mileage rate only for a car that you own. You must choose to use it in the first year you start using your car for your business. In later years, you can choose to use the standard mileage rate or actual expenses.

Each year, the IRS sets the standard mileage rate—a specified amount of money you can deduct for each business mile you drive. In 2006, for example, the rate was 44.5 cents per mile. To figure your deduction, multiply your business miles by the standard mileage rate for the year.

EXAMPLE: Ed handles all of the business and promotional work for EdNa, a two-man band. He drove his car 10,000 miles for band business in 2006. To determine the band's car expense deduction, he simply multiplies the total business miles he drove by 44.5 cents. This gives the band a $4,450 deduction (44.5 cents x 10,000 = $4,450).

If you choose to take the standard mileage rate, you cannot deduct actual operating expenses—for example, depreciation or Section 179 deduction, maintenance and repairs, gasoline and its taxes, oil, insurance, and vehicle registration fees. These costs are already factored into the standard mileage rate.

Band members can deduct any business-related parking fees and tolls—for example, a parking fee you have to pay when you visit a club promoter. But you cannot deduct fees you pay to park your car at your rehearsal space.

Actual Expenses

Instead of taking the standard mileage rate, you can elect to deduct the actual expenses of using your car for business. To do this, deduct the actual cost of depreciation for your car, interest payments on a car loan, lease fees, rental fees, license fees, garage rent, repairs, gas, oil, tires, and insurance. The total deductible amount is based on the percentage of time you use your car for business. You can also deduct the full amount of any business-related parking fees and tolls.

Deducting all these items will take more time and effort than using the standard mileage rate because you'll need to keep records of all your expenses. However, it may provide you with a larger deduction than the standard rate.

Note: When you claim actual expenses and use your car for both business and personal purposes, you must also divide your expenses between business and personal use.

EXAMPLE: In one recent year Laura drove her car 5,000 miles for her band business and 5,000 miles for personal purposes. She can deduct 50% of the actual costs of operating her car.

If you own only one car, you normally can't claim it's used only for business. An IRS auditor is not likely to believe that you walk or take public transportation everywhere except when you're on business. The only exception might be if you live in a place with developed transportation systems, such as Chicago, New York City, or San Francisco, and drive your car only when you go out of town on band business.

Also, when you deduct actual car expenses, you must keep records of the costs of operating your car. This includes not only the number of business miles and total miles you drive, but also gas, repair, parking, insurance, and similar costs. If this seems to be too much trouble, use the standard mileage rate. That way, you'll have to keep track of only how many business miles you drive, not what you spend for gas and similar expenses.

Finally, regardless of how much you spend for an automobile, your depreciation deduction is strictly limited. For example, for cars purchased in 2002, the annual depreciation deduction is limited to a maximum of $7,660 the first year, $4,900 the second year, $2,950 the third year, and $1,775 thereafter. These amounts change each year.

For more information about the rules for claiming car expenses, see IRS Publication 463, *Travel, Entertainment, Gift, and Car Expenses*. You can obtain this and all other IRS publications by calling the IRS at 800-TAX-FORM, visiting your local IRS office, or downloading the publications at www.irs.gov.

Travel and Touring Expenses

If you travel with your band—for example, you tour regularly—you can deduct your airfare, hotel bills, and other expenses. If you plan your trip right, you can even mix business with pleasure and still get a deduction for your airfare. However, IRS auditors closely scrutinize these deductions, because many taxpayers claim them without complying with the rules attached to them. This is why you need to understand the limitations on this deduction and keep proper records.

Travel Within the U.S.

Some musicians think they have the right to deduct the cost of any band-related trip they take. This is not the case. You can deduct a trip within the United States only if:

- it's primarily for band business
- you travel outside your city limits, and
- you're away at least overnight or long enough to require a stop for sleep or rest.

For your trip to be deductible, you must spend more than half of your time on activities that can reasonably be expected to help advance your band. For most bands on tour this is not a problem, since the band spends the bulk of its time either traveling, sound-checking, or performing.

You don't have to travel any set distance to get a travel expense deduction. However, you can't take this deduction if your band just spends the night in a motel across town. You must travel outside your city limits. If you don't live in a city, you must go outside the general area where your band is located.

Finally, you must stay away overnight or at least long enough to require a stop for sleep or rest. Again, for most touring bands, this is not an issue.

Combining Business With Pleasure

Provided that your trip is primarily for business, you can tack on a vacation at the end, make a side trip purely for fun, or go to the theater and still deduct your entire airfare. What you spend while having fun is not deductible, but you can still deduct your expenses while on business.

> **EXAMPLE:** The Bills fly to Austin for the South by Southwest show. The band performs and meets with record executives for two days and then spends one day in Austin enjoying the sights. Since The Bills spent over half their time on business—two days out of three—the cost of the flight is entirely deductible, as are hotel and meal costs during the first two days. The band may not deduct hotel, meal, or other expenses during the one vacation day.

Foreign Travel

The rules differ if your band travels outside the United States, and are in some ways more lenient. However, as with all expenses, your band must have a legitimate business reason for the foreign trip.

If your band is away no more than seven days, and you spend the majority of your time related to band business, you can deduct all of your travel costs.

However, even if your trip was primarily a vacation, you can deduct your airfare and other transportation costs as long as at least part of the trip was for business. You can also deduct your expenses while on business.

More stringent rules apply if your band's foreign trip lasts more than one week. To get a full deduction for your expenses, you must spend at least 75% of your trip on band business matters. Again, for most bands touring Europe or some other foreign location, this is not a problem.

However, if you spend less than 75% of your time on band business, you must determine the percentage of your time spent on business by counting the number of business days and the number of personal days. You can deduct only the percentage of your travel costs that relates to business days. A business day is any day you have to be at a particular place on business or in which you spend four or more hours on business matters. Days spent traveling to and from your destination also count as business days.

Deductible Expenses During Foreign or Domestic Travel

You can deduct virtually all of your expenses when you travel on business, including:

- airfare to and from your destination
- hotel or other lodging expenses
- taxi, public transportation, and car rental expenses
- telephone and fax expenses
- the cost of shipping your personal luggage or equipment or other things you need for your business
- computer rental fees
- laundry and dry cleaning expenses, and
- tips you pay on any of the other costs.

However, only 50% of the cost of meals is deductible. The IRS imposes this limitation based on the reasoning that you would have eaten had you stayed home.

You must keep good records of your expenses. You cannot deduct expenses for personal sightseeing or recreation.

Food

You can deduct your ordinary, necessary, and reasonable food expenses, or you can use a per diem system in which you utilize the per diem rates established by the federal government. These rates vary from city to city. To view the current rates, go to the U.S. General Services Administration (www.gsa.gov) and click Per Diem Rates.

If you are self-employed, you can use the meals and incidental per diem rates (M&IE). For example, if you were a self-employed musician on tour in Philadelphia in 2006, you could use the maximum Philadelphia per diem rates of $64 for meals and incidental expenses,

and you would not have to keep track of your meal receipts while at the show. If you claim per diems, you cannot also individually account for meals (you must use one system or the other). Also, any meal costs substantiated using the M&IE rate are subject to a 50% limitation on meal expense deductions. That is, you're allowed to deduct only 50% of your meal expenses—for example, if you spend $64 for a meal in a restaurant, you can deduct only $32. However, you must keep track of all you spend and report the entire amount on your tax return. Using the per diem system may simplify your record keeping and reduce your tax bill while still permitting you to deduct other related travel expenses.

Home Studio/Home Office

A home office deduction allows you to deduct a portion of rent, mortgage, or utilities for your music business. Unfortunately, the IRS has maintained the traditional position that performers in a band earn their income on stage, and therefore, the "home office" deduction may not apply if you use one room for personal practice. You can deduct expenses for a separate freestanding structure such as a studio, garage, or barn if you use it exclusively and regularly for your band business.

Songwriters who compose and record their songs at home, or musicians who maintain a home office for administrative tasks for the band—for example, a home office for keeping track of finances, booking, or promotion—may be able to claim the deduction. Under a tax law passed in 1999, you can claim the home office deduction as long you can show this is where the business' substantial administrative duties occur.

As a general rule, your band can't take the home office deduction unless you regularly use part of your home exclusively for one of these band purposes. Exclusive use means that you use a portion of your home *only* for business. If you use part of your home as your business office and also use that part for personal purposes, you do not meet the exclusive-use test and cannot take the home office deduction.

Satisfying the requirement of using your home office regularly and exclusively for business is only half the battle. It must also be true that:

- your home office/studio is your band's principal place of business, or
- you use a separate structure on your property exclusively for business purposes.

Here are some ways to help convince the IRS you qualify for the home office deduction:

- Take a picture of your home studio or office, and draw up a diagram showing it as a portion of your home.
- Have all your band business mail sent to your home office.

- Use your home office address on all your band business cards, stationery, and advertising.
- Obtain a separate phone line for your band business, and keep that phone in your home office.
- Keep a log of the time you spend working in your home studio. This doesn't have to be fancy; notes on your calendar will do.

In general, to qualify for the home office deduction, your home office need no longer be the place where you generate most of your band business income. It's sufficient that you regularly use it to administer or manage your business—for example, keep your books, schedule shows, prepare promotions, and order supplies. As long as you have no other fixed location where you do such things—for example, an outside office—you'll get the deduction.

How much you can claim toward your home office deduction depends on how much (what percentage) of your home you use as a home office or studio. For example, if you use 20% of your home, you can allot 20% of your home office expenses to the home office deduction. The main expenses that qualify are:

- your rent if you rent your home, or
- depreciation, mortgage interest, and property taxes if you own your home.

In addition, owners and renters may deduct this same percentage of other expenses for keeping up and running an

Tax Calendar

Date	Action
January 15	Your last estimated tax payment for the previous year is due.
January 31	If you hired independent contractors last year, you must provide them with Form 1099-MISC.
February 28	If you hired independent contractors last year, you must file all your 1099s with the IRS.
March 15	Corporations must file federal income tax returns.
April 15	You must make your first estimated tax payment for the year. Partnerships must file information tax return. You must file federal tax return (Form 1040). State individual income tax returns due in all states except Arkansas, Delaware, Hawaii, Iowa, Louisiana, and Virginia.
April 20	Individual income tax returns due in Hawaii.
April 30	Individual income tax returns due in Delaware, Iowa, and Virginia.
May 15	Individual income tax returns due in Arkansas and Louisiana.
June 15	Make your second estimated tax payment for the year.
September 15	Make your third estimated tax payment for the year.

entire home. The IRS calls these indirect expenses. They include:

- utility expenses for electricity, gas, heating oil, and trash removal
- homeowner's or renter's insurance
- home maintenance expenses that benefit your entire home including your home office, such as roof and furnace repairs and exterior painting
- condominium association fees
- snow removal expenses

- casualty losses if your home is damaged—for example, in a storm—and
- security system costs.

You may also deduct the entire cost of expenses just for your home office. The IRS calls these direct expenses. They include, for example, painting your home office or studio or paying someone to clean it. If you pay a housekeeper to clean your entire house, you may deduct your business use percentage of the expense.

The IRS Manual on the Music Industry

The IRS publishes a manual for tax examiners explaining how to audit musicians (*MSSP Entertainment: Music Industry*). If you'd like a copy of the manual, visit the IRS website (www.irs.gov). Under "Contents," click "Businesses." On the Businesses page, scroll down and click on the link to Market Segment Specialization Program. Then click "Entertainment-Music Industry" to access the guide.

A great source of information regarding business taxation is *Deduct It: Lower Your Small Business Taxes*, by Stephen Fishman (Nolo).

Tossing Your Tax Records

Have you been storing your band's cancelled checks from 1989 just in case the IRS audits you? Then it's time to climb up the attic stairs and get rid of that financial fire hazard. What tax records do you need to keep? Start with the basic rule that, with rare exceptions, the IRS is prohibited from asking you about returns that are more than three years old—that is, three years from the date of your last return. So, you need to keep records that relate only to the last three years. Bear in mind that tax returns may be based on financial records that date more than three years—for example, five-year depreciation on business equipment. So, keep records like these. For your personal income tax records, you will also need to hang on to information about capital gains and cost records for your house and improvements. There are some exceptions to the three-year rule—for example, you can be audited for six years if you fail to report more than 25% of your gross income, or you can be audited without any time limits if you file a fraudulent return.

How Likely Are You to Get Audited?

Partnership tax returns are audited less frequently than sole proprietorships (another advantage of filing a partnership tax return). Sole proprietorships with home business deductions are the number one target for audits, especially if your business is claiming a loss.

Is Your Band a Hobby or a Business?

Remember, the only expenses that can be deducted from your income are business expenses. If the IRS doesn't believe that the deductions are business-related, then they will not let you take them. Therefore, if the IRS doesn't consider your band to be a legitimate business, band-related expenses will not be deductible.

So what criteria does the IRS use to determine whether an activity is a business or just a hobby? Basically, the criteria are whether you are operating like a business (for example, the level of expertise and recordkeeping) and whether you have shown a clear and reasonable intention to make a profit. Evidence such as advertising for gigs, a business bank account, efforts to sell merchandise, or other attempts to make money will help to show that your band is in fact a business, even if you aren't making any profit. Technically, there's no time limit for how long your band can lose money and still claim deductions.

However, you should be aware that the IRS does operate under a presumption that any business, including a band, that loses money for three out of any five consecutive years is a hobby, not a business, and thus cannot deduct expenses. This is known as the 3-of-5 rule. It is important to note that the 3-of-5 rule only creates a presumption that your band is a hobby, not a final conclusion. This means that even if you lose money three out of five years, you still can demonstrate that your band is a business with a clear and reasonable intention to make a profit. If you have been losing money for several years, an auditor will want to know what you are doing to turn the business around and make a profit.

Some good indicators that you are treating your band like a business are that you:

- maintain a separate checking account for your band
- keep good business records
- make some effort to market your band—for example, seek out shows or create a website
- have band stationery and cards printed
- obtain a federal employer identification number
- secure all necessary business licenses and permits, and
- develop expertise in band business or in your field of music by attending classes and seminars.

The more time and effort you put into the band, the more it will look like you want to make money. So try to devote as much time as possible to your band, and keep a log showing the time you spend on it. If you cannot demonstrate an intention to profit, the band will be considered a hobby, and you will not be able to deduct your band's expenses from your personal tax return.

Payroll Taxes: When Your Band Hires Employees

If your band hires and pays someone for services (for example, a roadie, sound person, driver, or side musician), that person is either an employee or an independent contractor. Distinguishing between an employee and an independent contractor is very important for tax purposes. If your band hires employees, you will have to pay employment taxes (also called payroll taxes). No such taxes are required for hiring independent contractors. If you don't understand the difference between these two kinds of workers, you run the risk of miscategorizing your workers, which may land you in hot water for failing to pay the appropriate taxes.

Employee or Independent Contractor?

As a general rule, someone who receives a regular salary (for example, weekly or monthly payments) and must show up at all rehearsals and performances is probably an employee.

Some indicators that a person is an employee (not an independent contractor) are:

- the band tells the worker how to perform the job (this is one of the most important criteria!)
- the worker can quit at any time without any liability
- the worker can be hired or fired at will
- the worker receives employee benefits
- the band supplies equipment or facilities for the worker, or
- the band reimburses the worker for business and traveling expenses.

Workers who don't meet these criteria are probably independent contractors.

EXAMPLE: Bob and Mandy (a bass player and a drummer) are hired by the Velveetas, a nostalgia band. Bob and Mandy must practice with the band three days a week. They are paid $35 each for every practice. They bring their own instruments to band practices. Bob and Mandy receive $100 each for every show. For out-of-town shows, they travel on the band bus, and their hotel rooms are paid by the band. Bob and Mandy are given sheet music of what to play. Based on the degree of control and regular employment and pay, Bob and Mandy are employees.

The Employee/Independent Contractor Distinction Can Be Tricky

Making a distinction between employee and independent contractor can be difficult. The rules used by the goverment are discussed in detail in *Hiring Independent Contractors*, by Steve Fishman (Nolo). You may need to obtain the assistance of an accountant or tax preparer. You can also obtain advice from your state employment office, various government tax manuals, or the IRS.

Taxes for Employees vs. Independent Contractors

Your band must pay federal payroll taxes for every employee consisting of social security and Medicare payments (known as FICA) and federal unemployment taxes (known as FUTA). Your band will also have to deduct from employees' paychecks and federal income taxes (known as FITW). State payroll taxes consist of state unemployment taxes and state income taxes (except for Alaska, Florida, Nevada, South Dakota, Texas, Washington, and Wyoming, where there are no state income taxes). Five states (California, Hawaii, New Jersey, New York, and Rhode Island) also require that you pay state disability insurance. If you fail to pay payroll taxes or worker's compensation (see "Worker's Compensation," below), the owners/employers in the band may be personally subject to harsh fines and, on rare occasions, jail time.

Your band does not need to pay payroll taxes for independent contractors, because they pay income and self-employment taxes on their own. At the end of the year, your band gives a 1099 form to all independent contractors that it paid more than $600 that year. The independent contractor uses that 1099 form to pay his or her share of taxes.

Worker's Compensation

Every state requires that an employer pay for worker's compensation insurance for employees (not independent contractors). In some states, worker's comp payments are not necessary if you employ two or fewer employees. In some states, it's not necessary if you have four or fewer employees.

Usually, your band can acquire worker's comp insurance through private insurance carriers or from a special state fund (although, in some states, you *must* buy it from the state fund). Failure to pay for worker's compensation insurance can have very harsh repercussions for the employer, including stiff fines for which the employers may be individually liable.

How to Get a Federal Tax ID Number (FEIN) for Your Partnership

A federal employer identification number (FEIN) for a business is the equivalent of a social security number for an individual. You will need this number in order to file a partnership tax return, and you will probably need it to open a partnership bank account. (Record companies and music publishers may also request your FEIN before making payments to your band.)

In order to obtain a federal employer identification number, obtain a copy of Form SS-4 (Application for Employer Identification Number) by downloading it from the IRS website (www.irs. gov), getting one from the local office of the IRS, or calling 800-829-1040. The downloadable version is in a PDF "fillable" format, which means that you can type in your information using Adobe Acrobat Reader.

The form includes directions, but the following tips will help:

- **Space 1: Legal Name of Entity or Individual.** Insert the legal name of your partnership. This may be different from your band name. Usually, most bands take their band name and add the words "partnership" or "band partnership," for example, "Spyder Band Partnership." For more information on band names, see Chapter 9.
- **Space 2: Trade Name of Business.** Insert your band's name (for example, "The Spyders").
- **Space 7a: Name of Principal Officer, General Partner.** Someone in the band (one of the partners) must furnish their name and social security number. This person becomes the contact for the IRS.
- **Space 8a: Type of Entity.** Check the "Partnership" box.
- **Space 9: Reason for Applying.** Check "Started a New Business" and insert "Partnership" on the line.

- **Space 11: Closing Month of Accounting.** Usually this is December, but check with your accountant or tax expert in case you are using a different type of accounting year.
- **Space 12: First Date Wages Were Paid.** If you are not paying employees (see above), then write "Not Applicable."
- **Space 14: Principal Activity.** Check "Other" and write "Musical Services."
- **Space 15: Principal Line of Merchandise, Services.** Again, write "Musical Services."

After completing the form, you can get your band's FEIN right away by calling one of the TELETIN numbers on pages 2 and 3 of the form. If you cannot locate a number for your area, call 800-829-1040. The person who calls the IRS should be the person whose name is listed on Space 7a of the SS-4 form. The IRS operator will ask you questions about your completed SS-4 form and will then give you an FEIN number, which your band can use immediately. However, in order for the FEIN to remain valid, you must mail or fax your SS-4 form within 24 hours. Your FEIN is also used when filing your state tax return.

Canadian Income Taxes. Residents of Canada must file tax forms with Revenue Canada, the Canadian equivalent of the U.S. Internal Revenue Service (online at www.revcan.ca). Canadian residents must pay taxes by April 30 of each year and must have an SIN (social insurance number) when filing. The SIN can be obtained from the Canadian Department of Resources Development (www.hrdc-drhc.gc.ca). Income tax packages are available from Revenue Canada income tax offices, online, or at post offices in the province or territory where you live. Note that many of the rules described in this chapter regarding U.S. corporate, partnership, and other business taxation may not apply for Canadian bands.

Form **SS-4**	**Application for Employer Identification Number**	OMB No. 1545-0003
(Rev. February 2006)	(For use by employers, corporations, partnerships, trusts, estates, churches, government agencies, Indian tribal entities, certain individuals, and others.)	EIN
Department of the Treasury Internal Revenue Service	► See separate instructions for each line. ► Keep a copy for your records.	

Type or print clearly.

1 Legal name of entity (or individual) for whom the EIN is being requested

2 Trade name of business (if different from name on line 1)	**3** Executor, administrator, trustee, "care of" name

4a Mailing address (room, apt., suite no. and street, or P.O. box)	**5a** Street address (if different) (Do not enter a P.O. box.)
4b City, state, and ZIP code	**5b** City, state, and ZIP code

6 County and state where principal business is located

7a Name of principal officer, general partner, grantor, owner, or trustor	**7b** SSN, ITIN, or EIN

8a Type of entity (check only one box)

☐ Sole proprietor (SSN) _____
☐ Partnership
☐ Corporation (enter form number to be filed) ► _____
☐ Personal service corporation
☐ Church or church-controlled organization
☐ Other nonprofit organization (specify) ► _____
☐ Other (specify) ►

☐ Estate (SSN of decedent) _____
☐ Plan administrator (SSN) _____
☐ Trust (SSN of grantor) _____
☐ National Guard   ☐ State/local government
☐ Farmers' cooperative   ☐ Federal government/military
☐ REMIC   ☐ Indian tribal governments/enterprises
Group Exemption Number (GEN) ► _____

8b If a corporation, name the state or foreign country (if applicable) where incorporated | State | Foreign country

9 **Reason for applying** (check only one box)

☐ Started new business (specify type) ► _____
☐ Hired employees (Check the box and see line 12.)
☐ Compliance with IRS withholding regulations
☐ Other (specify) ►

☐ Banking purpose (specify purpose) ► _____
☐ Changed type of organization (specify new type) ► _____
☐ Purchased going business
☐ Created a trust (specify type) ► _____
☐ Created a pension plan (specify type) ► _____

10 Date business started or acquired (month, day, year). See instructions.	**11** Closing month of accounting year

12 First date wages or annuities were paid (month, day, year). **Note.** If applicant is a withholding agent, enter date income will first be paid to nonresident alien. (month, day, year) . . . . ►

13 Highest number of employees expected in the next 12 months (enter -0- if none). | Agricultural | Household | Other

Do you expect to have $1,000 or less in employment tax liability for the calendar year? ☐ **Yes** ☐ **No**. (If you expect to pay $4,000 or less in wages, you can mark yes.)

14 Check **one** box that best describes the principal activity of your business. ☐ Health care & social assistance ☐ Wholesale–agent/broker
☐ Construction ☐ Rental & leasing ☐ Transportation & warehousing ☐ Accommodation & food service ☐ Wholesale–other ☐ Retail
☐ Real estate ☐ Manufacturing ☐ Finance & insurance ☐ Other (specify)

15 Indicate principal line of merchandise sold, specific construction work done, products produced, or services provided.

16a Has the applicant ever applied for an employer identification number for this or any other business? . . . . . ☐ **Yes** ☐ **No**
Note. If "Yes," please complete lines 16b and 16c.

16b If you checked "Yes" on line 16a, give applicant's legal name and trade name shown on prior application if different from line 1 or 2 above.
Legal name ►   Trade name ►

16c Approximate date when, and city and state where, the application was filed. Enter previous employer identification number if known.
Approximate date when filed (mo., day, year) | City and state where filed | Previous EIN

Third Party Designee	Complete this section **only** if you want to authorize the named individual to receive the entity's EIN and answer questions about the completion of this form.	
	Designee's name	Designee's telephone number (include area code) ( )
	Address and ZIP code	Designee's fax number (include area code) ( )

Under penalties of perjury, I declare that I have examined this application, and to the best of my knowledge and belief, it is true, correct, and complete. | Applicant's telephone number (include area code) ( )

Name and title (type or print clearly) ►

Signature ►   Date ► | Applicant's fax number (include area code) ( )

For Privacy Act and Paperwork Reduction Act Notice, see separate instructions.   Cat. No. 16055N   Form **SS-4** (Rev. 2-2006)

Chapter 17

Help Beyond the Book

The chapters in this book cover most of the legal and business issues that musicians need to handle. Still, you may find yourself in a situation that will require additional research or information. This chapter will direct you to additional resources for musicians.

Music Resource Directories

The following directories all contain listings of record labels, management companies, and related services companies (such as CD manufacturers, promoters, and so on).

- *The Recording Industry Sourcebook* (www.recordingindustrysourcebook. com) provides information on record labels, management companies, and an extensive listing of recording facilities, producers, remixers, and duplicators.
- *Billboard Publications* offers many specialized music directories, including the following: *International Talent and Touring Directory; International Buyer's Guide; Record Retailing Directory;* and *Power Book Directory of Music Radio & Record Promotion.* Contact them at Billboard.com (www.billboard.com).
- *Euro Pop Book* and *Euro Jazz Book* are compiled and updated every two years by the French organization Centre d'Information

& Resource des Musizues Actuelles (IRMA) via a network of European music correspondents. These books offer information on European record labels, record distributors, booking agents, concert promoters, managers, entertainment lawyers, musicians, publishers, publicists, producers, and others in the European music industry. Available through Music Books Plus (www. musicbooksplus.com).

Internet Links

Throughout this chapter we have provided Internet addresses of interest to musicians. Websites are often here today, gone tomorrow, so by the time you try to connect they may have already moved on to cyberspace heaven. We'll do our best to keep the websites in this book as up to date as possible for future printings and new editions. If you have information about dead links or new sites that we haven't included, please let us know at cs@nolo.com.

Legal and Business Resources for Musicians

The following resources offer legal and business information of particular interest to musicians.

Equipment Insurance and Information

- *Harmony Central*, a site devoted to musical gear links (and stolen music merchandise) (www.harmony-central).
- If you're looking for a one-stop source of insurance for musicians, review the information at MusicPro Insurance (www.musicproinsurance.com), where your band can obtain insurance for instrument and equipment loss, tour liability, composer's liability, travel and accident insurance, health insurance, and term life.
- If you are a member of the AFM (www.afm.org), they offer on-the-road assistance. The U.S. AFM headquarters is located in New York; the Canadian headquarters is in Toronto. If you run into a problem while touring, the union advises members to call 1-800-ROAD-GIG (in the U.S.) and INFO-FED in Canada for union-related problems.
- For information about Carnet insurance coverage (see Chapter 5), visit the U.S. Council for International Business website (www.uscib.org) and click "ATA Carnet Export Service."

Touring Resources

- *The Touring Musician*, by Hal Galper (Watson-Guptil), provides help on preparing for and executing a successful tour.
- Festival Finder (www.festivalfinder.com) is a website with links and information about U.S. and Canadian music festivals.
- Pollstar: The Concert Hotwire (www.pollstar.com) is the website for *Pollstar* magazine, the official source of music concert information for the music industry.

Recording and Publishing Information

- *How to Make & Sell Your Own Recording*, by Diane Sward Rapaport (Prentice Hall), is the most popular guide for musicians and small labels that want to record and manufacture recordings.
- *Graphic Artists Guild Pricing and Ethical Guidelines*, by the Graphic Artists Guild (North Light Books), explains standard pricing for artwork preparation.
- *The Studio Business Book*, by Jim Mandell (Mix Bookshelf), provides information on how to run a recording studio.
- *A Songwriter's Guide to Music Publishing*, by Randy Poe (Writer's Digest Books), is a good, easy-to-

read guide on protecting songs and creating your own music publishing company.

- *The Art of Music Licensing*, by Al Kohn and Bob Kohn (Aspen), is a good guide to the business of music licensing. It includes a disk with many music licensing contracts.

Performance Rights Organizations

- BMI (www.bmi.com), 320 W. 57th Street, New York, NY 10019; 212-586-2000; in L.A., 310-659-9109; in Nashville, 615-401-2000.
- ASCAP (www.ascap.com), One Lincoln Plaza, New York, NY 10023; 212-621-6000; in L.A., 213-883-1000; in Nashville, 615-742-5000.
- SESAC (www.sesac.com), 421 W. 54th Street, 4th Flr., New York, NY 10036; 212-586-3450; in Nashville, 615-320-0055.
- SOCAN (Canada) (www.socan.com), 41 Valley Brook Drive, Don Mills, Ontario, M3B 2S6 Canada; 416-445-8700.
- The Harry Fox Agency (www .harryfox.com), which collects mechanical royalties, can be contacted at 711 Third Avenue, 8th Flr., New York, NY 10017; 212-370-5330.

Sampling Clearance Companies

To obtain a current listing of clearance companies, search "sample clearance" or "music clearance" using your Internet search engine. As of this edition, the following businesses offered sample clearance:

- Clear Music Now (www.musicclearance.com)
- Diamond Time, Ltd (www.diamondtime.net)
- Signature Sound (www.signature-sound.com)

Music Book Catalogs

If you can't find a specific book in your library or local bookstore, or would like to examine books on other music subjects such as songwriting or sound reinforcement, try Music Books Plus (www.musicbooksplus.com), a website devoted to books on or about music.

General Legal and Business Information

For some nitty gritty details of music law, you may need to conduct your own legal research. Finding an answer to a specific legal question generally involves reading legal books and finding applicable law and cases. Conducting legal research is not as difficult as it may seem.

Nolo publishes a basic legal research guide, *Legal Research: How to Find and Understand the Law*, by Stephen Elias and Susan Levinkind. It walks you through the various sources of law, explains how they fit together, and shows you how to use them to answer your legal question.

If there's a public law school in your area, it probably has a law library that's open to the public. Other public law libraries are often run by local bar associations or as an adjunct to the local courts. Law libraries associated with private law schools often allow only limited public access. Call to speak with the law librarian to determine what access you can have. You can always call your local bar association to find out what public law libraries are in your area.

Nolo's Legal Encyclopedia

Nolo's website (www.nolo.com) offers an extensive Legal Encyclopedia, which includes a section on intellectual property. You'll find answers to frequently asked questions about copyrights, trademarks, and other related topics, as well as sample chapters of Nolo books and a wide range of articles. Simply click on "Legal Encyclopedia" and then on "Patents, Copyright & Trademark."

Business Issues

For more information on how to organize the various types of business forms (partnerships, corporations, and limited liability corporations), review the following Nolo publications:

- *The Partnership Book*, by Denis Clifford and Ralph Warner
- *Form Your Own Limited Liability Company*, by Anthony Mancuso
- *How to Form Your Own California Corporation*, by Anthony Mancuso (also available for Texas corporations)
- *The Small Business Start-Up Kit*, by Peri Pakroo
- *Whoops! I'm in Business: A Crash Course in Business Basics*, by Richard Stim and Lisa Guerin, and
- *Working for Yourself: Law & Taxes for Independent Contractors, Freelancers & Consultants*, by Stephen Fishman.

Bands are considered "small businesses," and the Small Business Administration (SBA) (www.sba.gov) offers information and assistance.

Copyright Issues

- The Copyright Office (www .copyright.gov) has numerous circulars, kits, and other publications related to music that can help your band.

- Contact the Canadian Copyright Office (http://cipo.gc.ca) to download circulars about various copyright subjects as well as copyright applications and forms. (Circular 2, *Musical Works and Mechanical Contrivances*, is particularly helpful.)
- *The Copyright Handbook*, by Stephen Fishman (Nolo), primarily deals with written works, but it provides most of the basic information necessary to understand copyright law.
- *The Public Domain*, by Stephen Fishman (Nolo), tells you everything you need to know about how to find copyright-free music and artwork.

Trademark Issues

- *Trademark: Legal Care for Your Business & Product Name*, by Stephen Elias (Nolo), is an excellent guide for choosing and protecting a name.

- The U.S. Trademark Office's website (www.uspto.gov) includes the relevant applications and trademark office forms.
- For more information on Canadian trademark laws, contact the Canadian Intellectual Property Office (http://cipo.ga.ca).

Business Taxes

- *Tax Savvy for Small Business*, by Frederick W. Daily (Nolo), is a practical, easy-to-understand guide.
- *Deduct It: Lower Your Small Business Taxes*, by Stephen Fishman (Nolo), is a thorough guide to business deductions.
- The Internal Revenue Service website (www.irs.gov) offers downloadable IRS publications and forms.
- Revenue Canada (www.revcan.ca) provides Canadian tax forms and information. ∎

Appendix

How to Use the CD-ROM

Many of the forms discussed in this book are included on a CD-ROM in the back of the book. This CD-ROM, which can be used with Windows computers, installs files that you use with software programs that are already installed on your computer. It is *not* a stand-alone software program. Please read this appendix and the README. TXT file included on the CD-ROM for instructions on using the Forms CD.

Note to Mac users: This CD-ROM and its files should also work on Macintosh computers. Please note, however, that Nolo cannot provide technical support for non-Windows users.

How to View the README File

If you do not know how to view the file README.TXT, insert the Forms CD-ROM into your computer's CD-ROM drive and follow these instructions:

- **Windows 9x, 2000, Me, and XP:** (1) On your PC's desktop, double click the My Computer icon; (2) double click the icon for the CD-ROM drive into which the Forms CD-ROM was inserted; (3) double click the file README.TXT.
- **Macintosh:** (1) On your Mac desktop, double click the icon for the CD-ROM that you inserted; (2) double click the file README. TXT.

While the README file is open, print it out by using the Print command in the File menu.

Two different kinds of forms are contained on the CD-ROM:

- Word processing (RTF) forms that you can open, complete, print, and save with your word processing program (see below), and
- Forms from government agencies (PDF) that can be viewed only with Adobe Reader (see below). Some of these forms have "fill-in" text fields and can be completed using your computer. You will not, however, be able to save the completed forms with the filled-in data. PDF forms without fill-in text fields must be printed out and filled in by hand or with a typewriter.

See below for a list of forms, their file names, and file formats.

Installing the Form Files Onto Your Computer

Before you can do anything with the files on the CD-ROM, you need to install them onto your hard disk. In accordance with U.S. copyright laws, remember that copies of the CD-ROM and its files are for your personal use only.

Insert the Forms CD and do the following:

Windows 98, 2000, Me, and XP Users

Follow the instructions that appear on the screen. (If nothing happens when you insert the Forms CD-ROM, then (1) double click the My Computer icon; (2) double click the icon for the CD-ROM drive into which the Forms CD-ROM was inserted; and (3) double click the file WELCOME.EXE.)

By default, all the files are installed to the \Music Law Forms folder in the \Program Files folder of your computer. A folder called Music Law Forms is added to the Programs folder of the Start menu.

Macintosh Users

Step 1: If the "Music Law Forms CD" window is not open, open it by double clicking the Music Law Forms CD icon.

Step 2: Select the Music Law Forms folder icon.

Step 3: Drag and drop the folder icon onto the icon of your hard disk.

Using the Word Processing Files to Create Documents

This section concerns the files for forms that can be opened and edited with your word processing program.

All word processing forms come in rich text format. These files have the extension .RTF. For example, the form for the Band Partnership Agreement discussed in Chapter 2 is on the file Partnership.rtf. All forms, their file names, and file formats are listed below.

RTF files can be read by most recent word processing programs including all versions of MS Word for Windows and Macintosh, WordPad for Windows, and recent versions of WordPerfect for Windows and Macintosh.

To use a form from the CD to create your documents, you must: (1) open a file in your word processor or text editor; (2) edit the form by filling in the required information; (3) print it out; and (4) rename and save your revised file.

The following are general instructions. However, each word processor uses different commands to open, format, save, and print documents. Please read your word processor's manual for specific instructions on performing these tasks.

Do not call Nolo's technical support if you have questions on how to use your word processor.

Step 1: Opening a File

There are three ways to open the word processing files included on the CD-ROM after you have installed them onto your computer.

- Windows users can open a file by selecting its shortcut as follows: (1) Click the Windows Start button; (2) open the Programs folder; (3) open the Music Law Forms subfolder; and (4) click the shortcut to the form you want to work with.

- Both Windows and Macintosh users can open a file directly by double clicking it. Use My Computer or Windows Explorer (Windows 98, 2000, Me, or XP) or the Finder (Macintosh) to go to the folder you installed or copied the CD-ROM's files to. Then, double click the specific file you want to open.

- You can also open a file from within your word processor. To do this, you must first start your word processor. Then, go to the File menu and choose the Open command. This opens a dialog box where you will tell the program (1) the type of file you want to open (*.RTF); and (2) the location and name of the file (you will need to navigate through the directory tree to get to the folder on your hard disk where the CD's files have been installed). If these directions are unclear, you will need to look through the manual for your word processing program—Nolo's technical support department will *not* be able to help you with the use of your word processing program.

Where Are the Files Installed?

Windows Users
- RTF files are installed by default to a folder named \Music Law Forms in the \Program Files folder of your computer.

Macintosh Users
- RTF files are located in the Music Law Forms folder.

Step 2: Editing Your Document

Fill in the appropriate information according to the instructions and sample agreements in the book. Underlines are used to indicate where you need to enter your information, frequently followed by instructions in brackets. Be sure to delete the underlines and instructions from your edited document. You will also want to make sure that any signature lines in your completed documents appear on a page with at least some text from the document itself. If you do not know how to use your word processor to edit a document, you will need to look through the manual for your word processing program—Nolo's technical support department will *not* be able to help you with the use of your word processing program.

Editing Forms That Have Optional or Alternative Text

Some of the forms have check boxes before text. The check boxes indicate:

- optional text, where you choose whether to include or exclude the given text, or
- alternative text, where you select one alternative to include and exclude the other alternatives.

Optional text

If you **don't want** to include optional text, just delete it from your document.

If you **do want** to include optional text, just leave it in your document.

In either case, delete the check box itself as well as the italicized instructions that the text is optional.

Alternative text

First delete all the alternatives that you do not want to include.

Then delete the remaining check boxes, as well as the italicized instructions that you need to select one of the alternatives provided.

Step 3: Printing Out the Document

Use your word processor's or text editor's Print command to print out your document. If you do not know how to use your word processor to print a document, you will need to look through the manual for your word processing program—Nolo's technical support department will *not* be able to help you with the use of your word processing program.

Step 4: Saving Your Document

After filling in the form, use the "Save As" command to save and rename the file. Because all the files are read-only, you will not be able to use the Save command. This is for your protection. *If you save the file without renaming it, the underlines that indicate where you need to enter your information will be lost, and you will not be able to create a new document with this file without recopying the original file from the CD-ROM.*

If you do not know how to use your word processor to save a document, you will need to look through the manual for your word processing program—Nolo's technical support department will *not* be able to help you with the use of your word processing program.

Using PDF Forms

Electronic copies of useful forms from government agencies are included on the CD-ROM in Adobe Acrobat PDF format. You must have the Adobe Reader installed on your computer to use these forms. Adobe Reader is available for all types of Windows and Macintosh systems. If you don't already have this software, you can download it for free at www.adobe.com.

All forms, their file names, and file formats are listed below. These forms were not created by Nolo.

These forms have fill-in text fields. To create your document using these files, you must: (1) open a file; (2) fill in the text fields using either your mouse or the tab key on your keyboard to navigate from field to field; and (3) print it out.

Note: While you can print out your completed form, you will *not* be able to save your completed form to disk.

Step 1: Opening a Form

PDF files, like the word processing files, can be opened one of three ways:

- Windows users can open a file by selecting its shortcut as follows: (1) Click the Windows Start button; (2) open the Programs folder; (3) open the Music Law Forms subfolder; and (4) click the shortcut to the form you want to work with.
- Both Windows and Macintosh users can open a file directly by double clicking it. Use My Computer or Windows Explorer (Windows 98, 2000, Me, or XP) or the Finder (Macintosh) to go to the folder you created and copied the CD-ROM's files to. Then, double click the specific file you want to open.

- You can also open a PDF file from within Adobe Reader. To do this, you must first start Reader. Then, go to the File menu and choose the Open command. This opens a dialog box where you will tell the program the location and name of the file (you will need to navigate through the directory tree to get to the folder on your hard disk where the CD's files have been installed). If these directions are unclear you will need to look through Adobe Reader's help—Nolo's technical support department will *not* be able to help you with the use of Adobe Reader.

Where Are the PDF Files Installed?

- **Windows Users:** PDF files are installed by default to a folder named \Music Law Forms in the \Program Files folder of your computer.
- **Macintosh Users:** PDF files are located in the Music Law Forms folder.

Step 2: Filling in a Form

Use your mouse or the Tab key on your keyboard to navigate from field to field within these forms. Be sure to have all the information you will need to complete a form on hand, because you will not be able to save a copy of the filled-in form to disk. You can, however, print out a completed version.

Step 3: Printing a Form

Choose Print from the Acrobat Reader File menu. This will open the Print dialog box. In the "Print Range" section of the Print dialog box, select the appropriate print range, then click OK.

List of Forms Included on the Forms CD-ROM

The following files are in rich text format (RTF):

File Name	Form Name
ArtAgreement	Artwork Agreement
ArtAgreementShort	[Abbreviated] Artwork Agreement
Partnership	Band Partnership Agreement
PartershipShort	[Abbreviated] Band Partnership Agreement
LicenseNotice	Notice of Intention to Obtain Compulsory License for Making and Distributing Sound Recordings
Consignment	Consignment Form
Distribution	Independent Distribution Agreement
FirstRecording	Mechanical License and Authorization for First-Time Recording of Song
LabelAgreement	Independent Label Recording Agreement
LabelLicense	Independent Label License Agreement
Invoice	Invoice
Labelshopping	Label-Shopping Agreement
Management	Management Agreement
ManagementShort	[Abbreviated] Management Agreement
ModelRelease	Model Release Agreement
MusicianRelease	Musician Release Agreement
Performance	Performance Agreement

RecordBudget	Blank Recording Budget
SongSample	Agreement With Music Publisher for Use of Song Sample
MasterSample	Agreement With Record Company for Use of Master Recording Sample
TourBudget	Tour Budget

The following files are in Adobe Acrobat PDF format with fill-in text fields:

File Name	**Form Name**
fss4	Application for Employer Identification Number
formpai	Form PA
formcawi	Form CA

Index

A

C

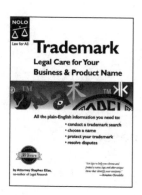

Trademark

Legal Care for your Business and Product Name
By Attorney Stephen Elias

Trademarks—the names and symbols that identify your business, brand and products in the marketplace—are important assets that you need to choose carefully and protect. With *Trademark*, you get the most up-to-date information you need to defend your creations. Includes all the forms and instructions you need to register a trademark or service mark with the U.S. Patent & Trademark Office.

$39.99/TRD

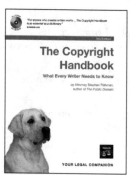

The Copyright Handbook

How to Protect and Use Written Works
By Attorney Stephen Fishman
Book With CD-ROM

This book provides the forms you need to protect creative expression under U.S. and international copyright law. It covers the Digital Millenium Copyright Act, the 20-year extension of copyright terms, *Tasini v. New York Times* and the resulting decision that affects all freelance writers—and more. All forms come as tear-outs and on CD-ROM.

$34.99/COHA

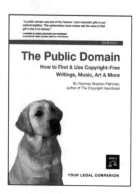

The Public Domain

How to Find Copyright-Free Writings, Music, Art and More
by Attorney Stephen Fishman

The first book of it's kind, *The Public Domain* is the definitive guide to the creative works that are not protected by copyright and can be copied freely or otherwise used without paying permission fees. Includes hundreds of resources, such as websites, libraries and archives, useful for locating public domain works.

$34.99/PUBL

CATALOG
...more from Nolo

BUSINESS	PRICE	CODE
Business Buyout Agreements (Book w/CD-ROM)	$49.99	BSAG
The CA Nonprofit Corporation Kit (Binder w/CD-ROM)	$69.99	CNP
California Workers' Comp: How to Take Charge When You're Injured on the Job	$34.99	WORK
The Complete Guide to Buying a Business (Book w/CD-ROM)	$24.99	BUYBU
The Complete Guide to Selling a Business (Book w/CD-ROM)	$24.99	SELBU
Consultant & Independent Contractor Agreements (Book w/CD-ROM)	$29.99	CICA
The Corporate Records Handbook (Book w/CD-ROM)	$69.99	CORMI
Create Your Own Employee Handbook (Book w/CD-ROM)	$49.99	EMHA
Dealing With Problem Employees	$44.99	PROBM
Deduct It! Lower Your Small Business Taxes	$34.99	DEDU
Effective Fundraising for Nonprofits	$24.99	EFFN
The Employer's Legal Handbook	$39.99	EMPL
Essential Guide to Federal Employment Laws	$39.99	FEMP
Form a Partnership (Book W/CD-ROM)	$39.99	PART
Form Your Own Limited Liability Company (Book w/CD-ROM)	$44.99	LIAB
Home Business Tax Deductions: Keep What You Earn	$34.99	DEHB
How to Form a Nonprofit Corporation (Book w/CD-ROM)—National Edition	$49.99	NNP
How to Form a Nonprofit Corporation in California (Book w/CD-ROM)	$49.99	NON
How to Form Your Own California Corporation (Binder w/CD-ROM)	$59.99	CACI
How to Form Your Own California Corporation (Book w/CD-ROM)	$34.99	CCOR
How to Write a Business Plan (Book w/CD-ROM)	$34.99	SBS
Incorporate Your Business (Book w/CD-ROM)	$49.99	NIBS
Investors in Your Backyard (Book w/CD-ROM)	$24.99	FINBUS
The Job Description Handbook	$29.99	JOB
Legal Guide for Starting & Running a Small Business	$34.99	RUNS
Legal Forms for Starting & Running a Small Business (Book w/CD-ROM)	$29.99	RUNSF
LLC or Corporation?	$24.99	CHENT
The Manager's Legal Handbook	$39.99	ELBA

Prices subject to change.

	PRICE	CODE
Marketing Without Advertising	$20.00	MWAD
Music Law (Book w/CD-ROM)	$39.99	ML
Negotiate the Best Lease for Your Business	$24.99	LESP
Nolo's Guide to Social Security Disability (Book w/CD-ROM)	$29.99	QSS
Nolo's Quick LLC	$29.99	LLCQ
The Performance Appraisal Handbook	$29.99	PERF
The Small Business Start-up Kit (Book w/CD-ROM)	$24.99	SMBU
The Small Business Start-up Kit for California (Book w/CD-ROM)	$24.99	OPEN
Starting & Running a Successful Newsletter or Magazine	$29.99	MAG
Tax Deductions for Professionals	$34.99	DEPO
Tax Savvy for Small Business	$36.99	SAVVY
Whoops! I'm in Business	$19.99	WHOO
Working for Yourself: Law & Taxes for Independent Contractors, Freelancers & Consultants	$39.99	WAGE
Working With Independent Contractors (Book w/CD-ROM)	$29.99	HICI
Your Crafts Business: A Legal Guide (Book w/CD-ROM)	$26.99	VART
Your Limited Liability Company: An Operating Manual (Book w/CD-ROM)	$49.99	LOP
Your Rights in the Workplace	$29.99	YRW

CONSUMER

	PRICE	CODE
How to Win Your Personal Injury Claim	$29.99	PICL
Nolo's Encyclopedia of Everyday Law	$29.99	EVL
Nolo's Guide to California Law	$24.99	CLAW

ESTATE PLANNING & PROBATE

	PRICE	CODE
8 Ways to Avoid Probate	$19.99	PRAV
Estate Planning Basics	$21.99	ESPN
The Executor's Guide: Settling a Loved One's Estate or Trust	$34.99	EXEC
How to Probate an Estate in California	$49.99	PAE
Make Your Own Living Trust (Book w/CD-ROM)	$39.99	LITR
Nolo's Simple Will Book (Book w/CD-ROM)	$36.99	SWIL
Plan Your Estate	$44.99	NEST
Quick & Legal Will Book (Book w/CD-ROM)	$19.99	QUIC
Special Needs Trust: Protect Your Child's Financial Future (Book w/CD-ROM)	$34.99	SPNT

	PRICE	CODE

FAMILY MATTERS

Always Dad	$16.99	DIFA
Building a Parenting Agreement That Works	$24.99	CUST
The Complete IEP Guide	$34.99	IEP
Divorce & Money: How to Make the Best Financial Decisions During Divorce	$34.99	DIMO
Divorce Without Court	$29.99	DWCT
Do Your Own California Adoption: Nolo's Guide for Stepparents & Domestic Partners (Book w/CD-ROM)	$34.99	ADOP
Every Dog's Legal Guide: A Must-Have for Your Owner	$19.99	DOG
Get a Life: You Don't Need a Million to Retire Well	$24.99	LIFE
The Guardianship Book for California	$34.99	GB
A Legal Guide for Lesbian and Gay Couples	$34.99	LG
Living Together: A Legal Guide (Book w/CD-ROM)	$34.99	LTK
Nolo's IEP Guide: Learning Disabilities	$29.99	IELD
Parent Savvy	$19.99	PRNT
Prenuptial Agreements: How to Write a Fair & Lasting Contract (Book w/CD-ROM)	$34.99	PNUP
Work Less, Live More	$17.99	RECL

GOING TO COURT

Beat Your Ticket: Go To Court & Win! (National Edition)	$21.99	BEYT
The Criminal Law Handbook: Know Your Rights, Survive the System	$39.99	KYR
Everybody's Guide to Small Claims Court (National Edition)	$29.99	NSCC
Everybody's Guide to Small Claims Court in California	$29.99	CSCC
Fight Your Ticket & Win in California	$29.99	FYT
How to Change Your Name in California	$29.99	NAME
Nolo's Deposition Handbook	$29.99	DEP
Represent Yourself in Court: How to Prepare & Try a Winning Case	$39.99	RYC
Win Your Lawsuit: A Judge's Guide to Representing Yourself in California Superior Court	$29.99	SLWY

HOMEOWNERS, LANDLORDS & TENANTS

California Tenants' Rights	$27.99	CTEN
Deeds for California Real Estate	$24.99	DEED
Every Landlord's Legal Guide (National Edition, Book w/CD-ROM)	$44.99	ELLI
Every Landlord's Guide to Finding Great Tenants (Book w/CD-ROM)	$19.99	FIND

	PRICE	CODE
Every Landlord's Tax Deduction Guide	$34.99	DELL
Every Tenant's Legal Guide	$29.99	EVTEN
For Sale by Owner in California	$29.99	FSBO
How to Buy a House in California	$29.99	BHCA
The California Landlord's Law Book: Rights & Responsibilities(Book w/CD-ROM)	$44.99	LBRT
The California Landlord's Law Book: Evictions (Book w/CD-ROM)	$44.99	LBEV
Leases & Rental Agreements	$29.99	LEAR
Neighbor Law: Fences, Trees, Boundaries & Noise	$26.99	NEI
Renters' Rights (National Edition)	$24.99	RENT

IMMIGRATION

	PRICE	CODE
Becoming A U.S. Citizen: A Guide to the Law, Exam and Interview	$24.99	USCIT
Fiancé & Marriage Visas (Book w/CD-ROM)	$34.99	IMAR
How to Get a Green Card	$29.99	GRN
Student & Tourist Visas	$29.99	ISTU
U.S. Immigration Made Easy	$39.99	IMEZ

MONEY MATTERS

	PRICE	CODE
101 Law Forms for Personal Use (Book w/CD-ROM)	$29.99	SPOT
Chapter 13 Bankruptcy: Repay Your Debts	$39.99	CHB
Credit Repair (Book w/CD-ROM)	$24.99	CREP
How to File for Chapter 7 Bankruptcy	$29.99	HFB
IRAs, 401(k)s & Other Retirement Plans: Taking Your Money Out	$34.99	RET
Solve Your Money Troubles	$19.99	MT
Stand Up to the IRS	$29.99	SIRS

PATENTS AND COPYRIGHTS

	PRICE	CODE
All I Need is Money: How to Finance Your Invention	$19.99	FINA
The Copyright Handbook: How to Protect and Use Written Works (Book w/CD-ROM)	$39.99	COHA
Copyright Your Software (Book w/CD-ROM)	$34.95	CYS
Getting Permission: How to License & Clear Copyrighted Materials Online & Off (Book w/CD-ROM)	$34.99	RIPER
How to Make Patent Drawings	$29.99	DRAW
The Inventor's Notebook	$24.99	INOT
Nolo's Patents for Beginners	$24.99	QPAT

	PRICE	CODE
Patent, Copyright & Trademark	$39.99	PCTM
Patent It Yourself	$49.99	PAT
Patent Pending in 24 Hours	$34.99	PEND
Patenting Art & Entertainment: New Strategies for Protecting Creative Ideas	$39.99	PATAE
Profit from Your Idea (Book w/CD-ROM)	$34.99	LICE
The Public Domain	$34.99	PUBL
Trademark: Legal Care for Your Business and Product Name	$39.99	TRD
Web and Software Development: A Legal Guide (Book w/CD-ROM)	$44.99	SFT
What Every Inventor Needs to Know About Business & Taxes (Book w/CD-ROM)	$21.99	ILAX

RESEARCH & REFERENCE

Legal Research: How to Find & Understand the Law	$39.99	LRES

SENIORS

Long-Term Care: How to Plan & Pay for It	$19.99	ELD
Social Security, Medicare & Goverment Pensions	$29.99	SOA

SOFTWARE Call or check our website at www.nolo.com for special discounts on Software!

Incorporator Pro	$89.99	STNC1
LLC Maker—Windows	$89.95	LLP1
Patent Pending Now!	$199.99	PP1
PatentEase—Windows	$349.00	PEAS
Personal RecordKeeper 5.0 CD—Windows	$59.95	RKD5
Quicken Legal Business Pro 2007—Windows	$109.99	SBQB7
Quicken WillMaker Plus 2007—Windows	$79.99	WQP7

Special Upgrade Offer
Save 35% on the latest edition of your Nolo book

Because laws and legal procedures change often, we update our books regularly. To help keep you up-to-date, we are extending this special upgrade offer. Cut out and mail the title portion of the cover of your old Nolo book and we'll give you 35% off the retail price of the New Edition of that book when you purchase directly from Nolo. This offer is to individuals only. Prices and offer subject to change without notice.

Order Form

Name _____

Address _____

City _____

State, Zip _____

Daytime Phone _____

E-mail _____

Our "No-Hassle" Guarantee

Return anything you buy directly from Nolo for any reason and we'll cheerfully refund your purchase price. No ifs, ands or buts.

☐ Check here if you do not wish to receive mailings from other companies

Item Code	Quantity	Item	Unit Price	Total Price

Method of payment

☐ Check   ☐ VISA

☐ American Express

☐ MasterCard

☐ Discover Card

Subtotal	
Add your local sales tax (California only)	
Shipping: RUSH $12, Basic $9 (See below)	
"I bought 3, ship it to me FREE!"(Ground shipping only)	
TOTAL	

Account Number _____

Expiration Date _____

Signature _____

Shipping and Handling

Rush Delivery—Only $12

We'll ship any order to any street address in the U.S. by UPS 2nd Day Air* for only $12!

* Order by noon Pacific Time and get your order in 2 business days. Orders placed after noon Pacific Time will arrive in 3 business days. P.O. boxes and S.F. Bay Area use basic shipping. Alaska and Hawaii use 2nd Day Air or Priority Mail.

Basic Shipping—$9

Use for P.O. Boxes, Northern California and Ground Service.

Allow 1-2 weeks for delivery.

U.S. addresses only.

For faster service, use your credit card and our toll-free numbers

Call our customer service group Monday thru Friday 7am to 7pm PST

 Phone
1-800-728-3555

 Fax
1-800-645-0895

 Mail
Nolo
950 Parker St.
Berkeley, CA 94710

Order 24 hours a day @ www.nolo.com

Remember:
Little publishers have big ears.
We really listen to you.

Take 2 Minutes & Give Us Your 2 cents

Your comments make a big difference in the development and revision of Nolo books and software. Please take a few minutes and register your Nolo product—and your comments—with us. Not only will your input make a difference, you'll receive special offers available only to registered owners of Nolo products on our newest books and software. Register now by:

PHONE
1-800-728-3555

FAX
1-800-645-0895

EMAIL
cs@nolo.com

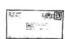
or **MAIL** us
this registration card

fold here

Registration Card

NAME _____ DATE _____

ADDRESS _____

_____

CITY _____ STATE _____ ZIP _____

PHONE _____ EMAIL _____

WHERE DID YOU HEAR ABOUT THIS PRODUCT? _____

WHERE DID YOU PURCHASE THIS PRODUCT? _____

DID YOU CONSULT A LAWYER? (PLEASE CIRCLE ONE)   YES   NO   NOT APPLICABLE

DID YOU FIND THIS BOOK HELPFUL?   (VERY)   5   4   3   2   1   (NOT AT ALL)

COMMENTS _____

WAS IT EASY TO USE?   (VERY EASY)   5   4   3   2   1   (VERY DIFFICULT)

We occasionally make our mailing list available to carefully selected companies whose products may be of interest to you.

❑ If you do not wish to receive mailings from these companies, please check this box.

❑ You can quote me in future Nolo promotional materials.
  Daytime phone number _____.

ML 5.0

Nolo
in the
NEWS

"Nolo helps lay people perform legal tasks without the aid—or fees—of lawyers."

—USA TODAY

Nolo books are ..."written in plain language, free of legal mumbo jumbo, and spiced with witty personal observations."

—ASSOCIATED PRESS

"Nolo publications...guide people simply through the how, when, where and why of law."

—WASHINGTON POST

"Increasingly, people who are not lawyers are performing tasks usually regarded as legal work... And consumers, using books like Nolo's, do routine legal work themselves."

—NEW YORK TIMES

"...All of [Nolo's] books are easy-to-understand, are updated regularly, provide pull-out forms...and are often quite moving in their sense of compassion for the struggles of the lay reader."

—SAN FRANCISCO CHRONICLE

fold here

- -

**NOLO
950 Parker Street
Berkeley, CA 94710-9867**

Attn: ML 5.0